THE WORLD'S GREATEST BLACKJACK BOOK

Revised Edition

THE WORLD'S GREATEST BLACKJACK BOOK

Revised Edition

Lance Humble, Ph.D.
Carl Cooper, Ph.D.

DOUBLEDAY & COMPANY, INC.
GARDEN CITY, NEW YORK, 1987

Library of Congress Cataloging-in-Publication Data

Humble, Lance.
  The world's greatest blackjack book.

  Includes index.
  1. Blackjack (Game)   I. Cooper, Ken.   II. Title.
GV1295.B55H86   1987   795.4'2   86-24387
ISBN 0-385-15382-1 (pbk.)

ACKNOWLEDGMENTS

We wish to thank all the gaming professionals who have participated in the evolution of the game of Blackjack, and who have so graciously allowed us to include their work in this book. We feel that the people and organizations mentioned here represent the finest body of experts on Blackjack in the world. In particular, we wish to thank Edward O. Thorp and Julian H. Braun for their original work and continuing contributions.

To the players, especially Nan and Bob.
Play by the book and you will realize your dreams.

FOREWORD

This is a fascinating, informative, and surprisingly extensive book.

During the past eighteen years, as a direct consequence of the work of Dr. Edward O. Thorp, myself, and others, numerous methods of winning at Blackjack by means of count systems have developed. For the serious player who will take the trouble properly to learn and use one of the better systems, the player can and should win over a period of time. Yet, many such players have failed to come anywhere near the mathematically proven reasonable expectations. There is more to playing the game than just knowing what is the mathematically correct play—much more.

Dr. Humble and Dr. Cooper have woven both factors into a fascinating and remarkably thorough account of just how really to succeed at casino Blackjack. This account includes a discussion of casino countermeasures, with recommendations on how to succeed in spite of such measures. There is much to learn in this book for both the novice and the experienced player.

JULIAN H. BRAUN
Chicago, Illinois

CONTENTS

SEVEN WINNING IN OCCASIONAL CASINO PLAY: HI-OPT I CARD COUNTING

PREFACE

An unknown philosopher once said that there are three kinds of people in this world: those who make things happen, those who watch things happen, and those who wander around braying, "What happened?" The purpose of this book is to keep you from falling into the "What happened?" category when you play Blackjack.

This book describes and teaches you how to win money in a casino. Strategies, techniques, and moves are explained that will enable you to win even under adverse conditions. After reading this book, you can approach a home or casino game with complete confidence. The methods that follow have won millions of dollars for our students in the last ten years, with the total growing daily.

Even if you never plan to step inside a casino, you can sit back and enjoy reading the inside story of one of the world's fastest-growing industries—gambling. If you are a gambler or hope to gamble someday, the following information will be invaluable:

how to choose the best place to play (from casino to chair);

proper casino etiquette;

how to control the dealer and not be cheated;

Blackjeck systems from simple playing to tracking cards;

playing tips for amateurs and professionals alike;

new strategies for winning at home Blackjack;

how to handle winning on junkets;

the fine points in playing Blackjack;

the future of Blackjack.

Although the book is written in first person for ease of reading, it is the collaboration of two unique individuals who share a common interest in winning money at Blackjack. One is a professor at a large Canadian university, teaching courses on gambling, and who has founded the International Gamblers Club to disseminate information to players worldwide. His students have won over $500,000 playing Blackjack. The second is a management consultant (and former IBM employee) who conducts memory techniques and communications skills training seminars through his own firm. Between us, we have over thirty publications covering a wide range of subjects. More important, we win when we play Blackjack.

There is something here for everyone. The nonplayer can find out what happens when the folding green hits the green felt. With new strategies, the home player will learn how to win consistently in that "friendly" neighborhood game. The hobbyist will see how to have more "funny money" on hand for the auction at the end of a "Vegas night." The occasional player can master the techniques to turn a stiff casino advantage into a tossup offering free drinks and entertainment. The serious player will be introduced to the Hi-Opt I system, a method that gains enough of a long-term advantage over the house to provide a profession.

The contents are arranged simply in three parts. The more you read from front to back, the better player you will become.

Chapters One through Five introduce the rules of the game and offer suggestions for play regardless of your level of knowledge.

Chapters Six through Nine develop a range of winning systems, from a simple "basic strategy" detailing how to play each hand, to the Hi-Opt I system for "counting" the cards and varying your playing and betting accordingly.

Chapters Ten through Twelve offer detailed tips for the serious player, analyze junkets, and outline the future of Blackjack.

This book is not theoretical. It presents a pragmatic approach to the often harsh realities of home and casino gambling, helping you *win* at the game, not just play it. The systems are based upon millions of hands of computer Blackjack, and proven in hundreds of hours of casino play. This book is not only accurate, it is also fun. Our personal experiences and those of hundreds of International Blackjack Club members are interwoven with the techniques, illustrating the many tips and suggestions for winning play.

You say you don't believe that Blackjack is a game of skill? We invite you to be the dealer. Any of the students of this book will be glad to demonstrate how easy it is to win. Dr. Humble has an open challenge to play any person or casino for any amount up to fifty thousand dollars. He has yet to be taken up on it.

LANCE HUMBLE, PH.D.
CARL COOPER, PH.D.

THE WORLD'S GREATEST BLACKJACK BOOK

Revised Edition

ONE

Cashing in on Blackjack Gold

You may have heard about the tourist vacationing in Las Vegas. He didn't have any money to gamble, so he just watched the games and bet mentally. In no time at all, he'd lost his mind.

HOLLY SHAW, Humorist

I've got a very important message for you that the gambling casinos of the world don't want you to know. They can be beaten. Not once, not occasionally, but consistently over a long period of time. Oh they would like you to think that only a genius with a photographic memory for cards can do it. Unfortunately for them, anyone can do it. *You* can beat them if you want. At the very least, you can make them quit beating you while you enjoy the comfort of their establishment. The game is Blackjack, and all the information you need is in your hands right now.

There are three participants in a game of Blackjack: you, the dealer, and the casino. To realize fully the benefits of reading this book, you must understand who usually foots the bill.

WHO PAYS FOR THE GLITTER?

It was summertime in Las Vegas, with the hot desert wind practically drying my eyes out between blinks, and I had decided to quit early after an exhausting night of play. I had stopped for an all-night session of Blackjack on the way to L.A., and even though it was only 4:00 A.M. and my plane was scheduled to leave at 9:00 A.M., I was through. I had been playing the dollar tables downtown at the El Cortez and had tripled my original stake in a night of experimenting with strategies. Time to quit. The big betting could come the next trip out now that I had validated certain ideas.

Tired and stiff from sitting too long, I thought I would then tour the Strip, stopping at each major casino to see how full the tables were and to observe any changes in their games since my last trip. Stretched out and awake again, I reached the casinos, needing only a short cab ride. As I hopped from one glittering palace to another, I saw very few winners.

I was pleased about my clothing, though. The Strip was flooded with hookers, finished with the bulk of their night's business and looking for a spare trick or two to complete the evening. On my Strip walk, I was propositioned only once. This trip I had worn my "tourist of modest means stopping in Vegas hoping not to lose too much and have to go home early" outfit. I had blended in at the casino and didn't seem too attractive to the other businesspeople in the area.

I ended my stroll at the MGM Grand, which meant I had unwittingly saved the most interesting for last. There was an enormous crowd, even at this hour, around one of the hundred-dollar tables. A handsome, tanned gentleman was playing five hundred dollars each on two hands per deal and staying even. In front of him were about forty stacks of hundred-dollar chips, five chips to a stack. The area was loaded with casino personnel, looking worried and watching every move he made. I began to keep track of the cards, and while he was not using a counting system, he was playing a good Basic Strategy (more later about both).

But the real story was not with this apparent winner. I began watching the other three bettors, all of whom were fairly poor players, and started seeing a lot of folding green. Folding green on the table is always a danger sign. It means that the players are losing and need more of their stake converted into chips. As I watched, the winner gained about two thousand dollars (merely four bets) and the others lost nearly ten thousand dollars. As Robert Blake (Baretta) might have said were he still on the air, "And that's the name of that tune." While there are always plenty of winners to be seen, somebody has got to be paying all those light bills on Glitter Gulch. If you've ever stepped inside a casino, it has probably been you.

WHY PLAY BLACKJACK?

In mid-1978, Resorts International opened Atlantic City's first casino. In the initial week, the casino "won" a paltry $438,504 *per day*. The gaming tables alone contributed $191,011 per day to this figure. The first week's summary reported that the average table player lost nearly $18 for every hour of play. For every $1.00 played at Blackjack, Resorts International returned to the player an average of only $.77.

By the second month, total casino winnings were up 25 per cent, with one day topping the $1,000,000 mark. The irony of these figures is that of all the casino games, Blackjack is the only one in which the player can consistently win money by using his or her own skill. There are many winning strategies for casino Blackjack, most based upon computer studies done over the past twenty years (one of the most simple and powerful systems ever devised is presented to you in Chapters Seven and Eight). All the other games—Craps, Roulette, Baccarat, keno, and the slot machines—are rigged to give the casino a permanent advantage regardless of your skill. There is no way you can win at these games over the long run. There is only one way to win: Get lucky and never play again once you are ahead. The longer you play, the more certain you can be that the mathematical percentages will grind you and your pocketbook down to nothing.

If you don't believe in computers and mathematics, then go to the casinos and watch the other games for an afternoon. You will soon see that they are losing propositions. No system has ever beaten those games, and no system will ever beat them under the present rules. If you want to be a winner in casino gambling, you

must choose Blackjack as your game. Otherwise, you'll be like
the grizzled New England farmer who, when asked what he
would do if someone gave him a million dollars, replied, "Well
. . . I guess I would just keep on farmin' till it was all gone."

THE EVOLUTION OF BLACKJACK SYSTEMS

Before World War II, Roulette and three-dice Hazard were the
featured games in the resort areas of Florida, Michigan, and Indi-
ana. In the thirties, Roulette held its own with Craps in Nevada,
with Blackjack running third. The casino advantage is a strong
5.26 per cent in American-style Roulette, so the players began to
gravitate to the Craps table for the simple reason that they lasted
longer and won more often. Now, with publications such as this
book showing that the casino advantage can be eliminated or
even reversed, Blackjack has become the winning game for the
casino player.

The origin of Blackjack is unknown. Like so many of the popular games today, it evolved from other games. And it is still
changing. Casinos are experimenting with multiple decks, providing seating for additional players at the table, and changing the
method of dealing. It will take years for Blackjack to develop the
stability that Craps has reached. As profitable as Blackjack has
been for the casinos, until recently they knew very little about the
game.

The operators have always depended upon each other for information. Like the sex "facts" passed in grade-school bathrooms,
this information was usually inaccurate. In 1930, Joe Treybal, a
respected dice and equipment manufacturer, published a book
titled *Handbook on Percentages*. Intended only for gaming operators, it devoted a mere page to Blackjack information, and that
was incorrect:

> The principle percentage in favor of the dealer arises from the fact
> that all busts (player exceeding 21) must pay the dealer irrespective
> of his own hand. Therefore, we have no definite figures as to the
> percentage, but guarantee it will get the money whenever you get
> any players to draw cards.

In 1953, there was a breakthrough. Roger Baldwin, Wilbert Cantey, Herbert Maisel, and James McDermott were stationed at the Aberdeen Proving Ground, an Army base in Maryland. Having a burning interest in Blackjack and much off-duty time, they began a detailed study of the game using desk calculators. After three years of incredibly painstaking efforts, they developed a very close approximation to a correct way to play without remembering or counting the cards that had already been played —a *Basic Strategy*. They published their work in the September 1956 issue of the *Journal of the American Statistical Association,* and a version for the general public was published by M. Barrows and Company in 1957. Unfortunately, the dramatic importance of this information was little suspected at that time.

Professor Edward O. Thorp was one who did take notice. He contacted the authors to study the methods they used, and then wrote a generalized computer program that could analyze Blackjack decks at high speed on an IBM 704 at MIT. After lengthy research, Thorp found that when the unused portion of the Blackjack deck had a disproportionately high number of 10-value cards in it, the *player* would actually have the advantage. His computations also refined the correct Basic Strategy. These results appeared in his first book, *Beat the Dealer. Beat the Dealer* was a sensation, even making the New York *Times* best-seller list one week in 1963. When Thorp received international publicity in *Life* magazine, the casinos became afraid that everyone would learn the system and beat them out of their money.

The results of the scare are common knowledge now. A number of the casinos changed some of the rules, making it harder to win. This lasted only two weeks. Too many players refused to play Blackjack with these unfavorable rules, and the win volumes dropped off dramatically. The casinos reacted to the law of supply and demand by quickly reinstating the old rules.

The casinos soon realized they had nothing to fear from players using "Thorp." What happened was that the publicity that Thorp's book provided turned out to be a boon for the casinos. The players kept losing at exactly the same rate as before, only now there were more of them. Most players who had purchased the book could not understand the difficult Ten Count it explained, and those few who could, did not take the time to master it. The casinos saw their Blackjack profits skyrocketing.

A second edition of *Beat the Dealer,* containing refinements brought about by Julian Braun's improvements to Thorp's computer programs, caused another boom in Blackjack profits for the casinos. Quick to capitalize on the success of Thorp, other books touting Blackjack systems began to appear. The popularity of Blackjack was growing tremendously. More casinos put in additional Blackjack tables until the game began to be a strong competitor with Craps as the most popular casino game in Nevada.

One of the most prolific producers of winning Blackjack systems almost single-handedly caused the next major increase in Blackjack's popularity. Griffith K. Owens of Las Vegas was the legendary "Lawrence Revere," and was also known as Leonard or "Speck" Parsons until the time of his death in April 1977. Using Braun's programs, he developed a number of strategies of varying complexity. In the early seventies, as a result of an aggressive advertising campaign, tens of thousands of his book, *Playing Blackjack as a Business,* reached eager readers. He had a system for everyone, mathematician or moron. Consequently, the casinos again feared that the scientific computer-devised systems would cut into their profits, so they changed from single- to multiple-deck games to counteract the card-tracking strategies.

As a result of the mushrooming popularity of Blackjack, researchers began to devise new, less complicated systems. The simplest, most powerful in terms of winning, and most popular point-count system to be published at this time was the Hi-Opt I. It was published in 1974 by International Gaming, Incorporated. The system was devised with the help of Braun's computer programs and an anonymous graduate student in mathematics at a large Canadian university. I estimate that there are several thousand purchased and pirated Hi-Opt I systems now in the hands of Blackjack players.

Hi-Opt I and the Revere Advanced Plus-Minus strategy (which is almost as simple as the Hi-Opt I but not as powerful) had a great impact on casino profits and procedures. These two strategies were responsible for more players winning more money than all previous systems combined. The increased winning was also responsible for the casinos introducing more multiple-deck games for a second time. Then along came Ken Uston, Blackjack teams, and the "Big Scare."

As detailed in his book *The Big Player*, Uston and his teammates won over a million dollars playing the game of Blackjack. Uston's team would sit down at tables and make minimum bets, keeping track of the condition of the deck. (In a Las Vegas conversation with Uston in December 1976, Ken told me how amazed he was that a simple strategy like the Hi-Opt I was so powerful. Evidently, in the latter part of 1976, a number of the team members were using the Hi-Opt I because of these features.) When the deck was favorable for the player, the flamboyant "Big Player" would be summoned with a hand signal to plunk down the maximum bet of five hundred dollars or one thousand dollars in a winning situation.

The casinos were happy to let this apparent wild man make enormous bets, jumping from table to table, because of the interest it generated. They also figured to win out in the long run as always. But Uston kept on winning. Finally, a clever casino employee deciphered the signals, much like a baseball coach stealing the opposition's signs, and identified the team. They were then barred from any further play in the casinos.

Shocked that a team using this approach could extract large sums of money from the tables, a number of the casinos who previously had single- and double-deck games immediately went to four-deck games. Some of the others went to five and six decks, even eight in their panic. At the present time, playing conditions in many Nevada casinos can be very tough. Despite these conditions, a number of professional and part-time players are still winning at the game. The purpose of this book is to tell you how and why.

THE LOSING FRAME OF MIND

Psychology tries to explain why people behave as they do. Gambling experts such as Oswald Jacoby estimate that less than one person in a hundred wins money from gambling in the long run.

The paradox is that although most people are consistent losers, they continue to gamble over and over again. Therefore, they *must* be gambling for psychological reasons rather than for the profit motive.

After twenty years of studying gambling, Dr. John Cohen of the University of Manchester came to the following conclusion:

> Analyses of the results and of gambling practices, age-old and worldwide as they are, suggest that we are dealing here with some of the most profound and complex features of the human mind. Repercussions extend far beyond the gaming table or the pace of cards into risk-taking and decision-making in all walks of life.

Gambling is nothing more than *adult play*. Winning is secondary. We *hope* to win money, but what we really enjoy is the *action*. Look at the language surrounding gambling. Gamblers are "players." They play cards, play the horses, play games, play the stock market, they even play around. Gambling is not a competitive sport. You don't play track and field, you run it. In a game, it's not your turn, it's your play. My research has shown that the play of gambling fulfills two basic human needs: the need to feel alive and the need to feel worthwhile.

The gambler feels alive by getting excited and aroused. Physically, gambling can speed up our heart rate, quicken our breathing, and increase muscle tension. There's no feeling like the one when our money hits the table. The emotions are a roller coaster of hope, excitement, euphoria, or anxiety, disappointment, frustration, sorrow, or regret. We can experience anger, hostility, aggression, and throw these emotions at spouses, the dealer, other players, or the gaming managers. One racetrack enthusiast said:

> You ask me why I gamble? I'll tell you. It's the thrill. I know the game is crooked and that I haven't got a chance. But when I put my money on the horse and hear its name on the speaker, my heart stands still. I know I'm alive.

A San Francisco gambler said:

> Only when I'm in the action do I feel truly alive.

Lem Banker, a professional football bettor, says:

> I live and die eight times on a Sunday afternoon.

Gambling makes us feel worthwhile. When we win, we react with pride, courage, and a strong sense of self-esteem. Gamblers describe their feelings with words such as "happy," "thrilled," "excited," "powerful," "brave," and "like a hero." They feel "full of energy," "in control of the situation," and "confident of winning." One gambler who had just picked a winner at the track put it best. His friends were making fun of him for his "undeserved" luck when he retorted, "Luck my ass. Who do you think I am, a nobody?"

While gambling fulfills these two needs, those fulfillments are not what makes gambling so addictive. Gambling releases us from the real world. We are isolated. There is no outside, no past or future, only here and now. Our whole being is focused on that next card. The gambler is transported into a play world, a fantasy where reality is suspended until the bankroll slips away unnoticed and unlamented until later.

While on this mental midway, we act, feel, and think with abandon. We suspend ourselves at a comfortable level of arousal. We are "high" or "spaced out." While in this state, we can courageously test our decision-making and predictive powers by trying to guess what to bet on or what bet will win. We are actors and actresses, the heroes of our own Walter Mitty drama. The uncertainty of the wager tweaks our childlike fascination with the unexpected, the surprise. We mentally scream our exhilaration at our successes, and because it is only play, feel safe from any real punishment for our failures.

Casino administrators are the best applied psychologists in the world. Every casino operator knows how to put his clients in a special frame of mind so that they will lose their money smoothly, effortlessly, and pleasurably. The accountant who spends two shopping days trying to save twenty dollars on his TV purchase calmly drops two hundred dollars in an hour at the tables while on vacation. The casino subtly grips his psyche with its polite service, free alcohol, gourmet dining, lavish entertainment, hint of sexual promise, and the yawning empty spots at the games.

If you want to gamble and win, you must become aware of the strong attraction that your psyche has to this frame of mind. By realizing how your needs are being satiated, you can better control your actions.

TEN REQUIREMENTS FOR WINNING AT BLACKJACK

While you have seen what happens to you when you gamble, you shouldn't feel that there is anything inherently wrong with gambling. My studies have shown that for most people, gambling is a natural and healthy activity. In one project, my students and I found that the average racetrack gambler spends twenty-two hours per week on gambling. You might think that people who spend this much time on gambling are "compulsive" gamblers. We found the opposite to be true. These people were psychologically more healthy than people who do not gamble. The gamblers had happier family lives, they were less hostile, less anxious, and less neurotic than the comparison group of nongamblers. We also found that the more often the gamblers wagered, the more confident and pleased they were with themselves as people.

I'm not suggesting that you begin gambling as therapy! I'm only revealing that people who gamble have been found to be at least as healthy (if not more healthy) than people who do not gamble. If you enjoy gambling, don't be ashamed to continue as long as it adds pleasure and excitement to your life. However, it never pays to go to extremes and gamble excessively. *Any* activity engaged in to excess is psychologically harmful. Gamble with control.

There are a number of prominent players who gamble a lot, but not excessively. In studying the lives of successful professionals such as Pittsburgh Phil and Nick the Greek, and in tapping my own experiences in developing winning gambling systems, I have found ten requirements that are necessary to play winning Blackjack:

1. A complete knowledge of the game
2. The keeping of records
3. Self-knowledge
4. Independence of thought and action
5. Mental readiness for sufficient concentration

6. Physical readiness
7. A basic knowledge of odds in cards
8. Self-control
9. A game plan
10. Experience

The following is a breakdown of each of these requirements:

1. A Complete Knowledge of the Game

You can't hope to win at something you don't understand. You need to learn everything there is to know about Blackjack before you can be assured of winning consistently.

I once saw one poor man who couldn't even *lose* properly because he didn't understand the game. I was playing in a downtown Las Vegas casino against a young, oriental female dealer. I was winning slowly but steadily while the other players bet with mixed results. An elderly oriental gentleman eased up to an empty seat and began to play. At first, his play was no worse than the others' at the table, although he did lose several hands in a row. When he purposely ruined a winning hand by taking an additional card, the players, including myself, began to look at each other in disbelief.

Finally, the man on my left leaned over across me and suggested to the gentleman that he shouldn't take another card when holding a winning hand. With an impatient wave, the old man shrugged off the advice and continued to lose hand after hand. In exasperation, my neighbor began berating the old man's play. The old man suddenly gathered up his chips, and in a heavy accent mumbled something about wanting the dealer to win. He had been losing on purpose because he thought the money was going to the dealer! The man should have *given* his money to the dealer if that's what he wanted. Instead, the dealer quietly let him enrich the casino.

You may not be that ignorant of the rules and procedures, but you will be playing no better than the old man if you don't know the game. This includes knowing the Basic Strategy, knowing a card-tracking system, knowing how to wager properly, and knowing how to protect yourself from cheating. All of these subjects are covered in later chapters.

2. The Keeping of Records

It is critical to keep records in playing Blackjack. A sample playing record sheet is shown in the figure below. Don't use a small, bulky spiral notebook or pad for this. It is a tipoff that you are not a casual player if the casino employees can see it. Draw it on the back of a blank check or other small piece of paper and carry it folded out of sight in a pocket. It's just as important not to carry a pen or pencil out in the open. Use one of the pencils from the keno area if you don't have a pencil tiny enough to hide on your person.

There are several reasons why you should keep this type of record sheet. You need to know where and when you played in case there is a casino pit boss or dealer working at that time who knows you are a winning player. If you have been winning regularly, you can avoid playing when they are present to identify you. This is where the "Dealer and Pit Boss Comments" column can be helpful. I always record the dealer's name, a description of him or her, and my impression of whether the dealer was honest or a cheat. I also record to what degree the pit boss was watching my play and whether he was keeping track of the cards with me or not. If the employees seemed suspicious, I avoid them by not playing again when they are present.

The won/lost record is an essential step in money management. By tracking the pattern of your winning and losing, you can both monitor your bankroll and identify casinos and dealers who are difficult to win against. Comparison with the results of other sessions and trips can help in planning your next outing.

3. Self-knowledge

You must know yourself as a gambler if you are to win consistently. Gambling is so psychologically powerful that it can totally transform you. You must closely watch your feelings as you play, so that you can learn, for example, whether you are the type of person who keeps gambling when behind or whether you can quit when losing. You should know how you relate to other players. Playing with people who upset you costs you money. Can you stay cool while playing against a dealer you don't like?

I saw one man let his irritation at the dealer interfere with his

The Playing Record Sheet.

DATE	TIME	CASINO	WON/LOST	DEALER AND PIT BOSS COMMENTS

game while playing at El Casino in Freeport, Bahamas. It was
early evening when the two of us sat down and the casino was
nearly empty. The man's wife was in an empty chair next to him
to watch the play. Since there were many empty seats, the dealer
let this pass. (Normally, if you sit down, you must play. Empty

seats attract players; nonplayers sitting at the table don't make any money for the casino.) After an hour and a half, the casino began to fill. I stayed at the table this long because I was winning.

Suddenly, in his British accent, the dealer asked the other player's wife to get up with the comment, "I'm sure you can use the exercise." Seeing the sudden nasty looks he got from the couple, he tried to smooth it over with, "Well, I read where you Yanks don't get enough exercise, you know what I mean?" This just earned him a heavier set of stares. Having blown any hope of tips, the dealer took his foot from his mouth and continued the game in silence.

I could see that the comments upset the man's wife and distracted his play because of the insult. He began to make bad plays and started chasing his losses. When I left, the couple's stack had dwindled to a single, forlorn chip.

When one of my students told me about the most expensive blouse he had ever seen, I expected to hear about one of the dancer's costumes. Instead, this costly piece of fabric was nothing more than a simple dealer's blouse. The student had been playing at a Reno casino with moderate success against a young male dealer. At the shift change, the new dealer turned out to be an attractive blonde who had forgotten one special piece of clothing, her bra. The fabric of the normal casino blouse is not particularly sheer, so when she leaned over to deal there was nothing to see. But as she stood up, or made certain turning moves, the fabric was pulled tightly across her breasts in a most distracting fashion for the men at the table. My student told me that he spent so much time trying to glimpse these brief fleshy flashes that he started losing track of the cards played and of the current level of his bankroll. He suddenly noticed that he was ten bets down at the ten-dollar level. As he got up, he ruefully realized that he had just seen a one-hundred-dollar blouse.

Find out what your reactions are to the various psychological and physical conditions in the casino. While I can endure sitting next to a cigarette smoker if the smoke isn't blowing in my face, I can't stomach a cigar smoker nearby. I immediately search for another game. Unfortunately, there is no easy or quick path to this type of self-knowledge. The only way to gain it is to start playing and pay attention to your feelings.

4. Independence of Thought and Action

Pittsburgh Phil, the legendary millionaire horseplayer, said, "A man who has not an opinion of his own has not one chance in a million to make money wagering." You must think for yourself, have confidence in your own judgment, and act independently. You cannot allow yourself to be influenced by others, be they friends, foes, dealers, mates, or whomever.

One weekend several summers ago, I learned this by being one of the influencers and seeing the harm I had done. I had planned to spend a quiet weekend at home working. My neighbor called me up late on Saturday and invited me to his country club's "Las Vegas night." He knew I was working on several new developments to my systems and thought I might like the chance to try them under fire. The rules were typical Vegas Strip rules, and twenty thousand dollars in chips would cost only five dollars, a real bargain.

That night, I sat down at one of the tables with my neighbors and several of their friends. No one knew I was a systems player except my host. He began to ask me how to play his hands, so I started describing the Basic Strategy and how it worked. I told him what the "best" plays were for his hands and explained how I was betting. The trouble was, it was just one of those nights. My success was running about average, nothing spectacular but with a slow, steady growth. My neighbor, on the other hand, was losing his shirt with my advice! No matter what the odds, he was exceeding 21 or losing with nearly every hand. I could see his mood darkening as he thought, "Why am I listening to this supposed expert? Any idiot could do this badly all by himself."

I quickly shut up and let my neighbor play his own hands no matter how poorly. His fortune turned and he began to hold his own. I ended the night moderately successful, taking my twenty thousand dollar stake into fifty-six thousand dollars. More importantly, I learned to keep my mouth shut. Everybody has the right to gamble the way he sees fit. I wasn't being fair to my neighbor to take his enjoyment away by gambling for him. In the casino, don't let anyone do this to you, or you'll have no better success than my neighbor. My answer now is standard. A woman saw I was winning and asked after she drew a 4 to a (9,8), "Was that the right play to make?"

I said, "Lady, when you win, it's *always* the right play."

5. *Mental Readiness for Sufficient Concentration*

Mental readiness is another psychological requirement you can acquire only through playing. Mental readiness not only means being alert, it is also the ability to concentrate on the cards regardless of what is going on around you. You must be proficient enough to track the cards and carry on a conversation with the dealer or the players at the same time. This is not as difficult as it seems, especially if you are using a simple system such as the Hi-Opt I point count. However, it does take practice.

While the final test is always at the tables, you can simulate a casino environment at home. I used to practice tracking the cards while sitting on the floor in front of the TV in the family room. The TV was on and I was right in the household traffic lane. I figured if I could accurately track the cards in this setting, the casino would seem like a library.

This was true to some extent, but I still had to adjust to the casino. While the environment wasn't anywhere near as hectic, the distractions were totally different. Instead of TV there were sirens and bells from the slot machines. Instead of children, there were distractions from the players and from behind the dealer in the pit. And above all, there was the tension of betting *the real thing!*

As surprising as it may sound, I did find one situation that is more *difficult* to play in than either my home or the casino. It is the typical Las Vegas night at your friendly church or club. On the night mentioned above, it was a system player's nightmare. Once I had mastered this Las Vegas night, the casino was child's play. Nobody knows what they are doing at a Vegas night, neither the players nor the dealers. Unlike the casino, everybody is talking to everybody else, the noise is enormous, the speed of play slow and erratic, and the level of expertise atrocious. The bets are often paid off incorrectly, so you have to count carefully after each hand. The card totals are misread, the cards are misdealt, and the mood is one of pleasant chaos for the serious player. All of this makes an ideal situation for mastering play in a real casino.

Whatever method you use for practice, the time spent in developing mental readiness will more than pay off. Before very long, you will find yourself being able to relax and enjoy the casino game, observing what is going on around you, while still tracking the cards. Like typing, something that once seemed slow and cumbersome will become second nature. Unlike typing, it can be quickly mastered.

6. *Physical Readiness*

Physical readiness means having your body ready to play at least four hours per day. This is a combination of not only good physical condition, but also getting an adequate amount of sleep. The problem with most casino sites is that it is very difficult to sleep there. You are often on vacation, when you don't want to waste your precious trip sleeping. The casino is a Disneyland for grownups. There are no clocks, no set mealtimes. It is very difficult to keep your biological balance in such an atmosphere.

When I gamble, I am careful to pay attention to my body. Most of us have a built-in "fatigue alarm." Whenever I am very tired and not concentrating well, I immediately stop playing and get some rest. I don't know what your "fatigue alarm" is, but all of my students seem to have one. Pay attention to it. When it goes off, get some sleep, no matter what time of day or night it is. And don't play again until you are fully rested. People who try "not to miss anything" usually end up missing only one thing: their money.

7. *A Basic Knowledge of Odds in Cards*

You need to understand card odds for several reasons. First, you will understand the effects of streaks and what to expect. Obviously, you will have runs of both wins and losses, with the long-term wins dominant. When you don't know what kinds of losing streaks can be expected, you are less likely to suspect a dealer of cheating. This lack of knowledge dulls your all-important sense of suspicion.

The second value of knowing the odds is in determining your beginning bankroll. You have to know the percentage advantage you have with each of the systems described in Chapters Six through Nine to determine your total bankroll, so that you aren't likely to lose an inadequate bankroll because of fluctuations in the game. Bankroll and betting levels are closely tied to your expected advantage. You will see exactly how these are related in Chapter Ten.

Finally, you must understand the percentage advantage you have so that you can determine if you are winning at the expected rate. If you are winning at a smaller rate over the long run, you are likely being cheated from time to time. One professional player's records showed that he had only broken even over hundreds of hours of play in single-deck games while winning at the expected rate in four-deck games. This was totally illogical since his advantage was four times greater in the single-deck games. His conclusion was obvious. He had been cheated regularly in his single-deck play. Without his knowledge of the odds, he would have been cheated in ignorance forever.

8. Self-control

Self-control is the most important *psychological* requirement in winning at Blackjack. No matter how strong a system you have, no matter how brilliant you may be, no matter how good your memory is, you can never win consistently without self-control.

This is particularly important when you are losing. You cannot be stubborn. When you lose, you must quit. The road from the Las Vegas Strip to the airport is paved with losers who couldn't stop, and sold their return tickets to "get even." One acquaintance had to cut a week off a family vacation because he couldn't quit. An old pilot's joke is, "You should never fly with the type of pilot who comes out of the john with his fly open." The gambler's analogy might be, "You should never gamble if your battle cry is, 'Just one more game, double or nothing.'" Knowing *when* to quit will be given in Chapter Five.

9. A Game Plan

In any endeavor, having a plan can be the difference between success and failure. This is especially true in Blackjack. There are many questions you can ask yourself about your reasons for playing the game. Are you certain you are reading this to win money at the game? Or is it because Blackjack is fun to play? If you are playing for enjoyment, then you don't have to concern yourself with winning, only the easier goal of breaking even. However, if you are playing cold-bloodedly to win, you must have an overall game plan.

The lack of a game plan can be deadly. A good salesman regularly takes advantage of his customer's lack of planning. When you go in to buy a simple family car, you often don't know exactly what you want. The dealer purposely stocks up on higher-priced models with the more profitable special features. When you ask for your plain model, the salesman shows you the fancy version with the suggestion, "It really doesn't cost that much more than what you originally wanted, and you can get it right away." Although you have been putting off buying a two-hundred-dollar piece of furniture for months, you readily agree to spend "only five hundred dollars" on a bunch of questionable features. These decisions made in the heat of battle frequently do nothing more than increase the heat. The best way not to regret a decision is to make it well in advance of when it might be needed.

In Blackjack, the decisions you should make concern the various aspects of your gambling. How many gambling trips do you intend to make this year? How many days will you be staying for each one? In what locations do you intend to play? How big a bankroll will you bring? How many hours a day should you play? When will you quit? Do you plan to socialize with people while you're there or will it be strictly business? These should all be answered in the planning stage. Without a game plan, the game will control you and not you the game.

10. Experience

There is no greater teacher, as the saying goes, than experience. There is only one way to get it in Blackjack, and that is to play under fire in every different condition you can find. Play in large casinos and in dust joints. Play against young dealers, old dealers, beautiful dealers and ugly ones, and dealers of different races. Play in Vegas, Reno, Tahoe, Atlantic City. Play in the Bahamas, England, Greece, Aruba, Canada, or Panama. Play in single-deck games, double-deck games, games with four, five, six, and even eight decks. Play in private games, or sit at the kitchen table and play against an imaginary dealer.

When I was developing my systems and was not yet certain of

the practical validity of my numbers, I played in every situation I could find. I followed the rules and broke every rule, just to see what happened (not being philanthropic in nature, I broke the rules at dollar tables only). The result is my utter assurance in what you will read. I have entrusted one of my most valuable commodities, my time, to the systems in this book. And certainly as high on my list in terms of value have been my wagers. Your experience will give you, too, the final lessons in playing winning Blackjack.

There you have my ten requirements for winning at Blackjack. I formulated these beliefs while struggling with trying to become a consistent winner. Once I put them into practice, my performance skyrocketed. I hope you will take the effort to apply them to your game so you can realize the same payoff.

THE ROAD TO WINNING

Here is the road to winning that this book maps out for you. It is a step-by-step summary of what you need to do in order to win money consistently in a casino.

FIRST:

1. Learn the Basic Strategy at home.
2. Learn to track cards at home with the Hi-Opt I card count.
3. Use the Hi-Opt I count to vary your bets, and play according to the Basic Strategy at home.
4. Keep records of your wins and losses.
5. Continue playing at home until you are at least five hundred betting units ahead (or keep playing until you are convinced you actually have a winning system).

THEN:

6. Accumulate a bankroll fifty times the size of your usual large bet.
7. Choose a casino that is in the top ten in terms of safety according to the list in Chapter Three.

8. Locate a table with the most favorable dealer (also as rated in Chapter Three).
9. Play against this dealer until you are showing a profit.
10. Keep playing as long as you are showing a profit.
11. Quit as soon as you begin to lose or when another dealer arrives.
12. After quitting, leave the casino quickly.
13. Record the events on your playing record sheet once you are away from the casino.
14. Find someone to cash your chips for you or come back at another time and cash them yourself.
15. Repeat the whole process in another safe casino.
16. For professional play, master the Hi-Opt I strategy presented in Chapter Eight.

THE ROAD TO LOSING

As important as it is to know the road to winning that this book presents, you should also know that it *does not* present the road to losing. But for those intellectually curious readers, or players with delusions of infinite wealth, I can show you how to lose your bankroll very quickly:

1. Skim this book; don't bother to learn it thoroughly.
2. Assume you know the Basic Strategy and the Hi-Opt I count well enough to win.
3. Ignore the chapters on cheating dealers since you "know" they couldn't possibly cheat in a big place like Las Vegas.
4. Rush to any gaming city with any kind of bankroll.
5. Find a blacklisted casino from Chapter Three.
6. Sit down at a higher-stakes table.
7. Make certain the dealer is a male over thirty years of age.
8. Buy chips with your entire bankroll.
9. Even though you are tired from the long flight and from a short night of sleep because of the excitement, play as well as you can.
10. Be prepared to return home within the next sixty minutes— you will have lost all of your money before the hour is up.

I am deadly serious about these rules. If you have fantasies of being Superman or Wonder Woman, try the road to losing. It is an unlimited-access superhighway with ten times more "on" ramps than "off" ramps. The road to winning is the Pike's Peak Hill Climb. You may feel like you're going around and around, but the direction is always up. Losing is fast. Winning is slow and steady. Like the casino, which over the long run will keep making money, you will be consistently *cashing in on Blackjack gold.*

T W O

The Game of Blackjack

If you don't know where you are going, you will probably end up somewhere else.

LAWRENCE J. PETER

I took a trip to Atlantic City about a month after Resorts International opened the first casino there. My expectations weren't very great because I had heard about the tremendous crowds of eager gamblers filling the casino to overflowing almost as soon as the doors opened. What I was totally unprepared for was the level of Blackjack play. I had rarely seen so many really *bad* players in one casino in my whole life. A typical example was a flashily dressed "dude" who sat down next to me at a $25-minimum table and began this conversation:

"Is this Blackjack?" he opened.

"Yes," I said.

"Aw good," he replied. "I want to play this game. What are those green chips?"

"Those are $25 chips."

"What are those black chips?"

"Those are $100."

"And the red ones?" he persisted.

"Those are $5.00 chips."

"What about those pink ones?"

"Those are $2.50," I said, bracing myself for the inevitable next question.

"That's funny," he said. "Why $2.50?"

"If you get a Blackjack for the $25 minimum bet, it pays $37.50 and they need the pinkies," I explained.

"OK," he said in his thick New Jersey accent, "now I know the game."

He didn't know the game. He started with $100 and lost that quickly. He pulled out another $60, lost, and pulled out another $100. When that was gone he left. Twenty minutes of play at a game he *knew* cost him only $260. He and his type will always be welcome at any casino they choose to play in.

W. C. Fields advised us, "Never give a sucker an even break." There's no even break from a casino. *You* have to give yourself the chance to minimize your losses or show a profit. And there is no way you can do that unless you truly *know the game*.

Even if you are an experienced gambler, I suggest you don't skip this chapter. Instead, skim through it. I believe you will find several topics that will be new and informative to even the seasoned player. If you are a beginner, then this chapter is of life-and-death importance to your gambling career. Don't you dare miss a word!

THE OBJECT

The object of the game of Blackjack is to obtain a total value of cards equal to or less than 21 that is higher than the dealer's card value. If the value of your cards exceeds 21, then you automatically lose. If your card value is less than or equal to 21, and the dealer's value exceeds 21, then you automatically win. If neither of the card values exceeds 21, then the higher value wins. In the case of ties (called a *push*), neither side in the casino game wins or loses.

THE EQUIPMENT

The game is played at a special table designed specifically for Blackjack. It is a kidney-shaped semicircle, with seats for up to seven players on the curved outside portion. The dealer stands behind the table in back of the chip tray. The following figure

shows the layout of a typical Blackjack table. The seat to the
dealer's extreme left is called *first* base and the seat to the far
right of the dealer is called *third base*. The table is covered with
green felt usually marked with common payoff ratios and the
dealer's playing rules in that casino.

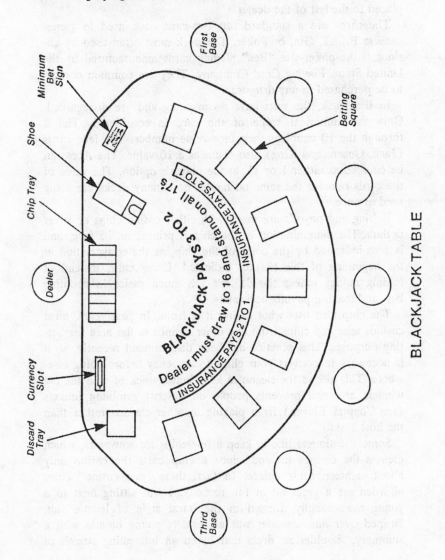

BLACKJACK TABLE

Where a casino uses more than two decks of cards in play at the same time, it is customary to use a dealing device called a *shoe*. The shoe holds the cards so that the dealer can distribute one card at a time without having to fumble with an excessive bulk of unplayed cards in his other hand. When used, the shoe is placed to the left of the dealer.

The cards are a standard fifty-two-card deck used in games such as Bridge, Gin, or Poker. The deck most often used by casinos is the poker-size "Bee" playing cards manufactured by the United States Playing Card Company. They are common enough to be purchased in any drugstore.

In Blackjack, the suits have no meaning and are disregarded. Only the numerical value of the card is considered. The 2 through the 10 count as their face-value number. The face cards (Jack, Queen, and King) also count as a 10 value. The Aces can be counted as either 1 or 11, at the player's option. The value of the cards remains the same no matter how many decks are being used at once.

Betting and payoffs are made with either casino chips or silver dollars. The denomination of the chip is printed on its face, and is also indicated by the color of the chip, as the conversation at the beginning of this chapter indicated. Using chips instead of folding money makes the dealer's job much easier in counting bets and making payoffs accurately.

The chip also lists what casino it is from. In past years, most casinos accepted chips from any other casinos in the area for betting purposes. This practice has been discontinued recently, so it is necessary to convert your chips to currency before going elsewhere. This allows the casino to keep better track of who the big winners are, and prevents people on no-cost gambling junkets (see Chapter Eleven) from playing in other casinos rather than the host casino.

Some vacationers like to keep a few chips for souvenirs, which pleases the casinos no end, since a chip costs the casino only about eighteen cents apiece. In fact, these "one casino" chips afforded me a great bit of fun recently. I was sitting next to a young man flashily dressed in the latest style of leisure suit. Draped over one shoulder was an equally young blonde with a summery, shoulderless dress that bared an interesting stretch of tanned skin. When they began to argue at the table, I couldn't help but overhear the problem.

"Can I have a few chips to take home, honey?" she purred.

"Hell no," he shot back. "Don't you realize that those things are money? I mean, it's like tearing up a dollar bill. You're just throwing your money away."

She was somewhat startled at his strong response, and also embarrassed at the attention the little interchange brought, so she shrunk back a little. The young man kept playing, pleased in his smug righteousness over his money management. At this point, I checked the ring fingers of both their hands and saw them empty. I looked at the young man again and saw that he was fairly slight, so I decided to have some fun.

I turned to the young woman with two chips I had been planning on tipping the dealer with and said, "Let me share some of my chips with you. Everyone ought to have something with which to remember a *good time* in Las Vegas." I emphasized "good time" to zing the young man's boorish behavior. With a flourish, I dropped the chips in her hand and returned to my game.

The young woman immediately began to rub it in to her companion. "See what a stranger will do?" she told him. "You're too cheap to let me have two lousy chips." He was staring daggers at my back, and everyone else at the table was having trouble keeping a straight face, including me. He finally got up, grabbed her arm, and marched off. As they walked away, the dealer observed, "She'll leave him soon."

Ah thank you, El Cortez, for providing the opportunity for me to exercise my "bird-dogging" skills (stealing someone's date) after so many years. Nothing is more fun than the "let's you and him fight" approach.

THE PEOPLE

Although there are seven seats at the table, Blackjack is not a group game. The players *do not* normally play as a team against the dealer. For each player, it is as though there were no one else at the table. You may be a big winner while the person next to you has lost hundreds of dollars. Instead of competing, Blackjack is a meeting place for people from all parts of the world. Ninety per cent of the players are recreation players, looking for enjoyment. Because of the game's pauses for shuffling and other gamblers playing their hands, there is more conversation at the Blackjack table than at any other casino game. And you are free to move to another table or casino if you feel ill at ease or are seated next to a disagreeable player.

Another person present is the dealer. From a playing standpoint, the honest dealer makes no decisions. Blackjack for the dealer is a mechanical game. He or she is merely a human machine who either pays or takes your bets depending upon the turn of the cards. The rules for playing the dealer's hand are written right on the green felt for all to see. The dealer need merely follow those rules.

It is also the dealer's job to answer any questions you may have about the rules of the game and to be generally helpful to the player. While the dealer won't tell you how to play your cards, he or she can assist you by pointing out your options or helping you count your card values. A young woman novice next to me once threw in her hand in disgust at having totaled 22, only to have the dealer return her cards to her. To her surprise, she had miscounted a four-card hand of 21!

There are two other casino people who can affect your Blackjack game: the *pit boss* and the *eye in the sky*. The pit boss is the dealers' supervisor and is the final authority for all problems or disagreements. It is the pit boss's responsibility to see that the games run smoothly and according to casino policies. The pit boss will be that sharp-eyed gentleman in a suit wandering around in the closed-off area behind the circle of tables.

The other observer has been dubbed the eye in the sky for reasons that will become obvious. The next time you are sitting at a Blackjack table, look up at the ceiling. You will see a series of mirrors above each table. Those mirrors are one-way viewing devices connected by a series of catwalks. Another sharp-eyed and well-trained individual patrols these catwalks watching play from an ideal overhead vantage point. The purpose of this is to discourage player cheating, since the player can never be certain he or she is not being watched or photographed breaking the rules. To be certain you don't accidentally break any rules, you should understand how the game is played.

BASIC PLAY

The first action you should take upon sitting down at the table is to change your currency into casino chips. Do not place your money in the marked betting square (or circle at some tables) or the dealer will think you are placing a wager on the next hand. In many casinos, you can place bets with currency. If the dealer shouts, "Money plays!" when your change is put out, then it is in the wrong place. Quickly ask for change or your first bet will be your entire buy-in.

Generally, the dealer doesn't like to make change for over twenty units. A twenty-dollar bill at a one- or two-dollar-minimum table will usually get you ten silver dollars and two five-dollar chips. During play, if you want to break down a larger-denomination chip, merely place it *beside* the betting square and announce "change." If you should run out of chips, you can buy more with currency.

There are no minimum buy-in rules at Blackjack. You can play with just one chip as long as it equals or exceeds the table minimum. You can carry your chips from table to table or even take them home overnight, or as a souvenir. If you have been betting more and more units and winning, the dealer will often pay you in larger-denomination chips, called *upgrading* your stack. While some think that this is an attempt by the dealer to get you to bet more and more by giving you larger chips, you can always obtain whatever change you need at any time at your discretion. The dealer is only making change the easy way by returning fewer but larger-denomination chips, or trying not to run short of his lower-value chips in the chip tray.

If you have sat down at the finish of a deck or shoe, the deal will stop. After a thorough shuffle of the cards, the dealer offers one of the players the option of cutting. (You may refuse this if you wish.) In a single- or two-deck game, the dealer offers the cards to a player. The player makes a one-hand cut, setting the cut-off portion on the table. The dealer then completes the cut. When more than one deck is used or the cards are dealt from a shoe, the dealer may hand you a *marker* card. You insert this solid colored plastic card edgewise into the deck for the cut. The purpose of all this is to assure you that the cards are well mixed and that everything is left to random chance.

After the shuffle and cut, the top card (the *burn* card) is usually taken out of play without being seen and put in the discard tray. After all the wagers are placed in the appropriate betting squares, the dealer then deals clockwise from first base to third base, one card at a time to each player. The cards may be dealt face down, in which case you are allowed to handle them to determine their value. If the cards are dealt face up, they are placed in front of your bet and are not to be handled. The dealer always has one card face up and one card face down (except in the English version, where the dealer takes one face-up card and takes the second card only after all the players' hands are completed).

After each player has two cards, the dealer goes back to first base and continues clockwise around the table, giving additional cards to players as they desire (called *hitting*), until the players wish no more cards (called *standing*) or have exceeded the 21 count (called *busting*). After collecting the bets of all players who have busted, the dealer reveals his down card (or takes a second card in the English version). He then hits or stands according to the casino rules and collects from or pays off the remaining players accordingly.

When your play is complete, you will want to take your casino chips and change them back into currency. The dealer cannot do this for you, since the currency slot at the table is a one-way path only. The casino will have a central cashier cage for changing chips. This not only reduces the chance of theft from the casino, it also helps the casino bosses identify big winners. If you were a big winner and don't want to fumble with a large number of small-denomination chips, ask the dealer to upgrade them for you before going to the cashier.

THE BLACKJACK

Any first two cards consisting of an Ace and 10-count card (10, Jack, Queen, or King) form a *natural* or *Blackjack*. This is an automatic winner if the dealer doesn't have a natural also. While all other payoffs in Blackjack are paid at even money (one to one), a natural is paid a premium three to two. A natural pays fifteen dollars on a ten-dollar wager, whereas a normal win pays only ten dollars on a ten-dollar wager. Whenever you hold a natural, you should immediately turn your cards over to be paid.

The dealer can also have a natural. The dealer is allowed to look at the down card whenever an Ace or 10-count card is showing (called *peeking*). If the two cards form a natural, the dealer automatically wins from any player not also having a natural. The player's natural is considered a push vs. a dealer natural and the wager is neither taken nor paid.

The English version creates a few variations, since the players' hands are completed before the second card is taken by the dealer. As you will see in the next section, there are certain situations where you may increase your bet during the play of a hand. If the dealer ends up having a natural, these additional bets are returned and the original bet amount is collected from any player not also having a natural.

PLAYER OPTIONS

One of the delights of Blackjack is that the player has so many decisions to make. The feeling of involvement is unmatched almost anywhere else in gambling. In most cases, you can communicate your decisions without having to say a word. In fact, dealers prefer that you use hand signals, and some casinos may require it. In the noisy and distracting environment of the casino, with slot machines whooping and bonging and conversations coming from all directions, the dealer can have a difficult time hearing your spoken signals. Hand signals let the dealers know your wishes without question and allow them to keep their eyes on the cards. Following are your six options and the techniques to signal them to the dealer.

STANDING

If your cards in a face-down game give you a satisfactory total, you should indicate stand by slipping your two cards under your stack of chips in the betting square. If you are playing in a face-up game, then all you need do is indicate a stand with a simple hand movement. I normally hold my hand palm down and move it sharply left and right in a wiping "no" motion several inches off the felt surface. This movement mimics the negative head shake and is clearly understood.

HITTING

To indicate a hit in a face-down game, you should grasp your cards and lightly scrape them toward you on the felt in one or two quick motions, much like brushing off a cigarette ash. The dealer will see this and will deal one card up in front of the betting square. If you want another card, repeat the scratching motion until you decide to stand or have busted (over 21). In a face-up game, you can indicate a hit by scratching your fingers rather than the cards over the felt. To make my hitting motion clearly distinct from my standing motion, I point to my cards with my index finger in a sharp movement that indicates "put it there."

SPECIAL TWO-CARD PLAYS

In standard Blackjack, you are always required to place your bet before receiving your first two cards. Blackjack would be very dull (and much more profitable to the casinos) if all there was to the game was betting, then hitting or standing. It would be much more fun if we could increase our bet when we appear to have an advantageous hand compared to the dealer. Here are a few ways in which the casino allows you to do this:

DOUBLING DOWN

After you have looked at your first two cards, you may feel you have a good hand that will become a very good hand with one additional card. This is an ideal time for the *double-down* bet. The basic double-down play means that you may make a second wager no higher than the amount of your original bet and receive one and *only one* additional card. This third card is usually dealt down. All casinos permit doubling on a two-card 11, most on 10, 11, and many on 9, 10, 11. Some even permit a double down on any two-card hand.

Where you may double down on any two-card hand, *soft doubling* comes into play. A *soft* hand is one that contains an Ace. Depending upon what the dealer up card is, you may wish to double down on A,7, for example.

To signal a double-down play to the dealer, all you need to do is move your double-down second wager into the betting square and set it *next to* your original bet. If you are playing in a face-down game, you must also turn over your cards so the dealer can verify that you have a two-card total that may be doubled. When you turn them over, place them on the dealer's side of the betting square.

PAIR SPLITTING

When your first two cards have the same point value, you have the option of separating them and playing them as two separate hands (face cards and 10s are usually considered pairs, but you would almost *never* want to split a 20). You may draw as many cards as you wish to split pairs (except split Aces—see below). Unlike the double-down play, where you can bet any additional amount up to the value of your initial wager, you *must double* your bet so that there is an equal amount wagered on each hand.

If you are playing in a face-down game, you can indicate your wish to split a pair by placing your two cards face up on the dealer's side of the betting square. You must then move a second stack of chips *equal to* the original bet up to the betting square and set it *beside* your first bet. The remaining cards will be dealt face up. In a face-up game, you need merely move your second wager up to the betting square since the cards are already face up in front of the dealer.

A special case of pair splitting involves Aces. The casino allows you only one more card, dealt face down, for each split Ace because it is such an advantageous card for the player. In addition, if you receive a 10 for a natural on one of the split Aces, it is paid off only as a 21-value hand (one to one) instead of as a natural (three to two).

In some casinos, you can combine doubling and splitting. One option sometimes available is called "resplitting." If you split a card and receive a third card of the same value, you can create a hand for another wager equal to your initial bet. Certain casinos also allow doubling down after pair splitting. Ask the dealer what is allowed where you are playing.

For example, I was playing at a downtown Las Vegas casino in a two-deck game and tracking cards when the deck turned favorable for me. The dealer's up card was a 6 (a very bad card for the dealer, good for me) and I held 7,7. My first bet was four units, so I split the 7s and bet another four units. I received a third 7 on the first hand and split again. At this point I had twelve units on the table. My first 7 drew a 3, which I then doubled down on for a third card. I now had sixteen units bet. My second 7 drew an A, and I doubled again. My third 7 drew a 4, which I doubled down on for a final combined total bet of 24 units. My heart sank when I saw the dealer's down card was a 5 for a two-card total of 11. The dealer hit with another 5 (16 total) and had to hit again. The fourth card was a 9 for a dealer bust. I collected my forty-eight units from the table and decided it was a good time for a break.

INSURANCE

When the dealer's face-up card is an Ace, play is stopped as the dealer asks, "Insurance, anyone?" Actually, the name "insurance" is misleading, because you are not insuring anything. You are making a side bet on whether or not the dealer has a 10-value card as his face-down card. The dealer must make the insurance offer before looking at his down card, so he has no idea what is there when he takes the insurance bets.

You can make an insurance bet in an amount up to one half of your initial wager in the betting square. The insurance bet is placed in the large semicircle so labeled. As the semicircle states, insurance pays off two to one. For example, if you originally bet ten dollars, and the dealer hand showed an Ace up, you could bet up to five dollars in the insurance semicircle. If the dealer's card turned out to be a 10, you would lose your original ten-dollar bet, but your insurance bet of five dollars would win the ten dollars back. If the dealer does not have a 10 as the face-down card, you lose your five dollars and play on; the hand continues in the normal fashion.

SURRENDER

The surrender option was introduced in Manila in 1958. Only a few of the casinos allow this play, so you will have to ask the dealer whether this is permitted. Surrender allows you to stop play on any hand under 21 and lose only half of your original bet (assuming the dealer doesn't have an Ace up). Some casinos restrict surrender to your first two cards, so again check with the dealer.

Surrender is the one option that requires you to speak to the dealer. If you wish to surrender your cards, merely say "Surrender" when it is your turn to hit or stand. The dealer may call out "Surrender!" to the pit boss and will collect your bet, returning half of it to the betting square.

This section on player options has made no effort to tell you *when* to make the various plays, only *how* to make them so you will feel comfortable in the casino. Chapters Six through Nine tell you exactly *what* plays to make *when* for whatever level of play you wish, from beginner to professional.

COMMON PLAYING MISTAKES BY ROOKIES

Everybody makes mistakes, even experienced professionals. But if you've ever made some innocent move (to you) and had the dealer harshly correct you, then you know how uncomfortable mistakes can be. In my years of play at the tables, I have categorized the more frequent and embarrassing novice errors. Once you understand the pitfalls and the reason behind the casino rules, you will be able to avoid making these errors.

BETTING ERRORS

One of the most foolish feelings in the world is to walk into a crowded casino, find one of the few empty seats, sit down, and throw out your five-dollar chip only to have everybody look at you in disgust. The dealer then says in a flat voice, "This is a one-hundred-dollar-minimum table, sir." With a red face, you get up and mumble, " 'Cuse me," and slink off. No wonder there were empty seats!

You should have a little empathy for the players at the high-limit tables. I've seen this type of interruption happen as often as once every two or three minutes on a busy weekend night at a crowded Las Vegas casino. After a while, the players and the dealer are fed up with having to state the table limit. The way to avoid this is to look for a little white-on-black plastic sign usually located to the dealer's left (your right). This sign will state the table minimum if it is different from the normal casino minimum. When in doubt, watch what the players are betting. At least half the players often will be betting the minimum in a higher-stakes game.

Another bit of carelessness that irritates the dealer and slows up the game is to throw several chips into the betting square. Your bet must be in a single stack so the dealer doesn't confuse your initial bet for a double down later on. In most cases, the dealer will arrange your bet before beginning to deal. Some dealers, though, will instruct you to keep your bet in one stack.

A terrible mistake is to touch your bet after the deal has begun. The dealers will react immediately and strongly, telling you, "Do *not* touch your bet." The reason for this response is that you are behaving like a cheater. Cheating players will attempt to *press* a good hand (add more chips when the dealer isn't looking) or *pinch* a bad hand (take chips off the stack when not being observed).

It is equally bad to place a double-down bet or splitting bet on top of your original wager. The cheat will add *more* than the doubled amount whenever possible. And once there is a single stack, the dealer can't be certain what the original bet was.

CARD-CARE ERRORS

You are *never* to touch the cards in a face-up game. If you do, or try to, the dealer can only assume it's because you wish to mark or deface a card. Cheaters have all kinds of ways to mark cards for later identification. They wear sharp rings to "cut" an edge, or they can do it with a fingernail. One cheater even tried to mark cards with a special ink that could be seen only through his treated glasses.

While you can handle the cards in a face-down game, you should be careful. The dealers, the pit boss, and the eye in the sky are much more alert to unusual player moves in the face-down game, since it is easier to mark the cards in play. A typical innocent mistake is to make the hit motion by brushing the cards too hard across the felt. This puts a bend in the cards that can be detected later. The dealer will stop you and ask that you brush the cards *lightly* for a hit.

VALUE MISCOUNTING

As in the example of the young woman throwing in a hand of 21, newcomers will frequently miscount their hand. In the flow of the game, you can forget your intermediate total as you take a hit or you make a simple addition error. If you have trouble adding up your cards, don't be afraid to take your time and read all the cards with each hit. This way you will be certain of their exact value.

Another problem is caused by mishandling Aces. I saw one man stand on A,4 because he was afraid of going over 21 on his next card. He forgot that A,4 could be either 15 *or 5,* so there was no possibility that he could bust his hand with one more card. I saw a woman throw in a hand of A,9 after hitting and receiving a 10. The dealer did a double take at the hand, raising his eyebrows in surprise. He then remembered his loyalties and obligingly scooped up the woman's cards and her money.

The best way to count Aces is to consider them a "1" and calculate your hand. When you reach a total, add a "10" for every Ace in the hand. For example, you are dealt A,3. This gives you a 4 or a 14 value. You hit and receive another Ace for A,3,A. Your values now are 5, 15, or 25 (a bust). You hit again and receive a 5 for A,3,A,5. First counting the Aces as "1," you now have a 10, and adding a "10" for the first ace, also a 20. Since 20 is a very good hand, you now decide to stand. By counting Aces as "1" first, then adding 10, you avoid standing on a soft hand because you are afraid of busting.

Another miscounting error involves chips. If you mix the values of your chips after getting your change, you may think you're betting ten dollars with two five-dollar chips and be betting thirty dollars with a twenty-five-dollar chip under a five-dollar chip. Or you may get your colors mixed up and think you're betting five dollars a hand and be betting twenty-five dollars a hand. When in doubt, look carefully at the face of the chips for their dollar value. Keep them in separate stacks in front of you and arrange them in some order such as low to high, left to right, for example. This way you will always know what you are betting.

PLAYING ERRORS

Many beginning players take hits for cards they never asked for because they are careless about the way they handle their cards. One such man sitting next to me in a face-down game would look at his hand and then set the cards back down. He was distracted for a moment and looked back to find the dealer and the other players looking at him, waiting for him to play his hand. He picked up his cards with a snap to review the hand, and the dealer hit him with a third card. The man protested that he hadn't wanted a hit, and before an argument could start, the dealer alertly called the pit boss over. Since the man had an obvious standing hand, the pit boss instructed the dealer to burn the hit card and asked the player to be more careful about the way he handled his cards. Had the hand not been such an obvious standing situation, the player might have had to accept the card.

Another playing mistake is to absent-mindedly stick your first two cards up near the area of the bet or up under the bet even though you may wish to take a hit. Suddenly you see the dealer giving cards to the person on your left, having passed you by. What you've done is to signal that you want no more cards. Once the dealer has gone by you and dealt to another player, it's too late. If you plan to hit, keep your cards away from the betting square.

A final playing mistake it to try to split nonpairs. The first time in the casino, a friend of mine tried to split an A,9 and couldn't understand why the dealer wouldn't let him. He had seen others splitting into two hands, but he hadn't noticed that the cards always were pairs.

By watching for these errors, you will make your Blackjack sessions much more enjoyable for you, the other players, and the dealer.

GENERAL TABLE ETIQUETTE

There are a few casino rules that don't fit under any particular aspect of play. The first of those is the infrequent *card-down* situation. Early in my career, I was playing at a full table when the dealer accidentally dealt a card to me over the edge of the table. Since it was very difficult for me to reach down under my stool to get the card, I thought one of the other players might get it. No one moved a muscle. Typical, I thought, of the modern version of John and Jane Q. Public. The dealer evidently hadn't seen what happened at first, but noticed I had only one card on the table as I started to bend down. He said, "Don't worry about it" and called, "Card down" over his shoulder. I went ahead and picked up the card with a helpful, "I don't mind."

When the pit boss arrived, the dealer handed him the card and pointing to me said, "He got it." The pit boss carefully looked over the card, then looked at me and gave it back to the dealer. Feeling stupid, I realized that players aren't supposed to retrieve cards from off the table. An experienced friend told me later that cheaters will mark or switch cards underneath the table whenever possible. I must have looked touristy enough that they didn't feel it was necessary to swap decks to see if I had pulled a switch.

Whenever a card goes off the table, tell the dealer and let the pit boss retrieve it.

Another rule goof I made nearly was in playing more than one hand at a time. At first, I picked up both sets of hands I was playing and was immediately informed by the dealer that I was not allowed to do that. When playing more than one hand at a time, you must fully play out the first hand before going on to look at the cards in the next hand. The only exception to this is when the dealer is showing an Ace up and asks for insurance bets. In that situation, you can look at all your hands to see which ones you might want to place the insurance side bet on.

The final area of general table etiquette is tipping. Even though the drinks are complimentary, the serving waitress is not. It is customary to tip the waitress for her service. I usually don't tip with every drink, but wait and tip a larger amount every other drink. The amount is up to you.

Another person who can be tipped is the dealer. *Why* you might want to tip dealers is discussed in detail in Chapter Four. This focuses on *how* to tip the dealers. The easiest way is simply to give the dealer a tip by placing the chip or money out on the felt between the betting square and the dealer and letting the dealer know it is for him or her. A method many dealers prefer, and one that nets the dealer more money if you are a winning player, is to bet your tip for the dealer. This is done by placing the dealer tip between your wager and the dealer on the line of the betting square. If you lose, the dealer collects both bets and will at least thank you in return. If you win, the dealer pays both bets separately, waits until you collect your winnings, and then picks up the tip and tip winnings.

Dealer tips are often placed to the right of the dealer (your left) in a stack. Periodically, the pit boss will take the tips away for safekeeping. This safekeeping is necessary because many casinos don't want dealers pocketing chips while dealing, and to keep the tips from being taken. Once when I was playing at El Casino in Freeport, I saw a player sitting at third base take the dealer's stack of chips. I believe it was an accident, though, because the player didn't try to hide it or mix the stack with his chips. The tip stack was very close to the player's chips, and the player was just fooling with the chips and picked up the second stack.

The dealer glanced over and noticed that his tips were missing and knew that the pit boss had not been by. Looking around, he spotted the second stack at third base and asked the player to return it. The player was extremely embarrassed, and returned the chips with a healthy tip as an apology. He then left after several hands.

THE CASINO ENVIRONMENT

There are a number of side features of casino Blackjack that are not directly related to the game. To understand fully what may be happening at your table, you need to be aware of the possibilities.

CASINO CREDIT

Marketing studies have shown that retail credit customers will buy more than cash customers. The casino industry has recognized this fact in gambling as well, and caters to players who use significant credit lines. A player using credit will be given a slip of paper called a *marker,* upon which he or she fills out an amount and then signs. (The marker is a negotiable instrument, which can be presented to the player's bank for payment.) The safest way for the casino to let the player use markers is to have the player deposit the gambling stakes in cash at the casino cage on arrival. The stake is then returned to the player minus any markers that were signed during the stay.

For most players, casino credit is similar to the check-cashing privilege you may have at the neighborhood grocery store. You fill out an application for credit, which is sent to Central Credit for verification. Once your credit is established, you are allowed to cash checks up to your credit limit. The typical procedure is to sign markers during your trip and then settle them with a single check at the end of your trip.

The problems arise when a player is unable to pay for his gambling losses. Having credit lines at several casinos can be the cause of this. For example, a player with a ten-thousand-dollar line of credit at five casinos could lose as much as fifty thousand dollars, well beyond his credit line and ability to pay. In most cases, the casino will co-operate with a valued player to the point of making compromises if there is a hardship in paying. Big bettors with credit problems can still be allowed to play on a cash-only basis if they agree to apply a portion of their winnings (normally 50 per cent) to the outstanding debt.

The occasional player who has written an insufficient-funds check will be the object of more vigorous collection efforts. A phone call or telegram will request that additional money be put in the account so that the check can be redeposited. If it bounces a second time, the casino will try more phone calls and letters. Important credit debts may be turned over to a lawyer or collection agency where the player lives. There is little need to worry about strong-arm tactics from the casino. Legally, the Federal Fair Debt Collection Practices Act, passed in 1978, bans the use of threats, telephone harassment, or other extralegal actions by credit collectors.

In fact, there is little legal basis for collecting a Nevada gambling debt at all. A casino debt is unenforceable in Nevada, and therefore unenforceable in any other state. Of course, filing a suit makes the debt public knowledge, which alone encourages many players to pay up. Also, if the defendant doesn't respond, the casino can win a default judgment against the player. Bahamian casino debts are also legally unenforceable. But in New Jersey and Puerto Rico, casino debts are legal obligations.

While casino collection tactics may be controlled, the danger lies in running up a bad debt on a junket. A junket is a specially chartered trip to a casino at the expense of the casino. Junket agents arrange for groups of large bettors to take these complementary trips asking only that the gambler play at the sponsoring casino for a certain number of hours at a specified betting level. Junket agents whose clients are credit problems risk cancellation of their profitable junket trips. Once fired by a casino, the junket agent has little chance of getting dates at other casinos.

Because the junket business is so competitive, some junket agents guarantee the debts of their clients. While the casino allows between 3 per cent and 5 per cent for bad debts, the junket agent must collect *all* markers he guarantees. A couple of high rollers with bad debts can put him out of business. So the

junket agent can be a tough man to owe, because he *must* have
your money.

I believe the best way to play Blackjack is as a cash player. I
don't want *anybody* connected with the casino to know how much
I have played, won, or lost. All casinos provide safe-deposit
boxes for valuables or money. Use those instead of the casino
cage, where your transactions will be watched. With casino credit,
you can lose what you don't have. With cash, you can handle the
game without anyone else's help.

PLAYER BENEFITS

One of the advantages of playing at the table, particularly if you
are playing with stacks of five-dollar chips or better, is show
passes (or other free services). If a show you wish to see at the
casino is "sold out," you should ask the pit boss if any reservations are available for players. These are normally reserved for
big losers, but you might be able to swing one. If you would like
to get into a show at a different casino, don't hesitate to ask the
pit boss where you are, as they routinely reciprocate reservations
at other casinos for their customers.

THIEVERY

Any place that attracts a large amount of people with money to
lose attracts thieves. In the first six weeks of play in Atlantic City,
there were two armed robberies in the rest rooms. I found out
what was possible quite by accident once while seeing a show at
the Stardust in Las Vegas.

Our party had excellent seats at the Lido show, a table at center stage front. One of the acts was a French pickpocket who
could take anything. He was walking by where we were seated
and suddenly dropped the mike. I grabbed and caught it, and as a
reward was invited onstage. Here I was, a winning Blackjack
player trying to take money out of the casino in obscurity up onstage during the Lido show! I thought I was going up to hold the
mike for him, but instead found that I was to be part of the act.
The pickpocket pointed to a spot on the stage and asked me to
stand there. I remember being terribly nervous because I noticed

I was standing directly on a trap door. He began to ask me questions and walk around me as I answered. Suddenly he whispered for me to hold onto my pants, which made me even more nervous. I knew he could take my belt off and drop my pants if he wanted to.

The next thing I knew he was holding a bag of jewelry (souvenirs for the home folks) I had in my inside coat pocket, my watch, my wallet, and my book with all the little phone numbers in it. All I could think about was, "When do I go through the trap door?" He finally let me step down and the act got a big hand. After the show, people were complimenting me because they thought I was part of the act, even though I tried to convince them that I wasn't. What started me thinking was the ease at which my valuables had been taken and how open an available purse or a rear-pocket wallet is to nimble and dishonest fingers.

Sometimes a little clever daring is all you need. A woman told me of losing an entire fifty-dollar jackpot at the dime slots. She had just finished filling up two cups with dimes from the jackpot and had begun playing again. Suddenly a well-groomed man immaculately dressed in an expensive-looking suit walked up, grabbed the cups, and said, "Let me cash these in for you." He then quickly turned and walked down the line of slots toward the cashier's cage.

The woman was momentarily caught off guard, thinking the man must work for the casino. When she realized a few moments later that a stranger had walked off with her money, she ran to follow. Rounding the corner where she had seen him last, she found only the typical casino crowd with no suited thief. She went to a nearby security guard, who immediately ordered the doors locked. The casino was searched, but the bandit was never found.

Although I sympathized with the woman, I had to laugh, thinking about a thief getting up, showering, dressing in a suit, kissing his wife good-bye in the morning and saying, "See you late this evening. I've got a heavy load of stealing to do today." One thing you can be certain of: Anywhere there are large sums of money, there will be countless swindle schemes in operation. If you're really intent on losing all of your money, at least get some enjoyment out of it and gamble it away.

Carry your valuables carefully, and watch your chips at all

times in the casino. I've seen chips "snitched" at the table, chips dropped, or just left somewhere only to disappear instantly. There's no reason to be a winning Blackjack player if you're going to give your winnings away.

PROSTITUTION

Although prostitution is illegal in Las Vegas, the authorities must allow it because there are so many and they're so obvious. Personally, I prefer to maximize the quantity of my gambling time rather than improve the quality of my sack time. But being the normal Western male who doesn't look like Sly Stallone or John Travolta, normally I don't get asked out too often. It's a change to listen to the lines women use to ensnare men instead of vice versa. What attracts these professional ladies is a high roller or a winner. I don't fit into the first category, but I consistently fit into the second.

A typical approach was one I heard in a small Las Vegas casino bar. The tables were too crowded for any worthwhile play, so I decided to wait until the show started and the casino cleared somewhat. As I sat there, a young woman took the seat next to me and smiled. She was very lovely, tall with long black hair and a clinging, long dress. I smiled back.

As I did, she asked, "Any luck?"

"No," I answered, "I haven't played here yet. It's too crowded."

"You look sad. Lonely?" she said, looking sympathetic. I shook my head no.

"On a scale from 1 to 10, how do you feel?"

"Oh about a 7," I said.

"Bet I can get you up to an 8!"

"Interesting. How do you do it?"

"Try me," she purred, her smile widening.

"No thanks," I ended. "As soon as I get a seat here I plan to win a few hundred dollars."

Once when playing at the Desert Inn, I won sixteen hundred dollars rather quickly, when the junket operator came over to chat. I stopped playing and stood next to my stool talking. At the sight of my winnings, the hookers congregated around the area very quickly. As I resumed play, one of my friends, Warren, sat down two seats away. Then three girls sat down, one between us and two bracketing us. The girl in the middle was very attractive, with golden hair curled loosely about her shoulders. She had evidently been drinking, and started talking loudly about being the best girl on the Strip (she was also very uninhibited about what details made her the best). Warren was taking all this in since this was his first trip to Las Vegas.

She noticed Warren's attention and gently put her hand between his legs under the table. I could see that Warren's playing (at least *casino* play) was over for the evening. The other two stayed for a while, but finding no action from me (why should I leave during a win streak?), soon departed. When I saw Warren the next morning, he grinned and told me that although he had little basis for comparison, she certainly did live up to her billing.

On a later trip, Warren and I had rented what turned out to be the dog of all rental-car dogs. It eventually broke down, but our luck was holding because we were right in front of a filling station. We nursed the car into the garage, where Warren decided to stay and see about getting it fixed. Since we were next to a very small casino, I decided to go in and play for a short time.

The place was so small it only had a couple of Blackjack tables. I sat down at one with a young female dealer and began to play. My fortune was still holding as I won about $450 in twenty minutes. The dealer was very nice, so I tipped her and quit before I lost my winnings back. You wouldn't have believed the look on the pit boss's face when I got up a big winner. The dealer saw it too and said, "Why don't you stay awhile? The fun is just starting." I declined and went to the cashier's cage.

As the cashier was counting out my chips the phone rang. Picking it up and pausing, the cashier said, "$450," then hung up. I looked out across the casino and saw the pit boss hanging up too. Evidently, he had wanted to know how much I walked out with. He then picked up the phone and made another call. I turned back to the cashier and counted my bills before leaving.

I walked outside and headed back to the service station to see how it was coming with the car. Just before I got there, a silver-gray Lincoln Continental pulled up beside me and stopped. A window noiselessly eased down and a gorgeous, dark-haired woman leaned out and said, "You interested in going to a party?" Curious why she picked me out, I looked around the street, finding it neither teeming with people nor bare. I thanked her but demurred, telling her I had to pick up my rental car with a friend. It later occurred to me that she may have been alerted by the casino that I was leaving with substantial cash. There was no other reason she should pick me out for her next client.

The gambling environment is designed to fulfill your every need. If you're short of money, the casino can help. Female companionship is available in abundance. Though men aren't out hustling on the street, male companions are often obtainable through escort services. And the casino entertainment is often free for players. As long as you remember that the entire system is designed to get all or part of your money, you won't go wrong, because this book tells you how to keep getting it back.

MYTHS OF BLACKJACK

Now that you know what Blackjack *is,* you should know what Blackjack *is not.* These myths have clouded the thinking of many potential winning Blackjack players. Each myth will be completely shattered by the time you master this book.

MYTH No. 1   You need luck in order to win at casino Blackjack.

This is completely false. Blackjack is the only casino game in which the *player* can actually get a permanent, long-term, mathematical advantage over the house using his or her own skill. True, over a few playing sessions, you may win or lose more than your advantage will dictate. But the long-term player who knows how to play the game according to this book will realize exactly the percentage of profit that is associated with whatever strategy from Chapters Six through Nine the player uses.

There is no need to prove this in casino play if you are skeptical. Learn one of the strategies, then play a few thousand hands at home, keeping track of the results. Or, if you have a computer at your disposal, as I do, let the computer do the playing. Either way, you will show a profit after playing this many hands.

MYTH No. 2   *You have to be a mathematical genius in order to learn how to win at Blackjack.*

This idea started after mathematics professor Edward O. Thorp published his best-selling *Beat the Dealer* in 1962. Thorp did have a very complicated strategy in his book called *Ten Count*. The press and other media focused on his being a professor and came to the conclusion that only an extremely intelligent person with a mathematical mind could win at Blackjack. This is now totally erroneous.

Thorp's 1966 edition of *Beat the Dealer* introduced a very simple point-count system where the player keeps track of large cards and small cards only. Being smart enough to count by 1s up to plus or minus 10 is enough. I have taught a ten-year-old girl and a twelve-year-old boy, on one holiday weekend, to play a winning game using the methods from Chapters Six and Seven later in this book. *Anyone* can learn to win.

MYTH No. 3   *You have to have a photographic memory in order to learn to win.*

I am often the "absent-minded professor." No photographic memory, or anything approaching such a memory, is needed. The most difficult part of learning to win is memorizing the Basic Strategy for playing the various possible hands. And for most people, all that's needed is a few hours of memory work.

You aren't memorizing the cards as you see them, you are merely counting the cards as they go by. If you can remember a single number, then you can track the cards. Chapter Six also contains hints in memorizing the Basic Strategy to help you shorten your study time.

MYTH No. 4   *Dealers deal too fast for players to keep track of the cards.*

While some dealers do deal extremely fast, they can never deal faster than you can play. That's because *no dealer can deal past you until you give the signal that you wish to stand.* Some dealers will try to get you into their rhythm of play by starting slowly and gradually speeding up, but *you* control the way you play your hand. He can never deal too fast for you to keep track of the cards.

MYTH No. 5   *It is impossible to win playing against four or six decks because there are too many cards to keep track of.*

Four or more decks all mixed together do seem formidable to play against. But it is not more complex, it only takes longer to keep track of 208 cards compared to 52 cards. It is also somewhat more fatiguing, because you don't rest as often. In a single-deck game, the dealer shuffles up, giving you time to rest. In a game of four decks or more, shuffling is more infrequent.

The complexity of tracking cards is the same. There are no different types of cards to track in a multiple-deck game, only more cards. You still track the cards with a simple plus-1 or minus-1 count, the same as in a single-deck game. If you are worried about maintaining your concentration long enough in a multiple-deck game, buy four decks and intermix them. If you practice keeping track of the cards, your counting will quickly become an almost effortless skill.

MYTH No. 6   *You need a bankroll of thousands of dollars in order to win appreciable amounts of money at Blackjack.*

All you need is a bankroll of two hundred dollars. With such a small start, you can win thousands of dollars. Admittedly, it will take much longer if you start small because you will only be able to make small bets at first, winning only small amounts of money. But you will win at the same *rate* as someone betting a thousand dollars per hand.

The more hours you play, the more money you will accumulate. Once you double your bankroll, you can bet twice as much on each hand, and so on. After the first fifty hours of play, you will be making bigger bets and will be well on your way to winnings in four or five figures if you stay with the game. I began with a bankroll of exactly two hundred dollars and have parlayed it up to over eighty thousand dollars. My former students have won much more.

MYTH No. 7 *There is no cheating in large Las Vegas casinos.*

It has been my experience that the larger the casino, the more expert the cheating dealers are. I have been cheated out of thousands and thousands of dollars by dealers in the largest casinos in the world. Chapter Four shows how this can be done.

MYTH No. 8 *They only cheat high rollers.*

A cheating dealer will cheat anybody he wants to, whether the person is betting fifty cents or five hundred dollars. Cheating dealers do not discriminate unless it is in their best interests because it is easier to deal themselves a good hand (hurting everybody) than it is to deal a particular player a bad hand.

MYTH No. 9 *Bad players hurt a good player's game.*

It has been proven mathematically that bad players at the table help a good player as often as they hinder him in actual casino playing. A winning player never blames another player for his losses. Instead, a winner thanks the bad player when the latter helps by playing badly.

MYTH No. 10 *The player sitting at third base can have a greater effect on whether the dealer busts or not than any other player at the table.*

This only appears to be true because he is the last player to draw and all the other players' attention is focused on him. Yet he has no more of an effect on the dealer than the players elsewhere at the table who hit, double, split, or stand. Every single play can change the order of the cards the dealer gets. Therefore, it doesn't matter who goes last. What matters, in terms of effect on the dealer's hand, is how many and what kinds of cards (large or small) are drawn by *all* the players *together*.

MYTH No. 11 *Casinos use shills in order to cheat players.*

Although the casino could cheat a Blackjack player in a number of ways, using a *shill* is usually not one of them (a shill is an employee of the casino who plays with house money). True, some casinos use shills to attract players to the table, but I have never seen a shill being used to cheat me in all my years of play. It's easy to spot shills, because they never double down or split. As Myth No. 9 pointed out, how other gamblers at the table play their hands has absolutely no long-term effect on a winning player's advantage or disadvantage. If a shill at your table makes you feel uncomfortable, you can ask him politely to leave.

It's not easy to shatter myths. If you have played Blackjack before, then you have probably been told that these myths are the "inside story." What you might be feeling now is "gambling culture shock." Culture shock occurs when you learn that what you were originally taught to believe is false. If you haven't had the playing experience yet, my experiences should prove instructive to you. At least you will be more alert as to what to expect in a casino.

This is the game of Blackjack. If you have read and understood this chapter, you will find little in the casino that can surprise you. You should now be able to sit down at a game anywhere and, after asking the dealer a few pertinent questions, play like an experienced gambler. You can avoid the costly and embarrassing rookie mistakes in your early play. Above all, you have taken the first positive step on the road to becoming a winning player. You know the game of Blackjack.

THREE
Choosing a Place to Play

It's the risk I like about owning a casino. Some days you win, other days you win more.

ONE CASINO OWNER TO ANOTHER

It was nighttime when I first saw the Las Vegas Strip. I was momentarily speechless, a condition unusual enough for me that one of my friends asked, "What are you thinking?"

I responded with the first thing that had come into my head. "This looks like somebody took one of Liberace's jackets and made a city out of it! I haven't seen so much to look at since Farrah Fawcett played tennis on the Superstars competition." I was like a kid in a candy shop with the standard worry: Underneath all that glitter, what am I going to get? In the candy shop, for every piece with a strawberry center, it seems like there are two that reveal half an ant after the first bite. Since the casinos likely hold equal perils, where do I start?

One approach to the problem is to wade on in. This might be OK for haircuts and harems, where time renews all resources, but it is an awful way to choose a place to gamble. Yet so many beginners do exactly this when they walk into a casino cold. They wade in eager to spend their money on the first table they see. "One Blackjack game is pretty much like any other," they rationalize, "so what difference does it make?"

To the player willing to take a more sensible approach to the game, it makes a lot of difference. There are over twenty options to the "standard" game of Blackjack. Each of these affects the player advantage, sometimes slightly, often dramatically. In addition, there are important intangibles that should temper your willingness to place your hard-earned bankroll just anywhere. You shouldn't want to wager indiscriminately any more than you would want to let a stranger carry your wallet or purse.

Without reading this chapter, you will be a "cradle to grave" player. You will walk into the casino a newborn innocent ready for the slaughter and walk out dead meat on the hoof. This chapter helps you lose your costly innocence forever, which is more fun to lose than your money. Rather than cradle to grave, your education will be "city to chair." You bought this book, so you've got the right game. Now get the right place. See how you can evaluate casinos, table options, and dealers based on information available only from the International Blackjack Club.

INTERNATIONAL BLACKJACK CLUB

In the early seventies, I found myself meeting a number of other serious players. There was no pattern or purpose; we just met through mutual interests, friends, at conferences, or by noticing each other using similar methods at the tables. Stories were eagerly passed around about how particular players did and about what playing conditions were at the popular casinos. I found these discussions immensely valuable, particularly when the information covered changes in rules or suspicions of cheating at various casinos.

But I was frustrated at the lack of real details or any assurance that the stories were reliable. There was no method of communication on a regular basis that was detailed or accurate. In fact, there was no communications of *any* type except for players' paths crossing randomly. These are the reasons I decided to found the International Blackjack Club (IBC).[1]

The IBC was designed to provide a central source for playing information and answers to questions, the club newsletter. The

---

[1] For information on the club and newsletter, write: International Gaming, Inc., Box 73, Thornhill, Ont., Canada L3T 3N1.

IBC Newsletter currently comes out four times per year and contains the latest facts and news about Blackjack from members and myself. For example, the early-surrender Basic Strategy given in Chapter Six first appeared in the newsletter. Member comments are passed on as well as general news of the game. Over the first four years of its publication, the newsletter published reports of player surveys showing winning and losing session results. The goal was to determine if there were significant differences from casino to casino in skilled-player win rates.

The surveys indicated a wide variety of card-counter win rates over hundreds of sessions. Unfortunately, there seemed to be no year-to-year consistency. A casino would be very highly rated, then appear in the bottom ten the following year. Most serious players now track casino playing conditions and rule variations. These factors are the most important in choosing a casino in which to play.

CHOOSING A CASINO

Theoretically, one casino should be just like another. They are normally regulated by the local government and periodically checked by agents for compliance with the rules. They play the "same" game. When the IBC initiated its first survey, we wondered if the playing results would bear this out. They didn't. That first survey, in 1975, showed a 24 per cent difference in the ratio of winning sessions to total sessions for casinos with enough playing reported for statistical validity. Club members in the Hilton (Las Vegas Strip) won 64 per cent of their sessions, while members in the Dunes (also on the Strip) won only 38 per cent of their sessions.

There are a couple of reasons that could explain the difference, one fairly normal and obvious and the other sneaky and insidious. The first reason, as mentioned earlier, is that Blackjack has not yet stabilized as a casino game. Roulette, for example, is very stable. The only difference in the games is the "European" wheel versus the "American" wheel. The European game has only one zero while the greedier Americans have a double-zero wheel. Craps, a game that seems to have been around almost as long as we have, shows essentially the same layout no matter where you play.

In Blackjack, each casino chooses which of the options described in Chapter Two it will allow and what restrictions it will place on those favorable to the player, such as doubling, splitting, or surrendering. The table below contains the options listed by effect on and importance to the player. The more significant options are at the top of each list.

EVALUATING RULES VARIATIONS   (In order of value)

Favorable for the Player

Early surrender
Doubling on any number of cards
Doubling on any three cards
Doubling on any two cards
Drawing any number of cards to split Aces
Doubling allowed after pair splitting
Surrender
Observer betting
Insurance

Unfavorable for the Player

Hard doubling restricted to 11
Two or more decks
Dealer hits soft 17
Hard doubling restricted to 10 or 11
No soft doubling
No dealer hole card (British style)
No resplitting of Aces

The rules allowed can vary drastically from location to location. Sint Maarten, for example, has nearly every rule listed in the table as unfavorable for the player in a four-deck game. Conversely, El Cortez in downtown Las Vegas offers doubling after split and surrender in a single-deck game while hitting soft 17 as the only unfavorable rule. So the first item of business in any new casino is to question the dealer as to the options in effect and the restrictions on any plays before putting your money out.

To help you plan your trips, the second table contains the playing rules for the various Las Vegas casinos that the club members frequent. The information in this table is supplied courtesy of Stephen Goldberg and Arnold Snyder. You should use this list as a guide only, because playing rules may vary between the time this is written and your trip. As you can see, the number of casinos in this part of the world is large enough that you should *never* have to play under unfavorable rules. As in any business, the law of supply and demand should help the casinos see how unprofitable it is to offer an inferior game.

ATLANTIC CITY

Standard Atlantic City rules currently are: double down on any two cards, no resplitting of pairs, double down allowed after splitting pairs, dealer stands on soft 17, no dealer-hole card.

Casino	Size	Decks	Double after Split	Late Surrender	Dealer Hits Soft 17
Atlantis	L	8/6	*		
Bally's	L	8/6	*		
Caesars	L	8	*		
Castle	L	8/6	*		
Claridge	M	8/6	*		
Marina	L	8	*		
Nugget	L	8	*		
Resorts	L	8/6	*		
Sands	L	8/6	*		
Tropicana	L	8/6	*		
Trump	L	8	*		

LAS VEGAS STRIP

Standard Las Vegas Strip rules currently are: double down on any two cards, no resplitting pairs, no double down allowed after splitting, and dealer stands on soft 17.

Casino	Size	Decks	Double after Split	Late Surrender	Dealer Hits Soft 17
Bally's Grand	L	6	*		
Barbary Coast	M	6/2			
Bourbon Street	M	4			
Caesars Palace	L	6	*	*	
Castaways	M	6			
Circus Circus	L	6/1			
Continental	S	6			
Desert Inn	M	6	*		
Dunes	M	6/2		*	
El Rancho	M	2			
Flamingo Hilton	L	6/2			
Foxy's Firehouse	S	6			*
Frontier	M	6	*		
Hacienda	M	5/2			
Holiday	M	6/2			
Imperial Palace	M	6/2			
King 8	S	4		*	*
Landmark	M	6/2/1			
Little Caesar's	S	5			
Marina	M	5/2/1			*
Maxim	M	4/2			
Nob Hill	M	4/2			
Paddlewheel	S	6			*
Riviera	M	2			
Royal	S	6/5/1			
Sahara	L	5/2			
Sands	M	6/4/2			
Silver City	M	4			*
Silver Slipper	M	6			
Slots A Fun	S	6			
Stardust	L	6/2			
Tropicana	M	4/2			
Vegas World	S	4/2			*
Westward Ho	S	6/1			

DOWNTOWN LAS VEGAS

Casino	Size	Decks	Double after Split	Late Surrender	Dealer Hits Soft 17
California	M	4/2			*
El Cortez	M	2/1	*		*
Four Queens	L	4/2			*
Fremont	M	4/2			*
Golden Gate	M	6/2/1			*
Golden Nugget	M	6	*		
Horseshoe	M	6/1	*		*
Lady Luck	M	6/2/1			*
Las Vegas Club	M	6	*	*	*
Mint	L	6/2/1			*
Nevada Club	S	2			*
Orbit Inn	S	6			*
Palace Station	M	6/2			*
Pioneer Club	M	6/1			*
Showboat	M	6			*
Sundance	M	2/1			*
Union Plaza	L	6/2			*
Western	S	6			*

RENO / TAHOE

Standard northern Nevada rules are similar to Downtown Las Vegas rules except that doubling down is restricted to two-card totals of 10 or 11.

RENO

Casino	Size	Decks	Double after Split	Late Surrender	Dealer Hits Soft 17
Bally's Grand	L	4	*		*
Bonanza	M	1			*
Cal-Neva	L	2/1			*
Circus Circus	L	4/2/1			*

Casino	Size	Decks	Double after Split	Late Surrender	Dealer Hits Soft 17
Comstock	S	2/1			*
Eldorado	M	1			*
Fitzgerald's	M	4/1			*
Harold's Club	L	4/1			*
Harrah's	L	4/1			*
Holiday	M	1			*
Horseshoe	M	1			*
Monte Carlo	S	1			*
Nevada Club	M	2/1			*
Peppermill	L	4/2/1			*
Pioneer	M	1			*
Hilton	L	4/2/1			*
Ramada	M	1	*	*	*
Riverside	S	4/1			*
Sands	M	6/2			*
Sundowner	L	1			*

TAHOE

Casino	Size	Decks	Double after Split	Late Surrender	Dealer Hits Soft 17
Barney's	S	6/1			*
Caesars	M	6/1	*		*
Harrah's	L	6/2/1			*
Harrah's Sports	S	1			*
Harvey's	L	1			*
High Sierra	L	6/1			*
John's Nugget	S	1			*
Lakeside Inn	S	1			*
Nugget	S	1			*

This list of selected casinos is most helpful in introducing the generally available casinos at various U.S. gaming locations. It is likely to be out of date as you read this, so it should be used as a guideline only. For up-to-date detailed information, you might want to obtain a copy of the *Casino Directory for Nevada*. It is published by RW Directories, P.O. Box 955, Draper, Utah 84020. This directory contains complete location and rules information on all Nevada casinos—over 30 cities and 150 casinos are listed. The directory details casino size, number of decks, blackjack rules and variations by casino, betting limits for all games, and additional game information such as poker offerings and betting ranges. This is an information-packed little booklet and, best of all, is available by sending only five dollars to RW Directories.

INTERNATIONAL LOCATIONS

This is a brief summary of rule variations for many international gaming locations. Due to the ever-changing nature of casino rules, the list should be used as a general guide and is illustrative of the variations common to foreign play. All playing rules are variations from the typical Las Vegas Strip rules.

Australia

This is a no hole card game. A major change is that you lose all double and split bets if the dealer ends up having a blackjack. (U.S. casinos refund the extra bet.) Doubling down is restricted to two-card hands of 9, 10, or 11, and there is no resplitting of pairs.

Austria

This is also a no hole card game where you lose all double and split bets to a dealer blackjack. Doubling down is restricted to two-card hands of 9, 10, or 11, and there is no doubling after splitting. An unusual restrictive feature is that if you double down with (A,8) and draw a 2, the total counts as 11 only (instead of 21 as in the United States).

The Bahamas

This is similar to the U.S. game except that doubling down is restricted to two-card totals of 9, 10, or 11 only.

Belgium

This is a no hole card game where you lose all double and split bets to a dealer blackjack. Doubling down is restricted to two-card hands of 9, 10, or 11, and there is no resplitting of pairs. If you double down with (A,8) and draw a 2, the total counts as 11 only.

Canada

Doubling is restricted to two-card totals of 10 or 11 only. There is also no doubling down after splitting pairs.

England

England is somewhat more restrictive than other European locations. You lose all double-down and split bets to a dealer blackjack. Doubling down is restricted to two-card hands of 9, 10, or 11 only. Splitting 4s, 5s, and 6s is not allowed, and there is no resplitting of pairs. Also, you may buy insurance only when you have a blackjack.

France

This is a no hole card game where you lose all double and split bets to a dealer blackjack. Doubling down is restricted to two-card hands of 9, 10, or 11 only, and doubling down after splitting pairs is allowed.

Germany

Germany also plays a no hole card game where you lose all double-down and split bets to a dealer blackjack. Doubling down is restricted to two-card hands of 9, 10, or 11 only. Resplitting pairs is not allowed, and the (A,8) double down when hit with a 2 is scored as 11 only.

The Netherlands

You lose all double-down and split bets to a dealer blackjack. Doubling down is restricted to two-card hands of 9, 10, or 11 only. Resplitting pairs is allowed.

Puerto Rico

As in U.S. casinos, you lose only your original bet when the dealer has a blackjack. Doubling on any two cards is allowed, and there is double down after splitting. Resplitting pairs is not allowed.

You can see that there is no shortage of places to try your skill at blackjack. The best approach is always to join a game and ask the dealer what the specific house rules are. That's how much of the information here was gathered. Many new players are afraid to ask, being embarrassed at not knowing what is going on or being fearful that it will tip off their systems play. Yet dealers know that an intelligent gamer wants to know the exact rules, and dealers get asked the question frequently. As for other players, they are often amazed to hear a string of unfamiliar rule variations. If you have carefully read this book, there will be little the dealer can say to you that will be unfamiliar.

ANALYZING TABLE CONDITIONS

After studying the options for the location you plan to visit, you should be able to identify several favorable casinos. Once you enter these casinos you will be confronted with more options to analyze, several varying from table to table.

NUMBER OF DECKS

In general, the more decks that are used, the worse it is for the player. One of the first moves the casinos made to counter Thorp's 10-count system in *Beat the Dealer* was to increase the number of decks. The casinos figured that trying to determine the ratio of 10s to non-10s would just be too difficult with up to 208 cards to keep track of. They were right, of course, until the second edition, in 1966, introduced the concept of a plus-minus count similar to the Hi-Opt I. Counting with multiple decks was no more difficult for the player; extra cards merely provided the player with fewer rest breaks as dealers shuffled.

What happens to the dealer advantage was unsuspected at that time. We now know that the dealer gains about .5 per cent in multiple-deck games. Even though the overall ratio of good and bad cards may be the same in either a single- or a multiple-deck game, the dealer has a larger pool of favorable cards to draw from with multiple decks. He busts less often as a result.

When you have a choice, play at a table with the fewest number of decks. Four decks is the common number currently played in most casinos, with some smaller houses still offering one- or two-deck games. Watch out for five-deck games masquerading as four-deck games! In the middle of 1977, one of the more successful Blackjack players phoned to warn me about this at the Stardust. As you will see, you must know the number of decks to properly use the Hi-Opt I system. In any case, a five-deck game is harder to profit from than a four-deck one.

A one-deck game, while offering the best statistical chance of winning, may not be the best game for you if you hope to generate substantial profits through heavy betting. Single-deck table dealers and pit bosses are extremely alert for systems players and will shuffle the advantage away at the slightest suspicion of card tracking. Since these games are available most often in smaller casinos needing to attract bettors, the typical betting levels are too small to generate enough profits for the high roller. But if you want to play for fun or to win a little loose change, a single-deck game is your best shot.

I recommend you stay away from six-deck games because they are extremely difficult to beat. Julian Braun estimated that to get a worthwhile advantage in a six-deck game with *any* powerful system the casino must deal out at least 4½ of the decks, and your bet range must be *at least 1 to 20* units per hand, a real eye-catcher with the pit bosses. The only possible approach to the six-deck game is to use team play and a very high-level professional system like the Hi-Opt II. When there are so many other places to play, the extra effort is not worth it.

For a time, the Castaways casino had an interesting nine-deck game with several advantageous rules. Braun calculated for me that a player would have a flat *advantage* of about .5 per cent using the Basic Strategy outlined in Chapter Six according to the last rules in effect. The player could grind out a small profit in the game with a flat bet. Alas, the increased traffic evidently didn't justify the liberal rules, so the Castaways discontinued the game.

Overall, the best type of game is one using the fewest number of decks when properly dealt.

METHOD OF DEALING

Originally, all Blackjack games used one deck with the dealer holding the unused cards in one hand. (Up to two decks can comfortably be dealt out of the hand.) With the introduction of four decks during the big scare Thorp caused, hand-held decks were no longer practical. A device was borrowed from the baccarat tables, called a *shoe*. The shoe is a box that holds the undealt cards for the dealer. A small window in the front allows the dealer to slide one card at a time out of the shoe onto the felt playing surface, freeing the other hand from its job of holding the decks.

There are advantages to a shoe game for both the casino and the player. The chances of cheating in a shoe game are minimal because it is nearly impossible to deal anything but the top card. While I have heard stories and seen diagrams of an illegal shoe (a *holdout shoe*) made by a small company in Las Vegas and exported to casinos outside the United States, the chance of encountering one in use is extremely small. It is far easier to cheat in a hand-held game, where an endless amount of sleight of hand can take place. If you have ever seen a "close up" magician do card tricks, then you are familiar with what can be done by hand with a deck of cards.

Another feature is whether or not the cards are delivered face up or face down to the player. An up game is much more advantageous for you since you see every card that has been dealt. The casinos like it because the players are never allowed to touch the cards. Keeping the cards away from the players provides less opportunity for the casino to be cheated by its customers. You can't mark or deface what you don't touch. If you must play a game with more than two decks, an up game is a better bet.

DEPTH OF DEAL

One of the most important considerations for winning blackjack players is the number of cards dealt before each reshuffle. This is normally expressed as a percent of deck dealt or "penetration" into the deck, that is, two thirds, one half, and so on. Arnold Snyder in his excellent book *The Blackjack Formula* showed that deck penetration was the single most statistically significant factor in determining win rate when using the level of system described in Chapter 7.

It is best to play in a game where the dealer reshuffles as infrequently as possible. Ideally, nearly all the cards should be dealt out before the shuffle. In practice with multiple-deck games, between one half and two thirds of the deck will be dealt before a shuffle. Dealers who continue on to the three-quarters penetration level provide significantly increased winning opportunities for the knowledgeable player.

For the casino, there is a continual trade-off between frequent reshuffling and high-deck penetration. Reshuffling slows up play and gives the house fewer hands per hour per table. Since most players are losers, house win rates go down. Shuffling after only half the cards have been dealt hampers knowledgeable system players and protects the casino. Yet dealers would rather play than shuffle—within the limits set by the pit boss. The result is an occasional situation where a dealer will give regular deep-deck penetration. This is a game you must not pass up.

TYPE OF CARDS

As previously explained, Blackjack is played with a simple set of poker-type playing cards. Despite the high-quality paper, rigid specifications, laminating, and enameling, the average deck lasts only about forty minutes of play. Cards quickly become smudged or bent and have to be replaced. Harold's Club in Reno, a relatively small place on the Las Vegas scale, uses nearly ten thousand decks per month! The cards used by Harold's (and nearly all other U.S. casinos) are the red-and-blue Bee Diamond-back introduced by the U. S. Playing Card Company in 1902. There are several reasons fair and foul, not involving cheating, why the casinos like to use them and why you should wish they didn't.

In the typical "I win, you lose" approach of the casinos to their customers, the Bee cards keep you from cheating and make it easier for the dealer to cheat. The continuous-pattern design of the cards makes it almost impossible to "mark" the backs of the cards because there is no reference point. In addition, two card colors are used so that a replacement deck is a different color. Adjacent tables are usually on a different color deck also. Imagine sneaking a card out of the game next door and putting it back in play at a new table (being a *crossroader*) only to find that your hand has the only red card in a blue-backed deck!

As mentioned, the other advantage of Bee cards is that it is easier for the dealer to cheat with them. The most common type of cheat is the dealer in a hand-held game who can deal "seconds"—that is, the card second from the top. I have seen card sharps demonstrate dealing all the way down to fifths! To deal a second, the dealer slides the top card out slightly but retains it with the thumb on the deck hand. He then slides the chosen card out to be dealt. By having the cards the same color, it is nearly impossible to see a second being dealt. If the dealer was using a bridge deck with a narrow white border, the white border would stand out starkly against the second's solid back being dealt out underneath.

The whole problem could be easily solved by making decks with the Bee design surrounded by a white border. The regular pattern would still be hard to mark and the dealing of seconds could be quickly spotted by players and pit bosses alike. With order quantities of thousands of decks per month, I imagine the U. S. Playing Card Company would be happy to oblige its customers' request for this design if there was any demand. I wonder why there is no demand from the casinos?

THE BEST DEALER

All right, you've carefully selected your target casinos and you are standing there after spotting which tables have the best playing options. The early show has just started so there are plenty of seats all around. The question now is: Which dealer should you pick? The answer is to pick the person you think you have the best chance of winning from. As a result of experience and from talking with other players, I had a good guess which type of dealer was easiest to win from. But for verification, I thought this was another question for the IBC members.

In 1975, I sent out the first survey asking: "What sex and age dealers have you had the best luck with in winning? Please rank them from 1 to 5—that is, give a rank of 1 to the kind of dealer you do best with and 5 to the kind you do worse against. Rank the other dealers in between." The accompanying table shows the results in 1975 and in subsequent surveys.

INTERNATIONAL BLACKJACK CLUB SURVEYS:
Dealers

| Dealer | *Average Rank* | | | | |
	1979	1978	1977	1976	1975
Young female (under 30)	1.75	1.42	1.60	1.86	1.80
Young male (under 30)	2.75	2.34	2.67	1.83	2.64
Middle-aged female (30 to 45)	3.25	3.14	3.27	3.13	3.36
Middle-aged male (30 to 45)	3.42	3.74	3.73	3.53	3.56
Older male and female (over 45)	3.92	4.06	4.33	3.86	3.60

It's obvious from the table that young female dealers have consistently been the best to play against through the years. Older dealers of either sex are the worst. This has been my personal experience also. A statistical test was applied to the numbers in the table to determine if the results could be the result of coincidence. Without going into all the mathematics, the differences were "significant" and not due to the vagaries of chance. The fact that the surveys agreed on five different occasions is further proof. Older dealers must be doing something the younger ones are not. You will see in Chapter Four what some of those things might be.

CHOOSING A SEAT

You are now ready to sit down and lay your money on the spot.
The final question in our casino-to-chair sequence is where to sit.
Go back and briefly review the illustration of a Blackjack table
before reading on. Since the dealer gives the players cards from
his left to right (your right to left), first base is the seat farthest
to the right. First base plays first. The last position, seat 7, is
called third base and plays last.

Seat 7 should be avoided. Although it allows a little more time
to think than the other seats, seat 7 has two disadvantages that
overshadow the value of the extra time. First, the line of vision is
poor from seat 7. You are right on the rope off to one side. If it is
a down game, there is little chance you will see anyone's hand as
they tip their cards to look at them. Counting a hand as it is laid
down and quickly picked up across the table is also more difficult.
Second, the dealer is more suspicious of a player in seat 7 than in
any other position because it is the preferred seat of most cheaters
and some counters. Remember the man who picked up the
dealer's stack of tips at El Casino in Freeport? The dealer might
never have seen him if he hadn't been watching seat 7 carefully.

Seat 1 has advantages and disadvantages. The greatest disadvantage is that seat 1 is under the gun. You are always somewhat
rushed because you must play first. However, some professionals
actually prefer seat 1 because the dealer is less suspicious of
them. Seat 1 is also next to the dealing shoe so that you can actually see *inside* the shoe and can get a very accurate estimate of
the number of cards left there and how far the game will go before hitting the red cut marker.

Seat 1 is the best if you can count cards very quickly. An up
game is ideal since you know every card that has been played or
dealt (except the dealer's down card) when you must make your
decision. If you sit farther down the table, there are double down
cards you may not see. Fortunately, most of the casinos in the
world (outside of Nevada) deal an up game.

For the developing player, seat 6 (next to third base) is preferable. You have a longer time to think about your best play because five people must finish their hands ahead of you. Although you aren't very far from third base, you have a much better view of the entire table without having to swivel your head excessively. Seat 5 is next best, but you are getting too near the middle of the table to be ideal. You've got hands on either side of you, keeping your head panning like a bank camera. Pit bosses know to watch closely anyone paying too much attention to the other players' cards. There's no need to cause yourself the extra work and attract the unwanted attention if a better seat is free.

In summary, remember that the suggestions in this chapter are guidelines, not hard-and-fast rules. They are based upon trends and percentages, not individual peculiarities. If you're sitting at third base with an old-codger dealer, ranging your bets like crazy in the worst-rated dust joint on the charts being dealt an eighty-five-deck hand held face down game with solid-colored cards *and winning,* stay there and milk it! As one grizzled gambler said to me, "I'll tell you what I think about your computers and averages. The average person in this world's got 1 boob, 1 ball, and 2½ kids!" But the charts show that if you play the games with lower win rates *over a long period of time,* you are less likely to walk away a winner.

What the advice in this chapter will do is to help give you an *edge* that exists in the game. You will be certain that you are doing everything in your power to get the best chance to win.

WHERE YOU CAN PLAY

Casino gambling is one of the fastest-growing industries in the world. In the United States, we've already added Atlantic City, New Jersey, to the list of gaming cities, with other financially strapped states seriously considering casinos of their own. At this writing, Playboy Enterprises has recently put another casino in the Bahamas. No matter where you travel—the United States, Canada, the Caribbean, Europe, or the Far East—you will be able to lay your money in the betting square. The reason? Casinos make money, big money! Big businesses like Hilton, MGM, and Playboy Enterprises are begging authorities to let them invest millions in luxurious facilities in choice locations. The governments are eyeing the tax income the casinos promise as a solution to immediate cash problems all the governments face. Consequently, your opportunities for playing have never been as great.

This section isn't meant to be a travel guide or catalog of every place in the world where you can find casinos. Such a guide would be out of date before you could finish reading the book. Instead, this section is intended to give you an overview of the major choices you have and some of the considerations in deciding where you want to play. In most cases, the information comes either from personal playing experience or from IBC members who have written me.

UNITED STATES

Nevada

Humorist Hod Shewell characterized Las Vegas as "The city of fish and chips: Some poor fish is always losing his chips." But given the choice of losing my money in the stock market or in Las Vegas, I think I'd take my chances at being a fish. Las Vegas is generally regarded as the most fabulous place for gambling in the world, and for no small reason. No other city can offer the same level of gambling alternatives, entertainment, or sheer action and glamor than this desert town.

The Las Vegas casinos are clustered into two main areas: downtown and the Strip. The Strip is the glamor center where the big bettors play. It offers the bigger stars and the more lavish shows. In any given month, Strip casinos can offer anything from a heavyweight championship prize fight or a tennis challenge match to the World Championship of Blackjack tourney.

The downtown casinos are smaller in size and type of operation. The big business in most of these casinos is slot machines, which tend to be more liberal (pay off better) than on the Strip. Betting limits are much lower than on the Strip, and heavy bettors rarer. There is no lavish entertainment downtown. Instead, small groups usually entertain in the bar or there is no entertainment at all.

At this writing, the Strip has generally become a very difficult place at which to play. All the casino personnel are on the lookout for any card tracking. Small signs are on display at each table, stating, "We reserve the right to bar counters." As Lillian Hellman observed, "Callous greed grows pious very fast." In other words, the casinos still aren't happy with their skyrocketing winnings. The lower average-player win rates as shown in the earlier tables (from 57 per cent to 55 per cent) are direct reflections of what has happened on the Strip.

The downtown casinos still offer worthwhile Blackjack opportunities if you are willing to live with the lower table limits and acceptable betting ranges. At times, though, I have had the dealer take countermeasures when I was betting only one to four dollars during a casual daytime playing session! Your best choice here and at the Strip is to stick to one of the highly rated casinos from the tables.

Reno is northern Nevada's largest city. Reno and nearby Sparks draw most of their gamblers from California. In general, Reno offers a less glamorous setting for the gambler than Las Vegas, with smaller casinos and less spectacular entertainment. Fortunately, this is beginning to change, with a new MGM Grand and Sahara (on the same scale as their Las Vegas predecessors) now open in Reno.

Lake Tahoe is really a gambling *area*. Located over six thousand feet up in the Sierra Mountains, the lake is politically divided down the center, with the west side in California and the east side in Nevada. The gambling is on the north and south ends of the lake on the Nevada side, and most of the hotels and local homes are on the California side. The ski season in the winter and water sports in the summer combine with the gambling industry to make this area ideal for vacationers all year round. The south shore is the most popular end of the lake and has the larger casinos, such as Harrah's, Harvey's, and the Sahara. The north shore offers less entertainment than the south, and has had an uphill struggle to compete with the large casinos. Consequently, the north shore seems to attract more vacationers and one-day players from California. You should be aware of the change to higher altitude in these locations. It may cause an adjustment problem for some people, increasing errors and decreasing the amount of time they can play before fatigue becomes a factor.

There are a number of other moderately sized casinos in Nevada, such as East Reno's Nugget or the Carson City Nugget, and numerous tiny "dust joints" throughout the state. You should be extremely careful in any of the dust joints because of their size. They can't afford to let anyone walk away a big winner—it takes too long to catch up (winnings that will let you walk away unnoticed in Las Vegas will make you a permanent house enemy in a small casino). Consequently, the pit boss will go to great lengths to see that you don't take your winnings with you. How that can be done is shown in Chapter Four.

The rules in Nevada vary greatly depending upon your location. The best rules are in Las Vegas. The main difference between downtown and Strip casinos is that the Strip casino dealer stands on any 17. The downtown dealer hits a soft 17 (a hand with an Ace counting as 11). Insurance is allowed in both locations, and any pair may be split. Split Aces may receive only one additional card. You can also double down on *any* two-card hand. In the Reno-Tahoe areas, the dealer hits soft 17, and you still may split any pair. Split Aces receive only one additional card each here, too. Insurance is allowed, but doubling is restricted to two-card hands of 10 or 11 only. For specific rules variations by casino, go back and review the table.

Atlantic City

I ran a headline in the July 1978 issue of the *IBC Newsletter,* "Resorts Casino in Atlantic City Is a Jungle." In 1978 Atlantic City was an extremely overcrowded location. Resorts International had a monopoly on the gaming there and made the most of it, with the gambling "take" frequently exceeding one million dollars per day! Prices were steep, table minimums kept high, and lines were continual in the fight for the next open seat.

In the intervening years, Atlantic City has stayed in the headlines. There have been suits and countersuits between systems players and the casinos. Allegations of casino mob ties, control commission improprieties, and community devastation have frequently been in the press. In retrospect, the boon gaming was to bring to Atlantic City citizens never seemed to materialize. And while there are currently many casinos open, the "captive market" population around the location results in a far less friendly gaming environment than in Nevada. Couple that with problems of street crime and see that Atlantic City is still a big gaming question mark currently rated "Don't Bother" by many blackjack experts.

CANADA

People seem to be surprised to discover that they can play Blackjack legally in Canada. Every year there are two hundred Blackjack tables open at the Calgary Stampede in Calgary, Alberta. The Stampede takes place during the first two weeks of July. In the second two weeks, there are about two hundred tables open at the Edmonton Exhibition in Edmonton, Alberta. All the games are played using four decks and typical Reno, Nevada, rules. However, the insurance bet is not available and the dealer doesn't take a hole card (British style). Betting ranges are from a minimum of $2.00 to a maximum of only $50. Two-hand play is $10 minimum each hand; three-hand play is $25 minimum. The game is played in Canadian dollars, and the casino cashier and dealers give even money only in exchange for American dollars. Since at this time the American dollar is worth slightly more than the Canadian dollar, you will want to exchange your money for local currency at the airport or a local bank before playing. Entry to the Calgary Stampede fairgrounds costs $2.50, and the casino is open from 10:00 A.M. to 2:00 A.M. Experienced casino personnel are brought in from Nevada to supervise the games, while the dealers are all local students. Some dealers deal out almost all of the cards, which is extremely favorable to the player. Minor dealer errors are common, and tipping is rare and unexpected. As you can imagine, the tables are usually crowded. For more information you can telephone the city of Calgary and ask for the Stampede Information Office.

Recent legislation in western Canada has also made it possible to play Blackjack six days a week throughout the year. If this proceeds satisfactorily, Blackjack may soon spread to all parts of Canada.

NEARBY FOREIGN CASINOS

A number of small countries near the United States have had casino gambling for many years. Eager not to fall behind in the race for the United States tourist dollar (no matter what its value), they have been expanding and promoting their casinos. One of the most popular of these countries is the Bahamas.

Bahamas

The Bahamas contain casinos located at Freeport, Paradise Island, and Nassau. If you love the warm weather like I do, then these might be excellent places for you to try. Instead of the around-the-clock blitz you experience in Las Vegas, Bahamas gambling seems much more civilized and European. The tables open at noon and stay open until the early morning hours. Play is light in the afternoon, and dress can be casual.

After six, beach-type attire is no longer welcome, although I've seen casually dressed players on long winning streaks play on into the evening unmolested. The action really seems to pick up about eight or nine o'clock at night. Unlike its American counterparts, who would let Phil the Gorilla play if he had the table minimum, the Bahamian casino retains its elegance at all times. The dealers are Europeans and very polite, and the players are relaxed after adjusting to the Bahamian pace of life.

The rules are somewhat more restrictive than in Las Vegas. All tables deal a four-deck game face up out of a shoe. At both El Casino in Freeport and the Resorts International on Paradise Island, the dealer goes to about one and one-half decks of the shoe. When the cards run down to a marker placed there, play is stopped for a reshuffle (except at El Casino in Freeport) and then the hands are continued. Play is essentially according to Strip rules, with doubling down limited to two-card hands of 9, 10, or 11. Table limits were $5.00 to $300 when I was there.

The $5.00 minimum causes some different procedures in playing at Paradise Island because there are no chips smaller than

$5.00 handled at the $5.00 tables. If you get a Blackjack when betting the $5.00 minimum, the payoff would be $7.50. Since no $2.50 chips were used at the table, the dealer pays off even money and "imprisons" a second $5.00 chip on your spot to wait for the next hand. If you win the following hand, you keep the chip. If you lose the next hand, the dealer takes the $5.00. In other words, you must automatically bet the 50 per cent premium you get on a natural on the next hand. This procedure is disadvantageous to you if you are using a winning strategy and raising your bets when the deck is favorable because the deck becomes less favorable after a Blackjack has been dealt out.

If you are betting the $5.00 minimum and wish to insure (which means you are using the Hi-Opt I count), the chip problem works to your advantage. Normally, you may only insure for half of your wager, since insurance pays off 2 to 1. But if you are betting $5.00, then you must insure for the full $5.00 minimum, allowing you to bet more in what your count shows is a favorable situation. As long as you are betting multiples of $10, these two peculiarities disappear. The last section will cover more on playing in the Bahamas. More about insurance in Chapter Six.

Haiti

Haiti offers a tough game with even tougher rules. Blackjack is four decks dealt face up out of a shoe to a full table of seven players. The dealer hits soft 17, and there is no soft doubling, no resplitting of any pair, and no doubling after splitting pairs. Hard doubling is restricted to 9, 10, or 11 only. Insurance can be bought, and surrender is available except versus a dealer Ace up. For more information about Haitian casinos, see the story in Chapter Eleven of my junket there.

Netherlands Antilles

There are four sister islands that have casinos: Aruba, Bonaire, Curaçao, and Sint Maarten. Of these four I have visited Aruba and Sint Maarten, both of which were delightful. I can't really think of these islands as gambling destinations, but rather as resorts with gambling as just an extra enticing feature. Blackjack once again is European in flavor, with tables opening up in the afternoon and early evening and play continuing until early morning or until the crowd dies out. The setting is plush, but on a much smaller scale than the Las Vegas gambling "warehouses" I'm used to.

Sint Maarten is located in the Caribbean about 120 miles east of St. Thomas. Sint Maarten's 37 square miles are divided into the Dutch portion in the north and the French portion in the south. The Dutch side is more heavily commercialized and all four casinos are located there. From the approximate largest to smallest they are the Mullet Bay, the Great Bay, the Concord, and the Little Bay. The Mullet Bay has the best beaches of the four and is located near several exclusive resorts.

The casinos open at 8:00 P.M. and close at around 3:00 A.M., depending upon the volume of play. Jackets are required for men. When I was there, the way people dressed on vacation was funny. Invariably, the women wore long evening gowns and jewelry, while the men, eager to shed their suits, wore Banlon shirts and jackets.

The casinos in Sint Maarten offer Craps, Roulette, and Blackjack. The Craps crowd was mostly American. There seemed to be an unusually large number of Roulette tables for the size of the casinos until I considered the number of French players from the other side of the island. The Blackjack table had a mix of nationalities. The most common table limit was $5.00, with a few $2.00 tables in each casino. The Mullet Bay has two "ladies only" Blackjack tables with $2.00 limits. The Concord has a rule that requires you to play two hands if alone at the table or else wait for a second player.

The game was played with four decks dealt face up out of a shoe to a maximum of six players at a table. The dealer takes no hole card. There is no doubling after splitting pairs, one card to split Aces, insurance allowed, and doubling on 10 and 11 only. There is no observer betting or surrender, and the dealer hits soft 17. The dealers are nice enough to show the players the burn card.

The dealers are very inexperienced and make lots of errors. Unlike Las Vegas, the pit bosses are very active, watching dealers one-on-one if the action is light, or constantly moving to the most active table if the casino is busy. But there is no "heat" on the systems player. The pit boss is watching for dealer mistakes rather than player winnings. Many of the women players had "cheat sheets" showing them how to play, often something that their husband armed them with before turning them loose. (By and large these were as useful as drinking lion's blood as a birth-control device.) Many players would hit or stand "by committee," asking a group with them what they should do. This would attract great pit boss attention in Vegas, but was tolerated in Sint Maarten.

There is no reason why the casinos shouldn't tolerate these antics, actually. Play was the common atrocious variety of a resort area. Many of the players seemed spur-of-the-moment types, splitting 10s versus a dealer 4, 5, or 6, or splitting 4s and 5s versus anything. Lots of them played "no bust" or "dealer mimic," too. Sometimes their cheat sheets gave them sort of an idea of what to do, but since they had no knowledge of the Basic Strategy or card counting, they played the hands incorrectly. There was a group of Japanese at my table for a short time. They were losing steadily, but no one could tell what they were saying to each other. All I could think of is that it would be a great way to have one person count and tell the others what to do.

I saw no signs of dealer cheating in Sint Maarten. The dealers were so inexperienced that it was all they could do to deal a proper game. Few locals played in the casinos, so there was little chance for collusion, either. Any cheating would probably get caught immediately by the alert pit bosses. I can't imagine a reason why the casinos would want to cheat. The rules are so restrictive and the players so terrible that cheating would be like dumping a bucket of water into Niagara Falls.

There was one final feature in the Little Bay casino that I've never seen anywhere else in the world. There was no cashier's cage. When you wanted to cash in, you shoved your chips at the dealer and asked for cash. The pit boss was called over to count your chips at the table. He then took them to a central cash dispenser and returned with your money. All the other casinos had the normal cashier's window.

In Aruba, the Blackjack rules are interesting. The dealer normally does not take a hole card (British style). All games use four decks dealt face up from a shoe. Although the dealer does not take a hole card, you aren't penalized for doubling or splitting. If the dealer ends up with a natural, your additional bet is returned to you. Insurance is available in all casinos. Doubling is restricted to 10 or 11 in most casinos, but there are exceptions. Ask if you are not certain what the rules are where you are playing. Pair splitting is allowed, but doubling is not allowed on split pairs.

I know I'm partial to tropical locations, but I found Aruba and Sint Maarten to be delightful. You'll find more on Aruba in the next section.

Other Locations

Using the methods in this book, you can win money at most casinos in the Caribbean. This applies particularly to the Bahamas, Haiti, and the Netherlands Antilles. But there are some locations you should avoid at all costs.

I do not recommend gambling in St. Andres Island, Panama, or Antigua. An issue of *Rouge et Noir News* reported that it is a policy for the St. Andres casino to cheat. Panama is dangerous. You may get robbed or detained should you have a lot of money on you. Antigua is not recommended because cards have been found to be missing from their shoes and because I have never heard of *anyone,* club member or friend, winning there.

Also avoid Puerto Rico—they have the worst rules in the world there. Doubling is restricted to 11 and you can split only certain pairs. (At least the game is dealt honestly because of a four-deck shoe.) With these restrictive rules, you would need at least a one to twenty bet range and a powerful strategy to stand any chance of winning enough money to pay for your trip. A one to twenty range will get you barred faster than you can get your next bet out. To top that off, the locals are extremely unfriendly despite the U.S. ad campaign to the contrary. If you don't know what else to do with your money other than play Blackjack in Puerto Rico, spend it on something more worthwhile, like buying the Brooklyn Bridge. Otherwise, don't say I didn't warn you!

AROUND THE WORLD

The list of casinos is long and growing constantly. What you will find here are brief descriptions of some of the better-known and more established places to play Blackjack.

Britain

The gambling industry here is strictly controlled by the British Gaming Board. The philosophy of the board seems to be to protect the players from themselves. Therefore, no irresistible temptations are offered, and some strange restrictions are imposed. There is no advertising, no entertainment, no drinking, no credit, no tipping, no shills (house players), few slot machines, and restricted hours (from 2:00 P.M. to 4:00 A.M.). The odds are strictly set so that the house advantage is precisely known. The standard plays at Blackjack are displayed at every table, and a player who needs it may ask the official controlling the game for help. Imagine asking a Las Vegas pit boss for help! I'd sooner invite a pickpocket to my wedding.

In addition, a so-called forty-eight-hour rule is imposed so that no one can walk in off the street and play. You must first join a licensed club and state your "intention to play." The cost to join is about twenty-five dollars. After forty-eight hours, you may then gamble. If you are from the United States, you may want to write to obtain forms in advance or ask your travel agent for them so that you can play on arrival. The only exception to this delay is when you are introduced by a current member who is on the premises. You can then play at once.

There are numerous small clubs and several large ones. Table limits at the small clubs are normally about fifty dollars. Some of the large clubs you may wish to visit are the Curzon House Club, Crockford's Club, Palm Beach Casino Club, International Sporting Club, and Victoria Sporting Club. Minimum bets range from one to five pounds, maximums from fifty pounds to two hundred pounds. The way the dollar has been going down, I'm afraid to tell you what the top limit is worth these days. Maximums used to be worth about five hundred dollars at the larger clubs.

With typical British control and precision, the games appear completely honest according to reports from IBC members. The dealers are quick and very businesslike, dealing one third faster than in Las Vegas. The rules are not ideal, but the game can be beaten with the Hi-Opt I. All games are four decks dealt face up out of a shoe. The dealer does not take a hole card (hence *British style*), stands on soft 17, and doubling is allowed on 9, 10, and

11 only. Insurance is allowed only on a player natural versus a dealer Ace up. Pair splitting is allowed except for 4s, 5s, and 10s. No resplitting of pairs is allowed, nor surrender, but doubling down after splits is allowed. No tipping is allowed, and there are no dealer refunds for doubling or splitting when the dealer Blackjacks.

The British casino people are aware of winning players and will bar them when detected, or not deal more than two of the four decks against a player they suspect. Because of the tight rules, you will have to use a betting range of either one to sixteen if you use the level of Hi-Opt described in Chapters Six and Seven, and one to eight if you incorporate the information in Chapter Eight. To keep from being detected you will have to disguise your betting as shown in Chapter Ten, then hide your winnings if you can.

French Riviera

There are casinos all along the French Riviera in Cannes, Juan-Les Pins, Deauville, La Baule, Touquet, and Evian. The most famous on the French Riviera is the old Casino of Monte Carlo. The Casino, with its lavish furnishings and decor, offers a variety of games in each of its salons. For example, there is the Salon des Amériques in which are found Blackjack, Craps, American Roulette, and a few slot machines for the homesick. Blackjack limits run from five dollars to one thousand dollars per hand.

Most IBC members report excellent playing conditions at Loew's Monte Carlo, located next to The Casino. Set into a steep cliff overlooking the ocean, Loew's offers the noisy American game and atmosphere of a Las Vegas casino, only in one of the most glamorous cities in the world.

If you want to mingle with the jet set, see a Grand Prix race, or play Blackjack in one of the most elegant settings anywhere, then the French Riviera could be for you. More and more people are taking advantage of a week-long travel package to Monte Carlo costing anywhere from seven hundred to fifteen hundred dollars. If your dream is to see the Riviera, you might check with your travel agent.

Germany

Casinos and gambling halls are very popular in Germany. The gambling halls (*Spielhallen*) are primarily slot-machine casinos.

The main game is Roulette, as in all European casinos. Fortunately, Blackjack is played in a number of the larger casinos, such as the Kurhaus in Baden-Baden and the casinos in Lindau and Konstanz.

There are a number of unique features of German Blackjack. At the Kurhaus, there is an admission charge with a sliding scale depending upon how many days you plan to gamble. The more days you play, the less the per-day cost. The Kurhaus is on the formal side, with coat and tie required. The casino also refuses to deal a game to less than three players. If the third player drops out, the game is halted until another player is found. This rarely proves to be a problem in the evenings, but weekday-afternoon games can be difficult to find. Also, you will never have the most advantageous situation: head-on play against the dealer.

The mechanics of the game are also slightly different. Instead of the hand signals preferred in the United States, the Germans play a "loud" game. Hits are requested by saying *Karte* (sounds like "card"), and standing is indicated by saying *raeste* ("rest" will get you by). All bets must be made in multiples of the minimum ten Deutsche mark (DM), which is somewhere between four and five dollars if the exchange rate has stabilized for a little while. All cards are dealt face up out of a shoe, and the dealer doesn't take a hole card. This is similar to the British style because the dealer *keeps* any additional bets made, like doubling down or splitting, when he deals himself a Blackjack. So as in British casinos, you have to be extremely cautious when playing against a dealer Ace or 10 up.

Another unusual Kurhaus rule is observer betting. An observer can bet any amount within the table limits on your hand if he so chooses. It can be extremely uncomfortable when making a borderline decision that will affect several bettors with 100 DM on your hand. Or worse, when you pull a 5 to your 16 and find an unwanted following for the rest of the evening because of it.

Another risk of German Blackjack is sitting in the third-base position. It is a common superstition among French and German players to expect the third-base player to "control" the dealer for the betterment of the table. The third-base player is supposed to hit for cards that would help the dealer and stand to leave the dealer busting cards. As you can imagine, there is no way an hon-

est player, even a Hi-Opt I card counter, could know exactly
what cards are going to the dealer. And as we've shown, it doesn't
make any difference anyway. Nonetheless, do yourself a favor
and avoid this hot seat in Germany.

Other Locations

Casino gambling is just about everywhere in the world. Madeira,
and Estoril (outside of Lisbon) in Portugal have been getting
some play from club members. Spain is into the casino business
now that Franco is gone. There is legalized gambling in Austria,
Chile, Ghana, Hong Kong, Italy, and Macao. You can use the information in later chapters anywhere in any foreign casinos. What
those travels might be like and what can happen during your
playing sessions are the subjects of the next section.

TYPICAL TRIPS AND PLAYING RECORDS

One of the splendid aspects of being a casino Blackjack player is
that I have an excuse to go somewhere else, preferably some
place warm when it's bitter winter where I live. In fact, the most
fabulous holiday I've ever had was just such a trip to Aruba.

BLACKJACK IN THE SUN: ARUBA

My wife had tried to get me to take a winter holiday for nearly
ten years. She had been suggesting Aruba for the last five of those
years when I finally gave in. She promised to pay for the trip,
eleven hundred dollars for the entire one-week stay. What an
offer! The price included round-trip air fare, a week's hotel accommodations, complete breakfasts daily, a cocktail party at a
different hotel every night, as well as glass-bottom boat rides, skin
diving, discount jewelry coupons, and free gambling-chip coupons. I needed a complete rest from my hectic teaching and
research, so I brought along only a small stake: one thousand
dollars in gambling money (my usual stake is five thousand to ten
thousand dollars). I couldn't pass up the opportunity to win some
money.

When we left home it was below zero with several feet of snow on the ground. After a pleasant but somewhat long (five hours) charter flight, we arrived in Aruba. It was sunny, temperature in the eighties, and everywhere we looked were smiling, friendly faces. We took an air-conditioned bus to our hotel, the Divi-Divi, named for a famous local tree that looks like a woman's hair in a windstorm. The leaves and branches of the divi-divi tree all flow in one direction because of the constant ocean breezes. The Divi-Divi Hotel is reputed to be the coziest spot on the island, and I highly recommend it. However, there are a number of other hotels, large and small, from which to choose.

The largest of several, all within walking distance of each other, are where the casinos are located. These are the Concord, Sheraton, Caribbean, Americana, and Holiday Inn. They share a tranquil cove, which makes swimming very pleasant. The only problem is that if you are staying at one of them, you might as well be staying in Chicago or any other large American city. If you want to soak up the native atmosphere, you're much better off at the Divi-Divi or some other smaller hotel. Wherever you plan to stay, it will take reservations as much as a year in advance, especially during the winter, since Aruba is becoming one of the most popular winter resorts in the world.

I was somewhat surprised by the people of Aruba. They didn't seem as bent on securing the American dollar as in so many places I've visited. There is no hostility or resentment against Americans—whites or anybody else. Everybody is treated equally and everybody is welcome. The natives seemed much more interested in enjoying life and in helping others have a good time. They are also well educated, taking English, Spanish, Dutch, and French in school, in addition to knowing their own native tongue, which is called *papeomento*. Everything moves slowly. The wait at restaurants is about twice as long as in the States—I was very content. After all, I was there to relax. If I want to go somewhere to hurry, I'll vacation in New York City.

The casinos are open at noon for slot-machine play. The table games at the Americana and Holiday Inn begin at 2:00 P.M., with the tables at the other casinos opening at 9:00 P.M. Jackets are required in all casinos after 9:00 P.M. Almost any type of jacket will do, even a windbreaker. Most of the time, playing conditions are very crowded. In the evening, every table in every casino is full, simply because there aren't that many tables in any of the casinos. The largest has only twelve tables, with the smallest containing six. Because of the crowds, the best playing time is in the afternoon and early evening.

The basic rules were not too different from what I was used to. Insurance is allowed at all five casinos. The dealer doesn't take a hole card, but refunds any additional doubling or splitting bets if he ends up with a natural. Surrender is allowed only in the Holiday Inn. No casino allows you to double after splitting a pair. The dealers put the plastic marker anywhere from two and one-half to three decks into the shoe, cutting off a deck to a deck and a half. Where a dealer cuts off more than a deck, he usually would keep on dealing past the marker until every player's hand had been resolved. Since the tables were always full, quite often the dealer wound up dealing down to the last half deck. This is extremely advantageous for the Hi-Opt I player.

All the other rules varied by casino. In one of them, the dealer said you could take as much insurance as you wanted—that is, you were not limited to taking insurance up to only half the size of your original bet. As I mentioned elsewhere, the more you can wager on insurance in the right situation, the better. I didn't find out about this rule until the end of my stay or I would have taken advantage of it. I first noticed it when one player took twenty dollars of insurance when he had only a five-dollar bet up. The dealer got Blackjack and the player received forty dollars in return. That will teach me to ignore my own advice and not ask the dealer for the local rules the first time I sit down to play!

There is no *heat* (casino pressure) on counters. The dealers and pit bosses are natives, and most of them were friendly and polite. This is more than I can say about some of the players. A number were quite rude to the dealers, who endured the poor treatment in anxious silence. After the first two days, I slowly stopped camouflaging my play and started to jump my bets rather prominently. No one paid any attention.

I also stopped tipping. I am so used to tipping that I do it automatically. In Aruba, I stood out by placing bets for the dealer. I quickly cut my tipping down to occasional bets when I had had a nice run. And then I would only tip a dollar or two, even though I was betting stacks of five-dollar chips.

The most startling feature of Aruba was the incredible quality of play at the tables. No wonder there is no heat! I have never seen more atrocious Blackjack playing anywhere in the world. These people would have lost their shirts playing Slapjack with the neighborhood kids. Most players would stand on totals of 13, 14, 15, or 16 against *any* dealer up card. Also, many stood on soft totals, such as A, 5 or A, 6.

One such poor player was a gray-haired woman playing third base at my table in the Caribbean casino. I was sitting immediately to her right and having a steady winning session. She kept advising me not to draw so often.

"Don't take so many cards," she said. "Let him bust, let him bust!"

Meanwhile, she was signing one traveler's check after another. Although I usually don't make a point of talking to other players at the table, I felt a little sorry for her losing all that money. So I said, "Well, the dealer keeps drawing until he gets 17, and I figure if it's good for the dealer it must be good for me. So I do it too." That shut her up, and she left shortly thereafter. In fifteen minutes, she managed to lose about two hundred dollars.

On the third day of my stay, I met a very funny gentleman at my table. He was a distinguished fellow with brilliant silver hair and a very expensive beige suit. He was also quite jolly, always smiling and talking to the dealers in Spanish. He kept on saying, "You've got to have *cajones* to win." He was by far the best Blackjack player I had observed on the trip. He played perfect Basic Strategy and at times he would even keep track of the cards! He told me that this was his fifth day in the casinos and he was "still up on them."

At this particular sitting, he said he was up sixty-five dollars. He had put fifty dollars away in his coat pocket and had fifteen dollars left to play with. As soon as he lost that he said he would quit. The fifteen dollars lasted about twenty minutes. All the time he kept on saying, "You've got to have *cajones* to win, you got to have *cajones*." Every time he mentioned *cajones* the dealer would grin with that famous, wide Aruba smile.

I couldn't stand it any more and finally asked him, "What is this *cajones?*"

"Oh," he said, "that's *balls* in Spanish."

He caught me by surprise and I burst out laughing. He never stopped talking while he was at the table. He told me he had read every book on Blackjack. He said he knew about Braun's work, "the guy at IBM." He also read Thorp's book, "the professor of mathematics," he added. I just kept nodding my head. I mentioned that there was a new book coming out by a couple of sharp guys named Humble and Cooper, and that I had read early versions, which looked pretty good.

He said, "Well, I don't think I need any more books, I think that I know everything there is to know about the game."

I had to laugh again. He was a very pleasant and entertaining fellow who was having a great holiday. His red, sunburned nose and silver hair made him look like a tropical Santa Claus. I hope he reads this story and recognizes himself. I also hope he had the *cajones* to quit a winner.

You may be wondering how I did on the trip. The results of my playing sessions are shown in the accompanying table. I had nine winning sessions and six losing sessions for a net profit of $920. Most of my playing was at crowded tables for fifteen to thirty-five minutes at a stretch. A couple of times I played for more than an hour. On one of these long sessions I suffered my largest loss: $265.

BLACKJACK PLAY IN ARUBA

Date	Time	Casino	Result	Bet Range
February 12	6:30 P.M.	Americana	− 50	2– 20
13	7:20 P.M.	Holiday Inn	+ 20	5– 20
13	9:20 P.M.	Americana	+125	10– 50
13	11:00 P.M.	Caribbean	+165	5– 60
14	10:00 P.M.	Caribbean	− 60	5– 60
14	11:00 P.M.	Sheraton	+175	5– 50
15	3:30 P.M.	Holiday Inn	− 50	5–100
16	2:30 P.M.	Holiday Inn	+335	5– 60
16	11:30 P.M.	Caribbean	+150	5– 40

Date	Time	Casino	Result	Bet Range
February 17	1:00 P.M.	Sheraton	−265	5– 80
17	3:30 P.M.	Americana	− 25	2– 20
17	4:00 P.M.	Holiday Inn	+145	5– 60
17	10:00 P.M.	Caribbean	+ 40	5– 60
17	12:30 A.M.	Americana	− 10	5– 40
18	1:00 A.M.	Sheraton	+225	5– 30

Won	+$1,380	Won	9 sessions
Lost	−460	Lost	6 sessions
Net	+$ 920		

My betting pattern was typical for a four-deck game. About 90 per cent of the time I was making the minimum five-dollar bets. Of the remaining time, two out of three bets were jumped to twenty dollars when the count was high enough. In the other one third of favorable situations, when the count was very high, my bet would be either forty or fifty dollars, or thirty dollars each on two hands. Once in a while I played two hands of forty or fifty dollars each. Because my winnings per hour were relatively high, I have to conclude that the gambling in each of the Aruba casinos is completely honest. I never saw anything suspicious at any time. This, coupled with the lack of heat, makes Aruba an excellent place to play winning Blackjack.

You may be wondering what happened to my wife during all this. Although she knows the strategies nearly as well as I do from helping me practice in my early days, she prefers to play the slots. She hit a fifty-dollar jackpot in the slot machines two nights in a row. Then she lost forty dollars and quit gambling for the week. Wise woman.

If someone is after you to go to an island paradise, and you like to win at Blackjack, don't pass up Aruba. It's growing all the time and more hotels are planned (they plan carefully and build only one hotel at a time). The food was excellent, and the vacationers friendly. However, I must disagree with my gambling acquaintance. You don't need *cajones* to win in Aruba; all you need to know is how to track the cards with the Hi-Opt I system. The rest is a heaven I'll be back to enjoy soon.

BLACKJACK ON THE BOARDWALK:
ATLANTIC CITY

Lest you think of all gambling as a relaxed romp in tropical splendor, I think you should hear about the early casino days of New Jersey. By the time you read this, the problem has lessened by having more casinos up and going.

The Resorts International Casino in Atlantic City had an official license to monopolize gambling in New Jersey in its first year of existence. Reports were that the whole town was concerned with milking the new wave of visitors eager to try the tables. Just to keep up on current events in the game, I visited Atlantic City so I could report to IBC members on the conditions.

I enlisted a fellow gambler to take the trip with me in the interests of helping humanity and getting in some decent playing time. We booked ourselves into the Holiday Inn so no one at the Resorts hotel could identify who we were. It was also cheaper than the casino hotel, but the prices were still as high as a New York City hotel. We each brought five thousand dollars, planning to hold our expenses down and to put as much of it into play as we could.

It turned out to be nearly impossible to hold our expenses down. In addition to the outrageous price at the Holiday Inn, parking one long block away from the casino was five dollars for three hours. Prices in the casino (once you got in) weren't any better. One beer and a gin and tonic on the rocks were five dollars.

Conditions were horrible. There was a line of several hundred people waiting at the door before the 10 A.M. opening. Looking around at the people in the casino, it seemed like every dreg and hustler on the East Coast was there (I wonder what we looked like to them?). Security was far from what it should be. By the time the casino was only two months old, there had already been three robberies in the washrooms. One of these netted the thief over four thousand dollars! At the cheaper tables, there were waits of over an hour to get a seat, even during the day. Fortunately, the twenty-five-dollar-minimum tables were fairly open. In the evening, the casino reversed the table mix so that 75 per cent of the tables were twenty-five-dollar minimums and 25 per cent were five-dollar tables. Even with the higher minimums, every seat was filled.

Some players were rude and obnoxious. I saw one poor tourist waiting patiently for nearly an hour for a seat. When the player in front of him finally got up to leave, the tourist moved back slightly to let him out. In the gap, a woman walking by the table quickly darted in and sat down to play. When the tourist complained that he had been next, the woman replied in typical Jersey fashion, "Look, buster, I'm sitting here now and if you touch me I'll scream my lungs off for security." A couple of the tourist's friends (male and female) were ready to drag the woman off the chair despite her threats when the pit boss stepped over. As he was listening to everybody talk to him at once, another seat freed up. The pit boss quickly directed the tourist to the empty chair in front of the other waiting people and beat a hasty retreat. What a place! It never ceases to amaze me when a little pushing and shoving starts how quickly people start acting like four-year-olds.

Resorts International made the Las Vegas casinos look like the Salvation Army. Resorts' goal was, "Everybody loses." Most casinos are happy to have winners floating around to keep the troops of losers motivated. Despite profits far outstripping anyone's wildest imaginations, Resorts didn't want *anyone* to win. Why should they when they had more players than they could handle?

A good example is what happened to me at the twenty-five-dollar tables on the second afternoon. By now I was playing alone, since my friend had gotten disgusted and retired for the trip. I chose a table with a young woman dealer and sat down. After a few minutes, she had a miserable run of luck, busting ten times in a row off the top of a freshly shuffled shoe. I won back all my previous losses in this string. The pit boss, looking like a three-hundred-pound penguin with his big belly and black suit, noticed our table's success and ran over. He leaned close to the dealer and whispered softly in her ear. I listened carefully and heard him say, "Cut the deck in half." She immediately shuffled and placed the cut card halfway into the four decks, leaving two decks to be undealt.

I had heard and seen enough. The casino didn't even want the players to have so much as a short run of *luck* if it could be avoided. There was no reason to cut the deck in half. Card counting didn't cause the dealer to bust ten times in a row. But Resorts was taking no chances. That was the last time I've played in Atlantic City and I don't intend to go back until there is more competition, or until the Casino Control Commission does something about the casinos' operations.

Casino Deals Card Counters A Losing Hand In Blackjack

ATLANTIC CITY, N.J. (UPI)—The Casino Control Commission said Wednesday that it has allowed Resorts International to ban professional card counters from its blackjack tables.

Resorts attorney Joel Sterns said 75 professional card counters from all over the world, including Yugoslavia, Czechoslovakia and the Philippines, have been identified by the company's security agents. He said some of the card counters are being backed with $100,000 bankrolls, and have been walking away from the casino's blackjack tables with up to $40,000 a day.

Seventeen card counters were thrown out of the boardwalk casino Tuesday night, Resorts officials said. Many of them showed up Wednesday afternoon at the commission's hearing on Resorts' application for a permanent gambling license in New Jersey.

Among those expelled was Howard Grossman, billed as the greatest blackjack player in the world. He said he had been at the casino for 10 days and "was just having a good time."

Resorts, the first legal gambling casino on the East Coast, received the permission in the form of a legal opinion by commission Chairman Joseph Lordi.

Commissioner Albert Merck said he has "very serious doubts about a casino blacklisting and identifying undesirables."

He said the real problem is that with professional gamblers, blackjack is considered a game of skill, not a game of chance.

If it is not a game of chance, then it "cannot qualify as a casino game," Merck said. "I don't think any level of skill should be kept out of the casino."

This article appeared February 1, 1979, months after my visit. It is a most incredible piece of propaganda. The casino interprets the rules both ways, as Commissioner Merck points out. Resorts claimed that Blackjack is a game of skill. If so, retorts Merck, it shouldn't qualify in a casino as a game of chance. But Resorts wanted it in the casino, so they claimed it as a game of chance as long as they could eject anyone who is skilled at playing it. Unbelievable!

The most disturbing point of the article is the way Resorts attorney Joel Sterns painted Blackjack card counters as ". . . walking away from the casino's blackjack tables with up to $40,000 per day." And the idea that counters were coming from all over the world to play at Atlantic City was questionable. Here is why those two statements make little sense.

First, the forty-thousand-dollar-winnings figure. Let's assume someone could actually maintain the concentration and have the endurance to track cards for eight hours per day (I don't know a single professional in the world who can do this without making numerous mistakes from fatigue, but let's assume it's possible). That means the counter would have to win five thousand dollars *per hour*. Next, let's assume that the counter plays one hundred hands per hour at the table in head-on play. Although head-on play at Atlantic City was virtually nonexistent (fifty hands per hour at a full table are more normal), let's give Resorts the benefit of the doubt. If the counter won *every* hand he or she played *all day,* the flat betting level would have to be fifty dollars each hand. Winning a still impossible 75 per cent of the hands increases the betting level to seventy-five dollars, etc.

But the counter's edge is not 50 per cent, (75—25); it is more like 2 to 3 per cent (which is enough to make it worth your while). With the realistic 2 per cent edge, you would have to be flat-betting twenty-five hundred dollars *per hand,* well over the table limits. If anyone walked away with forty thousand dollars, it was because of incredible luck and not counting skill. I frankly doubt that any counter made that type of killing consistently.

As you will see in Chapter Seven, most counters do not flat-bet. They bet smaller when the deck conditions are unfavorable, and larger in advantageous situations. Using this scheme, a counter could conceivably win five thousand dollars per hour more easily.

The problem is that the casinos are also aware of this, so that ranging bets widely attracts immediate pit-boss attention. If too big a bet suddenly goes out, the dealer shuffles the advantage away. I was shuffled up on occasion when ranging my bets from twenty-five dollars to one hundred dollars, an acceptable one-to-four range. To win five thousand dollars per hour, I would have to range my bets from five dollars to five hundred dollars and win *all* my bets at five hundred dollars. How long do you think the pit boss would let that occur if you were fortunate enough to have a run of luck? The word got out to the pros in the first two months: "Stay away!"

When Resorts initially opened in Atlantic City, three first-rate counters playing the Hi-Opt II (slightly more powerful than the Hi-Opt I) lost over sixty thousand dollars in less than three weeks, counting and signaling each other for the proper plays as a team. They were shuffled up on at both the twenty-five-dollar-minimum and one-hundred-dollar-minimum tables. They also swear they were cheated, but don't know how. I personally saw no sign of any cheating. I won two hundred dollars, but my trip cost four hundred dollars. Just as easily I could have lost two hundred dollars, so the results weren't too conclusive. I didn't need any further proof to play somewhere else.

Since my early visit to Atlantic City, the New Jersey Casino Control Commission has been thrashing around about the way the casinos may handle counters. After allowing the casinos to officially bar counters in January '79, the Commission continued to consider allowing counters to play. Then in October '79 the Commission ordered the Atlantic City casinos to allow counters to play unmolested as of December 1.

The Commission also permitted the casinos to institute countermeasures to minimize the risk in letting counters play. The casinos could reshuffle after dealing out only half the cards, and could shuffle upon seeing certain jumps in betting or upon seeing someone enter the game with a large opening bet. As you will see in Chapter Seven, these all thwart a counter tracking the cards and betting more in favorable situations. By December 14, 1979, the casinos had documented that counters still had an advantage (despite several counters' protests to the contrary) and were once again allowed to bar any Blackjack card counters they could detect.

This is the way it currently stands in Atlantic City. Identifiable counters are quickly barred. Winners for any reason are watched closely and countermeasures quickly taken regardless of the reasons for the win. It is still a problem of supply and demand. Once the casinos must start competing for players by offering better games (as in Las Vegas), then the player will have a better chance of finding a worthwhile game.

BLACKJACK IN PARADISE: PARADISE ISLAND

"Welcome to Paradise" flashed the sign as we crossed the bridge from Nassau to Paradise Island. Our limousine driver, Charlie the Great, assured us that we were truly entering Paradise. I use "the Great" when talking about Charlie because that's how he introduced himself to us when he picked us up at the airport. "The Great" may have referred to his mouth. He made Thomas Henderson (from Dallas Cowboys days) seem like a mute. Charlie talked almost nonstop during the forty-five-minute trip from the airport to Paradise Island. We arrived in the dark, so he couldn't show us the sights along the way. He did tell us all about good spots to eat, although he never ate out, he said, because it was too expensive. He also described interesting sights to see, but he didn't tell us about Joyce.

Joyce, the tour's representative, met us at the front door of the Flagler Inn as we arrived. Joyce was a beautiful Bahamian woman who looked like Farrah Fawcett with golden-brown hair. The next morning Joyce welcomed us with a rum-punch party and answered all the questions tourists typically have. She cautioned us about muggings, but I never saw any or felt in any danger. I told my wife I must have been too intimidating; she suggested I appeared too small a catch (if she's right, maybe that's what makes me more invisible at the tables).

I introduced myself to Joyce after the orientation—for strictly business reasons, of course! I mentioned that I was the author of several books and wanted to know if there was any possibility of getting them in any of the local Bahamian bookstores. That afternoon, she directed me to the largest book distributor in the Bahamas. My books were in the stores before the week was out. Thank you, Joyce!

On Monday afternoon, we visited the Straw Market, which is right on the dock in Nassau. There are a wide range of hand-crafted goods there, and locals enjoy a good haggle over prices. We also saw a number of fishermen selling conch (pronounced "konk"). Charlie the Great told us that conch was the local fish food, and that it cured everything from headaches to losing streaks in the casinos. I hope there is never a nuclear accident and the conches take over the world. They'll have a lot of getting even to do on the humans. We couldn't go anywhere that conch didn't appear on the menu in several different dishes.

Monday evening we went to the Neptune Room in the Holiday Inn and had a variety of seafood. The food was extremely expensive, as Charlie had promised, but was nothing special. Later that evening I managed to play Blackjack in the Paradise Island casino.

The casino has 26 tables, all dealing four decks out of a shoe. Most dealers cut off 1½ decks with the red plastic marker. When the marker is hit, the deck is immediately reshuffled before resuming play. The Blackjack rules at Paradise Island, like those of so many Caribbean locations, are less favorable than in Las Vegas. Doubling is allowed on 9, 10, and 11 only. Resplitting pairs is not allowed, nor is surrender. Insurance is allowed, and at the $5.00 minimum tables, you must insure for the total $5.00. However, the tables stock no $2.50 chips, so if you Blackjack on a $5.00 bet, your second $5.00 winning chip is "imprisoned" until the next hand.

The tables were full most of the time. In the early evening, when there are few players in the casino, only four to eight tables are open. In the late evening after 10:00 P.M., most of the tables are open, but conditions are so crowded that people were three deep waiting for a seat. Part of this problem was due to being there during the "season" in February, when the ocean liners bring thousands of tourists to Nassau. During this season, the best time to play is Sunday evenings and in the afternoons between noon and 3:00 P.M.

On Tuesday evening I won $345 in a short playing session. The young British dealer "innocently" asked if I kept track of the cards. I guessed that any offhand answer would be suspicious, so I lied. I told him I kept track of only the Aces because I knew that I had a better chance of getting a Blackjack if there were extra Aces in the shoe. I think he bought my story, but he continued:

"Do you play here often?" he asked.

"No," I said, "this is only the second or third time I've been here. I do most of my playing in Las Vegas." That was the truth.

My wife spent almost every day on the beach at the back of the Flagler Inn. I would spend the late morning and early afternoons with her before the sun got too hot. On Wednesday she introduced me to a whole family she met on the beach. Hank, the father, was a retired sergeant major who lives in St. Louis. I found he was an excellent gambler, like most noncoms, who played almost perfect Basic Strategy. He won a few hundred dollars playing with me on several occasions. Whenever Hank was leaving for the casino and his wife would ask him where he was going, he'd say, "Oh I'm going shopping." He brought back money every time from these shopping trips.

On Thursday evening while strolling through the casino with my wife, I bumped into "Bob." Bob is the most successful Blackjack player I know, having winnings of over five hundred thousand dollars in the past four years. When I talked with him, he was down close to ten thousand dollars, but was only a little concerned about it. He took us to dinner in the Bahamian Club, which served by far the best meal we had on the island. And it was all complimentary, thanks to Bob.

I saw Bob only once after that, near the end of the week. He had recouped all of his losses except for a couple of thousand dollars. He admitted that he had made a mistake coming to the Bahamas during the busy season. His original intent was to take a holiday in Florida, but the weather was so bad there he couldn't resist the casino on Paradise Island. Once a gambler, always a gambler.

On Friday, I played too much. I had a winning session in the early afternoon and then made the mistake of playing again a little later without sufficient rest. This led to the biggest loss of my trip: two hundred dollars. The conditions were crowded, I was tired, my psychological resistance was low, and I was making a few playing errors. Even though I was up twice during the evening, I didn't manage to walk away a winner. I was trying to win one thousand dollars on this trip and was pushing too hard. If only I were bionic at times!

On our last day I saw Hank and his family on the beach again. Hank told me he had played at my table the previous night and was astounded at the intensity of my concentration. He said I hadn't even noticed him at the table. He was right, I didn't notice him at all. I was preoccupied with the drunk sitting to my left, who was standing on all 13s through 16s and winning hundreds of dollars. Who says luck can't play some part in Blackjack?

Hank and I went "shopping" together for the last time that afternoon. The wonderful aspect of traveling is the fine people you can meet. Among our closest friends is a couple we met on a trip to Freeport. Of course, another consideration is the amount of money that can be made in the casinos!

BLACKJACK PLAY AT PARADISE ISLAND

Day	Time	Won/Lost	Bet Range	Comment
Sunday	Arrived 7 P.M.		Did not play due to jet lag.	
Monday	9:30 P.M. to 11:30 P.M.	−120	$5.00 to $40	Full table.
Tuesday	1:00 P.M. to 1:45 P.M.	+345	$5.00 to $60	Some head-on play.
	2:30 P.M. to 3:10 P.M.	−100	$5.00 to $30	Full table. Fast Italian dealer.
Wednesday	1:00 P.M. to 3:00 P.M.	+200	$5.00 to $80	The bet range did it.
	10:00 P.M. to 10:40 P.M.	+115	$5.00 to $40	Uncrowded table.
Thursday	2:00 P.M. to 2:45 P.M.	+235	$5.00 to $80	Uncrowded. With Hank.
Friday	1:15 P.M. to 2:10 P.M.	+240	$5.00 to $40	Dealer dealt out 3 decks.
	3:00 P.M. to 4:20 P.M.	−200	$5.00 to $60	Full table. Headache.

Day	Time	Won/Lost	Bet Range	Comment
	9:00 P.M. to 11:00 P.M.	− 70	$5.00 to $40	Was ahead twice! Got tired.
Saturday	6:10 P.M. to 9:00 P.M.	+ 20	$5.00 to $40	Full table. Was behind till the end.
Sunday	2:00 P.M. to 3:15 P.M.	+105	$5.00 to $80	Full table. With Hank.

$$Won= +\$1,260 \quad Won: \text{ 7 sessions}$$
$$Lost= - \quad 490 \quad Lost: \text{ 4 sessions}$$
$$Net= \overline{+\$ \ \ 770}$$

My playing record for the Bahamas trip is shown in the table. Although conditions were crowded most of the time, I won at a good rate. The reason is that the dealers were not paying attention to my bet range. I found I could very easily implement a range of one to eight or even one to sixteen without causing any disturbance. My impression this time was that the game in Paradise Island casino was completely honest. The playing conditions were not ideal, but this could have been avoided by coming sometime other than the height of the tourist season. The rules are not ideal, either. However, the honesty of the game and the location override the conditions. Charlie the Great, wherever you are I want you to know, "It's better in the Bahamas" means Blackjack, too.

Choosing where you play is part of the winning process. By now you've seen that the decisions you make about where to play can greatly effect *how well* you do with your money. Choose your location from anywhere in the world, find the right casino, pick the right combination of dealer and table rules, and sit down. Beginning with what you've learned in this chapter, you're getting ready to put your money on the betting square.

FOUR

Dealing with the Dealer

My rackets are run on strictly American lines and they're going to stay that way.

AL CAPONE

If I had to select the most important chapter in this book, I would choose this one. The honesty of the dealer is critical to winning. No matter how powerful your strategy is or how much of a mathematical genius you are, you will not win against a cheating dealer. The best cheats can deal in such a way as to win every hand if they want to. Author Mario Puzo observed, "The whole recorded history of gambling shows that when you have gambling, you have cheating." I estimate that approximately 10 to 20 per cent of Nevada dealers *can* cheat. It is discouraging guesswork to wonder about the number of those who *do* cheat. The purpose of this chapter is to show the different kinds of dealers, how to recognize them, and how to play them.

WHY BECOME A DEALER?

Dealing can be a good deal. When the Resorts International casino in Atlantic City was advertising for people to fill six hundred dealing positions, nearly three thousand applied. The job appears to have glamor and excitement. In reality, it is very hard work. The Atlantic City dealers worked nearly ten hours per day, six days per week in the early months of the casino's opening.

The job is very demanding. Dealers must work on their feet, forty minutes on, twenty minutes off, dressed in casino uniforms with no pockets (to insure honesty), facing a gambling public that can be rude, hostile, superstitious, or thieving. The dealer works under the strict supervision of a pit boss and under the ever-present eye in the sky.

Job security is nonexistent. If anyone on a shift is caught cheating, the whole shift is fired. Cheating on a shift is usually known by all the other dealers, whether or not they participate in it, so innocent dealers are fired for not speaking up against one of their number.

Dealing requires education, skill, manual dexterity, and good concentration. If dealer applicants show manual dexterity at handling the cards, good ability to concentrate, and knowledge of the rules, they are allowed to become apprentice dealers. The apprentice deals with an experienced dealer standing at his or her side correcting any mistakes and making comments on technique. Once the dealer is past the apprentice stage, the dealer can handle a game alone, usually very closely watched by the pit boss until the dealer convinces management of his or her competence.

In Atlantic City, since Resorts had to hire New Jersey residents, the dealers were put through a casino-sponsored "dealers school." In Las Vegas, new dealers must put themselves through a private dealing school. Even then, it is nearly impossible to get a job in a major casino without experience. New dealers must start at small casinos outside major areas such as the Strip.

Why would someone go to all this trouble to become a dealer? For some, the dealer's job is one with "class" in "part of the action." For others, it's the money. In an article appearing in *Gambling Times* magazine, Walter Tyminski (editor of the *Rouge et Noir News* gambling newsletter) analyzed figures from the *Nevada Gaming Abstract*. He found that the average salary of dealers working in a casino winning $20 million or more per year to be $12,370 per year. The average salary was this *low* because tips supplement wages. Average tips for Blackjack dealers at large Las Vegas Strip casinos are approximately $50 per day. On an annual basis, this amounts to an additional $12,500 per year! Dealing isn't such a bad way to earn a living after all.

THE DEALER'S JOB

The following set of rules, supplied courtesy of John Luckman at the Gambler's Book Club in Las Vegas, are given to newly employed Blackjack dealers in one downtown Las Vegas casino. Rules differ in each casino, and are listed here to give you an idea of the complexity of the game from the dealer's and casino's point of view:

1. $1.00 to $500, table limits.
2. Split any pair—or any two face cards. Split Aces—only one card is to be given on each, except player can resplit third Ace.
3. Double down on any two cards.
4. Dealer must spread and pay each hand individually; payment to be made while the hand is spread. Standoffs must be indicated while player's hand is still on the table.
5. If at all possible, make change for all bills before dealing. If player insists on leaving bills, they must be spread so the floorman and eye in the sky can see what amount is there.
6. Do not allow player to alter his bet after starting to deal.
7. When dealer breaks, count players' hands down close to make sure they are not over 21.
8. Dealer must hit soft 17 and stand on hard 17.
9. If a dealer should hit hard 17, the hit card is to be buried and the original 17 stands.
10. If player asks for reshuffle before the deck is played out, dealer will get OK from floorman before doing so. If this practice is once started of shuffling at player's request, you would be spending too much time shuffling. [Author's note: This is also a great way to get rid of a poor deck!]
11. The more hands you can deal without running over the players, the better game you will have. Keep a good, steady pace at all times.
12. Make sure all bets are inside box. Anything outside of box is not bet.
13. When hitting your hand, spread cards out, side by side. This way the floorman and "eye" can read all cards very easily.
14. Dealing cards will always be from left to right. Closely case the bets on the first and last hands. These are the most

likely spots for players to pinch (reduce) or press (increase) bets after receiving cards.

15. Right-handed dealers take and pay from right to left. Left-handed dealers take and pay from left to right. Leave Blackjacks on table and pay on final pickup.

16. A player playing more than one hand must play each hand in turn, although he may look at all of them, unless the floorman knows the player is a counter; then he cannot look at all of them.

17. A player doubling down must have the same bet as the original, unless you feel he is down to his last money; then he could double any part of same.

18. When paying bets, size into stacks. No capping of bets at any time when paying Blackjacks. Make two even stacks—size into same three times—then if you have an odd check, pay it last.

19. When player cuts cards, make sure he gives square cut; also, five or more cards.

20. At no time, for any reason, is the dealer to take his eyes off the deck, keeping one hand by the deck while it is being cut.

21. Never deal more hands than boxes on table.

22. A player may not take an exposed card; the dealer must.

23. If the dealer fails to give himself a hole card, he acts on all the other hands, then when he gets to his own, he takes the next card for his and finishes the hand.

24. If a player, after a deal, has more than two cards, the hand is void and has no action.

25. If the dealer fails to turn over a Blackjack, it will then be counted as 21. Any player having 21 would stand off.

26. Do not flip and hit cards off the deck with one hand. In other words, all cards coming off the deck will be with two hands.

These twenty-six basic items are but a fraction of the possibilities that require a decision. Good judgment takes over in most situations. As shown in No. 17, any progressive casino would rather modify the rules than lose a bet from a customer. (Players should question anything that isn't perfectly clear. And don't wait. Stop the dealer the instant there is any misunderstanding so that it can be explained.) For the high pay, the dealer must keep the game rolling under the most rigid of rules, constantly being watched by the pit boss or eye. A tough job.

CHEATING IN THE CASINOS

Before Thorp's *Beat the Dealer* was published in 1962, the question about cheating was, "Do they cheat in casinos?" Since the publication of that book, there has been much evidence of cheating in Las Vegas, in Reno, and in Lake Tahoe (as well as in casinos in other parts of the world). The question today is, "How much do they cheat in the casinos?" I'm going to limit the main discussion to Nevada casinos, since about 90 per cent of the world's Blackjack action takes place there.

ORGANIZED CRIME AND CASINO GAMBLING

According to an interview several years ago with an individual who is high up in the hierarchy of organized crime, the Mob has people placed in almost every casino in the state of Nevada. The people help the Mob take money out of the casinos by allowing certain other mobsters to win money while playing at their table. In order to balance the chips on the table, the honest players like you and me have to be cheated.

In the interview quoted below, taken from the 1976 January–February issue of *Rouge et Noir News,* we see strong evidence of this kind of cheating:

AN INTERVIEW

[Knowledge of the intimate details of organized crime's current activities in the world of casino gaming is limited to a handful of individuals. Our interviewee is one of these individuals, as you will find from the information he has provided.]

To what extent is organized crime active in Nevada casino gaming?

I have difficulty with that question because the term "organized crime" means different things to different people. Rather than get caught up in a philosophical discussion, let me say that the elements that were represented by previous owners are still active in Nevada casino gaming.

Let me explain that further. Our people may have solid hotel-casino operations, but we have our people in key spots. We're primarily interested in the areas of casino credit issuance and collection, junkets, and the supervision of table games.

Why the interest in supervision of Blackjack games?

Blackjack provides one of our biggest and safest sources of income. We have trained card counters who are "allowed" to play for large stakes without being barred. It isn't necessary for us to cheat. The decks don't get shuffled up as often for our players, and house personnel don't overreact to large increases in our bet size.

The scam is so simple and effective that we've spawned a bevy of competitors. So many insiders now have working arrangements with card counters that it has become necessary to bar unaffiliated counters to protect the bottom-line performance. Unfortunately, the "boys" are getting too greedy for their own good.

What do you see as organized crime's future in Nevada?

Casino gaming is small potatoes compared to sports betting. Our long-range plan is to become more active in the promotion of sports events in Nevada. We're particularly anxious to feature events of national interest wherein we promote the event and house the participants. When we can house, feed, and entertain the "cast," the results can be affected in any number of ways without anyone becoming the wiser.

When we want to throw a participant off we can offer sex of the quality and quantity that is hard to refuse; the room can become uncomfortable and/or noisy; subliminal techniques are being tried; food can be doctored, etc. We don't have to balance the betting books on such operations, and the acquiescence of participants is not required.

I don't have to spell out how we use casinos in influencing participants in nonarena sports events. You are smart enough to figure that out for yourself.

If you are wondering about the accuracy of the above interview, just think for a moment how important Las Vegas has become as a site for major sporting events, from tennis to boxing, in the past few years. The plans of the Mob seem to be well in place and working at an accelerated pace.

There's an old joke about the accountant applying for a job and being asked, "Do you know double-entry bookkeeping?"

"Hell yes!" says the accountant, "And I can go that one better. I'm an expert in triple-entry bookkeeping, one for you showing the real profit, another for your wife showing a slight profit, and a third for the IRS showing a loss."

In my days with a large computer company, I had the opportunity to speak with a salesman who nearly starved covering the hotels-casinos in Las Vegas in the early days of accounting machines. He was having no success selling hotels cash-management systems there when they were popular all over the rest of the country. All the casinos would buy were reservations systems. Keeping accurate track of the funds flow in the casinos was a *disadvantage* to the old-time casino owners. Even though ownership has changed hands, you might wonder if organized crime is still that big a factor in the casinos of Nevada. If the behavior of the "little people" who work there is any indication, it is.

I spoke with a sales manager who told me an interesting story about Las Vegas. He was on a trip to the West Coast with two of his salesmen when they decided to stop in Vegas for an all-night gambling spree. The manager, coincidentally named Luciano, was a short, dark Italian who grew up on the East Coast. One of the salesmen was an enormous fellow, about 6 feet, 5 inches and 250 pounds. The second man was a slight Jewish man with horn-rimmed glasses. About halfway through the evening, they decided to try to get into the main show at the Strip casino where they were staying.

Walking up to the showroom doors, they found an enormous line waiting to get in. The manager, in true East Coast fashion, brashly walked up to the doorman and demanded, "What do you have to do to get into this thing?" What happened next took the three completely by surprise.

The doorman started to brush them off when his eyes suddenly got very large. He looked at the manager, the big salesman, and the small salesman, and gulped, "This way please."

Without seeing what the tip was, the doorman took them down to center front next to the stage where there were no tables, just lounge chairs. The manager tipped the doorman twenty dollars and sat down in wonderment. This was where Frank Sinatra or

the like sits when he comes to a show. About twenty minutes after
the show started, three beautiful young women noiselessly joined
them.

That's when the sales manager figured out what happened and
started laughing so hard he could barely stop. As he explained to
the others later, what the doorman saw was an older, forceful
Italian mobster, his hulking bodyguard, and his faithful accountant. Even without knowing who they were, the doorman was taking no chances.

A similar bit of intimidation worked for Larry, a friend of mine
who had heard that story before he went to Las Vegas on a con-
vention. Larry was an executive for a large manufacturing company at the time. His boss was at a meeting at the Landmark
Hotel, although the boss was not staying there. Larry had been
asked to drop the boss's luggage off at the front desk during the
meeting upstairs so the boss could quickly pick it up afterward
and catch his plane. Here's the conversation that ensued between
Larry and a troublesome bell captain.

"I'd like to store these bags here for several hours. Can you do
that?" began Larry.

"Are you a guest of the hotel, sir?" responded the bell captain.

"No, but these are for my boss, who is here at a meeting."

"Is your boss a guest of the hotel?" persisted the captain.

"No, but he's here at a meeting," Larry repeated.

With a satisfied smile, the bell captain then said, "Well, I'm
sorry, but we can't store luggage for anyone not a guest of the
hotel. You'll have to make other arrangements."

"But my boss told me to bring his luggage here to him," Larry
protested.

"That's not my problem, is it?" ended the bell captain.

Larry told me later that he suddenly remembered the above
story and considered the Italian name of his boss in a moment of
inspiration.

"No, that's not really my problem," Larry countered. "It's
going to be yours."

At this change in the conversation, and in Larry's tone of
voice, the bell captain suddenly became alert.

"My boss, Mr. Travaglini, is going to be very upset when he
finds that his bags aren't here for him."

"Am I supposed to know him?" asked the bell captain.

"He's from the East, and at first he's going to be mad at me, but after I tell him what happened here, he'll be mad at you. And I don't think having Mr. T. mad at you is a very wise thing to do."

Larry told me that the bell captain looked him over for the first time, seeing someone in a five-hundred-dollar suit running bags for his "boss," gulped, and said, "I'll watch them. Gimme the bags."

"Oh by the way, Mr. T. doesn't like to have his bags messed with."

"They'll be here when he's ready, sir," finished the now fully cowed bell captain.

You think there's no Mob influence in Las Vegas? You'll never convince Larry or those three salesmen! And for good reason, too. On March 14, 1979, the St. Louis *Post-Dispatch* ran the following article:

Aladdin Hotel Convicted of Aiding Crime Figures

The Aladdin Hotel Corp. . . . was convicted Tuesday in U. S. District Court in Detroit of helping Detroit crime figures secretly gain an interest in the corporation, which owns a Las Vegas, Nev., hotel and gambling casino.

The jury, which deliberated six days, also convicted four Detroit men, several of them described by authorities as associates of underworld figures. They had been charged with violating federal anti-racketeering statutes . . .

Convicted were: No. 1, an ex-convict who is entertainment director of the Aladdin; Detroit bail bondsman No. 2; No. 3, executive director of the Aladdin; and No. 4, a pit boss at the Aladdin.

The Nevada Gaming Commission several years ago identified No. 1 as a member of the Detroit underworld. No. 2 was denied a license in 1971 for the Aladdin because of his organized-crime associations. . . .

The four defendants and the corporation are expected to appeal their convictions.

At the time this is written, the Aladdin is currently under the direction of the Nevada Gaming Commission. In whose hands the casino will land is anybody's guess at this point.

About the same time as the problems with the Aladdin, the

Nevada Gaming Commission was forced to take action against the companies which operate the Stardust Hotel. Nevada authorities had uncovered a 3.5 million dollar slot-machine skimming operation. The Gaming Commission revoked the licenses of the companies that operate the Stardust and levied a five-hundred-thousand-dollar fine, the largest in Nevada history. In addition, the corporations were ordered to pay one hundred thousand dollars to the state as reimbursement for the cost of the action and another hundred thousand for taxes due on the stolen money.

Las Vegas may not be the only place influenced by crime figures either, as is indicated in this UPI article:

THE TRENTONIAN, THURSDAY MORNING, JANUARY 25, 1979

NJ PRODUCES EVIDENCE
Resorts Caught in Mob Tie Lie?

BY JOHN RHODES

ATLANTIC CITY (UPI)— The state Wednesday produced evidence strongly contradicting claims by Resorts International it completely severed ties to an employee linked to organized crime and banned from the Bahamas.

Assistant Attorney General G. Michael Brown said Edward Cellini, the first manager of the company's Paradise Island casino, was given checks totalling $190,500 up to 20 months after the Bahamian government ordered Resorts to end its relationship with him.

Brown presented the evidence during the 11th day of Casino Control Commission hearings on Resorts' request for a permanent gambling license.

The evidence seemed to contradict testimony by Resorts' president I. G. "Jack" Davis. Davis has repeatedly denied the company retained Cellini after the severence order from the Bahamian government and that Cellini had links to organized crime.

Cellini was manager of the Paradise Island casino from late 1967 to December 1969 before he was banned from the Bahamas as an "undesirable" who was tied to organized crime by his brother Dino.

When the Bahamian government insisted Cellini be severed from all company operations, Resorts said his employment would be end Dec. 31, 1969.

Brown, however, pointed out

that five checks totalling $190,500 were paid to Cellini through Resorts' subsidiary, Paradise Enterprises, Ltd., in 1970.

Brown challenged Davis further, saying not only did Cellini receive the five checks, but Resorts also paid for trips he took throughout the Caribbean islands. Brown charged Cellini was allowed to take advantage of a company car leasing plan.

Davis, in sworn testimony before the Division of Gaming Enforcement last month, said Cellini's expenses were paid in return for his "opinion" regarding Resorts' "imminent involvement in other islands."

When questioned by Brown Wednesday, Davis rescinded his sworn testimony.

As you can see, Resorts International, the Atlantic City casino owner, was reported as paying $190,500 to a man banned from the Bahamas as an "undesirable" (for his Mob ties through his brother). This was in return for his "opinion" regarding Resorts' "imminent involvement in other islands." A man commanding $190,500 for opinions is not to be laughed at.

Unfortunately, the president of Resorts had testified earlier that the "undesirable" was no longer on the payroll until the New Jersey assistant Attorney General produced evidence to the contrary. When presented with the evidence, the president rescinded his sworn testimony of the previous month. And while we're thinking about Atlantic City, let's don't forget the alleged involvement of state gaming officials in the ABSCAM inquiry.

CHEATING AND BLACKJACK

You should have noticed in the mobster interview that winning money from mobbed-up dealers has been *the most lucrative method for obtaining money from the casinos*. When the Mob says lucrative, they means millions of dollars. Dealers must consistently show a normal table win rate despite dishonestly losing to their friends. In order to recover dishonest losses, honest players like you and me must pay for it. How else can Blackjack tables show a profit on the "bottom line," as he claims they do? The dealers must be cheating.

Nevada newspapers frequently report the arrests of dealers at small and large casinos alike. The dealers are usually charged with "dealing from other than the top of the deck," fined several hundred dollars, and fired by the casinos. The casinos always deny any knowledge of the fact that the dealer was cheating, which may or may not be true, depending upon the dealer and the casino. Here are two typical articles from my files describing cheating at two small Nevada casinos in the midseventies:

Cheated at '21'

LAS VEGAS SUN, *August 29, 1974, page 11*

CARSON CITY (UPI)— The Nevada Gaming Control Board has filed a complaint against ——, owner of the Owl Club in Yerington, alleging he cheated customers in his "21" game in July and August.

The Control Board asks that the gaming license of —— be revoked and he be fined 10,000. —— has 15 days to answer the complaint.

The board said its undercover agents discovered —— peeking* at the cards in the deck and dealing "seconds"† in the game on more than five occasions between July 26 and August 15.

The State Gaming Commission last week issued an emergency order closing the games and slot machines.

Tonopah Casinos Shut by Gaming Authorities

Las Vegas SUN, *Tuesday June 11, 1974, page 9.*

Carson City (UPI)—The Nevada Gaming Commission has closed down the gambling at two Tonopah casinos because of alleged cheating and other irregularities, it was announced Monday.

Philip Hannifin, chairman of

---

* "Peeking" means stealing a look at the top card of the deck.

† "Seconds" means the dealer kept the top card and dealt the second card from the top.

the State Gaming Control Board, said the Commission granted a board petition to close the table games, seal the slot machines and pull the gaming licenses of the Tonopah Club and the Tonopah Belle.

The board petition for emergency closure followed seven

months of surveillance by gaming agents, he said.

The board alleged dealers looked at their hole card when neither an ace nor a 10-value card was face up,‡ peeked in various fashions at the unused portion of the deck, and dealt "seconds"—that is, other than the top card.

Some of my former students (whom I've taught to play winning Blackjack) and I have pooled skills and managed to win slightly over five hundred thousand dollars playing Blackjack in the past few years. We should have won in excess of three million dollars according to the mathematical advantage we have and the level of betting we used. We played as a team, so we know the difference was not due to making excessive playing errors. We were rarely shuffled up on or suffered any other type of house pressure. There is only one explanation for why we did not win the full amount: The reason can only be dealer cheating.

Player-dealer partnerships, for the benefit of the Mob, the casino, or an individual, are corroborated in Mike Goodman's 1975 book, *Your Best Bet*. Goodman, a veteran pit boss in Las Vegas, says:

The ideal setup, one that counters and cheaters dream about, is talking a dealer into becoming a partner. It's happening more and more as the gambling business continues to mushroom. Reliable casino employees are becoming much harder to find. In Nevada, it's safe to say that almost every large casino is being victimized by one or more dealers who are working with agents on the other side of the table.

---

‡ The dealer is only allowed to look under his up card when the up card is an Ace or a 10-value card—this is to see whether he has a Blackjack. If he does have a Blackjack then there is no further play for that round, he wins; all the players lose except those who also have a Blackjack. They tie the dealer.

Goodman goes on to say, "Even today there's no telling how much leakage or cheating is going on in clubs still using single decks."

I was lucky enough to observe a skimming operation at a famous Strip casino. I was strolling by looking for a good table at about ten-thirty one morning when I saw something that made me stop. A man in his fifties, balding with gray hair, wearing a blue shirt with polka dots, was having the time of his life. He was playing three hands at five hundred dollars a hand, five black chips. I also noticed that he had about eight thousand dollars' worth of black chips in front of him. He had drawn a tremendous crowd around him. I asked the young fellow standing next to me how long the man had been playing. The man had bought a thousand dollars in chips about twenty minutes before.

I stood there and watched him play. When I looked up at the dealer I couldn't believe my eyes. I had played against that dealer on and off for over four years and had never won more than fifty dollars from him. This morning the dealer couldn't do anything right. He was busting about 80 per cent of the time.

I began watching the player carefully to see how good he was. The man played a fairly accurate Basic Strategy but kept no track of the cards. He was betting big money sometimes when the deck was favorable, other times when the deck was unfavorable.

I waited until he quit forty-five minutes later, ahead thirty-one thousand dollars. In the same casino I have seen a young man up five hundred dollars while playing with a small reference card attract three pit bosses like vultures over their carrion. With this older man, the dealer had been smiling the whole time, while a single pit boss was watching happily. I'm certain the pit boss was in on this skimming operation, because it is his job to keep anyone who is not one of the "boys" from winning any appreciable amount of money. When someone does win a lot of money quickly, and he or she is not supposed to, the pit bosses get very, very upset. I saw the exact opposite in this situation.

If you ever see this happening and there are some seats open, sit down and start betting. It's an easy way to win quick money. Over the years I had observed similar skims in several Las Vegas casinos, but I didn't realize what they were at the time. I thought the players simply got lucky. I realize now that you don't get lucky against a cheating dealer in a casino.

Throughout the years, I have seen numerous examples of dealer cheating in Las Vegas. On one occasion, my friend Nick and I caught a female dealer giving herself Aces. There were three of us at the table when I sat down at third base. The others, including Nick, were grumbling because they were losing. They began to make fun of the dealer, who was young but somewhat plain. One of the players said her chest was like a surfboard. She got red in the face but said nothing. She merely gathered up the cards, shuffled several times, dealt, and came up with the Ace of Diamonds as her up card. She asked for insurance, which no one took. She didn't have a Blackjack.

As soon as we all played our hands she reshuffled immediately instead of dealing two more rounds, as she had been. After the shuffle, she again had the Ace of Diamonds as her up card. We played, she reshuffled again, and guess what card she dealt herself? Right. The Ace of Diamonds for the third time. This time she had a ten underneath for a Blackjack. We all stood up in one motion and left the casino.

Actually, she was being nice to us. She could have cheated us out of our money without arousing our suspicion. Instead, she just wanted us to know who was boss, who was in control. Moral? A dealer's chest should never be likened to a surfboard, no matter how close the resemblance.

On another occasion at a different casino, my friend Joe and I got a much more expensive education. Joe and I were playing late one night when I decided to go to bed. Joe wanted to stay for a little while longer, so I nodded my good-bye and left.

As I walked into the casino the next morning, who do I see playing but Joe. He had been playing all night and was down about eight thousand dollars in a single-deck game. He played all night because the dealer was showing him both the burn card and bottom card at every shuffle, and because the dealer dealt out *all* the cards. This is ideal for the counter.

I tried to get Joe to quit because he was very tired. Joe wanted to get even, so I decided to help him by sitting down, playing myself, and correcting any of Joe's playing errors. Joe was not making any mistakes, his count was the same as mine, and his betting was accurate most of the time. I lost five hundred dollars in about twenty minutes while Joe lost another twelve hundred dollars. I realized that George, the dealer, was cheating us. I was so mad I said, "George, stop cheating." George smiled, then broke out laughing at me. I quit.

We were definitely cheated by George. It was impossible for us, particularly for Joe, who had been playing for hours, to lose that much money with the advantage we had. Our strategy was the most powerful that computers could generate up to that time. We had won in excess of ninety thousand dollars with it in playing in private games in our hometown. But our skill and system meant nothing when matched against a dealer who could cheat. The only way to protect yourself against the cheating dealer is not to play against him.

WARNING SIGNS OF A CHEATING DEALER

A general statement about cheating comes from former casino owner Harold Smith, Jr. He states in his book *I Want to Quit Winners,* "We could cheat all the time and they [agents of the Gaming Control Board] would never know it. We're far more expert at this business than they are." If Smith's statements are true, then how can the average player ever hope to spot the cheating? The answer is, he can't. The important skill you can develop is how to spot a potentially cheating dealer or how to detect the fact that you are being cheated without actually seeing it.

There are a number of ways to spot the potentially cheating dealer. Some involve common sense, others require a little bit of inside information to understand. All of them can save you money.

EMPTY TABLE

One sign is a dealer who is standing behind an empty table. Usually this is a dealer who has cleaned out all the players. If he is consistently alone, that means he keeps on cleaning out any new players as soon as they sit down. They lose quickly and leave his table empty.

I have found this to be particularly true at the five-dollar-minimum tables in downtown Las Vegas, Reno, and Lake Tahoe. These tables are usually empty. I've also noticed that the dealers at these tables are always older than the dealers at the one-dollar tables in the same casinos.

This empty-table sign is one of the reasons why people will join you so quickly if you are playing alone. Not only do most players dislike playing alone with a dealer, but also insiders know an empty table can be a sign of a dealer who is too successful for the players' good.

TWENTY-FIVE-DOLLAR-MINIMUM AND HUNDRED-DOLLAR-MINIMUM TABLES

The twenty-five-dollar-minimum and hundred-dollar-minimum tables are traps for the unwary player. These tables can contain cheating dealers an extremely high percentage of the time. Such tables are most often found on the Las Vegas Strip (the five-dollar tables in downtown Las Vegas are analogous to the higher-priced Strip tables).

It's much better to cheat at the higher-minimum tables, which attract the high rollers, because the net gain per cheating maneuver is so much more. It makes more sense (and is less risky) to cheat a high roller once for a hundred dollars than tourists twenty times for five dollars each.

In addition to signs from the casino table, closely observing the dealer can give further information about the honesty of the game.

TOUGH-LOOKING DEALERS

You will find a lot of ugly, tough-looking dealers in Nevada casinos. It doesn't seem logical, yet I have found that tough-looking dealers are more difficult to win money from than attractive dealers. Correspondence from IBC members backs me up on this. A lot of the tougher ones look like the bad guys you see in an old cowboy movie. They look ugly and brutal and I'm sure they repel a lot of players.

Why don't casinos hire only good-looking dealers, like the Playboy Enterprises casinos or some of the Caribbean houses? I think it would be much better for their business. The answer is that these tough-looking dealers (and others not so tough-looking) may often be mobbed up. The former manager of a Nevada casino told me that his most difficult problem was trying to get mobbed-up dealers off his payroll. He said that they were very difficult to get rid of because they had *juice* (connections). His casino went bankrupt within a few months of its opening.

JEWELRY

A telltale sign of some cheating dealers is wearing expensive watches and rings. The rings are usually studded with diamonds, or have a ruby or other precious gems in the middle. While being a dealer won't exactly make you poor, in these inflationary times with diamond and gold prices soaring, expensive jewelry should not be particularly common to dealers as a group. The more ostentatious and expensive the personal effects of the dealer, the more you should be wary of playing at his or her table. The dealer may have an "outside" source of income—you!

TIME-WATCHING

Another sign of cheating is a dealer who too frequently turns his wrist in order to check the time. The real reason the dealer does this is to take a peek at the top card in the deck to decide if it should be dealt or not. This move is immediately suspect because of the type of job the dealer has.

Dealers work forty-minute shifts with twenty-minute breaks in between. After a few months on the job, the dealers develop such a fine sense of time from this pattern that they could tell time within several minutes without looking. There is no real need to know the time anyway, they're not going anywhere until they are relieved. Always avoid a time-watching wrist twister.

There are a number of playing signs that can also alert you to the cheating dealer. The game of Blackjack is one of probabilities with swings both in the direction of the player and the dealer. But when a particular swing consistently favors the dealer, it's time to be careful.

DEALER/BIG WINNER COMBINATION

As you saw in the earlier example, when a Blackjack player is betting five hundred dollars to one thousand dollars per hand, playing several hands, and *winning,* you can be fairly certain that you are witnessing a skimming operation. If there is a big winner at the table and the casino personnel are giving the fortunate soul all sorts of unfavorable attention, then you have a good indication of an honest game with a lucky player. In either case, *take a good look at the dealer* in this situation and remember him. He is going to be money down for his shift at the table.

As I mentioned, it is often advantageous to sit down during a skimming operation and get some of the action. And sitting with a lucky high roller can often let you play unobserved in his shadow. But avoid that dealer later. After any type of heavy losing session, honest or dishonest, the dealer will be wanting to even up his or her "bottom line" win/loss statistics kept by the casino by recouping the losses as soon as possible. The skimming dealer must do it to keep his job, and the dealer losing because of a bad run of cards will be tempted to cheat to keep the pressure from the pit bosses off. So avoid a dealer after a heavy losing session.

NO-BUST DEALER

Sometimes you will see a dealer having an incredible winning session. Malcolm X warned, "If you see someone winning all the time, he isn't gambling, he's cheating." This is probably true of a dealer who seldom busts. The best way to deal no-bust hands is by dealing other than the top card. One woman playing at a Strip casino asked the dealer in front of me, "Don't you ever bust?" The dealer just smiled.

It's easy to see the contrast by playing on the Strip and then jumping into a taxi and speeding to the downtown area to play. The difference is remarkable. Downtown dealers do seem to bust more often. If you want absolute proof, stand away from a table and merely count the number of times a Strip dealer busts in every fifty hands. Then do the same thing downtown. Compare five to ten Strip dealers to any five to ten downtown dealers and you may have your proof.

10 OFF THE TOP

You can make a similar type of measurement with another common cheating indicator. This practice is for the dealer to give himself a 10-value (or Ace) up card right after the shuffle. This sleight of hand is easy to learn and gives the dealer a large-percentage advantage over the players.

One of the most highly respected gambling authorities in the world, Professor Peter Griffin, actually went around from casino to casino and counted how often the dealer came up with a 10, Jack, Queen, or King, or Ace immediately after the shuffle. He found that it occurred over 40 per cent of the time. Statistics show that it should happen only 38 per cent of the time (20 tens and Aces divided by 52 possible cards).

Griffin reported his findings at the Second Annual Conference on Gambling, held in Lake Tahoe in May 1975. This professor is an excellent Blackjack player and is still allowed to play in Nevada. Yet he does not win often possibly because he is known to the casino personnel as an expert. "Ten off the top" could be just one of the reasons for his change of "luck."

BLACKJACKING DEALER

Another trick after the shuffle is for the dealer to have an immediate Blackjack. Many more Las Vegas Strip dealers deal themselves Blackjacks right off the top than do downtown dealers. If you find that a dealer deals himself a Blackjack as soon as you sit down to play, or that the frequency of dealer Blackjacks is higher than about one in twenty, find another game. You are probably being Blackjacked intentionally.

LOSE DOUBLE DOWNS

Cheating dealers prefer to win as much as possible while cheating as infrequently as possible to reduce the risk of being discovered. One of the most common ways to do this in a hand-held one- or two-deck game is to win a high percentage of a player's big wagers from doubling. In one such situation, I found myself losing a large amount of double downs when the deck was very rich in 10-value cards by being dealt a small card on my hand of 9, 10, or 11. This is improbable for both me and the dealer. Yet the dealer kept on finding small cards somewhere in the deck in order to make his own hand without busting.

Since bringing this to the attention of the International Blackjack Club members, I have received many letters confirming high doubling losses as a common cheating approach. If you are losing an inordinately high percentage of your doubled hands, once again, take your play elsewhere.

The above ten warnings signs help you identify the potentially cheating dealer and stay clear of a probable loss. There are a number of other signs that indicate for certain that the dealer is a cheat.

METHODS OF CHEATING

The most common way of cheating is through sleight of hand. By sleight of hand, I mean the use of manual dexterity to manipulate cards or deal from other than the top of the deck. The most common type of sleight in casino Blackjack is dealing seconds.

DEALING SECONDS, ETC.

Seconds means dealing the second card from the top of a hand-held deck while leaving the top card unchanged. What the dealer must do to effectively deal seconds is get a look at the top card, called peeking. A clever dealer peeks while adjusting his chips, paying players off, or looking underneath his up card (when it is an Ace or a 10) by moving the deck at different angles. On these occasions he has a chance to crimp the top card and take a peek at it. Once he knows what the top card is, he can decide whether or not to deal seconds in order to save the first card for his own hand.

Most dealers who can deal seconds can also deal *bottoms*— that is, the bottom card from the deck. Many dealers can also deal thirds and fourths from the top. In large and small casinos alike, these sleight-of-hand dealers are so expert that it is impossible for the average player to detect when they are dealt other than the top card. Therefore, don't worry about trying to spot such cheating. Learn to detect cheating in other ways described in this chapter.

If you want a demonstration of this cheating, you can purchase one for as little as fifty dollars, as a friend and I did in Las Vegas. Through a third party, we paid a dealer to come up to our hotel room to show us what he could do. He "showed" us how to deal seconds, thirds, fourths, and bottoms. My eyes were about ten inches away from the deck in his hands and yet I could not see that he was cheating. It looked as though every card were coming off the top. I later saw a similar demonstration from Lawrence Revere in Las Vegas and from a professional magician in San Francisco. You have to see it to believe it.

STACKING THE CARDS

Another common method of cheating is *stacking*. Cards may be stacked in two main ways: as they are being picked up, or while they are being shuffled. In casino Blackjack, it is rare that you'll see the dealer picking up the discards in a random or haphazard order, such as a high card, then a low card, then a high card, then a low one. The dealers are trained to pick up cards from left to right (or right to left for left-handed dealers) all in one sweep. This keeps the cards for each player's hand together so that the hand may be reconstructed later should there be a dispute between the player and dealer.

However, I did spot a dealer at a Las Vegas Strip casino picking up the cards and arranging them in a high–low stack in a four-deck game. He did this stacking so very smoothly that I would not have noticed it had I not been warned by a friend to look for it from this dealer. I had been on two junkets to this casino and had come back a loser both times. I was suspicious, and my suspicions were confirmed. With the high–low stack, the dealer could guess about the value of the next card with no small degree of accuracy, particularly after a light shuffle. I have never been back to this casino to try for a third loss.

Cards can also be stacked through careful shuffling. If the dealer notices that there was a large number of 10-value cards out on a particular round, he can note the location of the clump on the discards. Then when the deck is reshuffled, the dealer can cut and mix the cards so that the clump comes out near the front of the deck. He can make note of that and vary his dealing accordingly. On a smaller scale, this is how Aces and 10s magically appear as the dealer's up card off the top of the deck so frequently. Such nonrandom dealing is more common in four- and six-deck games.

NO SHUFFLE

Many dealers do not mix the deck very thoroughly, shuffling only twice before dealing after the cut. This is really a method of stacking the cards, which takes advantage of the way Blackjack players hit their hands—that is, by not shuffling very much, the dealer preserves the order of the cards as they were played. This is usually a high–low sequence rather than a random distribution, since the players are trying to hit 21. For example, two 10s dealt to one player in the first deal will result in adjacent players receiving tens in the second. This increases the chance of poor player-busting hands of 12 to 16.

Richard A. Epstein, in his book *The Theory of Gambling and Statistical Logic,* states that the shuffle operation must be repeated *at least* five times, and more likely twenty to thirty times to achieve complete randomization. Obviously, the last two numbers would slow up the game, but the typical shuffle operation in the casino results in a far from random deck.

HOLDOUT SHOE

Another way to cheat is to use a holdout shoe. This is a special shoe that holds the top card in place so that the second can be dealt. The shoes are made by a Cuban man who lives in Las Vegas. He gave one of my former students a demonstration in his home. It is nearly impossible for you to recognize this special shoe. The only visible difference between it and an honest shoe is that the holdout shoe has a face plate about one-quarter inch higher. This allows the dealer to pull the first card up and deal the second one without the player realizing it. Of course, the dealer has to have a way to identify whether he wants to deal the first or hold it back. The top card can be identified with a little mirror or prism placed in the shoe. These allow the dealer to get a peek at the top card from his vantage point to the side of and slightly behind the face of the shoe.

You may detect such a shoe from the way the dealer pushes out the cards. In order to keep the top card in place, he must hold it steady through the hole with one finger while pulling out the second card from the slit in the bottom with another finger. The telltale sign is a dealer using two fingers to deal but moving only one finger. At the Second Annual Conference on Gambling, a veteran gambler reported that there was a special dealers' school in Las Vegas where dealers learned how to cheat with the shoe.

CARD-HIDING

Late in 1977, an IBC member reported to me that the dealers in the Hyatt Lake Tahoe and at the North Shore Club were hiding cards. The dealers would pick up the unexposed two cards of a busted hand without showing them to the players by turning them over. This may not be cheating in the strict sense of the word, but it hurts the player who is trying to track cards.

Another card-hiding practice is to burn groups of cards between hands. The dealer takes a small clump of undealt cards and places them in the discard tray without letting the players see them. It's impossible to keep an accurate count of the cards, which foils the systems player. Your single recourse when faced with this is to take your money elsewhere. The casino will stop these practices only if it sees its business reduced because of the inferior game it provides.

HELP

Help refers to the dealer assisting the player by signaling what down card the dealer holds. If you should ever want to find a dealer who will help you, you must get to know someone in the Las Vegas underworld. There are agents who line up players with dealers for a percentage of the take. The usual charge is 33 per cent, which is split among the dealer, agent, and sometimes the pit boss.

I met a high-stakes gambler in Las Vegas several years ago who told me how he set up one of these arrangements with a woman dealer in Lake Tahoe. She and the player worked out a set of signals ahead of time so that he would know the exact identity of each down card whenever she had a 10 or an Ace up and had to look underneath. The man told me he played for over three hours and that her signals did in fact correctly identify every down card to him.

There was only one problem: He lost twelve thousand dollars. Even though he knew the dealer's exact hand over 38 per cent of the time, he lost. It's mathematically improbable to lose that much with such help over a period as long as three hours. So, if you want to make money at Blackjack, don't depend upon honor among thieves.

MY POSITION ON DEALER CHEATING

Some casinos are infested with cheaters. Others are relatively free of the lice. Some dealers cheat for the Mob, some for the casinos, and some cheat for themselves. No matter who it is done for, the effect is the same: You are separated from your hard-earned money.

Twenty-five years ago, Edward Thorp suggested a number of ex-

cellent ways in which cheating could be eliminated. His suggestions
fell on deaf ears. Cheating would be dangerously difficult for the
dealer if he or she dealt under the rules of Atlantic City and most
foreign casinos: no hole card and no hand-dealt games. Why
hasn't this been adopted in the state of Nevada? If cheating were
too difficult, then the people controlling Blackjack games could
not steal money from their employers. When will the owners
wake up to what is going on, or are they all part of the skimming
operation?

Allan Wilson, author of an excellent book on gaming, *The Casino Gambler's Guide*, wrote to me:

> I made the mistake of putting my photo on the book jacket, and
> that has had an impact on my ability to find a "good game" in Ne-
> vada. I've had enough "negative" sessions in Las Vegas over the
> past dozen years to suspect strongly that you may not be too para-
> noid about the cheating situation after all.

The way you can protect yourself is to avoid unsafe casinos
and dealers. As the casino and dealer ratings in Chapter Three
showed, winning players do not win very often in certain casinos
and against certain types of dealers. This is indirect but scientific
evidence of foul play. If you are a serious gambler, playing by the
up-to-date information in those ratings is the best way (and possibly the *only* way) to find a potentially safer game. The information in this chapter will then help you make certain it *is* safe.

INDICATORS OF A SAFE GAME

There are two very simple indicators of a safe game. The first is
an apprentice dealer. The apprentice is the only dealer you can be
positive about in terms of honesty. You can always recognize an
apprentice because there is an older, experienced dealer standing
right beside him or her at the table. The older dealer is watching
the novice run the game, giving pointers on how to handle the
cards, how to pay off the players, how to shuffle, and so on.

Apprentice dealers are most often found in downtown Las
Vegas and rarely found on the Strip. Once I did find one such
dealer learning at the two-dollar tables at a Strip hotel in 1975.

He still deals at the same tables but he is no longer a novice. He may have been taking special lessons because I can't beat him anymore.

Apprentice dealers are a systems player's dream. They aren't experienced enough to know how to cheat, and the casino wouldn't waste another dealer at the table if they could. I once passed a table and heard the young woman dealer suddenly turn and ask the pit boss, "Is this how I should handle this play?" I immediately sat down and had a nice winning session. I have done this every single time I have been fortunate enough to find such a situation and have come out a winner in 80 per cent of these sessions.

Another very good sign of an honest dealer (or more precisely, of a dealer who is dealing honestly at a particular time) was told to me in 1973 by "Dash," an old-time dealer. He said the first thing to look for is a table where the players are winning money. This will be a table where the dealer is honestly busting quite frequently, or is dishonest and busting to help someone. Sit down quickly, because like the novice dealer's table, this one will fill up immediately. If there's "money on the table," you can be a little more sure about there being nothing "under the table."

ESTABLISHING RAPPORT WITH THE DEALER

As far as the casino is concerned, the person on the other side of the table from you is supposed to be a mindless automaton. The dealer follows without variation a set of rules such as the ones presented earlier in this chapter. Like a computer that follows a "program," the dealer runs the Blackjack game. So much for theory.

In reality, the dealer is just like you and me. The dealer is working at a job dealing with (and to) the public, which on some days can be rotten. The last thing you want to do is increase the dealer's dissatisfaction while you are playing.

I remember seeing a dealer take care of an obnoxious player once in a two-deck hand-held game in Las Vegas. The man sitting to my left was a real whiner, complaining when anybody else

Blackjacked or drew a good hand that it never happened to him.
If the dealer drew to a hand that beat him, that earned more
whines. If he won, he would grumble that it was "about time" or
"it probably won't happen again." I wanted to tip his chair over
in the hope that the show line behind us would trample him.

The dealer was a jovial Indian (from India, not Oklahoma)
with extremely quick and smooth hand motions. After about ten
minutes, the whiner made a double down play and the dealer
gave him his third card face down, per the casino rules. The
dealer drew an 18, then started the payoffs with the whiner. Before the dealer turned over the player's card he said "bad." The
down card was a 2. The other people at the table chuckled while
the whiner just groaned. I couldn't believe my ears.

Several hands later, three us doubled down. The dealer took
out only one set of chips, then starting with the whiner's down
card went from hand to hand and said, "bad, good, bad." Fortunately, I was the "good" (I had been tipping). Sure enough, I
had a 10 down, the other two doubled hands pulled a 5 and a 6.
The dealer grinned and giggled, "I'm guessing good tonight." I
knew he couldn't be guessing that accurately, but the other
players were too ignorant of the game to understand what was really happening. This "good/bad" routine continued with perfect
accuracy until a pit boss wandered over on a casual tour.

At the end of the dealer's session, he walked off with a wide
smile at the whiner. The dealer had seemed to have had fun entertaining us, mystifying the players as to how he did it. The people at the table marveled at *how* he could guess those cards, and
someone even mentioned ESP. I knew there was little guesswork
involved. I was more amused at *why* we were privileged to see
this little show. When the whiner walked off after giving most of
his chips to the little Indian dealer, I knew why.

GET PERSONAL

For your sake, don't ever complain to dealers; they hear it all the
time. It's very depressing when multiplied by the many hundreds
of people they see day after day, week after week, year after year.
Try to cheer the dealer up without being too obvious about it.
One approach I have found that really works with a female dealer

is to smile. It's very good to smile as you walk up to a table where a woman is dealing. Just smile, keep on smiling, and make a few pleasant remarks. Most of them will smile back and become cheerful and friendly toward you.

If you are a woman, a smile can have the same effect on a male dealer. In the April 1979 issue of *Playboy* magazine, the "Playmate of the Month," Missy Cleveland, was described as visiting Las Vegas and returning a winner at Blackjack. She observed, "It's easy to double your money, just smile at the dealer." Even though most players don't have the smile (or other tools) of a *Playboy* model, a smile is still an excellent way to "get personal."

I actually do have a great time when I'm playing Blackjack—win or lose, the excitement is exhilarating. If you react the same way, why not share your feelings with the dealer?

If you have learned a system from this book well enough so that you can engage in conversation while playing, it is a very good idea to get personal with the dealers. You might start asking how long they have been dealing, where they have dealt before, where they are from, and so on. If you are good at it, tell a few stories, crack a few jokes. This softens up the honest dealers and makes it more difficult for the cheating dealers to keep their mind on the difficult maneuvers. It helps if you can tell a few sexy stories; then they really lose their concentration.

I was playing with an exceptional joker one time at Caesar's Palace. At first, the table was quiet. We were both losing and the dealer was making hand after hand. Then this other guy started to joke around. He was so funny that the pit boss came over laughing and started telling stories himself. Everybody was having a good time. Another player sat at the table; we all continued laughing and started winning. I kept winning until the dealer was relieved; then I quit because the replacement was an old gray-haired man. The table comedian had made us all some money with his dealer-distracting humor.

Try to avoid a dealer who is in a bad mood. I don't like to be around negative people unless I have to anyway, but the unhappy dealer has the opportunity to take out his or her frustrations on the players like the "surfboard dealer" did. When I was on my disastrous Atlantic City trip, I ran into a dealer whose mood was visibly black. Since his table was the only one with empty seats I sat down anyway and tried to "get personal." As we played, he was extremely agitated and upset. I finally got out of him what had happened.

He was near the end of his shift when I was playing, but at the start of his shift, three deaf players sat down at his table. The entire time he dealt, they never spoke to each other. Instead they "signed" as they played—that is, used the hand speech developed for the deaf. The three did so well that they followed this dealer from table to table all day. By the time I got to him, he was nearly frantic from dealing all shift to these completely silent players furiously talking with their hands. It was all I could do to keep from falling out of my chair laughing when I heard his sad story.

TIPPING THE DEALER

There is a good bit of controversy among Blackjack professionals on whether or not tipping the dealer is wise. The people against tipping declare that the honest dealer is only a card-issuing machine at the table and cannot help or hurt any player. And the dishonest dealer won't be swayed by tips anyway. This would be true if dealers weren't as human as the players.

For example, I had an attractive young blond dealer at the El Cortez cheat for me because I was tipping. I was playing one Saturday evening with a table full of stiffs. They were all having an excellent run of cards and winning. Throughout the hot run for the other players, I was only holding my own, as can often happen with the turn of the cards. Nonetheless, I was the only one tipping.

I wasn't going to make the dealer rich with my tips. I would bet any of my half-dollar chips from Blackjacks and an occasional dollar chip from time to time, but I was tipping. Just before the shift change, I had a horrible run of cards, surrendering four hands in a row. The cards should have been good on the last hand by my count, so I had $25 out. When I announced "surrender" the dealer made a move I had never seen before. She gave me $25.

What happened was this. If you have ever been in a casino, then you have seen how the dealers' arm movements are very fluid and circular as they pick up cards and bets and pay off winners. When I announced "surrender," the young woman reached her arm out as if to pick up my twenty-five-dollar chip, but instead of grabbing it, flicked it into my stack of chips with the fingernail on her middle finger. The flick was covered by her hand motion so the only sign of what she had done was a faint "click" as the chip hit my stacks. She brought her hand back to the chips tray and returned $12.50 (my surrender payoff). I had just "won" $25.

She gave me a knowing glance and continued the game with none of the cheap stiffs at the table the wiser. At the shift change, she walked off to the lounge area and I quit the game. Before she was out of sight, we caught each other's glance and I gave her a return "thank you" smile. She had taken a chance to show her appreciation, and I didn't want her to think it had gone unnoticed.

While having the dealer initiate cheating in your favor is not the typical benefit of tipping, knowing when and how to tip a dealer can be critical to your winning. First of all, it is a good practice never to *give* the dealer a tip. Instead, place a bet for the dealer as described in Chapter Two, placing the money on the upper part of the betting square toward the dealer. All dealers know exactly what this means and realize that only if you win your hand will they receive money. They will pay off your bet and the tip separately and then pick the latter up when all player payoffs are completed.

There is a purpose to betting for dealers. One very important reason is to tell the dealers that you are on their side, that you are looking after them. If a dealer is a cheat, it may make the dealer think twice before beginning to cheat you. You will be cheated anyway if you are winning money or if the policy in that casino on that shift is for them to cheat the players regularly. However, the dealer may wait a few minutes before beginning to cheat you to show appreciation for the fact that you have made a tipping bet.

If you are playing against an honest dealer, it is still a good policy to tip because the dealer may deal farther down in the deck instead of shuffling away the advantage more quickly. As soon as I win a big bet or several small bets, I immediately place a bet for the dealer. The idea is to do this as quickly as possible after you start winning so that the dealer will not begin to cheat your or to shuffle up on you.

Tipping can be a clever way to get the dealer to deal out one more round than normal before shuffling away any advantage. If you have a favorable deck composition, it is a very good idea to place a bet for the dealer before the next round of cards is dealt. Four out of five times the dealer will deal that extra hand, especially when you are playing alone or with one other player and there are enough cards in the deck to cover your hands. This use of tipping will give you a substantial extra advantage.

It is important that you tip the proper amount. Since tips are usually pooled and divided up equally among the dealers on each shift, overtipping can be a waste. I prefer to tip more often with smaller amounts. You might think of the betting-chip-to-tip ratio as about four to one or five to one. If you are betting twenty-five-dollar chips (twenty-five-to-one-hundred-dollar wagers) you might tip a five-dollar chip; one-hundred-dollar-chip bettors (one-hundred-dollar-to-five-hundred-dollar wagers) would tip with a twenty-five-dollar chip, etc. The exact amount and frequency are up to you.

You should feel more confident now about going into a casino and finding a safe game. You have the tools to determine if the dealer is friend, foe, or neutral. With your understanding of the dealer's job, tricks of the trade, and motivations, you are almost ready to begin systems play. All you need is the fine tuning about the game, which you will get in Chapter Five.

FIVE

How to Play Smart (Without a System)

Many vacationers who go to Las Vegas to get away from it all soon find that Las Vegas gets it all away from them.

MARK BELTAIRE

You've come a long way in four chapters. You've learned about the roads to winning and losing. You have learned how, where, and with whom to play. You now know how to protect yourself against a cheat and how to handle the dealer. But there are still more tricks you need to learn before you are ready to prove the above quote wrong and begin winning. These tips concern how you should manage yourself, how to stay ahead of the dealer, and how to keep clear of the casino. Once you master these, you are ready to become a winning player using the systems in the next four chapters.

MANAGING YOURSELF

I've always remembered a quote attributed to eighteenth-century English author Horace Walpole:

> The world is a comedy to those that think, a tragedy to those that feel.

The man writes like a true gambler. In Blackjack, where the steady application of your skills can result in consistent winnings, controlling your emotions becomes all-important.

CONTROL OF EMOTIONS

Many players lose because they become emotionally involved in the game. When they are losing, they start steaming and begin to chase their losses. The problem with chasing your losses is that they will catch you before you catch them. Your hormones won't help you win money at the tables; your head will.

Talk to some of the dealers about losing. Most of them are not from the West; they're from the East Coast. Many of them didn't come out to deal, but came out as players. A casino employee named Rudi told me he used to own a clothing store in Buffalo, New York. He got caught up in gambling and lost his business. As a Blackjack dealer he has met many people working under the same circumstances.

The best way to quit chasing losses is to play like a man I saw when I was on a junket at the Hilton. I was playing alone when a black guy in a beige suit, funny red hair, and reddish sunglasses came up to play. Sitting down, he reached into his coat pocket and dumped a large pile of chips on the betting square. The dealer straightened out the chips and dealt both of us hands. Suddenly I realized it was Redd Foxx. Foxx looked at his cards, took another, and stood. I stood and then watched the dealer draw to a 21. All Foxx said was a loud, "Sheeeit!" and walked away. Now, that's the smart way to gamble: He lost and left.

There is a good technique you can learn to help control yourself. *Allow the emotional arousal to act as the signal for you to quit.* You must pay attention to your emotions. As soon as you feel yourself getting emotionally aroused, STOP PLAYING. Be like the basketball coach who calls a time out when the team is getting blown out. In the sports world, this is called "settling down." In gambling, it is called "keeping your money."

You may get your emotional signal in a variety of ways. It could be physical, a tenseness in your stomach, chest, face, throat, or hands. My signal is impatience. I want the dealer to get the cards out faster so that I can play more hands and win my losses back. The type of feeling will vary from person to person. It will only take you a few sessions of paying attention to your emotional state to learn how and where to locate your emotional

signal. However, once mastered, it will save you thousands of
dollars in your gambling career.

STOP-LOSS LIMIT

Another way to keep from chasing losses is to have a "stop-loss
limit." As soon as you start to lose, RUN. I like to quit after losing three or four big bets in a row. You may want a different limit
for yourself, but you must have one. Whenever you sit at the
table, you should know exactly how much you will allow yourself
to lose before leaving.

A friend of mine, let's call him Ron, has a stop-loss limit of
two thousand dollars. Ron plays Blackjack for a living, usually
earning in excess of fifty thousand dollars each year. Although he
is a professional, he is not perfect. He told me that it is sometimes
hard for him to quit after being down two thousand dollars. He'll
continue to gamble. According to his records of the past three
years, Ron found that he would be up thirty-four thousand dollars *more* if he had always stuck to his loss limit. Ron's a believer
now in following his own rules on quitting.

Whatever you make your stop-loss limit, stick to it. If you do,
you will never lose any big money. If you don't, you will never
win any big money, and the probability of losing money will
quickly reach 100 per cent. Gambling expert Oswald Jacoby has
produced a diagram that gives you a good idea of when to quit.
This "quitting curve" is shown in the figure below. If you memorize and *use it,* you will rarely lose very much money while gambling. The Chinese have an ancient saying: "Before you start any
game, you must decide on three things: the rules, the stakes, and
the quitting time." By keeping your head in control of your emotions, you will be countering the casino psychology of trying to
separate you from your money as painlessly as possible.

NEVER QUIT WHEN WINNING

If you are a perfectionist, then you can ignore this paragraph. If
you are the normal serious Blackjack player whose chief aim is to
win money, then repeating this piece of advice will help you. As I
said in Chapter Three: NEVER QUIT PLAYING IF YOU ARE

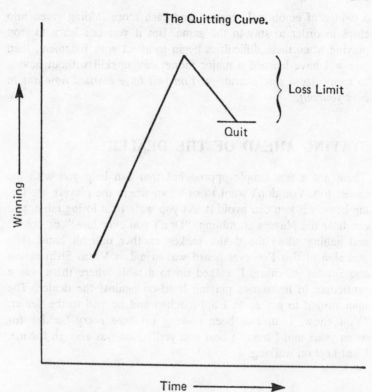

The Quitting Curve.

Loss Limit

Quit

Winning →

Time →

WINNING, NO MATTER HOW BAD THE CONDITIONS OR YOUR EMOTIONAL STATE. If a drunk sits down beside you and starts swearing, put up with him *if you are winning*. If the dealer begins to hide the cards on you so you can't track them, keep playing *if you are winning*. Do you get the idea? The name of the game is to win money. Take it under any and all conditions. However, as soon as you hit your stop-loss limit, take your money and leave no matter how good the conditions appear to be.

Appearances can be deceiving. It's not easy to maintain emotional control when the dealer keeps taking your hard-earned money out of the betting square and never puts any back. It's not easy to watch a stack of cute plastic chips disappear with detached logic. It's even harder to pull out a wallet or purse without a twinge of emotional reaction and cash more folding green into chips in order to stay in the game. But if you can learn to stop playing when these difficulties begin to affect your judgment, then you will have learned a major money-saving skill without having to memorize a single strategy. *You will have learned how not to beat yourself.*

STAYING AHEAD OF THE DEALER

There are a few simple approaches that can help you with the dealer too. You don't want to sit down where the players are losing heavily if you can avoid it. As you walk by a losing table, you can hear the players grumbling, "Don't you ever lose?" or oohing and aahing when the dealer makes another difficult hand. The best sign of this I've ever heard was at a Las Vegas Strip casino one Sunday morning. I walked up to a table where there was a gentleman in his sixties playing head-on against the dealer. The man started to get up as I approached and he said to the dealer, "You know, Lou, I've been coming up here every Sunday for seven years and I haven't beat you yet!" That was enough for me. I just kept on walking.

"IS HE HOT?"

Another sign of a winning dealer is when there are few chips on the table in front of the players. A very good question to ask of the players at this type of table before you join is, "Is he hot?" If one of the players tells you something like, "Yeah, he's hot. He keeps on getting Blackjacks," or "I've never seen anyone pull so many 20s and 21s off stiff hands," then don't bother sitting down. Just walk to another table, or better yet, to another casino.

There are lots of reasons why the dealer could be "hot." It could be part of the normal runs that can be expected in the game, or it could be due to the dealer's skill at affecting the outcome of the hands. In either case, you don't need to be part of it when the players are losing. This question is useful whenever you are unsure whether the players have been winning or losing at the table.

TALK TO THE PIT BOSS

Another valuable approach before you begin to play is to talk to the pit boss. Dealers are usually afraid of the floor men or pit bosses they work with because a dealer can lose his job if his boss doesn't like the way he deals. So dealers must respect these people even though they may not like them. Ian Andersen's book *Turning the Tables on Las Vegas* is largely devoted to methods of interaction and ingratiation in the player-dealer-boss triangle. One of the methods he uses is to get to know the pit bosses and speak with them *before* he sits down. If the dealers feel you have some "pull" with the pit bosses, the dealers may think twice about cheating you or giving you a hard time tracking the cards. Or they may delay trying any tricks until they are more certain of your relationship with their boss.

GET CHANGE FOR TIPPING

Once you sit down, it is an excellent practice to take one of your chips and get it changed into smaller chips right away. The dealer will automatically know that the reason you asked for the change was for tipping. He then knows that you intend to take care of him if you begin to win. If the dealer is a cheat, he is less likely to cheat you when you get change early.

HIT AND RUN

I've found that most dealers deal honestly when you first sit down to play. I'm not really sure why this is the case. Perhaps they are waiting, wishing that you would win and place a few tipping bets for them. Or perhaps they are waiting to see how good a player you are to determine if they should take countermeasures against your tracking of the cards. Whatever their thinking, I have found that on a lot of occasions I win money after ten or fifteen minutes at the table. Then hands turn around and I begin to lose money, especially on double-down or large bets.

When this happens consistently, the evidence points to dealer cheating. The dealers are told not to let anyone win any appreciable amount of money. Yet as we saw in the last chapter, half of the dealer's income is from tips. Nobody makes a bet for the dealer during a losing streak (unless they are crazy). The dealer is caught between the casino's demands for house wins and the dealer's need for player wins. So the dealer may deal honestly at first, hoping that you will get up a few units and make a bet for him. Then later on, he knows that if he is to keep his job, he must gradually (or very quickly) take the money back that you have won. *This is when to run.*

This "hit and run" approach can help make you a more regular winner. Play for that first ten or fifteen minutes; then as soon as you lose two or three large bets, quit immediately. Don't keep playing, hoping for another hot streak. It rarely comes in most casinos.

READING THE DEALER

An advantage that *any* player, systems or nonsystems, can gain comes from reading the dealer for information about the hole card. The only time this information may be available is when the dealer has an Ace or 10 up and must check the hole card to see if there is a Blackjack. If there is a Blackjack, which is about 5 per cent of the time, then there is nothing to worry about; you have probably lost. But if there is no Blackjack with an Ace or a 10 up, which is about 33 per cent of the time, then the dealer now knows something that can help you.

The casino has trained the dealer to be an automaton, giving no information to the player about the game other than the rules. But as any experienced card player knows, there are many ways to tell what a person is thinking or what cards are in a player's hand. As Yogi Berra said, "You can observe a lot just by watching." While the dealer isn't going to tell you what the down card is, the dealer may unwittingly tip off its value by his or her actions. The book *Nonverbal Communication for Business Success* details a scanning technique for observing and interpreting the nonverbals. This section shows the results of applying those techniques to the game of Blackjack.

I first became aware of how important the dealer could be from the attractive blonde who had so graciously given me back my

twenty-five-dollar surrender bet. I noticed that she was helping
me play my hand whenever she had looked at her down card. Once
when she had a 10 up and I held a 13, she paused for only a brief
moment before going on to the next player. I didn't even have
time to give her my signal, but she acted as if I had said, "stand."
When the players' hands were completed, she turned over a 6 and
proceeded to bust with a 7. Another time I had a 16 to her 10 up
when she paused and looked me directly in the eye. The message
to hit was clear. I hit (and busted anyway). She turned over another 10 for a 20 total. What can I say except that I was sad
when the shift ended and she went home. I was doubly sad that I
could stay only a single day, and wouldn't be able to find out if
this would continue.

Choosing a Readable Dealer

If you want to find a readable dealer, there are a number of features to look for. In general, the less experienced and competent
the dealer, the better. Apprentices and slower, clumsier dealers
tend to make more mistakes that can be read by the observant
player. An emotionally involved dealer, whether friendly or
unfriendly, is a good victim. The friendly dealer, like the one
above, may be willing to let information "slip" in the search for
tips. The unfriendly or competitive dealer may also project feelings about how good or bad a hand is, much like the poker player
who is losing badly will let his anxiety advertise his cards. You
should avoid intelligent-looking dealers. I've found that the
smarter the dealer, the less likely he or she is to project any information the player can use. But if you have the right dealer, here
are the signs to look for.

Clumsy Repeek

Some of the inexperienced dealers, when they have a 10-value
card up, will look clumsily underneath to see if they have an Ace.
Because of their inexperience, they often look so quickly that they
don't remember what the hole card is, or they don't see enough of
it to tell its value. So they look again. This "repeek" is a good indication that the down card is not a face card but a smaller-value
card.

Face cards are very easy to see: They have a lot of paint on them. But it is just as easy to mistake a small card such as a 4 for an Ace. So the dealer checks again to be certain. When you see the dealer look twice, you can be fairly sure that the card is a nonten-value card. Since there is a 10 on top, then the dealer is likely to have a busting hand. Depending on your hand, you may want to double, split pairs, or stand on your stiff more often than you normally would with a dealer 10 up.

Friendly Dealer

If you have a dealer like the Sunoco advertisement—"I can be *very* friendly!"—then you want to give this dealer plenty of time to get the important down-card information to you. In the case above, I began to play slower so that I could let the dealer pass me by or get the "hit" message before I committed myself with a hand signal. If you are playing head-on or are brave enough, you can smilingly (and half jokingly, for your safety) ask the dealer what you should do with your hand. Do this out of earshot of the pit boss, though, because many of them get quite unreasonable, thinking that this is cheating.

Involved Dealer

There doesn't seem to be any difference in competitiveness between men or women dealers. I've seen men who feel that a prolonged win streak by a player is an affront to their *macho* self-image. I've seen women dealers who are jealous of a woman player or determined to strip a chauvinist from his money. Your best bet is to find a dealer who seems a little caught up in the game. The ideal type would be like the nervous Don Knotts character, whose every thought was displayed like a neon billboard.

A nervous or involved dealer will be showing tension, anger, disgust, or dismay at a poor hand, and relaxation, pleasure, satisfaction, or relief at a good hand. The best time to look for these reactions is immediately as the dealer looks at the down card. It may come out as a facial expression, a change in posture or stance, or possibly in the way the hands are held.

Depending upon what your philosophy of gambling is, you can even *create* an involved dealer if you want to. Any reaction that gets an emotional response from the dealer will help. You can act drunk, fresh, friendly, dumb, insulting, you name it. Although the story of likening the dealer's breast development to a surfboard got the wrong results, it did succeed in getting the dealer involved.

Don't think that the dealers don't "play" the gamblers like a fisher with a trout on the line. I've seen some of the smoothest hustling in the world from the British dealers in the Bahamas lining up some action from vacationing single girls looking for a little romance. I also saw a woman dealer in Las Vegas play an older man for tips. The woman noticed him eyeing her closely with no little amount of good, healthy lust. He was tipping generously and smiling at her.

She began to make an unusual move with the deck I'd never seen before. She would turn her wrist and bring the deck close to her chest in a brushing motion. This caught my eye because the dealers are taught to keep the deck well away from their body in a hand-held game to minimize the chance of sleight of hand. I was waiting for a reprimand when the pit boss came over and she made this move in front of him. You can imagine my surprise when he watched it and a little smile showed up at the corners of his mouth. He turned and walked off without a further word.

I finally figured out what was going on. It was difficult to see what was happening from my seat, but I eventually noticed that the dealer had long fingernails. What she was doing was casually brushing her nail across her nipple to keep it erect. This was keeping the old guy happy and tipping. The pit boss had immediately seen what was happening, chuckled inwardly, and let the dealer get away with the break in procedure. So be aware of what is being done *to* you and *for* you.

Individual Signals
One of the important concepts in nonverbal communications is that no single sign means anything in and of itself. Because you are playing with individual dealers, there are really no common signals that can give you any information about the hole card. But there may be a reliable signal from an individual dealer that you can use to your benefit. What you have to do is adopt the mentality of a baseball coach who watches the opposing pitcher for any tipoffs of what pitch is coming up next.

The first thing you do with any new dealer is to watch him or her for a period of time. This is best done before sitting down to play. You have enough to keep track of without trying to analyze the dealer at the same time. Look for any changes in movements that seem to agree with the run of the cards. What you are looking for are the three r's in reading the dealer: relationship, reliability, and regularity. When you have spotted a relationship between cards and dealer movements, you should next begin using it to predict the down card. If this proves accurate, then you have a reliable signal.

The final requirement is that the dealer makes the move regularly. If the dealer tips off the down card only once in ten times, then you are being helped 10 per cent of 33 per cent, or on only 3 per cent of the hands. This is hardly worth your time and effort, since the tip is approximate anyway. But if the dealer does it with regularity, then you are getting help for as much as one third of the hands. Your advantage could be enormous. If the dealer were to tip off the exact down card *perfectly,* you would have as much as a 9.9 per cent *advantage* over the house in playing these hands. Since you are only getting an indicator, your advantage must be somewhat less, but in the range of 0 to 10 per cent for the hands where you can read the dealer.

A common sign in which some dealers give themselves away is in the way they place their hands after looking at the hole card. If they have a card underneath that makes up a good hand, some dealers will place their fingers (or their hip) somewhere away from their card—that is, when they have a solid hand they don't have to draw another card to, they leave the hand alone. They may place their hands or the deck closer to your cards. But when they know they have to hit (when they have a small card under there), they usually place their fingers and/or body close to the up card so that when they turn the cards over they are ready to hit. You might look for hand position, deck location, or how the dealer turns to see if any of these show a relationship to the down cards.

Another tip can come from the dealer's eyes. Researchers have found that the pupils in our eyes dilate when we see something interesting. This was first discovered by watching the reactions of male college students who were being shown pornography. One of their first physiological reactions was dilation of the pupils. Although you need fairly sharp eyesight for this because of the casino lighting, you can watch the dealer's eyes for this response.

Another sign to watch for is what the nonverbal-communication experts call "flashing." Each of us can make over two hundred thousand separate and distinct facial expressions. Although this number is enormous, we are all good at interpreting these signals. But when the dealer is trying to maintain a "poker face," the normal expressions are suppressed. If the dealer is in any way involved, though, it will be nearly impossible to control *every* facial sign *all* the time. What will happen is that the dealer will "flash" the expression briefly when looking at the down card. The result may be a slight upward movement of the eyebrow, tensing of the forehead, unconscious clenching of the teeth, or any number of other movements. Where these become useful is in the case of a reliable pattern relating to the down card.

So there is a wide range of information the dealer may be sending you for one hand in three. Your main concern is that you observe carefully so as not to be mislead. Also, don't be obvious about your observations by staring at the dealer. This is often enough to make the dealer self-conscious enough to change the all-important behavior. Also, don't ever tell the dealer what you have observed. Even if the dealer is trying to be helpful, no one wants to be foolishly transparent. One mention of what you know is enough to stop a tipoff forever and eliminate the terrific advantage of being able to read the dealer.

READING BENT CARDS

There is another trick the professionals use to gain a slight advantage over the house. The number of times is usually small, but you should be aware of them in case you run into a favorable situation where this trick can be used. It also involves getting information from the dealer looking at the hole card. What you are looking for here are bent cards.

Think for a moment about how cards might get bent in a Blackjack game. If it is a face-down game, you could bend them while you hold them, but this is considered cheating (it's like marking the cards). Or the dealer can bend them while shuffling and checking his hole card for a Blackjack. Since the dealer must check his hole card for every Ace or 10 up, these cards get bent after being in play for a while. The Ace or 10 gets bent face up like a rocking-chair rocker, while the hole card gets bent in the opposite direction. But while the hole card is picked from the whole deck, the up card is *always* an Ace or 10. If you begin seeing any cards that have the rocking-chair curve, however slight, you can be fairly certain they are Aces or 10s. Since there are four 10s for every Ace, 80 per cent of the bent cards will be 10s.

You can use this information to your advantage when you notice that the dealer has a bent down card. This gives you a fairly accurate estimate of the dealer's hand. You have to see this before the dealer checks for a Blackjack, or else the slight bend will be gone. If you are tracking the cards in a face-down game, you can also use the bent-card information to guess what the other players are holding and modify your play accordingly.

The problem with this bent-card strategy is that its application is so infrequent. If the dealer does not take a hole card, such as in Britain, then there is no bending of the cards. If the dealer gives the cards a hard shuffle, the bending is destroyed. A four-deck game also reduces the amount of bending that is likely to take place for an individual Ace or 10. Also, if the casino is sharp and rotates a new deck in the game every hour or less, the cards probably will not have had enough time to get noticeably bent.

It is best to locate a single-deck hole-card game where the dealer really bends the hole card back during his peek. Try to find a table where the deck is a little dirty around the edges from handling. This tells you that the deck has been in play for quite some time. Make certain the dealer doesn't shuffle the decks too hard. A soft, easy shuffle doesn't destroy the cards' "memory" for a bend. And if there are only one or two players at the table, this is ideal. The fewer the players, the more dealer hands that have been dealt, and the more often the dealer has had to bend the Aces or 10s checking the hole card. Reading whatever bend is in this type of game gives you another edge in becoming a winning Blackjack player.

Now that you have learned how to control yourself and the dealer, and get whatever useful information the game has to offer you, you are ready to find out a little bit more about the other participants in your Blackjack game, the pit bosses.

KEEPING CLEAR OF THE CASINO

The pit boss is the first line of managerial defense in protecting the casino's money. Unlike the dealer, the honest pit boss has no betting stake in whether or not the player is winning. Pit bosses are never tipped. But it is the pit boss's job to see that the casino makes as much money as possible. A good pit boss would rather shoot himself in the foot than let you walk away a winner. Unfortunately for the player, the pit boss has a number of approaches to keep you from winning, or to make you want to leave if you manage to avoid his tactics. I've alluded to a number of these previously, but you'll see them fully explained here.

CASINO COUNTERMEASURES

People have been going to casinos with "winning" Blackjack systems for years. The casino management never worried about any of these "systems" because they were convinced all of the casinos' games were unbeatable. As a result, once the Las Vegas casinos realized that the method outlined in Thorp's *Beat the Dealer* was a legitimate winning system, they panicked. For the first time in years, they changed some of the basic rules of Blackjack. Doubling was restricted to two-card totals of 11 only, and a pair of Aces could no longer be split, which added to the house advantage by about 1 per cent.

The results were dramatic and immediate. Play at the Blackjack tables fell off drastically as the gamblers recognized an inferior game when they saw one. But worse, play at all tables fell off as the flow of tourists to Las Vegas decreased. In only two or three weeks, the casino management realized that it was winning the battle against card tracking at the expense of the entire casino. It quickly removed the new restrictions and play resumed at prescare levels. It was better for the casinos to live with card tracking than to close down without it.

The rules twist that has become most popular in the seventies is the multiple-deck game. Most of the world's casinos now use four decks exclusively. Single-deck games are still available in some Nevada casinos, but even they are intermixed with games having two or more decks at the higher-stakes tables. Using multiple decks seemed more acceptable to the gambling public than fiddling with the rules. So the casinos thought their problems with systems players were over. "No one would ever be able to keep track of four decks of cards," was their reasoning.

In fact, the addition of three more decks did help the casino, but not for the expected reason nor as much as the modified rules helped during the "panic" in 1964. Four decks didn't stop the systems players; it merely slowed them down. The additional decks add to the house advantage by about .5 per cent, and produce fewer favorable betting situations for the player. But the additional decks in no way eliminate the ability of a dedicated player to beat the game.

This is where we stand today. The profits from the Blackjack tables have been increasing in a most satisfying manner for the casinos under the current rules. Most current players are still suckers. Fortunately, the game can be beaten with consistency by a knowledgeable player. Rules changes proved to be too costly for the casino, so the only option left is to discourage the systems player in other ways. These casino "countermeasures," which don't alienate the other players, are the subject of the next sections.

Shuffle-up

The primary weapon to thwart the systems player or discourage the winning player is the shuffle-up. The dealer is instructed to shuffle whenever he feels a player has an advantage or whenever the pit boss orders it. If the dealer can track cards, he will eliminate any favorable situations for the player. If a pit boss thinks *you* are successfully tracking cards, he may order the dealer to shuffle after each hand no matter what the situation. In either case—early or immediate shuffling of the deck—the opportunities to find advantageous playing conditions are greatly reduced or eliminated.

Like most winning players, I get shuffled up on quite a bit. For example, I like to play at the Royal Inn when I am in Las Vegas.

It's a small place, single-deck game, clean, honest, and lots of local people. One pit boss there has a vendetta against systems players. I was playing alone against the dealer letting my winnings ride from one to two to four units in favorable situations. After noticing my winnings, the boss stood there tracking cards with me. Every time the deck was favorable, he would tell the dealer to shuffle up. I left soon thereafter.

The same thing happened later in the trip at the Cal-Neva. A pit boss there looked like Rodney Dangerfield, except that he was going to get respect because he was bigger, fatter, and very ugly. I put a two-hundred-dollar bet out once in a favorable situation thinking that the pit boss might have the dealer shuffle up. When he did, I left the bet out there, figuring that I had at least an even game with my knowledge of Basic Strategy. As luck would have it, the dealer dropped me a Blackjack paying three to two. I collected my five hundred dollars in the betting spot and walked off laughing as the boss steamed. It was great fun and extremely satisfying.

There is a disadvantage to the casino in shuffling up. If the table is full with only a single systems player there, the casino risks chasing away the other six players. The frequent shuffling slows up the game and irritates the "paying customers." Sometimes it is easier to let a systems bettor play unbothered in order to keep the others at the table happy. If the systems player isn't winning too heavily, then this isn't a bad financial situation either.

As you will see in Chapter Seven, the systems player bets more heavily when there is a player advantage. The casinos know this and will have the dealer shuffle up whenever a large bet is suddenly placed on the table. You can use this zealousness to your benefit if the dealer is only faking the ability to track cards. As you play, you may detect unfavorable deck situations from time to time. When the deck gets very poor, you can put a large bet out on purpose. If the dealer is running true to form, he will shuffle up, thinking you are betting on an advantage. What he has done is to play into your hands by eliminating a *casino* advantage. This is about the only worthwhile aspect of the shuffle-up. If you find this countermeasure too bothersome, your only choice is to take your game elsewhere.

Cut-off Dealer

Thorp pointed out a strategy of betting called *end play*. The casinos used to let every card in the deck be dealt out. They felt that the number of people who could memorize each card as it was played and compute the odds on the remaining cards was so few as to be safely ignored. They were right about the number of people who could do that, but they were wrong about the safety in doing so.

The strategy behind end play was to take advantage of the drastic swings of the composition of the deck when only a few cards remain. By composition, I mean the makeup of cards that result in a dealer or player advantage. End play is a method of maximizing the frequency of favorable deck conditions.

Let's say, for example, that you are playing in a single-deck game. There are only sixteen cards remaining to be dealt, and they contain mostly cards that are *unfavorable* to you. If you were playing alone against the dealer, correct end play would be to bet five hands at the table minimum of five dollars. This would force a reshuffle as you played out your hands. As soon as the reshuffle occurs, stand on any remaining hands. Now you will have bet only twenty-five dollars into an unfavorable situation. Since the "unfavorable" cards are on the table, the newly reshuffled remaining thirty-six cards have a favorable composition. You would now bet five hundred dollars per hand on all seven betting spots, thirty-five hundred dollars into a *favorable* situation. Every hand would have a better-than-even chance of winning. Conversely, if the remaining sixteen cards were highly favorable, then you would bet five hundred dollars on only one hand at a time until the reshuffle. In either case, you are betting heavily into favorable situations.

After reading Thorp's book and getting stung a few times by players quick to take advantage of any new ideas, the casinos got wise to end play. They quit dealing down to the end of the deck in all games. Now, when someone is suspected of tracking cards, the dealer will be instructed to "cut the deck off." In a four-deck game, a cut-off dealer may reshuffle after only two decks have been played. In a single-deck game at a full table or with a lone player betting on multiple hands, the dealer may reshuffle after each round to eliminate any possibility of end play. And if you are tracking cards, cutting the deck off greatly reduces the number of favorable betting situations. Once again, your only option is to find another game.

Card-hiding

Obviously, if you are trying to track the cards, you must see them. In an "up" game, this is no problem. The cards are there for all to see. In a "down" game, this can be somewhat more difficult, as many players protect their cards like poker players from the others at their table. As a countermeasure, the dealer will let you see as few cards as possible through card hiding.

The most common form of card hiding is the burn card. It is customary to take one card and turn it upside down on the bottom of the deck in a hand-held game or put it in the discard tray in a shoe game. Sometimes the dealer will show you this card, but he is more likely to burn it unseen. What is not customary is to burn more than one card. Some casinos will discourage card tracking by burning anywhere from five to ten cards off the top of the deck, particularly in four-deck shoe games. Or they may burn the same number of cards between each dealing round. This makes it impossible to track cards accurately.

Another card-hiding trick is to pick up player-losing hands without looking at them. This is most often done for busting hands with a shill in the game playing with house money. The dealer knows that the shill won't be miscounting and won't complain about not having his cards looked at. The dealer may also pick up player bets and cards when holding a natural and fail to expose the players' cards.

Don't be part of this card hiding when you play in a down game. I don't make a point of openly showing my cards to everyone at the table, but I am extremely careless with how I hold and turn them. Anyone who wants to know what I am holding can see if he or she want to. I feel this is just courteous play, since we're all betting against the dealer. I am only hurting the other players by keeping my cards from them. The dealer doesn't care what I have unless he's a cheat. And if he's a cheat, I won't win anyway.

If you are playing with friends, you can show your cards openly if you aren't betting at high levels. I once sat down with an unusual pair of friends, Rich and Mohammed, one Jewish student and one Arab exchange student vacationing in Las Vegas on spring break. As I sat down, Rich turned to me and said, "We're playing as a team here. Anybody who sits with us has to join our team and show us his cards." I laughed and told them I would be happy to be on their team. Under the circumstances, I kept my betting at modest levels so as not to alarm any of the pit bosses. A fourth man sat down and received the same request. The four of us played this way for nearly an hour before the two young men left with their winnings. All in all, it was a very enjoyable session. Everyone was talking to each other, the dealer was being tipped, and the ice was broken among strangers by the two pleasant young students.

As they walked off, I couldn't resist asking one question: "How did you two ever get to be such good friends? In these days, you've got to be a rarity." They both laughed and Mohammed told me in his clipped English, "We actually have quite a lot in common, particularly in Las Vegas. We both love women and money." With this they turned and left laughing uproariously.

Shills

I mentioned shills earlier. A shill is a casino employee who plays with house money. A shill will play the basic game, usually following some house-prescribed strategy. Where a shill can hurt someone tracking cards is by diluting a favorable deck. If you are playing alone against the dealer and winning, really the best situation for tracking cards and winning, the casino can send a shill to join you. The shill won't hurt your play, but the shill will be taking half of your cards in favorable situations. Of course, the shill will also be taking half of the unfavorable cards, too, but the shill is "losing" house money, you aren't.

A shill can also be used to cheat you. One of these uses is called an *anchor man*. The shill sits at third base so he takes the last cards before the dealer hits. If the dealer is peeking, the dealer can signal the anchor man whether to hit or stand. If the next card is bad for the dealer, the anchor man hits no matter what. If the next card is good for the dealer, the anchor man stands. In this way the dealer can make his hands without risking dealing seconds, or when seconds can't be dealt, such as out of a shoe with only a prism for peeking.

If you are playing in a game and the person at third base is playing erratically, watch out. If the player is hitting 17 or more, or standing on impossibly low cards versus good dealer up cards, the player could be a drunk, a dolt, or an anchor man. When in doubt, find another game.

Heat

As I reminded you earlier, if you are winning despite all the unfavorable conditions and casino countermeasures, keep playing. If you follow that advice, then you are likely to feel a little heat. Heat refers to psychological pressure put on a winning player by the pit bosses. This can be very uncomfortable for you.

I received one kind of heat in 1975 when playing at a downtown Las Vegas casino where they are not used to twenty-five-dollar-chip bettors. I was betting twenty-five-dollar chips and was ahead over four hundred dollars when the pit bosses started to buzz around the table like hornets. Finally, they surrounded my table. Two of them stood on each side of the dealer and two more of them stood behind me, one on either side. That was heat! All they were trying to do was to pressure me into quitting.

If this should happen to you, my advice is that you keep playing as long as you are winning in spite of the pressure, if you can stand it. I decided to leave with my winnings when I lost three hands in a row. I played another ten minutes. When I got up, the pit bosses trotted off to wherever pit bosses go to wait for the next problem. I had my money and they had my absence so we were both happy.

Barring Players

If you are winning in too threatening a manner, the pit bosses may skip the soft stuff and get to the ultimate countermeasure: barring. I have been officially barred in only one casino, and that not because of my play, but because they made a connection between my appearance on their island and the subsequent appearance of my first Blackjack book on their island's bookshelves. I have been asked to leave casinos several times. If you are asked to leave a casino, do so. But take down all the details of the encounter. Get the date, time, and casino. Record the dealer's name, the pit boss's name, and any conditions of play, such as your betting pattern and winnings. You may want this information at some later date for legal action (for more on the legal status of barring certain players, see Chapter Twelve).

Don't consider being barred a badge of accomplishment. I think being asked to leave before I am ready is a sign of losing the overall game. The only time I can accept being discovered and barred is when I don't intend to come back, and wish to win as much as possible before the casino takes action. And even if I'm asked to leave on one shift, there are two other shifts with different personnel for me to play against who have likely never seen me or been told about me. In Chapter Ten you will see all the techniques for winning without getting barred.

WHAT YOU CAN DO

These are the weapons the casino has in making your gambling life difficult. Without knowing how to track cards and use the information to vary your betting and playing strategy, there are only two methods you can use to counter them.

Hide Your Winnings

If you are skillful with your hands, it is a good idea to hide as many chips as you can from your winnings. There are a number of ways to do this. You can get the smaller denominations changed into larger chips so that it will appear to the pit boss that you've got fewer chips in front of you. You can also cover the larger-denomination chips, such as those for twenty-five dollars, with smaller chips, such as those for one dollar or five dollars. Another thing to do is simply to pick up several large-denomination chips and slip them into your shirt pocket when the pit boss isn't looking.

One technique that I have found successful when I am on a junket and required to draw five hundred or a thousand dollars' worth of chips at a time is to switch tables. As I am walking from one table to the next with several hundred dollars' worth of chips in my hands I just put a few in my sports-jacket pocket. It's very difficult for the pit boss or the dealers to notice what you are doing when you are hopping from table to table. Some players slip a chip or two into their cigarette package when it's lying on the table. You may feel like a walking treasure island with chips hidden all over your body, but you will disguise the fact that you are a winner.

Be a Woman

Blackjack author Lawrence Revere stated that a woman who learns how to play winning Blackjack can win a million dollars by virtue of being female. I have found this to be true, particularly in Las Vegas. Casino personnel are among the most chauvinistic in the world. They do not respect women as gamblers. I once had a pit boss tell me, "If you let a woman out of the kitchen or the bedroom she gets confused." They do not feel that a woman has the mentality or inclination to be a professional Blackjack player. I know some men players who even disguise themselves as women to take advantage of this situation. If you are a woman (or can make yourself look like one) and like to play Blackjack, you have a very profitable future ahead of you.

PSYCHOLOGICAL PITFALLS IN GAMBLING

You are now nearly ready to learn how to beat the game of Blackjack. You have explored the psychology of the game, learned its rules, determined how to choose a game, seen how to handle the dealer, and been introduced to a few playing tips. Before you can appreciate the exacting analysis that follows in the next four chapters, you should recognize what Professor Richard A. Epstein called "gambling fallacies" in his book *The Theory of Gambling and Statistical Logic*. These errors are the result of what the uneducated gambler calls "intuitive logic." Superstitions like lucky socks, "hot" dice, the dealer's attitude, ESP, or streaks help rob the naïve player of his money. What you will see in the upcoming sections on winning Blackjack systems will eliminate these errors once and for all.

ERROR NO. 1   *Betting expensive "long shots" and ignoring small "sure things."*

There is a tendency for most gamblers to overvalue the benefit of betting a long shot and undervalue the good chance of a small gain. For example, one of the major magazine sweepstakes has a seventeen-million-to-one chance of hitting the one-hundred-thousand-dollar first prize. The cost is a single fifteen-cent stamp. So you might guess that you have an expected value of one hundred thousand dollars divided by seventeen million, or about six-tenths cent in probable winnings. Would you bet fifteen cents to win six-tenths cent very often? Evidently people do in great numbers. Everyone remembers when they won a jackpot, but forget how long they built it up. This tendency to overrate the ridiculously small possibility of winning a large sum of money is what keeps all the bad bets of the world such as state lotteries, numbers rackets, and keno profitable for the house. John Cohen, a British gambling researcher, observed that most gamblers bet on the *possibility,* not the *probability* of winning.

Bettors will frequently pass up the chance of a small gain with higher probability. Some slot machines offer you a shot at several hundred thousand dollars for a single-dollar bet. Blackjack presents much smaller maximum winnings for higher bets. Yet Blackjack is the better gamble because you have a small *advantage* at steady winnings rather than a disadvantage at enormous winnings.

ERROR NO. 2   *Believing that "things even out."*

Many bettors think that after a long run of successes, a failure is inevitable, and vice versa. I'll never forget waiting in line for a show one evening by a roulette wheel. As I watched, a red number came up nine out of ten spins of the wheel. I couldn't resist playing for fun, so I began to put one-dollar bets on red. I won fifteen dollars in several minutes. Black numbers started coming up more frequently, but I continued to bet red. After nearly twenty minutes I was down to my original dollar, so I quit. I returned to the line happy with my twenty minutes' worth of free entertainment.

The husband of the couple we were with couldn't resist rating my play. "I could have told you you would lose your winnings back. The wheel couldn't keep turning up red forever. It had to start hitting black sometime. You should have switched to black right away." I started to explain the concept of probabilities and independent events to him, but gave up when I saw how firmly he believed the nonsense he told me. There is no reason why a trend should reverse or things should even out in gambling.

ERROR NO. 3   *Betting optimistically.*

We all tend to overvalue the chance of something good happening and undervalue the chance of something bad happening. For example, if the chance of drawing a winning lottery ticket is the same as dying from a heart attack next year, we will all consider winning the lottery ticket more probable than having a fatal heart attack. Pleasant events tend to stick out in our minds; unpleasant events are quickly wiped out. We can all remember drawing a 4 to a hard 17, but tend to forget how often we lose standing on a 16 versus a dealer 10 up. The optimistic bettor is always saying, "Yeah, but it won't happen to me," or "Everybody's got to get hot sometime." The probability of winning a million dollars in one North American lottery is the same as getting struck by lightning twice!

ERROR NO. 4   *Making current playing decisions based upon the results of similar decisions made previously.*

A man sitting next to me once in Aruba told me, "I'm through hitting 12s. Every time I hit a 12 I get a 10 card and bust. I'm done busting on 12 tonight!" If I would have had the time, and if the man had wanted to listen, I would have explained that whether he had busted or not on 12 all night had nothing to do with any 12 he held in the future. The only thing that matters is the chance of beating the dealer based upon what cards have been dealt off the deck and what the dealer shows as his up card. As poet Robert Frost said, "The past is a bucket of ashes."

One of the frequent sources of this error is the insurance decision. Buying insurance is a bad bet unless you are tracking cards. Yet all of us have felt the chagrin of twenty-twenty hindsight after the dealer has asked, "Insurance anyone?" and seeing him turn up a 10 card for Blackjack. We don't seem to pay as much attention to those times when we didn't buy insurance and he didn't have a Blackjack. So not only is our memory defective, but also the past and the present are not connected from shuffle to shuffle as far as the cards are concerned.

ERROR NO. 5 *Preferring to be a "high roller."*

It is more exciting to bet a hundred dollars with a chance of doubling your money than it is to place five consecutive bets of twenty dollars with the same chance of doubling your money. I will never forget my first trip to Las Vegas. I had played the dollar tables all evening at Binion's Horseshoe downtown and had won about eighty dollars on a stake of twenty dollars. I was flushed with the excitement of the winnings as I returned to the Strip hotel where we were staying. As I walked through the lobby, the hundred-dollar table caught my eye. At that time, a five-dollar bet for me was outrageously extravagant. Yet those hundred dollars were hot in my pocket.

I walked over to the table and watched two players there winning and losing, but mostly losing. I didn't know a system then, so I had no idea the game could be beaten. I finally turned from the table and decided to go to bed a winner. My fear level is now quite a bit higher than the table limits. I've doubled plenty of five-hundred-dollar bets since then, but none of them was ever as expensive-feeling as that tempting hundred-dollar-minimum bet so many years ago. Since then, I've never forgotten the lure of trying to roll higher than my bankroll justifies, and neither should you.

ERROR No. 6 *Remembering "streaks" and ignoring "runs."*

Once again, our mind is magnificent at editing perceived reality. Because of the enormous amount of information that is shoved into the mind in everyday life, our brain quickly learns to edit out the unimportant, commonplace, or familiar. That's why you may not notice a new couch in the living room or that a friend shaved off his mustache. You've quit observing these familiar features closely.

Gambling is much the same. You notice only the unusual or the uncommon. Long winning or losing streaks stand out vividly in your memory. Smaller runs, good or bad, just don't register. For this reason, the extremes are remembered as occurring more frequently than they actually did, and the runs are thought to occur fewer times than they did. What matters in winning Blackjack is not the big winning or losing sessions (although you should minimize the latter). What matters are all those sessions netting you small gains. They mount up slowly and surely, as the playing records show in Chapter Three.

ERROR NO. 7 *Overestimating the importance of skill.*

The most I have ever won at the Blackjack tables in a single sitting (to date) is sixty-seven hundred dollars. I won it in about three hours in a Caribbean casino. I'd like to think I won that much because I am such a superior player. Although I was betting heavily, those winnings are far in excess of what my advantage should have earned me. I realize I experienced one of the "streaks" or "runs" that will happen in the game. The important thing is that I didn't become overconfident and begin to expect that level of winnings in all my sessions. Many players have followed that logic to the poorhouse.

There is a very dangerous tendency to overestimate the degree of skill involved in Blackjack, where both skill and chance are involved. "Probabilities direct the conduct of a wise man," as Roman statesman Cicero advised nearly two thousand years ago. The only results you can count on are the long-term-performance estimates found in Chapters Six, Seven, and Eight. In the short run, anything can happen and probably will. But in the long run, your rate of winning should conform approximately to the numbers in those chapters. This leads to the next error.

ERROR NO. 8 *Placing too much faith in the short run.*

When Julian Braun began testing various Blackjack systems about fifteen years ago, he worked with a minimum of one million computer hands for each study. To put this in human terms, if you played head-on with the dealer at 100 hands per hour, you would have to spend 10,000 hours at the tables or the equivalent of 13½ months in round-the-clock play. This is the *minimum* number of hands Braun used to evaluate systems.

As far as the research statistics are concerned, even the most

avid Blackjack player is seeing only short-term results in his playing sessions. This is why you should place your trust not in what
you have observed or kept track of at the table, but in what the
scientific analysis of the game has proven. Informed guesses
aren't worth the price of a roll of toilet paper, but hard facts are
priceless. The only way to have hard facts is to use results
generated over millions of hands.

ERROR NO. 9   *Confusing unusual events with unlikely events.*

Whether or not a particular turn of the cards happens is not a
function of how *probable* it is. For example, getting an ace-high
straight flush in poker is no more statistically unlikely to happen
than to get any other, lower-scoring hand. Each hand in any card
game is as probable as any other hand. The rules of the game
make the straight flush important and therefore more unusual.

Getting Blackjacks of (A,10) off the top of the deck five
straight times is no more unlikely than getting stiff hands of (10,
6) five straight times. The chance of an "unusual" sequence of
cards should be figured strictly by the probability of that sequence
occurring.

ERROR NO. 10   *Believing in luck.*

An old German proverb cautions us, "Too much luck is bad
luck." The only truly "lucky" individual I have ever heard of is
Walt Disney's Gladstone Gander, and he is fiction. Too many
gamblers are playing with Stone Age emotions in a computer
world. The days of goat bones and chicken entrails, talismans and
evil spirits are over, at least for winning players. Too many people think luck is a tangible commodity, something to be saved or
used, taken advantage of or cursed. To the winning player, luck is
nothing more than an uninformed rationalization of the short-run
turn of the cards. In its worst form, the belief in luck is the excuse of a player too lazy to learn how to win.

What you will find in the next four chapters will eliminate your
dependency on luck forever. The strategies for winning at Blackjack will keep you from making any of the above errors by showing you how to play correctly each and every hand you will encounter in any casino in the world or in a private game. You've

come a long way in building your knowledge of the game. Now it's time to build your confidence and control over what is happening at the table. You are about to become the only type of player in the world of gambling whom the casino is afraid to let play: a card counter.

SIX

Having Fun on Vacation: Basic Strategy

If you can't manage your money and your emotions, you have no business at the table.

NICK THE GREEK

As I begin this chapter on Basic Strategy, I can't help thinking about a pair of T-shirts I recently saw. An attractive young couple was walking along arm in arm, their shirts displaying these signs: Hers said, "He's mine because I deserve the very best." His boldly stated, "I *am* the very best." They were both fortunate to know *and agree on* what was the very best. As a Blackjack player, you too deserve the very best. What you will find in this chapter *is* the very best.

There's an almost undefinable sense of confidence and security in *knowing* that you can make the correct play no matter what hand the dealer gives you. There are even tangible feelings of superiority tempered with sympathy in watching other players make mistake after mistake as their money dwindles. Playing Blackjack without the information in this chapter is like trying to play golf with only a putter. You can play the game, but you just won't get anywhere. Unfortunately, very few people know "the very best" plays in Blackjack when they see them.

I was my usual nondescript, rumpled self playing a one-deck game quietly in a downtown Las Vegas casino when the classic stereotype of the "sweet little old lady" sat down on my left. I had been playing for nearly a half hour there because the young woman dealing was extremely nice, and a man betting heavily at the table was attracting all the attention. The older woman, who later told me her name was Marge, quickly asked for change and put a minimum bet out. Then began one of the most unusual string of hands I've ever had.

My first hand was A,7 against a dealer 6 up card. Marge looked over at me sharply when I slid another stack of chips out to the betting spot for a double-down wager. My third card was a 4 for a total hand count of 12. The dealer turned over a 4 and then drew a 7 for a standing hard total of 17. Marge had pushed with the dealer and sat there shaking her head at me.

I drew 9,9 on my next hand against a dealer 9. I once again slid another stack of chips out and signaled a pair split. My first 9 busted with a 5 and a 10, and my second 9 drew a 10. The dealer proceeded to bust, so I was two units down at this point.

My next hand was 10,3 versus a dealer 2 up. Marge looked at me in almost total disbelief as I stood on my 13. The dealer turned over an 8 and drew a 7 for 17. The dealer collected my bet and paid Marge. At this point, Marge evidently couldn't stand it anymore and finally spoke.

"Son, you're just throwing your money away! You break up two good hands and then stand on peanuts."

"How should I play them?" I asked innocently.

"Don't hit or split those good hands. I play like the dealer unless I get a 10 or 11 I can double on. That's the only way you can make money at this game. That splitting is for the birds."

I thanked Marge for her friendly advice, but told her I would try my approach for a little while longer. My string of unusual cards continued. My next hand was 10,5 against a dealer 10. I surrendered the hand and the dealer took half of my bet. Marge looked with amazement at my making a play she'd never even seen. She kept watching me. She lost when the dealer drew to a hard 21. At this point I was 2½ units down, with Marge down 1 unit. Intimidated by the surrender play, she was blissfully silent for the next hand.

I drew a 5,3 against a dealer 5 and doubled down. Marge busted by hitting a hard 15. My third card was a 10 for a hard total of 18. The dealer turned over a 9 and then drew a 10 to bust.

My last hand in this series was A,2 against a dealer 4 up. I doubled and drew a 6 for a soft total of 19. Marge stood on 8,8.

The dealer turned over an Ace and drew a 3 for a soft 18. I was now ½ unit up and Marge was 3 units down. While none of the rest of the hands were as unusual as the first six, Marge continued to pepper me with chatter about how "lucky" I was. I finally had to leave to give my ears a rest.

I don't blame Marge for being bothered by my playing decisions. I can empathize with her. I too am continually dismayed by the apparent generosity of typical Blackjack players like Marge. Because of their ignorance of the game, they are paying entirely too much for their evening's entertainment at the tables. It's like going to the movie theater and *insisting* on paying $10 for a $4.50 seat. Marge was getting upset with me because I knew how to get in free! You see, I was playing according to Basic Strategy.

THREE LOSING "STRATEGIES"

These are three commonly known strategies for playing Blackjack. The first is the *no-bust* strategy. It doesn't take too many rounds of trying to improve a hand and busting, then watching the dealer bust, before a player tries the no-bust approach. The table below shows the probability of busting when hitting various hand values. Even the lowly 12 has nearly a one-in-three chance of busting.

PROBABILITY OF BUSTING

Hand Value	% Bust if Hit
21	100
20	92
19	85
18	77
17	69
16	62
15	58
14	56
13	39
12	31
11 and under	0

Before long, the problems with playing the no-bust strategy become readily apparent from your dwindling playing bankroll. While you do win each and every hand in which the dealer busts, you find you are losing money steadily. The reason is that the dealer doesn't bust often enough to justify your always standing on low values. The next table illustrates what happens. The dealer will bust less than 30 per cent of the time. He will achieve a standing hand in nearly 72 per cent of the hands.

DEALER FINAL-HAND PROBABILITIES

Dealer Final-hand Value	%	Cumulative % Total
Natural 21	4.83	4.83
21 (3 or more cards)	7.36	12.19
20	17.58	29.77
19	13.48	43.25
18	13.81	57.06
17	14.58	71.64
Bust	28.36	100.00

Now look at the third table to see what this means. If you are playing the no-bust strategy, 61.3 per cent of the two-card hands will play themselves—that is, natural 21, hard-standing 17–20, or hitting without danger of busting; 38.7 per cent of the hands, the 12–16 values, will lose if the dealer doesn't bust. Since the dealer doesn't bust 71.6 per cent of the time, the no-bust strategy will over the long run lose 27.7 per cent (71.6 per cent times 38.7 per cent) and win 11.0 per cent (28.4 per cent times 38.7 per cent) of these hands. This is a 16.7 per cent dealer advantage for this category of hands alone.

TWO-CARD-COUNT FREQUENCIES

Two-card-count	% Frequency
Natural 21	4.8
Hard-standing (17–20)	30.0
Decision hands (12–16)	38.7
No-bust	26.5
	100.0

You can't win by standing on low values. You won't even beat the dealer by trying to stand on *higher*-value hands. If I offered you a Blackjack game where I would guarantee you a constant hand of 18, would you take it? You shouldn't.

The table of dealer-hand probabilities shows you will lose to the dealer in the long run if you get an 18 on each and every hand. Look at the figures. The dealer will beat you with a 19 or better 43.25 per cent of the time and lose to you with a 17 or bust 42.94 per cent of the time. The other 13.81 percent of the hands will be a tie. You will be losing .31 per cent of the hands (43.25—42.94) with a constant 18. It takes a consistent hand of *19 or better* to beat the dealer. A no-bust strategy can't hope to benefit you when a guaranteed 18 won't.

Because there are other factors that determine the total advantage for the house, such as paying three for two on a natural, the overall house advantage against no-bust strategy is estimated by Thorp to be between 5 and 8 per cent. You can determine how accurate Thorp is by trying this approach and seeing how quickly your bankroll disappears.

A second seemingly logical approach to playing Blackjack is the *dealer-mimic* strategy. "If it's good for the dealer," you reason, "it's good for the player." Your odds are the same as the dealer's for holding any final-hand value, so the game appears even. The problem again lies with how player and dealer busts are handled.

You always lose when you bust. The dealer loses on a bust *only* when the player hasn't busted. Those times you *both* bust, the dealer wins. You can never recover from this disadvantage by mimicking the dealer because you must hit or stand first. As calculated by Thorp, the house advantage with the dealer-mimic strategy is nearly as bad as with no-bust strategy: 5.7 per cent (Peter Griffin says 5.5 per cent).

Based upon my observations over the years, a third losing system is still popular among many players. This system is WAG. WAG (Wild-assed Guessing) is the decision process of the typical rectal engineer. Do you need an answer? They know where to get it. In my early playing days as a youth betting pennies in neighborhood games, I was a WAG player. Fortunately, so was everybody else. The casinos are not entities to WAG with. They will courteously and with excellent service send you home broke. They love WAGers, because WAGers line their pockets.

A word of caution is needed. There is a modification to WAG called SWAG (Systematic Wild-assed Guessing). The only difference between SWAG and WAG is that you are wrapping the garbage in Christmas wrapping paper instead of newspaper. SWAG strategies cloak themselves with labels such as ESP or betting progression. Any system that is not based upon the Basic Strategy presented in this chapter does not merit even your passing interest. The systems in this book are the simplest and most powerful available.

DEVELOPMENT OF AN ACCURATE BASIC STRATEGY

Basic Strategy is the term applied to a system of play providing the highest betting yield without keeping track of the cards already played. It was the search for such a strategy that led Messrs. Baldwin, Cantey, Maisel, and McDermott to spend three years pounding calculators. As covered in Chapter One, their work attracted the attention of Professor Thorp and was improved by him through the use of an MIT computer. Later Julian Braun of IBM assisted Dr. Thorp in refining his calculations for the second edition of Thorp's *Beat the Dealer* (Braun is also the developer of the Basic Strategy presented here).

These events show the two ways to determine Basic Strategy decisions: calculation and simulation. Baldwin et al. used a calculation method that was extremely laborious. To determine a correct strategy of play, you must consider *every* possible combination of cards that can be dealt, calculate the probability, and determine whether the hand wins, loses, or pushes. I doubt whether the four original researchers calculated the probability of the dealer getting a hand of A, 2, A, 2, 7, A, A, 6 in that order. The chance of getting this hand is very remote, yet skipping this and other rare combinations reduces the accuracy of the results.

For this reason, Braun wrote a program to cycle through EVERY possible interactive combination of player and dealer hands. Although the program was complicated to devise, once developed it was a simple task to accurately determine the Basic Strategy by using the computer to do a *complete* combinatorial analysis. This was much faster than actually playing millions of Blackjack hands in an effort to determine the Basic Strategy.

Braun also wrote a simulation program to evaluate the performance of count systems. In a simulation, the computer actually "deals" hands to itself randomly and records the results. Performing millions of calculations per second, an enormous number of hands can be "played" and recorded in a short amount of time. Every system developed or evaluated in this book has had *at least* one million hands simulated to determine the correct performance figures. (Details of Braun's computer programming technology can be found in the Appendix of his report, "The Development and Analysis of Winning Strategies for the Casino Game of Blackjack," available from the Gamblers Book Club or Rouge et Noir.)

One of the first results of these studies was to confirm mathematically something many gamblers had guessed from experience: The player's advantage depends upon the dealer up card. The table shows the probabilities that the dealer will bust with each possible up card and the corresponding player advantage with the correct Basic Strategy.

PLAYER ADVANTAGE VS. DEALER UP CARD

Dealer Up Card	Dealer Bust %	Player Advantage % with Basic Strategy
2	35.30	9.8
3	37.56	13.4
4	40.28	18.0
5	42.89	23.2
6	42.08	23.9
7	25.99	14.3
8	23.86	5.4
9	23.34	− 4.3
10, J, Q, K	21.43	−16.9
A	11.65	−36.0
Overall	28.36	0.0

As the table indicates, although the dealer is most likely to bust with a 5 showing, the player has the greatest advantage with a dealer 6 up. (This table assumes a one-deck game played with typical Las Vegas Strip rules.) The numbers vary only slightly with multiple decks and rules variations. The Basic Strategy shows how to play every hand you can receive in Blackjack depending upon what the dealer up card is. This strategy is designed to help you in one of three ways by showing you how to: lose less, win more, and win instead of lose.

BASIC STRATEGY CASE I: Lose Less

You Hold	Dealer Holds	Your Decision	Amount Wagered
A, 7	10	Stand	$1.00
A, 7	10	Hit	$1.00

Your Win %	Dealer Win %	Net %	Net Result
41	59	−18	−$.18
43	57	−14	−$.14
		Gain	$.04

Case I shows a "lose less" situation. All hands assume a single-deck game with a $1.00 initial wager. If you were following a dealer-mimic strategy holding A,7, you would stand. If the dealer has a 10 up, you will lose with this play 18 per cent more often than you will win. This means for every $1.00 you wager in this situation, in the long run you will lose $.18. If you follow Basic Strategy and hit A,7 versus a dealer 10 up, you will still lose more often than win, but your expected loss will be $.04 less. Basic Strategy helps you *lose less* in this situation.

BASIC STRATEGY CASE II: Win More

You Hold	Dealer Holds	Your Decision	Amount Wagered
A, 7	6	Stand	$1.00
A, 7	6	Double	$2.00

Your Win %	Dealer Win %	Net %	Net Result
63	37	26	$.26
59.5	40.5	19	$.38

Gain $.12

Case II illustrates how you might not be winning as much as you could be with one of the loser strategies. Again you are holding A,7, only this time the dealer has a 6 up. You already know that this is the best possible situation for the player. If you follow dealer mimic (also no-bust) and stand, you will win 26 per cent more often than you lose for an expected win of $.26. If you double, as I did in the first hand in my game with Marge, your net win decreases to 19 per cent. But since your bet increased to $2.00, the expected value of this play is your win percentage times a doubled wager: .19×$2.00=$.38. Your net gain from doubling is $.12. Basic Strategy has helped you win more.

BASIC STRATEGY CASE III: Win Instead of Lose

You Hold	Dealer Holds	Your Decision	Amount Wagered
6, 6	4	Stand	$1.00
6, 6	4	Split	$2.00

Your Win %	Dealer Win %	Net %	Net Result
42.5	57.5	−15	−$.15
51	49	2	$.04

Gain $.19

Case III identifies a situation where you might be losing instead of winning. Following the no-bust strategy, you would stand with a 6,6 to avoid the 31 per cent chance of busting. Your expected result in this situation is a $.15 loss. However, if you split the pair of sixes, thus doubling your initial bet by playing two hands, you gain a slight 2 per cent advantage on each hand; 2 per cent of your doubled wager equals an expected value of $.04. Your gain from splitting over standing is a hefty $.19.

Each entry in the Basic Strategy tables that follow has been chosen because it provides one or more of the above improvements in net gain. For example, you might hit, double down, or split (4,4), or you might stand, hit, or double down on A,7, depending upon the casino rules and the dealer's up card. If you use the Basic Strategy in single-deck casino games, you will have an exactly even chance with the house. In a four- or a six-deck game, the casino will have only .5 per cent advantage in the long run (Chapters Seven and Eight will show how to gain a permanent long-term advantage over the house). Another reason the Basic Strategy is so important is that you will be using it to play 75 per cent of all the hands you will ever get even when using the Hi-Opt I count and play strategy described in following chapters.

Memorizing the Basic Strategy and executing it in actual play are the critical first steps toward learning to win at Blackjack.

ORGANIZATION OF THE BASIC STRATEGY

As you saw from the three examples above, the correct Basic Strategy decisions were made by evaluating a particular player hand versus a specific dealer up card. The entire Basic Strategy shows the proper playing decision for every possible hand against all ten of the dealer up cards. In addition, it provides guidelines for making a side bet such as insurance, and for varying the strategy for optional casino rules such as permitting doubling down on split pairs, or for surrender. As you see, the Basic Strategy can present a considerable amount of information to learn and retain.

This chapter is organized so that you may reach the level of performance you desire with the least amount of effort. The more tables you decide to master for use in the casino, the more you will reduce the casino advantage. For example, the occasional player can cut the house advantage in half by learning only seven rules. Memorizing doubling rules shown by four numbers on a ten-item line further reduces the casino odds to about .5 per cent, and so on. You see the value of what you can reasonably retain and use in the casino, or you can determine how much you need to master to achieve the playing odds you desire. Learning the Basic Strategy is a step-by-step process you adapt to your abilities and playing-performance goals.

To make certain you are learning the most important and profitable information first, you must know the answers to three questions:

1. What are the options for which there is a Basic Strategy?
2. How often are each of them encountered?
3. How profitable is knowing how to correctly play each option?

With these questions answered, you can choose the options that are most likely to occur in casino play and that have the highest profitability for you, then learn them first.

The Basic Strategy options are:

Hard hitting and standing (hands with no Aces or pairs)
Soft hitting and standing (hands containing an Ace)
Hard doubling (no Aces, no pairs)
Soft doubling (hands with one Ace)
Pair splitting
Pair splitting where doubling is allowed after splitting
Insurance
Surrender

The following table shows the frequency with which these options will be encountered in your first two cards. For simplicity, all frequency percentages in this chapter assume a two-card hand. The table decisions, however, assume any hand unless otherwise noted. *Notice that simple hitting and standing make up over two thirds of the hands you will be dealt.* Pair splitting and hard doubling round out the 100 per cent total of all possible hands. Don't include surrender or soft doubling in adding toward 100 per cent, because they are duplicated in other categories. Insurance also doesn't count in the total, since it is a side bet.

BASIC STRATEGY FREQUENCY OF USE AND RESULTING BENEFITS

Two-card Basic Strategy Decisions	% Frequency	% Player Advantage
HITTING AND STANDING		
Hard nonpairs	53.1	
Soft (A, 2 through A, 10)	14.5	2.45
DOUBLING		
Hard nonpairs (5–11)	19.3	1.59
Soft (A, 2 through A, 9 vs. dealer 6 or less)	3.7	0.14
PAIR SPLITTING		0.46
Doubling Allowed After Split	13.1	0.10
INSURANCE	14.9	0.00
SURRENDER ALLOWED	3.6	0.06
Early surrender allowed	10.4	0.62

This table also shows the relative benefits of learning the various parts of the Basic Strategy. The figures assume a single-deck game played with typical Las Vegas rules (dealer stands on any 17, no surrender). The player advantage of 2.45 per cent is a composite figure for both hard and soft standing. The frequency of 13.1 per cent for pair splitting applies whether doubling is or is not allowed. The number of hands that could be split stays the same; only the strategy varies.

The sequence in which the various strategy tables will be presented in this chapter is shown in the table below. The recommended order of learning the standard plays and options is based upon frequency of occurrence, player benefit, and ease of learning. For example, although insurance Basic Strategy gives you no additional statistical advantage, it is so easy to learn that everyone should use it in casino play because it will save you money.

CUMULATIVE ADVANTAGE WITH BASIC STRATEGY

Casino Rules	% Player Advantage	Cumulative % Player Advantage
HOUSE ADVANTAGE	−6.97	−6.97
BLACKJACK PAYS 3:2	2.33	−4.64
COMMON RULES		
Correct hitting and standing	2.45	−2.19
Hard doubling	1.59	−0.60
Insurance	0.00	−0.60
Pair splitting	0.46	−0.14
Soft doubling	0.14	0.00
OPTIONS		
Pair splitting (double allowed after split)	0.10	+0.10
Surrender	0.06	+0.16
Early surrender	0.62	+0.88

I believe that each person who plans to play should learn the correct hitting and standing strategy. This takes just a few moments and reduces the house advantage by half. One-time players who plan to play more than a few hands should also learn the simple hard-doubling strategy. This addition cuts the advantage by over a factor of seven. For occasional players, learning the first two rules in pair-splitting tables lets you play what is nearly a break-even game. If you plan to play more seriously or use the Hi-Opt I, you should learn the complete set of tables.

The strategies in the next ten tables look very imposing at first. The tables are presented in their complete form for purposes of explanation only. The final sections of this chapter will show how to organize the information and learn it with the least amount of effort. So don't try to remember what you are reading at first; only make certain you understand how to read the tables and how much the various strategies will benefit you.

THE CORRECT BASIC STRATEGIES

There is one factor you must know before choosing a Basic Strategy: how many decks are used where you intend to play. I advise that you learn the Basic Strategy for four-deck games first. You will be using this strategy most often since the majority of the world's casinos use four decks. You can learn the few differences between single- and multiple-deck play later on. Many accomplished players use the multiple-deck strategy in *all* games (including single-deck games). The reason is that it is easy to make a mistake by confusing two strategies, especially under the pressure of actual play moving from casino to casino where the rules may vary. Using one set of tables is a sound practice, since the differences in terms of performance are so slight that you lose only a few hundredths of a per cent using the four-deck tables in a single-deck game.

The multiple-deck strategy is also safer to use if you are concerned with the honesty of the dealer because it is more conservative. You double down and split pairs less often with the multiple-deck strategy. Therefore you risk less of your money. This chapter will use the four-deck tables for the presentation of the correct Basic Strategy. Corrections for one- or two-deck games are shown, and complete charts for all decks and playing options are provided in Appendix C.

The tables are easy to read. The numbers indicated along the top of the charts represent every single value the dealer could have as his "up card"—the card that lies face up on the table. All Basic Strategy decisions are based upon the dealer's up card and your hand.

Your possible hands are listed on the left side of the table, and are made up of *two or more* cards. To find any decision, simply go down the left side of the table until you find your hand, then go across the page to the right until you are under the column representing the dealer's up card. You will find the correct play where the player's row intersects the dealer's column. The four types of plays you will find are: hit, stand, double, or split a pair.

STANDING AND HITTING

The first table shows the proper strategy for hitting or standing when holding any hard, nonpair hand that could bust if hit. The entire table can be summarized with four simple rules, listed in their order of two-card frequency:

1. Always HIT 12 through 16 vs. dealer 7 or higher (23.1 per cent)
2. Always STAND on 17 or higher (15.7 per cent)
3. STAND on 12 through 16 vs. dealer 6 or lower (13.1 per cent), except vs. dealer 2 or 3
4. HIT 12 vs. dealer 2 or 3 (1.2 per cent)

BASIC STRATEGY: 4 Deck Hard Standing & Hitting.

YOU HOLD	DEALER UP CARD									
	2	3	4	5	6	7	8	9	10	A
17 or more	S	S	S	S	S	S	S	S	S	S
16	S	S	S	S	S	H	H	H	H	H
15	S	S	S	S	S	H	H	H	H	H
14	S	S	S	S	S	H	H	H	H	H
13	S	S	S	S	S	H	H	H	H	H
12	H	H	S	S	S	H	H	H	H	H

S = STAND   H = HIT

The division of the table between the dealer 6 and 7 is important. As shown earlier, the odds of the dealer busting take a large drop between a 6 up and a 7 up. All the tables will contain this division. Also notice the small frequency of Rule 4. You can eliminate this rule if you wish with an acceptable reduction in performance.

The next table gives the strategy for hitting or standing when holding any soft hands with three or more cards, or any two-card hands that may not be doubled. The table can be summarized with three rules, listed in their order of two-card frequency:

1. STAND on soft 19 or more (7.2 per cent)
2. HIT soft 17 or less (6.0 per cent)
3. a) STAND on soft 18 vs. dealer 8 or lower
   b) HIT on soft 18 vs. dealer 9, 10, A (1.3 per cent)

You can remember Rule 3 in either the hit or stand version, whichever is easier. Once you know one, the other automatically follows. You now know how to make correctly all basic hitting and standing decisions. If you play by these two tables alone, you will have more than halved the casino advantage! As you play, watch how few bettors have even this beginning knowledge of the correct plays in Blackjack. If you go back to my game with Marge, you will see that she was mad at me for making a proper standing decision on the third hand.

BASIC STRATEGY: 4 Deck Soft Standing & Hitting.

YOU HOLD	DEALER UP CARD									
	2	3	4	5	6	7	8	9	10	A
19 or more	S	S	S	S	S	S	S	S	S	S
18	S	S	S	S	S	S	S	H	H	H
17 or less	H	H	H	H	H	H	H	H	H	H

S = STAND   H = HIT

HARD DOUBLING

If you think of Blackjack from the viewpoint of a sporting event then hard (that is, without Aces) doubling is much like taking advantage of the "breaks" of the game. As a Texas University bumper sticker proclaimed during its football team's long unbeaten streak of the late 1960s, "If you've got it, flaunt it!" With doubling, you take advantage of a good hand versus a less valuable dealer up card to increase your winnings. The table below describes the proper playing strategy for the next most important player decision, hard doubling.

BASIC STRATEGY: 4 Deck Hard Doubling.

YOU HOLD	2	3	4	5	6	7	8	9	10	A
	DEALER UP CARD									
11	D	D	D	D	D	D	D	D	D	H
10	D	D	D	D	D	D	D	D	H	H
9	H	D	D	D	D	H	H	H	H	H
8 or less	H	H	H	H	H	H	H	H	H	H

D = DOUBLE   H = HIT

You are allowed to double only two card hands in most of the world's casinos, so the frequency percentages are completely accurate. The table can be summarized by these rules:

1. Always HIT 8 or less (7.2 per cent)
2. DOUBLE 11 vs. dealer 10 or less (4.8 per cent)
3. a) DOUBLE on 10 vs. dealer 9 or less
   b) HIT 10 vs. dealer 10, 11 (3.6 per cent)
4. a) DOUBLE 9 vs. dealer 3 through 6
   b) HIT 9 vs. dealer 2, and 7 through Ace (3.6 per cent)

By adding this table to your casino playing strategies you will have learned only eleven rules and will have dropped the casino advantage to well under 1 per cent.

INSURANCE

As mentioned in Chapter Two, the insurance bet is misnamed. It insures nothing. It is merely a side bet on whether or not the dealer has a 10-value card under his Ace up card. The Basic Strategy for this play is simple:

NEVER BUY INSURANCE

Insurance is a sucker bet for the average player. Some so-called "smart" bettors insist that you should always insure if you hold a natural 21 against a dealer's Ace up. They reason that if the dealer also has a natural, you can't lose. For example, if you have bet two dollars, you can insure for one dollar. If the dealer has a natural, your normal two-dollar bet is lost, but the one-dollar insurance wager pays off two to one, winning the original two dollars back. But if the dealer *does not* have a natural, you lose your one-dollar insurance bet. The question is: Does the dealer have a 10 under his Ace often enough to justify risking another dollar? *The answer is:* NO!

If you ignore any cards that have been played (which is the original Basic Strategy assumption), the odds of the dealer having a 10 down can be calculated exactly. There are fifty-two cards in a deck, sixteen of which have a value of 10. Thirty-six cards are therefore non-10s. Three cards are visible to you: your Ace, the dealer's Ace, and your 10. So there are 49 unseen cards in the deck, fifteen of which are 10s and thirty-four of which are non-10s. Here are the long-term results of this situation:

15 hands dealer has 10 down$\times$\$2.00 payoff
=\$30.00 won
34 hands dealer has non-10 down$\times$\$1.00 bet lost
=\$34.00 lost
_____
$ 4.00 net loss

The problem is that in this situation, the payoff for an insurance bet is won fifteen times every forty-nine hands, while you are betting it will happen fifteen times every forty-five hands. This four-hand difference accounts for your net loss. The best possible insurance situation you can face without tracking the cards is still a loser. If you don't hold a natural or a 10 the calculation is:

16 hands dealer has 10 down$\times$\$2.00 payoff
=\$32.00 won
33 hands dealer has non-10 down$\times$\$1.00 bet lost
=\$33.00 lost
_____
$ 1.00 net loss

The only time you might want to make an insurance bet is when you are tracking the cards. Chapter Seven will tell you when the insurance bet is probable enough for you to wager profitably on it.

At this point, you haven't reduced the house advantage any farther, but you have saved yourself a few poor bets over the course of your play. If you are a one-time player, you now have enough knowledge to make your money last quite a while longer. You are now paying about $.50 for that $4.50 movie. You are also well along the way to learning how to become a consistent winner.

PAIR SPLITTING

The table on page 169 tells us that the next most important option of Basic Strategy to master after doubling is pair splitting. With the addition of the proper splitting strategy shown in the table below, we can reduce the house advantage to within a few tenths of 1 per cent.

BASIC STRATEGY: 4 Deck Pair Splitting.

YOU HOLD	DEALER UP CARD									
	2	3	4	5	6	7	8	9	10	A
A,A	SP	SP	SP	SP	SP	SP	SP	SP	SP	SP
10,10	S	S	S	S	S	S	S	S	S	S
9,9	SP	SP	SP	SP	SP	S	SP	SP	S	S
8,8	SP	SP	SP	SP	SP	SP	SP	SP	SP	SP
7,7	SP	SP	SP	SP	SP	SP	H	H	H	H
6,6	H	SP	SP	SP	SP	H	H	H	H	H
5,5	D	D	D	D	D	D	D	D	H	H
4,4	H	H	H	H	H	H	H	H	H	H
3,3	H	H	SP	SP	SP	SP	H	H	H	H
2,2	H	H	SP	SP	SP	SP	H	H	H	H

S = STAND　　　H = HIT　　　D = DOUBLE　　　SP = SPLIT

The rules that summarize this table are listed by frequency of occurrence:

1. NEVER SPLIT 10,10; 5,5; and 4,4 (10.0 per cent)
2. ALWAYS SPLIT A,A and 8,8 (.9 per cent)
3. a) SPLIT 2,2 and 3,3 vs. dealer 4 through 7
   b) HIT 2,2 and 3,3 vs. dealer 2, 3, 8 through A (.9 per cent)
4. a) SPLIT 9,9 vs. dealer 2 through 6, 8, and 9
   b) STAND on 9,9 vs. dealer 7, 10, and A (.5 per cent)

  5. a) SPLIT 6,6 vs. dealer 3 through 6
     b) HIT 6,6 vs. dealer 2, 7 through A (.5 per cent)
  6. a) SPLIT 7,7 vs. dealer 7 or less
     b) HIT 7,7 vs. dealer 8 or more (.5 per cent)

(The percentages don't quite add up to the 13.1 per cent total occurrence listed in the earlier table for pair splitting because of rounding off of the frequency values for rules 1, 4, 5, and 6.)

Every Basic Strategy player should be familiar with and follow the first two rules of pair splitting. For example, even though split Aces receive only a single additional card, you turn a lowly 2 or a weak 12 into a powerful set of 11s, giving you an advantage of over 40 per cent when splitting Aces. As with the entire Basic Strategy, each correct splitting play helps you win more.

SOFT DOUBLING

If the casino allows it, you can also decrease the house advantage by doubling down on certain two-card hands that contain an Ace. The only time this is beneficial is when the dealer shows a 6 or less as an up card. The strategy for soft two-card hands not doubled has already been discussed. Rules summarizing the soft-doubling decisions shown below are:

BASIC STRATEGY: 4 Deck Soft Doubling.

YOU HOLD	DEALER UP CARD				
	2	3	4	5	6
A,8 or more	S	S	S	S	S
A,7	S	D	D	D	D
A,6	H	D	D	D	D
A,5	H	H	D	D	D
A,4	H	H	D	D	D
A,3	H	H	H	D	D
A,2	H	H	H	D	D

S = STAND   H = HIT   D = DOUBLE

1. STAND on A,8 and A,9 (1.0 per cent)
2. DOUBLE A,6 and A,7 vs. dealer 3 through 6 (.9 per cent)

3. DOUBLE A,4 and A,5 vs. dealer 4 through 6 (.9 per cent)
4. DOUBLE A,2 and A,3 vs. dealer 5 and 6 (.9 per cent)

Although soft doubling gains a small additional advantage of .14 per cent, with this last table you have turned the typical Las Vegas Strip single-deck game into a no-cost session of entertainment.

But you're not through yet. There are further tables you can learn to take advantage of two playing options permitted in a number of the world's casinos.

PAIR SPLITTING (WHEN DOUBLING IS ALLOWED AFTER SPLIT)

If you are allowed to double down on either side of a hand that has been split, you have a further advantage of approximately .10 per cent. This favorable rule makes it desirable to split more frequently than was shown before. The table below illustrates this more liberal splitting strategy. Actually, these two strategies are so similar that the summary rules are not listed again. Instead, the *differences* in the two strategies are highlighted with italics and summarized below.

BASIC STRATEGY: 4 Deck Pair Splitting (when double down allowed after split).

YOU HOLD	DEALER UP CARD									
	2	3	4	5	6	7	8	9	10	A
A,A	SP	SP	SP	SP	SP	SP	SP	SP	SP	SP
10,10	S	S	S	S	S	S	S	S	S	S
9,9	SP	SP	SP	SP	SP	S	SP	SP	S	S
8,8	SP	SP	SP	SP	SP	SP	SP	SP	SP	SP
7,7	SP	SP	SP	SP	SP	SP	H	H	H	H
6,6	*SP*	SP	SP	SP	SP	H	H	H	H	H
5,5	D	D	D	D	D	D	D	D	H	H
4,4	H	H	H	*SP*	*SP*	H	H	H	H	H
3,3	*SP*	*SP*	SP	SP	SP	*SP*	H	H	H	H
2,2	*SP*	*SP*	SP	SP	SP	SP	H	H	H	H

S = STAND   H = HIT   D = DOUBLE   SP = SPLIT

When doubling is permitted after pair splitting, you should *also:*

1. SPLIT 2,2 and 3,3 vs. dealer 2, 3
2. SPLIT 4,4 vs. dealer 5, 6
3. SPLIT 6,6 vs. dealer 2
4. SPLIT 7,7 vs. dealer 8

These hands would then be played separately, with any doubling decisions made by following the Basic Strategy as applicable for each hand.

SURRENDER

If the casino where you plan to play allows surrender (the option to throw in your hand and give up half your bet), then follow the table below for the two-card hands that make this decision profitable.

BASIC STRATEGY: Four-deck Surrender

Dealer Up Card	Surrender Holding	Frequency %
Ace	9,7 and 10,6	.5
10	9,7 and 10,6	3.7
	9,6 and 10,5	
9	9,7 and 10,6	.5

No three-card surrender plays are shown because most casinos allow surrender on the first two cards only. The surrender Basic Strategy for three or more cards is extremely complex and results in too small a gain for the amount of memory effort involved.

Early Surrender

A recent variation to the surrender play described above is "early surrender." This more liberal surrender rule allows you to throw in your hand and lose half of your original bet *before* the dealer either looks at or deals a hole card. In Las Vegas, for example, you may surrender only when the dealer has determined that he does not have a natural 21. At the time this is written, early surrender is being offered in Atlantic City.

BASIC STRATEGY: Multiple-deck Early Surrender

Dealer Up Card	Surrender
Ace	ALL Hard 5–7
	ALL Hard 12–17
10	ALL Hard 14–16

This table shows the correct early-surrender strategy for *any* multiple-deck game. Following this strategy in a four-deck game will give you an extra .62 per cent. This will wipe out the built-in four-deck advantage to the house of .54 per cent and give the player a slight .08 per cent expected gain.

MODIFICATIONS TO FOUR-DECK BASIC STRATEGY

As you may have noticed, the performance figures quoted in the earlier tables were for a single-deck game. In the many mathematical studies of Blackjack, a single-deck game played with Las Vegas rules is typically used as the performance base. To simplify the presentation in this text, only the four-deck Basic Strategy is given in table form (the one-, two-, and six-deck strategies can be found in table and simplified form in Appendix A). The next table describes the changes to the four-deck Basic Strategy for the single-deck game.

BASIC STRATEGY: One-deck Modifications

Hard standing and hitting
  STAND on 7,7 vs. dealer 10

Soft standing and hitting
  STAND on A,7 vs. dealer A

Hard doubling
  DOUBLE hard 11 vs. dealer A
  DOUBLE hard 9 vs. dealer 2
  DOUBLE hard 8 vs. dealer 5
    or 6

Pair splitting
  STAND on 7,7 vs. dealer 10
  SPLIT 6,6 vs. dealer 2
  DOUBLE 4,4 vs. dealer 5 or 6
  SPLIT 2,2 vs. dealer 3

Soft doubling
  DOUBLE A,8 vs. dealer 6
  STAND on A,7 vs. dealer A
  DOUBLE A,6 vs. dealer 2
  DOUBLE A,3 and A,2 vs.
    dealer 4

Pair splitting (when doubling
   after split allowed)
   SPLIT 7,7 vs. dealer 8
   STAND on 7,7 vs. dealer 10
   SPLIT 6,6 vs. dealer 7
   SPLIT 4,4 vs. dealer 4

Surrender
   PLAY 9,7 vs. dealer A
   SURRENDER 7,7 vs. dealer 10
   PLAY all hands vs. dealer 9

In general, you stand, double, and split more often in a single-deck game, and hit or surrender less often. As a result, the single-deck game is .54 per cent more profitable for the player. Go back to my game with Marge and see the unusual single-deck hands I was dealt.

BASIC STRATEGY: Additional Modifications

1. For Two Decks

   Hard doubling
      DOUBLE 7, 4 and 6, 5 vs. dealer A
      DOUBLE hard 9 vs. dealer 2
   Surrender
      DON'T SURRENDER vs. dealer 9

2. For Six Decks

   Surrender
      SURRENDER 8, 7 vs. dealer 10

These additional modifications show the minor changes to the four-deck Basic Strategy when playing in two-deck or six-deck games. The two-deck game requires only three changes, while the six-deck game requires a single infrequent play variation. This is another reason why the four-deck Basic Strategy is the best to learn and use first. If you will be playing at those casinos that still offer a single-deck game, you can learn the modifications at a later time.

CALCULATING THE HOUSE ADVANTAGE

With the vast amount of computer work done, we now know exactly how advantageous it is to play for every variation in the game. There are a number of variations to the common rules of Blackjack that affect the long-term house odds. The following table presents the percentage changes of each such variation.

EFFECTS OF RULES VARIATION

Variations from Typical Las Vegas Strip Rules	*Player Advantage % with Basic Strategy*
Early surrender—four decks	+ 0.62
Doubling on any number of cards	+ 0.20
Doubling on any three cards	+ 0.19
Six-card bonus—four decks	+ 0.17
Drawing any number of cards to split Aces	+ 0.14
Doubling allowed after pair splitting	+ 0.10
Six-card bonus—one deck	+ 0.10
Surrender —four decks	+ 0.06
—one deck	+ 0.02
Dealer wins ties	— 9.00
No doubling on 10	— 0.56
Four or more decks	— 0.54
Two decks	— 0.38
Dealer hits soft 17	— 0.20
No doubling on 9	— 0.14
No soft doubling	— 0.14
No dealer hole card	— 0.13
No resplit of pairs	— 0.05
Cheating dealer	—100.00

The table assumes as a base that you are playing Basic Strategy in a single-deck game with dealer standing on any 17, doubling on soft or hard hands, no doubling after pair splitting, and no surrender. In this situation, your advantage is exactly 0 per cent (an even game). Notice the negative effects of using multiple decks. Two- or four-deck games are two of the most unfavorable player variations. The other common changes make a small difference in the final advantage.

Calculations to determine the player advantage for a sample downtown Las Vegas casino offering a single-deck game with surrender and doubling after split are:

Basic single-deck game	0.00%
Dealer hits soft 17	−0.20%
Surrender	+0.02%
Double after split	+0.10%
Player advantage	−0.08%

A sample Las Vegas Strip casino has the following odds:

Basic single-deck game	0.00%
Two decks	−0.38%
Double after split	+0.10%
Player advantage	−0.28%

In Atlantic City, the player actually has a slight long-run advantage over the house:

Basic single-deck game	0.00%
Four decks	−0.54%
Early surrender	+0.62%
Double after split	+0.10%
Player advantage	+0.18%

In general, the casino advantage will rarely be over 1 per cent when you are playing according to Basic Strategy. This is usually good enough for the occasional player.

Two students of mine, an older couple, are ardent Blackjack players. They had spent their yearly vacations driving their camper up to the Reno/Tahoe area, gambling, and seeing the sights. Several of their vacations were cut short by gambling losses, and on many they lost their limit well before their vacation was over. Showing them the Basic Strategy was one of the more satisfying things I have ever done. They likened their former style of play to driving without headlights.

On their next trip, lasting three weeks, the couple played over three hundred individual hours betting from one dollar to five dollars a hand. Up until the last two days, they were only a hundred dollars down. (In those last two days they lost two hundred dollars playing at a small casino. In their ignorance, they had ignored a friendly dealer's plea that "I feel hot tonight.") Overall, they lost an average of a dollar an hour, which *included dealer and waitress tips*. The man's comment to me when he returned was that they received much more than three hundred dollars' worth of enjoyment, drinks, and shows. In addition, they didn't lose their limit, nor did they cut short their vacation.

The two are now learning to track cards so they can win on next year's trip. If you, too, are ready to learn Basic Strategy, continue reading.

HOW TO LEARN BASIC STRATEGY

Most of us are like the little girl who said, "Memory is what I forget with." After seeing all the Basic Strategy charts, which contain about 150 individual entries, you may be wondering if it is practical to learn Basic Strategy for a single vacation trip. Take heart! The individual play charts are the worst possible format for memorization. If the rules summaries weren't enough to help you organize the material for learning, don't worry. This section shows you other ways to learn the Basic Strategy well enough to use it in casino play.

Everybody claims to have a bad memory, but we always seem to remember what we want to. The little neighbor boy who can't remember his multiplication tables can reel off the numbers, playing history, and batting averages of the local major-league team. The woman who can't remember her shopping list can recite what everyone had on at a party three weeks ago. The businessman will forget a meeting with a client but never forget a tee time. The first rule in remembering anything is that you must *want to*. When the desire is there you can remember anything.

Since you are already reading this book, the problem of desire is largely solved. You next need to have more confidence in yourself. We are always awed by people gifted with good memories. Napoleon could call every officer in his army by name. Broadcaster Joe Garagiola knows hundreds of baseball stories. As a catcher, he would resume a specific conversation with a batter after not seeing him for weeks. Memory expert Harry Lorayne can remember every last name in a five-hundred-person audience.

You have the same capabilities. As the griot replied to Alex Haley's amazement at the prodigious amount of tribal history he had memorized, "Western man has forgotten the power of the human mind." Your memory is fully able to retain the appropriate Basic Strategy. Here's how you can make your learning as simple and efficient as possible:

1. Get in the Right Physical Environment

You learn much faster if you have the proper physical environment. Everyone has a "right place" to study in. It might be propped up in bed or in a favorite chair, but it is the one location where you are fully relaxed and can concentrate. Make certain that you study the charts in this location whenever possible. It should also have good air circulation. Studies have shown that poor air circulation reduces the amount of learning that takes place because the flow of oxygen to the brain is reduced.

For the same reason, don't study on a full stomach. The digestion process requires more blood to the stomach, so we get drowsy from reduced oxygen flow to the brain after heavy meals. An empty stomach is also bad. Hunger sensations are distracting, and our energy level is low from lack of food. Fatigue also slows our learning process, so don't study after heavy exercise. The best periods for learning the charts (or anything else, for that matter) are several hours after meals, when you are rested and have a proper location.

This isn't as restrictive as it might seem. One student learned the entire Basic Strategy in the mornings while commuting on the train to New York City. He ate a light breakfast, and found that he had excellent concentration from being ignored by strangers in his car and from the uniform background noise of the train. A woman student told me her best study time was directly after she put the children down for their afternoon naps. She had about an hour a day lull in which she learned to play Blackjack for a coming vacation instead of watching TV.

2. Minimize Memory Interference

"Interference" is a psychological term for our tendency to confuse two subjects we are studying simultaneously. Interference also takes place when we study something and then go on to do anything else. Our other actions interfere with what we have learned, and less is remembered the next day. The ideal way to counter interference is to study right before you go to bed. This way there are no other events to interfere with the Basic Strategy you have learned, and the subconscious can work all night on the information. This is perfect for me, since I am a "night person" whose most productive times are those late-evening hours.

Another way to fight interference is to know your absorption rate. Don't try to learn more than you should at one time. If you are memorizing a speech for the club or learning a new job, postpone studying the Basic Strategy until you can devote your full memory powers to one subject.

How you plan your recall trials will dramatically improve your retention. As a college instructor, I know that my students remember most what they *missed* on a test. I always go over the correct answers immediately after the test is completed. I once gave a twenty-question multiple-choice test again after a week, and nearly 90 per cent of the students marked all twenty correctly. Minimize the delay between your study and a recall trial.

After a short study session, immediately ask yourself practice questions to test your retention of the Basic Strategy. For example: 12 vs. 2: Do I hit? Answer, then check your chart. On 9 vs. 3: Do I double? Again, answer, then check. This question-asking recall trial is a mnemonic technique called the *inquiry method of instruction* by education specialists. It is a quick and powerful way to learn book material. The method forces you to think and makes it difficult for you to forget what you have already learned. Always use it.

Finally, don't study another table or another subject until you have tested yourself on the first table. Otherwise, you will confuse the different tables. When you separate learning sessions from recall trials, the brain seems better able to organize and catalog the information.

3. Schedule Your Time for Learning Efficiency

Time-management experts tell us that we all have good and bad times of the day as far as productivity is concerned. Periods of high mental alertness and possible concentration are called "internal prime," and times of low energy and alertness are called "external prime." You will save a great deal of time studying at your internal prime. In writing this book, I can turn out as many pages in two hours after 10:00 P.M. as I can in the four hours from 1:00 P.M. to 5:00 P.M. All my study sessions take place after 10:00 P.M. Study at your personal prime time.

Make certain you allow enough time for rest between study sessions. The longer you rest between sessions, the more learning takes place because the brain has had time to assimilate and consolidate the information. Also, work a little on it each day. If you try to feed a baby its formula too quickly, most of the formula ends up being rejected after a few pats on the baby's back. Learning is the same way.

Researchers had two groups of students memorize a long list of nonsense words. One group had to memorize the list in one day and needed sixty-eight repetitions. The second group tried over a three-day period and took a total of only thirty-eight repetitions. The effort was cut in half by spacing the learning.

The last time saver in scheduling your learning is to study in units of complete tables each time. It's better to attempt to learn a large amount of information in repetitive sessions than to learn smaller chunks at a single sitting and integrate them at the end. For example, study *all* of the hard standing and hitting rules each time. Don't try to learn a rule each day; it will take longer at the end to associate them.

4. *Organize the Material into a Pattern*

If we could somehow sort out what our brain held, we would find that 90 per cent of what we know was learned visually, 9 per cent auditorially, and 1 per cent from the rest of our senses. We would also see that most of the information was organized in some manner. Organizing the Basic Strategy for easier retention is the next step. Since you are learning to play Blackjack through book form, we will be dealing with the best source for learning, visual.

Even so, it is difficult to remember which of 4 letters goes where in a matrix of approximately 150 spaces. Fortunately, there are 3 other methods for organization that make your learning easier. You have already seen one form of simplifying organization. With each chart, a list of rules summarizing the decisions was given. Some people remember words the easiest. If you are one of these, then you might use the table below to study from. There the rules are listed by frequency of occurrence.

BASIC STRATEGY: Four-deck Rules by Frequency of Occurrence

Rules	Frequency %	% Total Hands Covered
1. HIT hard 12–16 vs. dealer 7 or higher	23.1	23.1
2. STAND on hard 17 or higher	15.7	38.8
3. STAND on hard 12–16 vs. dealer 6 or lower (except 2 or 3)	13.1	51.9
4. NEVER SPLIT 4s, 5s, or 10s	10.0	61.9
5. STAND on soft 19 or higher	7.2	69.1
6. HIT hard 8 or lower	7.2	76.3
7. HIT soft 17 or lower	6.0	82.3
8. DOUBLE 11 vs. dealer 10 or lower	4.8	87.1
9. DOUBLE 10 vs. dealer 9 or lower	3.6	90.7
10. DOUBLE 9 vs. dealer 3–6	3.6	94.3
11. STAND on soft 18 vs. dealer 8 or lower	1.3	95.6
12. HIT 12 vs. dealer 2 or 3	1.2	96.8
13. ALWAYS SPLIT Aces and 8s	.9	97.7
14. SPLIT 2s and 3s vs. dealer 4–7	.9	98.6
15. SPLIT 9s vs. dealer 2–6, 8, and 9	.5	99.1
16. SPLIT 6s vs. dealer 3–6	.5	99.6
17. SPLIT 7s vs. dealer 7 or lower	.5	100.0

Others are shape-oriented. Letters and numbers have little impact, but a picture is easily retained. If you are this type, then the charts in Appendix C will be of great help. These charts are like the earlier tables in that they can be shaded where appropriate. The resulting shaded shapes are easier to remember than the location of individual letters.

The third method or organization may be easiest of all to remember. Most of us are accustomed to dealing with numbers, if only in balancing our checkbook. In some cases, whole charts can be reduced to a simple line of numbers such as in the following table.

BASIC STRATEGY: 4 Deck Summary (no double after split).

YOU SHOW	DEALER UP CARD									
	2	3	4	5	6	7	8	9	10	A
min hard std #'s	13	13	12	12	12	17	17	17	17	17
min soft std #'s	18	18	18	18	18	18	18	19	19	19
min hard doubling	10	9	9	9	9	10	10	10	11	—
pair splitting										
9,9	SP	SP	SP	SP	SP	S	SP	SP	S	S
7,7	SP	SP	SP	SP	SP	SP	H	H	H	H
6,6	H	SP	SP	SP	SP	H	H	H	H	H
3,3	H	H	SP	SP	SP	SP	H	H	H	H
2,2	H	H	SP	SP	SP	SP	H	H	H	H
soft doubling										
max #'s	—	18	18	18	18					
min #'s	—	17	15	13	13					
surrender	(9,7), (10,6) vs. dealer A, 10, 9									
	(9,6), (10,5) vs. dealer 10									
early surrender	hard 5 to 7, hard 12 to 17 vs. dealer A									
	hard 14 to 16 vs. dealer 10									

NOTES: ALWAYS Split (A,A) and (8,8)
NEVER Split (10,10), (5,5) and (4,4)
NEVER take Insurance

The first line of the previous table represents the hard standing and hitting decisions outlined earlier. The numbers shown are the minimum hard standing numbers. You should STAND on any hand equal to or higher than those values for each dealer up card. For example, you would STAND on 7,5 versus a dealer 4 but not a 3. You would always STAND on a hand of 17 or higher. All you need remember to master that hard standing and hitting table is the position of three numbers in a ten-item line (which is made easier by the divider between dealer 6 and 7).

The second line showing minimum soft standing numbers is read similarly. You would STAND on a soft 18 or higher for every dealer up card except 9, 10, and Ace. Against 9, 10, and Ace you STAND on soft *19* or higher. To master these earlier tables you need only remember the positions of five numbers on two ten-item lines.

The third line organizes the doubling rules from the hard doubling table. Again, doubling *includes* the number listed as a minimum. You DOUBLE a hand of 9 or more versus a dealer 3 through 6. Note that you DO NOT DOUBLE a two-card hand of 11 against a dealer A.

Pair splitting is not so simply organized. It is possible to reduce the number of individual playing lines from ten to five by utilizing summary rule Nos. 1 and 2 as shown in the "Notes" section. If you want to approximate the remaining lines, you can follow the rule below with only a small loss in advantage:

"Always SPLIT against the same dealer card or lower." You will only misplay six out of fifty hands with this approximation. But if you plan to use the Hi-Opt I count and strategy in the next two chapters, take the time to learn the correct splitting decisions.

Soft doubling requires both low and high limits to be specified. Note that you DO NOT DOUBLE soft hands against a dealer 2. Against a dealer 5, for example, you would double any hands between and *including* A,2 and A,7.

The surrender strategy can also be simplified. Since you know that 8,8 should always be split, you can follow these rules and make only one insignificant mistake:

1. SURRENDER a hand of 16 versus dealer A, 10, 9
2. SURRENDER a hand of 15 versus dealer 10

The mistake is in surrendering 8,7 to a dealer 10, a play that will occur less than once per thousand hands.

In summary, if you follow these rules, you will spend the least amount of time memorizing the Basic Strategy:

1. Find your "right place" that is comfortable and provides good air circulation.
2. Be well rested when you study.
3. Don't study on a hungry or full stomach.
4. Know how much you can learn at one time.
5. If possible, study before you go to sleep.
6. Otherwise, don't study something else before testing yourself.
7. Test yourself as soon after your study session as possible.
8. Study a little each day.
9. Allow rest between same-day study sessions.
10. Spread your reviews over as many days as possible.
11. Learn each table as a whole.
12. Pick the organization that is easiest for you to remember and begin studying the hard standing and hitting decisions.

Learning the Basic Strategy is one of the most difficult parts of this book. Yet the strategy is not hard to learn, it is just tedious. Focus on your goal of winning at Blackjack and keep saying to yourself, "IF I LEARN THE BASIC STRATEGY, THE REST WILL BE EASY."

PUTTING THE BASIC STRATEGY INTO PRACTICE

In learning the charts, it is quickest if you actually get a deck of cards and play Blackjack at home. Keep the book beside you and refer to it as you play. Always guess the correct play first, *then* check your decision by looking at the chart. It takes anywhere from one hour to fifteen hours of practice to memorize the Basic Strategy well enough to play it. Any pure studying of the charts you do can reduce this time significantly.

Use the inquiry method to practice the hands given in the table below. This table contains almost every hand you will ever get in a Blackjack game. In each column, the player's hand is on the left and the dealer's up card is on the right. "X" stands for 10-value cards, and "A" means Ace.

BASIC STRATEGY PRACTICE TABLE.

A7 4	A9 3	A9 6	A7 5	14 A	A7 6	A9 5
99 2	99 A	99 4	99 6	99 3	99 7	92 8
65 A	74 5	92 6	83 3	16 4	14 9	15 A
15 9	13 A	16 A	16 9	A5 3	83 X	99 5
A7 A	77 6	77 8	77 3	77 5	77 4	77 2
16 X	16 3	16 6	14 X	74 2	15 X	A5 4
A5 5	A5 6	A3 5	A3 6	16 7	A3 3	53 3
14 8	15 7	14 7	15 8	A9 4	16 8	72 6
72 3	54 8	63 5	54 2	72 7	63 4	66 4
88 X	66 7	66 3	66 5	66 2	66 6	15 3
A6 3	A3 5	A8 2	A8 4	A8 6	A8 3	22 2
22 8	22 6	22 5	22 3	22 7	22 4	65 7
74 A	83 9	82 6	73 A	A4 2	55 7	A4 6
14 5	14 3	15 2	15 4	15 6	16 5	13 4
44 3	62 5	44 2	88 9	44 5	44 4	A7 2
A4 4	A6 6	A6 4	A6 5	A7 3	A6 2	33 6
33 5	33 3	33 7	33 2	33 4	33 8	A8 5
13 3	15 5	13 5	14 6	14 4	13 6	13 8
AA 2	AA X	AA 7	AA 8	AA A	AA 9	44 6
55 2	64 X	82 4	73 8	64 5	73 3	10 9
A2 6	A4 3	A4 5	A2 5	A2 3	A2 4	14 2
16 2	12 4	12 3	13 2	12 5	12 2	AA 3
53 5	53 6	A7 X	44 7	62 6	53 4	12 6

Some players still have trouble memorizing the Basic Strategy. If you are one of these, go ahead and use a "crib sheet" in the casino until the Basic Strategy is reliably committed to memory. The last page of this book contains a small representation of the Basic Strategy in a format developed by the Gambler's Book Club. Four copies in two sizes are given.

You can take the larger version and slide it behind the cellophane of your cigarette pack. Even if you are a nonsmoker, you can still leave the pack on the table in front of you. The smaller

version could be glued to the inside of a matchbook. Some
players have even had charts engraved on their cigarette lighters,
money clips, and other items having "fondle value" while playing.

The beauty of knowing the Basic Strategy is that it always gives
you a powerful weapon against the house. With the information
in this chapter, the house advantage is virtually wiped out. Even
if you decide not to use a winning method that involves keeping
track of the cards, you stand an excellent chance of almost breaking even in the long run if you play the Basic Strategy. You can
now enjoy playing Blackjack and all the amenities that go with
being a player in a casino (complimentary drinks, meals, shows)
without the risk of losing large sums of money.

SEVEN

Winning in Occasional Casino Play: Hi-Opt I Card Counting

You watch sixteen 10s and what do you get? Another day older and deeper in debt.

ANONYMOUS

Thank goodness for a deck of cards! If Blackjack were played somehow with dice or a spinning wheel, there would be no reason to write this book. Cards are superior to dice or wheels for one very important reason: Cards have *memory*. Mathematicians call the dealing of cards "dependent sequential events." I call it "making money."

The problem with games like Craps or Roulette, the next two most popular casino games, is that consecutive bets have no relationship to each other. The chances of throwing any "point" on the dice or hitting any number on the wheel are theoretically the same on each trial. Statistically, these actions are "independent sequential events." Nick the Greek observed, "Three things are sure to get you eventually: death, taxes, and the house percentage." He went on, "Logically, the only sound advice regarding the game of dice is: Don't play it. The best long-term attack I know is to play the 'don't pass' line and take the odds. Using that method, I've lost several million dollars. . . ." The built-in house advantage is inescapable in these games, since the odds in favor of the casino never change with each bet.

The odds in Blackjack *do* change with each bet as the cards are dealt out. For example, if your first hand versus a dealer 10 up in a single-deck game consisted of A,A,A,A,10,10, you would bust with a 24. However, the odds would thereafter be very different for you. With all of the Aces out of the deck, your chance of getting a Blackjack with its premium payoff would be eliminated. As you will soon see, the appearance of the three 10s also reduces your chance of winning for all remaining hands dealt before a shuffle-up. Conversely, if your first hand off the top of a deck was 5,6,5,5 and the dealer pulled a 5,9,9 to bust, you would have a large *advantage* for the subsequent hands dealt from the deck before shuffling. This is why Blackjack is the only beatable casino game. The odds for or against you are continually shifting with the value and number of cards already put in play.

This chapter will show you how to evaluate the cards you see played in order to determine when the remaining deck presents an advantageous betting situation for you. When the composition of the remaining cards in the deck favors you, you will place large bets. When the remaining cards are against you, you will be placing minimum bets. Sizing your bets based on the cards that have already been seen is called "counting."

POOR ALTERNATIVES TO COUNTING

When I was in college, we had a running joke about the difficulty of material. Whenever a particularly involved mathematical or statistical proof was omitted in a text or in a lecture, the author or professor would tell us the proof "took several pages and was beyond the scope of this text" or it would "fill up several boards and take too much class time." As you can imagine, we began to rate everything as to how many pages it took. "You should have seen the transmission job I did on my old clunker this weekend; it must have been a five-page repair." When stumped on a test we were always quick to point out that "the answer takes several pages and is beyond the scope of this student." Although it never helped our score, it beat leaving a blank space.

Well, the mathematical background that proves the material in this section takes several pages and is beyond the scope of the average Blackjack player. If you are the type who needs to see the equations and proofs for yourself, you'll find them in the following two books: *The Casino Gambler's Guide* by Allan N. Wilson and *The Theory of Gambling and Statistical Logic* by Richard A. Epstein. Rather than make you wade through the formulas, I have broken down what you need to know into basic facts and then applied them to common betting systems in Blackjack (and gambling in general).

DOUBLE UP AND CATCH UP

One of the most common methods of betting in all of gambling is a progression sometimes called a "Martingale." The theme is that you increase your bet after a loss in order to catch up. As long as you win your last bet, you will be slightly ahead. If you use the "double up" progression, where you double the value of your last losing bet, you will end up one unit ahead after finally winning. For example, if you start with one unit and keep losing until you win a 16-unit bet, your final position will be $16-(1+2+4+8)=16-15=1$ unit ahead.

In theory, playing a progression system seems to make sense. You will always recoup your losses by winning the last bet. In practice, progressions are very dangerous to the player. With the eventual long losing streak, you run out of money before you win again. The casinos know this and love to see a progression player come in to try out a new system. I was in the MGM Grand in Las Vegas one afternoon when a young man and his father came over to my table. The young man sat down next to me, and the father chose a seat at the next table. They both pulled out a little card, bought about $500 worth of chips, and started playing.

At the appearance of the reference cards, the pit bosses quickly came over to watch the two play. In a little over 20 minutes, the son had about $1,700 in front of him and the father about $900. The pit boss at my table watched the son's betting pattern for a while and finally asked the young man, "Betting progression?" The player nodded his head. The pit boss then politely asked, "May I see the card?" The young man handed it over and the pit boss examined it closely with a blank expression. He then silently handed it back and went over to the pit boss at the next table and whispered in his ear. They both smiled, turned, and left. After that, they gave the two no more than normal attention. Why weren't they upset by these "systems" players who were winning? Because the pit bosses knew in the long run that they would clean the two out. Here's why.

FACT No. 1 *If the house has the advantage, NO betting method will break even or have an advantage. (Wilson)*
Let's examine the case for doubling up. One of the problems with this approach is that the casinos have set a limit on the amount any player can place on a single bet. Let's say we are playing at a casino with a $500 table limit. We see below what happens with doubling up for two casino advantages and two player bankrolls. The casino advantages approximate a player using dealer mimic or Basic Strategy. With a bankroll of $511, you can lose only nine consecutive times before reaching the table limit (1-2-4-8-16-32-64-128-256). You can't make the next bet of $512. With a bankroll of $63, you can double after only six consecutive losses before running out of money.

Now, each sequence that you win before either running out of money or reaching the table limit, you net a $1.00 gain. Each time that you lose up to the table limit or until your bankroll is exhausted, you lose all the previous bets. In evaluating doubling up, we can compare the probability of winning $1.00 to losing everything. To make these odds easier to compare, I've calculated ratios. In line one of the table, for every 304 sequences, you will win 303, for a gain of $303. But once every 304 sequences you can expect to lose all $511. The net long-term loss for this approach is $208.

As you can see, the less the casino advantage, the smaller your expected losses. But they are losses nonetheless. Also, there is a chance that your busting string of losses can happen more (or less) than once every 304 hands. Converting this to Blackjack time, you can still expect to lose your $511 bankroll in this situation once every 4 to 6 hours at the table. It could happen right away. So, no matter what the table limit or your bankroll, the figures show that winning those doubled sequences will never pay back the infrequent but disastrous single string of losses.

RESULTS OF DOUBLING UP

CASINO ADVANTAGE	PROBABILITY OF SINGLE LOSS	PROBABILITY OF LOSING PROGRESSION SEQUENCE	PROBABILITY OF WINNING PROGRESSION SEQUENCE	P(win) TO P(lose) RATIO	BANKROLL	LAST BET	SINGLE LOSING SEQUENCE LOSS	WINNING SEQUENCE GAIN	NET LOSS
-6.0%	.53	.0032997	.9967003	303:1	$511	$256	$511	$303	—$208
-.5%	.5025	.0020427	.9979573	489:1	$511	$256	$511	$489	—$22
-6.0%	.53	.0418195	.9581805	24:1	$63	$32	$63	$24	—$39
-.5%	.5025	.0320390	.9679610	31:1	$63	$32	$63	$31	—$22

FACT No. 2 *For any even game, ANY betting system leads to the same results. (Epstein) Therefore, NO progression is better than any other betting scheme. (Wilson)*
If you're playing in an even game, using a betting progression can be lots of fun and keep you busy, but it won't help you. You'll get the same results with SWAG, flat betting, or anything else your imagination can conjure up.

REVERSAL OF TREND

Many players think that there is some kind of luck that is like a troubled insomniac, turning from side to side. They keep waiting for the next indication of a turn so they can bet on it. The trouble is, you can't bet on a trend to reverse.

FACT No. 3 *LAW OF LARGE NUMBERS: While a statistical percentage will converge on the theoretical, the absolute difference is likely to get larger.*
It is perfectly possible, and very likely, that your losses could keep increasing in an even game. This in no way violates the statistical theory, but it does show the fallacy in waiting for a trend to reverse. The next table shows how your net losses could be getting larger and larger even though you are getting closer to the expected theoretical percentages in an even fifty–fifty game.

"LAW OF LARGE NUMBERS" IN EVEN GAME

Hands	Hands Won	Hands Lost	% Won	Net Loss
10	4	6	.40	2
100	43	57	.43	14
1,000	460	540	.46	80
10,000	4,900	5,100	.49	200

Even more startling are the calculations that are shown in the following table. In an even game, you would think that each side should be ahead for about half the time (which is consistent with the idea that "things even up"). Surprisingly, this is the *least* likely result.

FACT No. 4   *There is no tendency for wins and losses to even up. (Epstein)*

It is much more probable that one side or the other will lead for the majority of the time. Wilson presented a study of coin flipping taken from the classic *An Introduction to Probability Theory and Its Applications* by William A. Feller. Feller showed that in an even game, like theoretically flipping a coin once a second for a year (about thirty-one million flips), the eventual loser would likely be ahead only a small per cent of the time.

UNLIKELIHOOD OF COIN FLIPS "EVENING UP"

Maximum Length of Time Loser Holds Lead	Chance %
1 day	6.6
2.2 days	10
19.9 days	30
53.5 days	50
100 days	70
154 days	90

So as you can see in the last two tables, you could starve waiting for your trend to reverse in an *even* game, and do *worse* when you are at a disadvantage.

JUMPING IN AND OUT OF THE GAME

Some Blackjack players like to treat a deck of cards as if it had a life and will of its own. They like to monitor whether the deck is "hot" or "cold" and play accordingly by jumping in and out of the game.

FACT No. 5   *There is no advantage to jumping in or out of the game. (Epstein)*

If you are playing Blackjack *and are not tracking* the cards, jumping in or out will be of no benefit to you. You might be leaving with favorable conditions or betting when you have a disadvantage; you will never know.

PICK YOUR "BOLDNESS"

If you want to double your bankroll and you face a *disadvantage,* the best way to do it is to fold your money over and put it in your pocket. If you are intent on betting it, this next table shows you what to do. Bet it all on one shot.

CHANCE OF DOUBLING BANKROLL BEFORE GOING BROKE

Player-Advantage %	Bankroll to Be Doubled (in betting units)				
	1	10	20	50	100
−2.0	.490*	.401	.310	.119	.018
+2.0	.510	.599	.690	.881	.982†

This table shows the probability of doubling your bankroll before going broke for a disadvantage and advantage. When the casino holds the advantage, your best wager is to put your whole bankroll on a single bet. The Las Vegas term for this type of bettor is a "plunger." The more betting units you try to double, the smaller your chances. In this case, you have a 49 per cent chance of doubling a hundred dollars on a *single* bet, but only a 1.8 per cent chance of doubling the hundred dollars *betting one dollar at a time.* Epstein dubbed plunging the "maximum boldness" strategy.

When you have an advantage, the situation reverses. You have a 51 per cent chance of doubling your hundred dollars in a single bet, but a whopping 98.2 per cent chance of doubling your hundred-dollar bankroll betting one dollar on each hand. This is the "minimum boldness" strategy. With minimum boldness you take little risk and let your advantage slowly grind out the profits. This is analogous to the casino's approach in setting table limits. The house's bankroll is practically infinite compared to the bankroll of the average player. Since the house limits the size of

---

* "Maximum boldness"   † "Minimum boldness"

individual bets (and many of the bets, like "red" and "black" at Roulette, cancel each other), the house is taking the "minimum boldness" approach by risking a tiny portion of its "bankroll" over hundreds of thousands of bets. The success of this can be seen in the soaring annual profits of the casino industry.

What you must know as a player is the relationship between your advantage or disadvantage and the chance of going broke. The table below shows the classic "Gambler's Ruin" graph for a range of pertinent Blackjack percentages. The Gambler's Ruin chart gives the figures for doubling your bankroll with the various percentages you may encounter using the Blackjack systems in this book (the Roulette and Craps figures are included for reference).

Gambler's ruin.

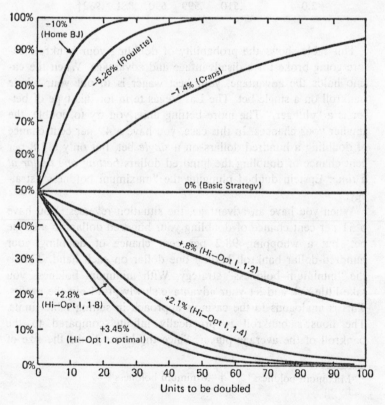

Units to be doubled

Notice how the advantages you can obtain with a Blackjack system greatly decrease your chances of losing your bankroll. Playing dealer-mimic strategy in a Blackjack or a Roulette game is totally futile if you want to double a hundred-unit stake. Craps is hopeless. Even the Hi-Opt I can't guarantee success, but it can certainly reduce your chance of failure. With less than a 1 per cent advantage, you should successfully double your hundred-unit bankroll about five of every six attempts. This may be hard for you to believe, but this relationship between advantage and risk has been proven and demonstrated by hundreds of mathematicians and statisticians in the past twenty years.

KELLY CRITERION AND COUNTING

Trusting for now that you can gain an advantage with a counting system, the real question becomes: How should you bet in order to maximize your profits while minimizing your risk? Once again, the mathematicians have answered this one for us. According to Professor J. L. Kelly in 1956, *the optimal betting method is to bet a percentage of your total bankroll that corresponds exactly to the per cent advantage you have at any particular time.* Professor Kelly and other scientists have proven both mathematically and in practice that this "Kelly Criterion" is the most profitable long-run method of wagering.

First applied to Blackjack by Thorp in *Beat the Dealer,* the Kelly Criterion can be used in all gambling games, not just Blackjack, in which the player has an advantage and knows what it is in percentage terms. It is up to the gambling system to determine how much of an advantage the player has and when it exists in order to bet properly. This is the benefit of a Blackjack count like the Hi-Opt I. More on this later. Let me show you how winning Blackjack systems evolved.

DEVELOPMENT OF BLACKJACK COUNTING
SYSTEMS

The wide range of Blackjack counting systems available today is the result of two truly original research efforts. As I discussed briefly in Chapter One in "The Evolution of Blackjack Systems," the first breakthrough was made by Messrs. Baldwin, Cantey, Maisel, and McDermott. In 1953, they reasoned that there should be a "best" strategy in which to play Blackjack and went about trying to compute it with hand calculators. Their results were made public in 1956.

Professor Edward O. Thorp noticed their work and refined their calculations using a high-speed IBM computer at MIT. The first Basic Strategy was now in existence, the most accurate version of which you saw in Chapter Six. Thorp's creativity and insight into the game caused him to ask a second question, which changed the game of Blackjack into a beatable game for the first time. He knew that the cards had "memory," and wondered what would happen in the game as various cards were played out.

With the computer programs used to determine the Basic Strategy as a base, he began calculating the results of playing with a depleted deck. With each computer run, he removed all the cards of a single value from the deck and computed the results of playing Basic Strategy. Fortunately, the findings justified all this work. Thorp observed that a shortage of any cards valued 2 through 8 benefited the player. Conversely, a shortage of 9s, 10s, and Aces benefited the dealer.

The most recent study validating these results was performed by Professors John M. Gwynn, Jr., and Armand Seri in their paper, "Experimental Comparisons of Blackjack Betting Systems," presented to the Fourth Conference on Gambling in Reno in December 1978. The following table shows the results of their ten-million hand-simulation run used to determine how much change in Basic Strategy expected gain would result from the removal of a single card of given value. The game was simulated with a single deck and northern Nevada rules. In this run, 2 through 7 helped the player, and 9, 10, and Ace helped the dealer (The value for 8 was experimentally 0 per cent).

Thorp had essentially the same results before him and noticed that a shortage of 5s presented the most benefit to the player. He then devised a simple "5-count" strategy that suggested a variable betting scheme and modified Basic Strategy when the player knew there were no more 5s in the deck. The problem with the 5-count was that it identified favorable situations only about 6 per cent

ESTIMATED CHANGE IN BASIC STRATEGY
EXPECTATION FOR SINGLE-CARD REMOVALS
(ten-million-hand simulation with Reno/Tahoe rules)

Cards Benefiting Player When Removed		Cards Benefiting Dealer When Removed	
Card	Est. % Change	Card	Est. % Change
5	+.64	10	−.53
4	.52	A	−.49
6	.45	9	−.13
3	.44		
2	.37		
7	.30		

(or less) of the time if there was more than one person at the table. So Thorp also suggested keeping track of whether or not the deck was "5 rich" or "5 poor"—that is, whether the proportion of 5s in the deck was higher or lower than normal. This increased the identification of advantageous betting situations, although betting in a rich-poor situation was not as advantageous as betting when all 5s were out of the deck.

Thorp then went to his famous 10-count system, which is still used by some players in casinos today. As the table shows, Thorp saw that removing a 10-value card greatly affected the player's expected gain. More importantly, there are 16 10-value cards, which allow for a greater potential fluctuation in "richness" or "poorness" than only 4 5s. For the player, the more 10s that are left in the deck, the better.

The 10-count system keeps a running count of the number of 10s and non-10s seen as the cards are played. There are 36 non-10s in the deck, and 16 10s in the deck. This means that the normal ratio of non-10s to 10s is 36:16 or 2.25. Thorp reasoned that any time this ratio fell under 2.25, the player would have an advantage. The farther the ratio fell, the greater the advantage and the heavier the player should bet.

The problem with the 10 count is that it requires keeping a count of two numbers—the tens and the non-10s—and calculating a difficult ratio within .1 accuracy. For example, if you see 4 10s and 11 non-10s, you have to calculate the ratio $25 \div 12 = 2.08$ quickly and make your bet. Shortly after the publication of *Beat the Dealer,* many players recognized this shortcoming and began devising simpler systems from the data in the book. The first of these players to announce a system publicly was Harvey Dubner at the 1963 Fall Joint Computer Conference in Las Vegas.

Dubner proposed a simple Hi-Low point-count system where the high cards would be balanced by the low cards. Whenever there were a disproportionate amount of high cards left in the deck (excess low cards had been removed), the player would have an advantage. Dubner suggested that each Ace or ten be counted as —1 when it was seen, and that each two through six be counted as +1 when seen. Whenever the total at any point in time was above 0—that is, whenever there were more low cards out of the deck than high cards—the player would know he had an advantage and could bet more heavily.

Braun took Dubner's idea, and with the help of speed digital computers, determined the correct betting and playing strategies for such a count. This newer and simpler system appeared in the second edition of Thorp's *Beat the Dealer* in 1966. Blackjack players everywhere examined the simple Hi-Low approach and began looking for even more powerful and simple count systems to use in the casino. The years since have seen an incredible number of Blackjack systems hit the market, each one promising more simplicity or accuracy at the tables. The next table illustrates the most well-known or well-advertised systems. One of these, however, stands out in its simplicity above the rest as an excellent system for all players.

In 1968 Charles Einstein wrote *How to Win at Blackjack,* in which he proposed keeping a count of the number of *3s through 6s versus the number of 10s* seen. Peter Griffin examined this simple count in 1973 and thought that it would be excellent with a properly developed playing strategy.

At this time I approached Braun to help me construct a simple but powerful strategy for the average player. Braun was gracious enough to loan his computer programs to me, and in 1974 the

CARD COUNT SYSTEMS.

SYSTEM	CARD COUNT VALUES									
	2	3	4	5	6	7	8	9	10	A
Hi-Opt I (Einstein)	0	1	1	1	1	0	0	0	−1	0
Gordon (DHM)	1	1	1	1	0	0	0	0	−1	0
Braun + − (Dubner, Thorp, Revere, Wong)	1	1	1	1	1	0	0	0	−1	−1
Revere Advanced + −	1	1	1	1	1	0	0	−1	−1	0
Ita (Systems Research)	1	1	1	1	1	1	0	−1	−1	−1
Hi-Opt II (Stepine)	1	1	2	2	1	1	0	0	−2	0
Revere Point Count	1	2	2	2	2	1	0	0	−2	−2
Revere Advanced Point Count − 73 (Uston)	2	2	3	4	2	1	0	−2	−3	0
Revere Advanced Point Count − 71	2	3	3	4	3	2	0	−1	−3	−4
10 − Count (Thorp, Roberts)	4	4	4	4	4	4	4	4	−9	4
Thorp Ultimate	5	6	8	11	6	4	0	−3	−7	−9

complete strategy was derived and given the name Hi-Opt, an abbreviation for "highly optimum." The computer work was done by Mr. G., a graduate student of mathematics at a large Canadian university.

As Julian Braun wrote in his 1975 paper "The Development and Analysis of Winning Strategies for the Game of Blackjack":

To the best of my knowledge, this count was original with Mr. Einstein. He is to be congratulated for his insight in picking this count as recent research reveals that optimum playing results for a simple +1, −1 count system are achieved by an optimized system based upon this count.

. . . Mr. Einstein produced a good system in 1968, but it lacked many refinements, and contained some errors in its strategy tables.

Eventually, a substantial improvement in results over the earlier Einstein system was achieved. The Hi-Opt I system was sold privately for several years at two hundred dollars until pirated copies were common enough to diminish sales. It is the basics of this system that you will find in the coming pages.

CHOOSING A SYSTEM

Up until the past five years, choosing a Blackjack system was much like determining which was the No. 1 college football team. The systems developers all advertised "We're No. 1," and Blackjack players would informally gather to discuss the merits of each system based upon the games they had seen or the system they used. As in the race for a national collegiate football championship, the *real* "No. 1" was impossible to determine concretely.

Fortunately, the mathematicians and statisticians picked up the challenge Thorp's work provided and have greatly increased our knowledge of winning Blackjack systems. While I sullenly regarded my math and stat instructors at college as all being the type of men who still live with their mothers, I now find I owe them a debt of gratitude (I have even managed to find the subjects they taught quite likable as applied to my field of psychology, and I don't live with my mother). Their work has been invaluable in helping establish "who is No. 1."

Julian Braun was one of the first to tackle the problem of systems performance. The results presented in his previously mentioned paper were the first to reflect the comparative performance of the popular count systems. These figures will be discussed in Chapter Eight. Peter A. Griffin, currently professor of mathematics at California State University at Sacramento, was the second to analyze Blackjack systems performance. In December 1976, he presented his paper "Use of Bivariate Normal Approximation to Evaluate Single-parameter Card-counting Systems in Blackjack" to the Third Conference on Gambling at Las Vegas, Nevada. These calculations for the systems in the previous table are presented below:

DIFFICULTY OF SYSTEMS VERSUS PERFORMANCE

System	Level	Number of Values	Betting Correlation	Playing Efficiency
Hi-Opt I	1	5	.88 (.96)	.615 (.635)
Gordon	1	5	.86	.574
Braun + −	1	7	.97	.510*
Revere Adv + −	1	7	.89	.592
Ita	1	9	.96	.532*
Hi-Opt II	2	7	.91	.671
Revere Pt. Ct.	2	8	.98	.527*
Revere APC (73)	4	8	.92	.657
Revere APC (71)	4	9	.995	.523*
10 count	n/a	10	.72	.621
Thorp Ultimate	11	9	.996	.525*

NOTES: Figures with an asterisk show system including Ace in Hi-Low count.

Figures in parentheses show value with Ace side count.

Look over these two tables carefully. Familiarize yourself with the counts they present and the relative-performance statistics they contain. You will need this information for the next section.

FACTORS IN SELECTING A BLACKJACK COUNTING SYSTEM

There are five criteria for selecting the right Blackjack system. I am presenting them in the order of most to least importance from my experience. For example, I place cost of the system last. My reasoning is that you may repay the difference in systems costs in your first sitting at the table. You may view it differently depending upon your budget. Here's what you should consider in choosing a system.

1. Ease of Use

You can have the greatest system in the world, but if it is too hard for you to apply in the casino, then it is only so much junk. You might as well have spent your money on a movie because afterward you'll at least have your memories. Also, a difficult system can turn a dandy slice of excitement playing Blackjack into a chore. I don't want to be a slave to my system. I want to enjoy the game. Finally, the difference in performance among advanced, professional, and expert Blackjack systems is only about a single mistake per hour from level to level. If your system is so difficult that you are making playing errors trying to implement it in a casino, then you could be wasting your time.

The difficulty of a Blackjack count is measured in two ways. The first is the "level" of the system. The level is the highest point value assigned to any single card. For example, the counts in the card-count systems table are divided into first-, second-, fourth-, and more-than-fourth-level systems. Fourth-level systems like the Revere Advanced Point Counts are extremely difficult for very bright people, much less average gamblers. Imagine trying to assign one of six numbers to nine card values at the speed of a Blackjack game and make all the additions and subtractions correctly! An hour of that in the casino and friends would drag you out babbling.

The number of card values counted also affects the difficulty of the system. For example, in the first-level systems, you count only five card values for the Hi-Opt I or Gordon counts, while the Ita/Systems Research count requires you to track nine values. Making those extra four additions or subtractions every thirteen cards or so increases both mental fatigue and the risk of errors.

What you want to look for is a system that has the lowest level, preferably a first-level system, and tracks the fewest number of card values.

2. Performance

You will be using the results of your counting system in two ways. The first, which is what this chapter is about, is determining the proper size of your bet with each hand. The second, which will be covered in the next chapter, is determining when and how to vary from the Basic Strategy when the composition of the remaining deck changes from normal. Using advanced statistical and mathematical techniques on the computer, Griffin computed two measures of count-systems performance called the *betting correlation* and the *playing efficiency*.

The betting correlation indicates how accurate the count is in identifying the timing and value of advantageous betting situations. A perfect betting correlation is 1.00. The playing efficiency indicates how good the count system is in identifying the gain from varying from Basic Strategy compared to the total gain available, assuming perfect knowledge of the deck composition. The upper efficiency limit for single-parameter (no side counts) point counts such as those shown in the previous two tables appears to be about .700.

The proper relative importance to attach to betting correlation and playing efficiency depends on several factors, such as the amount of the deck cutoff and the amount you can increase your bets without casino heat. In general, you can see in the card-count systems table that the higher the betting correlation within one level, the lower the playing efficiency. Also, the performance figures tend to improve somewhat with higher-level systems. Griffin did show that level-five systems and beyond offered little improvement over level-four systems, so the practical limit for consideration is only fourth-level-and-under counts.

In general, what you want to see in a system is a good balance between betting and playing performance, depending upon your style of play. If you play where you can range your bets widely, then a system with a high betting correlation will be the most help to you. If you must keep your bets relatively flat because there is casino pressure or you are betting near table limits, then you must have a system with a high playing efficiency. For the average player, you will want to choose a system that is near the top in both categories.

3. *Thoroughness*

As you saw in Chapter Two there are a surprising number of options in Blackjack. Some of them, such as surrender or early surrender, are played at only a few of the U.S. casinos. Whatever system you choose should have basic and counting strategies developed for *all* of the possible Blackjack options worldwide. If the system is incomplete, then you might find yourself in a casino like Resorts International in Atlantic City not knowing how to handle the early-surrender option.

4. *Growth Possibilities*

If there is one trait that seems to characterize the Blackjack player, it is the drive to get a bigger and bigger edge over the casino. That's why so many of the ridiculously complicated systems in the table have found a buying public. But owning one of these systems and *using* it are two different matters. A better approach is to begin with a simple system that can be improved as your abilities to play the game increase without having to learn a whole new system.

The way to improve a system is to begin tracking cards that formerly had a 0 value. Therefore, the more cards your initial system counts, the less it can be improved. The best example of why you might want to keep track of certain cards separately is the Ace. As Griffin points out in his 1976 paper:

> Blackjack gurus seem unanimous in the opinion that the Ace should be valued as 0 since it behaves like a small card for (playing) strategy variations and a big card for betting (variations) strategy.

Griffin's calculations then prove his point. Notice the systems in the last table, which include the Ace. In nearly every case, the betting correlation is slightly higher by a few hundredths, but the playing efficiency is approximately .10 lower than similar counts ignoring the Ace. The most accurate way to use the Ace information is to not include it in the basic count. Instead, you should keep a side count of the Aces if you wish the added accuracy.

With a system counting as few cards as possible, you are also able to keep side counts of all other cards. These side counts can then be used to modify the basic count shown in the card-count-systems table. Griffin originated the concept of using side counts to adjust the basic count for the zero-value cards and presented the playing rules in "Multiparameter Tables." Correctly using these tables can improve a simple count advantage by as much as 20 per cent.

So the fewer cards that are counted, the more improvement is possible in the system. You can build on the basics later.

5. Cost

Because of the high amount of work needed to develop Blackjack systems, and the need for great amounts of expensive computer time, the costs of Blackjack systems have been high in the past (this doesn't hurt the seller, since there are a certain number of serious gamblers who will buy every system put out no matter what the cost in the hope of finding one new piece of information that will help them). Then there are the quick-buck artists trying to undercut the expensive systems with worthless or pirated information sold mail order for small amounts of money. So if you're looking for a system, you can pay anywhere from ten dollars to two thousand dollars for Blackjack information, with the average cost of a good private system about two hundred dollars.

WHY THE HI-OPT I?

Now you can understand why this book presents the world's greatest Blackjack system for the average player. *The Hi-Opt I is the most powerful simple system available.* If you examine the last table, you can see that the Hi-Opt I is the lowest-level system and counts the fewest cards. This means that you add or subtract in single units and that you perform these calculations fewer times than in any other system (except Gordon). For example, the Braun $+ -$ requires 25 per cent more calculations, and the Ita count requires 50 per cent more. Although you must watch all the cards with any system, the Hi-Opt I requires the least mental effort and can be played with fewer mistakes.

The performance of the Hi-Opt I system is excellent. The betting correlation is in the range of any of the other simple systems not counting Aces. The playing efficiency is somewhat higher than that of other level-one systems, and much higher than the counts including Aces, regardless of their level. This balanced performance results in very high playing gains for the simplicity of the system. Since 1974, a few hundred players have won several million dollars with the Hi-Opt I system. Chapter Eight will show detailed playing-gain information.

The Hi-Opt I system also has good growth possibilities. With the addition of an Ace side count (figures shown in parentheses in the table), the Hi-Opt I balanced performance is near any other system listed. In fact, Griffin showed that there is little improvement to be gained beyond the third level. And a higher-level system is not necessarily better than a lower one. The optimal fifth-level system is worse than the best level-four system. The Hi-Opt I system gives the best combination and trade-off of simplicity, betting correlation, and playing efficiency.

The possible performance of the Hi-Opt I is probably beyond most players' ability to take advantage of it. If you could keep side counts of all the 0-value cards, the A, 7, 8, 9, and 2, the playing efficiency would be a remarkable .891 and the betting correlation a near-perfect .98. Griffin remarks that this is within hundredths of the ultimate capability of a human being playing an honest game of Blackjack from a single deck. There is plenty of room for improvement with the Hi-Opt I.

The Hi-Opt I system is one of the most complete available today. Playing and betting strategies for all the major playing options have been researched and determined. Full multiparameter tables are available for all the 0-value cards. Current playing options such as early surrender are continually being analyzed as they occur and are added to the system immediately.

Finally, you can't beat the cost or convenience. The basics of the Hi-Opt I system are in your hands right this minute.

CARD COUNTING WITH THE HI-OPT I

Learning to count the cards is essential in becoming a winning player. Computer studies by both Thorp and Braun showed that the player who uses Basic Strategy wins more hands than the dealer when a lot of small cards have been dealt out of the deck. Thus, when you know you are likely to win more than the dealer in the upcoming hands, you would wager more money than usual. This gives you a profit in the long run. Conversely, when more small cards than large cards are left inside the deck, the dealer wins more hands. In this situation, you would bet as little as possible or stop playing.

The earlier table indicates which are the important small cards and which are the important large cards. The important small cards are 3s, 4s, 5s, and 6s. The 10s and Aces are nearly equal in value, but the Aces are not counted for reasons you've already read. So the important large cards are those with a value of 10: the 10s, Jacks, Queens, and Kings. No other cards need be kept track of in the basic count.

To become a feared card counter, all you need do is keep track of the large and small cards using the Hi-Opt I counting system. Every time you see a small card (3, 4, 5, 6) out of the deck, count it as a plus one (+1). Count each 10-value card you see as a minus one (−1). These increments up or down are combined to give you the Hi-Opt I count. The combination rule is that each +1 cancels out each −1 as you are counting. For example, if two small cards came out of the deck, your net count would be +2 (+1 added to +1). If the next card was a high card, your net count would be +1 (+2 minus 1). Whenever your net count is plus, you should place a larger bet on the next hand because you have the advantage. When your net count is 0 or negative, bet your minimum wager.

The Hi-Opt I count is shown in this table. First, make certain you understand which cards count +1, 0, and −1. Then examine the practice-card combinations. If you don't understand how the net counts were derived, ask someone to help you. You *must* understand this table to know the Hi-Opt I counting system. There are three different ways you may keep track of the count and wager, presented here in increasing difficulty and accuracy. All assume that you play the hands according to Basic Strategy.

PLUS-COUNT WAGERING

Plus-count wagering can be used when you are first counting in casino play, or when you are having trouble remembering the count while playing. With plus-count wagering, you bet more when there is *any* positive count from hand to hand. The procedure is to count the cards in play starting with a 0 count for each

HI–OPT I CARD COUNT

CARD VALUE: 2   3   4   5   6   7   8   9   10   Ace
POINT COUNT: 0 +1 +1 +1 +1   0   0   0   −1   0

PRACTICE CARD COMBINATIONS

CARDS		NET COUNT	CARDS		NET COUNT	CARDS		NET COUNT
2,3	=	+1	2,3,4	=	+2	2,3,4,5	=	+3
3,4	=	+2	3,4,5	=	+3	3,4,5,6	=	+4
4,5	=	+2	4,5,6	=	+3	4,5,6,7	=	+3
5,6	=	+2	5,6,7	=	+2	5,6,7,8	=	+2
6,7	=	+1	6,7,8	=	+1	6,7,8,9	=	+1
7,8	=	0	7,8,9	=	0	7,8,9,10	=	−1
8,9	=	0	8,9,10	=	−1	8,9,10,A	=	−1
9,10	=	−1	9,10,A	=	−1	9,10,A,2	=	−1
10,A	=	−1	10,A,2	=	−1	10,10,A,A	=	−2
3,10	=	0	A,2,3	=	+1	10,10,3,4	=	0
4,10	=	0	A,3,4	=	+2	10,A,2,3	=	0
5,10	=	0	A,7,8	=	0	A,2,3,4	=	+2
6,10	=	0	2,7,8	=	0	10,10,10,A	=	−3

hand. This way you don't have to remember the count from hand to hand. If there is a plus count, then you bet more on the next hand. This is somewhat useful when you are playing at a table with three or more players.

There are two patterns in counting cards: during the hand and at the end of the hand. With the "during" pattern you count each card as you see it turned up. This way you have the accurate count at any point in time for the cards you have seen. The disadvantage is that you may sometimes get confused as to which cards you have not already counted and which should be skipped. This can easily happen when a player tosses his down cards on top of his hit cards after busting. You suddenly see a pile and can't remember which of them were up cards that you have already noted.

With the "end" pattern, you wait to count the cards until the round is complete, counting "during" only the cards that are in busted player hands (the dealer collects these before continuing to deal to the next player). This method of counting eliminates the confusion of which cards to count. The problem with counting the cards at the end of the hand is that you must count them quickly, as the dealer turns the hand over and scoops up the cards. It's easy to make a mistake counting this quickly. Another problem is in using the count to modify Basic Strategy (as you will learn to do in Chapter Eight). Without the current count, you will be making playing decisions based upon the condition of the deck many cards ago. With a full table, your count for playing strategy is likely to be dangerously inaccurate.

I suggest that you start with the "end" pattern for plus-count wagering. You can easily move to the "during" pattern as your ability keeping the Hi-Opt I grows and as your level of systems play requires a more accurate count.

The advantage of plus-count wagering is that you don't need to remember the count for the entire time between shuffles. This is less fatiguing and easiest to master. The disadvantage is that you will be betting inaccurately a significant portion of the time because you will be ignoring the results of previous hands. For example, if the first hand off a newly shuffled deck had resulted in a —3 count, and the second hand showed a +3 count, with plus-count betting you would bet heavier on the next hand because of the +3 count of the current hand. The actual net count at this point is 0 (+3 minus 3). You should be betting a minimum amount because you have no advantage. A much better betting method, and one that everyone can master with a little effort, is the running count.

RUNNING-COUNT WAGERING

The running count must be kept from the time the dealer begins after shuffling until he stops to reshuffle. Instead of starting with a 0 count for each hand, you start with a 0 count off the top of a shuffled deck and remember the count from hand to hand. This way you know *exactly* the relative number of large and small cards that have been put in play up to the next reshuffle.

With running-count wagering, the larger your plus count, the greater your advantage over the dealer. The simplest method is to bet the same number of chips as your running count. If the running count is 0 or negative, you should then make the minimum table bet.

Keeping the running count requires only a little more effort than observing a plus count. You count the same number of cards, so you make the same number of additions or subtractions, but you only need to remember the count obtained from the previous hand as your new starting point. This is a small price to pay for the accuracy of the running count. With a little casino experience, this can be done with slight memory work or by mechanical tricks (as you will see). In fact, many occasional players may decide to go no farther and use the Basic Strategy with a running-count-bet variation.

TRUE-COUNT WAGERING

The running count is fine for a single-deck game, but can be misleading in a multiple-deck game because it may overestimate your advantage. For example, the running count doesn't differentiate between a +6 count with a half deck remaining to be dealt or a +6 count with 2 decks left. Yet one is *4 times* better than the other for betting purposes! Here's why.

The +6 running count with half a deck remaining means that there are 6 more 10s than low cards left in the undealt 26 cards. Then there are 11 10s and 5 low cards remaining (assuming the normal mix of 0-value cards). Going back to the old 10-count strategy, the non-10s-to-10s ratio is 15:11 or 1.36. This is heavily in favor of the player (the more under 2.25 the better, remember?). The +6 running count with 2 decks remaining means that there are 6 more tens than low cards in the remaining 104 cards. Once again, assuming that the normal ratio of 0-value cards are present, there are 35 10s and 29 low cards. The non-10s-to-10s ratio is 69:35 or 1.97. While still under 2.25, this is much less favorable than 1.36.

By keeping a *true count,* these differences in advantage due to different undealt deck levels can be easily monitored. The *true count* is determined by dividing the running count by the number of decks remaining. This calculation gives you the "running count per deck," which is the correct value to use in sizing bets. In the example above, +6 ÷ 2 decks = +3 true count. In addition to being mathematically accurate, +3 is intuitively correct also. It stands to reason that having a certain excess of tens in two decks is only half as good as having the same excess of tens in a single deck. Thus, in multiple-deck games where the shuffle point is at more than one deck remaining, the true count will always be *less than* the running count. If you bet using the running count only, you will be overestimating your advantage. This is dangerous to your bankroll.

In the second part of the above example, $+6 \div \frac{1}{2}$ deck $= +12$ true count. This requires what the mathematicians call "division by a fraction." The algebra of it is:

$$\text{true count} = \frac{\text{running count}}{\text{No. of decks remaining}} = \frac{+6}{\frac{1}{2}} = +6 \times \frac{2}{1} = +12$$

Again, it stands to reason that an excess of 10s in half a deck is the same as twice that excess in a full deck. Thus, in a single-deck game where less than a full deck is remaining, the true-count number will always be *higher than* the running count. Betting the running count in multiple-deck games will cause you to wager more than your advantage merits. Betting based upon the running count in single-deck games will cause you to bet less than optimal in favorable situations. So instead of two $+6$ counts, we actually had true counts of $+3$ and $+12$, one *4 times* the other. This difference indicates the importance of learning to keep a true count.

PERCENT OF RUNNING AND TRUE COUNTS BETWEEN LIMITS FOR HI–OPT I (10,000 deals)

COUNT LIMITS	1 DECK		4 DECKS	
	RUNNING COUNT	TRUE COUNT	RUNNING COUNT	TRUE COUNT
AT 0	18.1%	17.9%	9.9%	22.4%
BETWEEN ±1	50.3	40.0	27.3	55.7
BETWEEN ±2	72.1	57.4	42.0	72.2
BETWEEN ±3	86.4	69.3	54.5	84.4
BETWEEN ±4	94.1	76.6	63.8	91.6
BETWEEN ±5	98.1	82.2	71.8	95.6
BETWEEN ±6	99.6	87.2	79.5	97.3
BETWEEN ±7	99.9	90.3	85.6	98.1
BETWEEN ±8	99.9+	92.6	90.1	98.7
BETWEEN ±9	99.9+	94.7	93.1	99.3
BETWEEN ±10 or more	100.0	100.0	100.0	100.0

The figures in this table show how great the error between running count and true count can be with the Hi-Opt I system. The figures were obtained from a computer simulation of 10,000 deals, relatively short by simulation standards but enough to give you an idea of the differences. Three quarters of the deck was dealt in the single-deck simulation before shuffling, and the 4-deck simulation was reshuffled with 1 deck remaining.

You can see in the single-deck game that the running count does indeed give lower values than the true count. Slightly over 98 per cent of all the running counts were between +5 and —5. Only 2 per cent of the time the running counts ranged outside of ±5. But the true count ranged outside ±5 17.8 per cent (100 per cent minus 82.2 per cent) of the time, showing that the true count generates higher betting numbers in the single-deck game.

The reverse is true in the 4-deck game. Once again taking the ±5 range, the running count was outside ±5 28.2 per cent, while only 4.4 per cent of the time was the true count outside the ±5 range. In the 4-deck game, the running count generates higher betting numbers than are justified by your advantage. So the true count must be used if you want to be completely accurate in your betting.

Examples of how to calculate the Hi-Opt I true count are shown in the following table. As in the Hi-Opt I card-count table, you *must* understand this table to compute correctly the true count for betting purposes. The calculations are shown in increasing accuracy of estimated remaining deck. As the table indicates, you always round off to the nearest whole number. True counts of X.5 *and over* are rounded *up; under* X.5 are rounded *down*. For example:

$$\frac{+6}{4 \text{ decks}} = 1.5 = +2 \text{ true count} \qquad \frac{+4}{3 \text{ decks}} = 1.33 = +1 \text{ true count}$$

For purposes of the division operation, the + or — sign can be ignored. All you need to do is carry the sign through the calculation so that you end with the same sign you began with. Once again, if you don't understand this table, get your calculator out and work the computations in decimal arithmetic or get someone who hasn't been away from algebra as long as you have to help you. Once you convert several running counts to true counts, you will see that it is not as difficult as it first appears.

TRUE-COUNT PRACTICE TABLE

Running Count	No. of Decks Remaining	True Count
+6	3	+2
−4	2	−2
+6	4	+2
−5	3	−2
+4	3	+1
−1	2	−1
+1	3	0
−5	2½	−2
+4	2½	+2
−7	1½	−5
+4	1⅔	+2
−5	3⅓	−2
+3	1¾	+2
−5	2¼	−2
+8	3¼	+2
−3	½	−6
+3	⅔	+5
−1	⅓	−3
+5	¼	+20
−4	¾	−5

SIZING YOUR BETS

If you can play according to Basic Strategy, can count the cards, and can compute the true count, then you know almost enough to be a complete Blackjack player. The final step is to use the Basic Strategy and true count to determine the size of your next bet. As you read earlier, betting according to the Kelly Criterion provides the most long-term profit with the least risk. You determine your advantage for the next hand and then bet that percentage of your bankroll. For example, if you know you have a 3 per cent advantage and your bankroll is $1,000, then you would bet $30 on the next hand. All you need to know is the relationship between the Basic Strategy expectation for the casino's rules, the current true count, and your advantage. You already know how to compute the Basic Strategy Expectation from Chapter Six. You have just learned how to keep the true count. Now you will see how to determine your advantage.

Few Blackjack counts have ever been directly tied to the player betting advantage. Thanks once again to Professor Peter A. Griffin, the Hi-Opt I provides another assist for the player. The formula you need is:

Player Advantage (in per cent) = Basic Strategy Expectation
+ .515 × True Count

The first insight this formula provides is that every increment in the Hi-Opt I true count is worth approximately .5 per cent (.515) to the player. When the true count is +2, you have gained about 1 per cent *relative to* the dealer. The formula also takes into account that the rules variations from casino to casino change your *absolute* advantage over the dealer. For example, the Basic Strategy Expectations (BSE) for various casinos are:

BSE =   .17%   Caesar's single-deck
BSE =   0%   Stardust single-deck
BSE = −.19%   Las Vegas downtown single-deck
BSE = −.34%   MGM Grand (Las Vegas) four-deck

The exact advantage with a +2 true count at Caesar's is:

Player Advantage = .17 + .515 × 2 = +1.2 per cent

The exact advantage with a +2 true count at the MGM Grand in Las Vegas is:

Player Advantage = −.34 + .515 × 2 = .69 per cent

Adhering strictly to the Kelly Criterion, with a $1,000 bankroll you would wager $12 on the next hand at Caesar's Palace and $7.00 in the same situation at the MGM Grand across the street. This betting approach will net you the greatest winnings with the least amount of risk (using the above formula to determine bet size, it is safe to generalize that you should always bet your minimum if the count is negative or 0). If this method of winning at Blackjack—counting, computing the true count, calculating the advantage, and betting that portion of your bankroll—seems too

complicated a job, take heart. You'll see how easy it is to learn in
a coming section. Until then, here is another reason why counting
is so valuable.

THE INSURANCE BET

If you learned your Basic Strategy, then you know that "Insurance" is a bet for philanthropists. You're better off giving your
money to a college; they may name something other than the
team mascot after you. For the counter, though, the insurance bet
is a winning opportunity worth attention because it is so easy.
The only comparison of how well various count systems identify
the proper insurance play (insurance efficiency) is once again
provided by the ever-busy Professor Griffin. He computed the
correlation between the correct insurance play and the play indicated by the count for several systems:

Count System	Correlation
10 count	1.00
Hi-Opt I	.85
Braun + −	.79
Ita	.72

The 10-count system will identify each and every insurance bet
accurately since it keeps track of the non-10s-to-10s ratio. Any
time this ratio is under 2.00, insurance is warranted. While the
Hi-Opt I count is not perfect for insurance, it identifies almost all
of the proper insurance plays better than two other common systems. You should insure 1 in 73 hands (once every 5.6 chances)
in 4-deck games, and 1 in 44 (once every 3.4 chances) in single-
deck games. The insurance rules will add .12 per cent to your advantage with flat betting in a single-deck game (only .035 per
cent for 4 decks), more if you are ranging your bets.

Take Insurance If:

True count is greater than or equal to +2 (single deck)
True count is greater than or equal to +3 (multiple decks)

Correct insurance play is another edge over the casino. I was playing at a downtown Las Vegas casino when the true count creeped up to +6. The two other players at the table were ahead and we were all having a good time talking to Sally, the cordial dealer. I had been winning enough that I was disguising my play whenever the pit boss came over. The next hand after the +6 count left me with a stiff and Sally with an Ace up. She asked for insurance and after a short exchange of doubt between the other two, everyone at the table took it.

Sally turned over a 10 after peeking and said, "Yeah, insurance was a good bet because there were so many 10s left in the deck." She looked at me with a smile and started to gather up the cards. I had been tipping so she had taken no countermeasures, but it was obvious she was counting or at least following both me and the flow of the cards in the single-deck game. We each knew for certain that the insurance bet was a good one because of our ability to track the cards. So will you when you learn to count.

THE ACE SIDE COUNT

As you saw in the section "Choosing a System," there are improvements in performance of the Hi-Opt I from keeping an Ace side count in addition to the running count. *This is an advanced technique and shouldn't be tried until you have totally mastered counting with the Hi-Opt I.* It will take a bit of extra work to keep a separate count of Aces, but the Ace adjustment will add further to your advantage over the house.

The Ace acts as a high card for betting purposes and a low card for playing decisions (except in certain double-down situations). As with 10s, the more Aces that are left in the deck the better off you are. You should expect to see one Ace for each quarter of a deck dealt. The general rule is that for each *extra* Ace that is *left in* the deck, you add +1 to the *running count* for betting purposes. Conversely, you add a −1 for every *extra* Ace that is *out of* the deck. Notice that you add these numbers to the *running count*. This means that an Ace adjustment can be used in either running-count *or* true-count wagering.

For example, you have just sat down at a single-deck game and played two hands. No Aces came out. Let's further assume that the Hi-Opt I running count is 0 at this point. Without the Ace side count, you would believe this to be an even game where you have no advantage. However, since there is an extra Ace in the deck (four Aces left with about three quarters of the deck remaining), you have a slight advantage. Your running count is now +1 and your true count is also approximately +1. You could make a larger-than-minimum bet.

Now suppose that you have sat down at a table with two other players. The dealer reshuffles at the sight of a well-heeled player such as yourself and begins the round. You and your two playing companions all pull Blackjacks while the dealer busts with a 2,3,5,6,9. What is the current-count situation? You count the dealer's cards and get a +3. The three player Aces count 0 and the three 10s count −3 for a running count of 0. You appear to have an even game once again. Wrong. You have been keeping an Ace side count and realize that three of the four Aces have been played while only a little under a quarter of the deck has been dealt. The deck is proportionately short two Aces. Therefore your running count is −2 and your true count is rounded to −3. Your "break-even" situation was really a case where the dealer had the advantage.

The Ace adjustment is somewhat harder to compute in a multiple-deck game than in a single-deck game. With 4 decks, there are 16 Aces to count instead of 4. You will generally see about 12 Aces before the shoe is shuffled, so your side count must start higher and be remembered longer. In addition, the Ace excess/shortage situation is harder to compute. If 2½ decks are remaining, then you must know quickly that an Ace count over 10 gives you an excess. Similarly, with 1¾ decks the base number is 7; with 3¼ decks the base is 13.

Since you always need to know the number of Aces left in the deck, and for purposes of keeping the true count, you always must determine how much of the deck is left, the easiest way to keep an Ace side count is to count backward. In a single-deck game, start at 4 and subtract 1 for each Ace you see played. In a 4-deck game, you would start at 16; 2 decks at 8, etc. If you count upward starting at 0 you will have to make an extra mental step to determine the amount of deck that has been *played*. Since the true-count computation uses the amount of deck that is *left,* you have information that is of no further use to you. Count backward and save the additional effort.

HOW TO LEARN AND IMPLEMENT THE HI-OPT I COUNT

If you are like many of my students, at this point you may be thinking, "Who is this guy kidding? I'd have to be a cross between HAL the computer and Mr. Spock from *Star Trek* to do all this while short-skirted ladies are plying me with booze and pit bosses are eyeing me with suspicion." I don't blame you if you feel this way because you've only seen the "what" and not the "how" of counting.

I liken learning to count with the Hi-Opt I count to learning to type ten to twenty words per minute. If you have ever had a typing class, then you remember feeling at the start, "There is no way this will ever be faster than writing." Yet at some point you quit thinking about the details, and the words started appearing on the page. Once the keys are learned, *anyone* can manage ten to twenty words per minute with a little practice. If you have never had a typing class, then you know the above feeling of disbelief when typing with your hunt-and-peck system. Yet you *know* you could learn to type because you've seen too many slow burners learn it with ease.

Blackjack is much the same. You've got to go from your hunt-and-peck method of play to Basic Strategy and counting cards if you want to win. It's far easier to do than learning to type. It also pays a lot more than typing once you master it. And unless you work for a brewery, you can't drink for free while you're at it. In my memory classes, I've taught every imaginable type of person to count. While the amount of time it takes to get up to casino speeds has varied, not one has ever said, "I can't do it" or "I don't understand how to count." *Anyone* can learn to play the important part of Basic Strategy and use at least a plus count. Even you. Here is how you can master everything in this chapter:

1. Learn the Hi-Opt I Values

Go back and review the Hi-Opt I card-count table. Go through the practice-card combinations until the relationship between the cards and the net count becomes boringly obvious. You want to get to the point where if one of your friends walked up to you on the street and said, "3," you would respond, "+1" without breaking stride.

Next get a comfortably used deck of cards. Stay away from brand-new decks or cards with that hard plastic coating because they will be too difficult to handle without distraction. We're working on the mental effort here, not the manual one. Check to make certain all the cards are in the deck. I'll never forget a student who came to me in exasperation because he could keep the right count only about 20 per cent of the time. This is the normal error rate, so when he told me he kept coming up plus, I checked the deck. Sure enough, his deck was missing the Jack of Clubs (the late Lawrence Revere told me he would remove a card from his students' practice deck to keep them coming back for more lessons). You've heard of playing without a full deck? Don't let people say that about you.

Now find a place where you can get some uninterrupted quiet for at least twenty minutes. It's important that this first session be a good one because the habits you start with will likely carry into the casino. If you are heavily distracted, you're not going to get the positive start that you need. If you are a night person, begin this after everyone is in bed. Day people, get away from the phone or other uncontrolled interruptions. If you have to, sneak away to the library or find an empty office and hide there. Mothers, shove the kids off on someone and tell them you're working on a business venture. That will keep them guessing and couldn't be more accurate.

Once you are in your retreat, here's what to do. Begin going through the deck one card at a time keeping a running count. This takes concentration, so you can see why I wanted you to have a good place to work. Go very slowly, checking back with the card-count table if you are having trouble remembering whether or not a certain card should be counted. Look at every single card in the deck. The Hi-Opt I is what is called a "balanced count," so at the end, your running count of the deck should be 0 (sixteen tens and sixteen low cards). If your count does not equal 0 and the deck is complete, you have made an error. Don't worry about it. Shuffle, cut the deck, and go through it again more slowly. Do this until you get a 0 count at the end.

From now on you will start keeping track of your result each time you go through the deck. Don't try to deal Blackjack and don't try to increase your speed. Keep looking at the deck card by card in a steady pattern. Speed and play will come later. What you are striving for at this point is accuracy. At the end of each run-through, mark whether or not you end on 0. Quit after a half hour. That's about all the steady counting the average person can take before blanking out.

Start carrying the deck of cards with you. Anytime you have a few minutes, pull out the deck and start counting. Instead of being stuck reading *Family Mouth Hygiene* at the dentist's office, you can work on your game. Any idle time can be used to solidify your lock on the Hi-Opt I. Keep this practice up until you achieve 80 per cent accuracy at the end of the deck—that is, until you end up with a 0 count four out of five times. I've seen some people with a lot of card sense do this immediately; others take a few weeks of on-and-off practice.

At this point you are ready to begin building your speed. Time yourself at the speed you've been practicing. This will be your base time. When you practice, keep trying to beat it. Don't go so fast that you sacrifice accuracy. When you can beat your old base time with at least 80 per cent accuracy, change the base time. First shoot for about fifty seconds, or a card a second. When you can get down to thirty seconds for the deck, there won't be a game in the world you can't keep up with. With practice, it's reasonable that you can count the cards as fast as you can go through the deck, your mind working much faster than your fingers.

Next go through the deck two cards at a time, then three, then four. This is more like the way you will count at the Blackjack table. You tend to see clumps of cards with seconds of time in between. The clumps are easier to count because often high and low cards cancel each other out and don't affect your running count.

Going through the deck in clumps makes it easier for you to break thirty seconds.

When counting a single deck quickly is a snap no matter how many cards at a time you examine, then move on to four decks. Start the process over. Go through the deck one card at a time, etc., always keeping in mind the 80 per cent accuracy requirement. When you can do four decks in under 2½ minutes, go for 100 per cent accuracy. Then you will have mastered the Hi-Opt I count forever. Like riding a bike, you will have a skill you will never forget. If you don't play regularly, then a little drill will be all that's needed to work your speed up before your next trip to the casino.

You can be doing this step while you are learning the Basic Strategy. The Basic Strategy takes longer to learn than the Hi-Opt I count, but shouldn't hold up your becoming a winning player. After you have learned the first six rules of the four-deck rule table in Chapter Six, you will know how to play enough hands so that you can begin to practice playing and counting while you finish memorizing the complete Basic Strategy.

2. Implement Plus-count Wagering

You are now ready to begin playing and counting. To ease the transition from merely going through the deck to acting the part of the dealer and the player, start with only plus-count wagering. Deal two player hands and a dealer hand from a single deck so that you will see enough cards to count reasonably for the next bet. Bet one unit on each hand when the count is +1 or lower and, ten units when the count is +2 or higher. Keep track of the results. You shouldn't see any great winnings. You may see none at all mainly because you will see a high-plus betting situation so infrequently.

The real value of this exercise is to get you used to counting and dealing. A side benefit is that you learn to add the value of the hands, both dealer and player, more quickly. You will find your dealing and Basic Strategy decisions getting faster and faster. In fact, learning to count is a great way to master the Basic Strategy strictly because of the number of practice hands you work through.

3. Implement Running-count Wagering

When you are comfortable with dealing and counting each hand, begin carrying the previous hand's count over for the running count. Wager the same way, one unit or ten units, depending upon the count. Deal the last card out and check to see if your count is 0. Since you are nearly ready for casino play, try to achieve complete accuracy. If you are making too many errors, stop playing whether you want to or not. This is the same discipline you must impose on yourself in the casino. The time to learn when to quit is *now*.

Keep track of your wins and losses from session to session. Play until you are at least five hundred units ahead. That should convince you that counting with Hi-Opt I is a winning system. Up to this point, it may seem like you have put in a lot of work—and you may have. A few hours of practice or even a few months of practice is a very small price to pay for learning how to obtain a permanent advantage over the casino. Such knowledge has earned me, my former students, and others millions of dollars. This knowledge is not too difficult to implement in relation to the reward.

When I was first learning to count cards, I didn't have the opportunity for casino play until I had reached this stage of expertise. I've said you are ready for casino play, yet you may wonder how good you really are. My first trip as a card counter to a casino was a fairly normal experience based upon my conversations with hundreds of players.

I decided to start in one of the downtown Las Vegas casinos where I could bet one-dollar minimums and range from one to four dollars without attracting any attention. I felt this would allow me a fair test of counting. I was very concerned about my ability to track the cards in an actual game. I had my single-deck count-through down to twenty-five seconds from dedicated practice and fear of the unknown. I knew the Basic Strategy comfortably and had been playing practice hands until I was bored with winning on paper. I wanted to walk out with a thicker wallet.

My first hour of casino counting was quite an experience. I had the usual problems of the novice, forgetting the count between hands (nothing to do but start over at 0), missing cards, forgetting which cards I counted, and plain distraction in the casino. But the second hour was quite different.

There's something wonderfully special about the first time you do anything. The first time up on skis, the first breath of SCUBA air under water, the first childbirth, whatever. Playing Blackjack is no different. After about an hour, I had finally worked out the mechanical problems of what approach to counting worked best for me. The initial excitement and nervousness had worn off. I found my counting rhythm. As hand after hand came off the top of the deck, I began to get a tremendous surge of feeling. For the first time in my life I truly understood the game and what was happening.

It was almost as if I were in control of the game. I could watch the other players breaking Basic Strategy rules and losing their money. I could tell who the good and the bad players were after a few minutes. More importantly, I had a *feel* for the deck. Oh I never knew exactly what card was coming out next (nor do I now), but I knew what was likely to happen. When somebody was due a 10 because the count was so high plus, more often than not they got it. Instead of a disappointing mystery, Blackjack had become a fascinating ebb and flow of controlled fortune.

I had started late that night with a whopping twenty-dollar stake. Playing nearly all night on glands alone, I finished with eighty dollars. This didn't make me a marked man with the casino, I'll admit. But for someone who had always measured the success of my playing sessions by how long it took to lose all my stake, it was a triumph beyond imagination. I knew the mathematics of counting were right, but to see the results in U.S. currency is another matter.

So don't expect instant success when you first start counting in the casino. There will be an adjustment period of varying length depending upon your style of play and current skill. But when it clicks, you'll know it. And that's what this book is all about.

4. *Implement True-count Wagering*

You will find that keeping the running count and playing according to the Basic Strategy will not take your total attention as you become more experienced in the casino. You will find it fairly easy to watch people, eavesdrop on conversations, and relax as you play. When this happens, it is time to improve your play by keeping the true count.

To calculate the true count you must learn how to size the remaining deck accurately. In a single-deck game, this is not too difficult. The ideal way is to count how many cards have been put in play and then determine what per cent of the deck remains. A more practical method that doesn't require keeping this separate count involves estimating the amount of deck remaining to the nearest fraction. Typically this is halves or fourths.

Get three decks of cards and create four stacks containing thirteen, twenty-six, thirty-nine, and fifty-two cards. Put them next to each other. What you are doing here is becoming familiar with the relationship between deck thickness and number of cards. Look at the stacks from all angles, front and side, that might be used when sitting at the Blackjack table. Now take a fourth deck and try to cut off thirteen cards just by grabbing the proper thickness. Count the cards and see how you did. Even up the deck and try again. You should get to the point where you can consistently cut off between eleven and fifteen cards. Next try it with twenty-six cards. Your margin here should be twenty-three to twenty-nine cards. Finally put two decks together and try for thirty-nine cards. A three-card error one way or the other is acceptable. When you can make these cuts consistently within the limits, then you know how to estimate the remaining single deck by sight. Get a deck right now and try it. It's much easier than you think.

You want to build up the same ability for four decks, only not to such accuracy. The normal player estimates the remaining deck to the nearest whole deck, the good player to the nearest half deck. Very few players can accurately guess four decks to the nearest quarter deck. Most players who want that type of accuracy prefer keeping a separate count of the exact number of cards played. You can take a four-deck stack and cut it off at various levels to get the visual "feel" for the number of cards remaining.

The accuracy you want with four decks is limited by how well you can handle the division step. It doesn't make sense to guess the remaining cards to the nearest quarter of a deck if you can't divide by 3¼ properly. Start with adjusting to the nearest whole deck and get more accuracy only if you feel you need it. Since you are rounding to the nearest whole true-count number, there is some approximation built in anyway. In actual casino play, perfect true-count calculation is nowhere near as important as the casino playing conditions, such as how much the house will let you range your bets.

With true-count wagering, you compute the true count only once per hand, just before you place your bet. The ideal time for this is when all the hands have been completed and you have seen every card that has been put in play (except possibly the burn card). The only reason you may not want to wait to place your bet is discussed in Chapter Ten. The casinos know that the counter wants to see every card before betting and will watch for anyone who consistently waits to place the next bet. Because of this, you may wish to vary when you place your bet, even if it means not having a complete count. Nonetheless, you will still only need to calculate the true count once per bet. Since it's usually done between hands, when you aren't counting, this refinement can be done during an idle moment in your counting effort.

Once you are adjusting the running count to the true count, you will have better betting information. Because the casino won't let you bet the one-unit-to-ten-unit range you practiced with, you will have to let your bets range more gradually. A simple method is to bet the same number of chips as your true count. If your true count is less than or equal to 0, you can bet the table minimum. If you are under scrutiny from the pit bosses, then you will have to resort to more sophisticated betting techniques, such as those in Chapter Ten.

5. Implement Kelly Criterion Wagering

If you are not forced to disguise your bets as shown in Chapter Ten, the best betting approach is the Kelly Criterion. This adds an addition and another division operation at the end of the true-count division. It also requires that you familiarize yourself with the effects of the rules-variation table in Chapter 6. These tell you how much each playing option affects the Basic Strategy Expectation (BSE). To know your exact per cent advantage, you must use Griffin's formula for the Hi-Opt I. In casino play, you can approximate it by dividing the true count by 2 and adding the result to the BSE. So when you walk into a new casino, you either know the rules beforehand and can come with the BSE in mind, or you can quiz the dealer and estimate it on the spot.

Knowing your bankroll and your advantage with each upcoming hand, you then multiply these and determine your next bet. I started out with a bankroll of two hundred dollars and very small bets. My bankroll is now many hundred times that and still growing. As your winnings accumulate, your bankroll will grow too. And while your overall advantage doesn't change, the bigger your bankroll, the bigger your bets, and the more money you will win. I now can win as much in one sitting as I used to win in one trip because my wagers are correspondingly bigger.

6. Keep an Ace Side Count

This final step is for the advanced player. Try this only when you can play the Basic Strategy error-free in the casino and *comfortably* keep the count without missing cards. Keeping an Ace side count requires more effort. So if you don't have enough spare time in the basic Hi-Opt I count, then trying to add an Ace count will be disastrous. What you eventually want is to be able to count, keep the Ace side count, play with Basic Strategy, and still be able to talk to the dealer. This can be done with practice, but only by players who have mastered the first four steps.

If you implement everything in this chapter, here is what you will be doing at the table:

CONTINUOUSLY:
1. Keep the running count
2. Keep an Ace side count (optional)

ONCE EVERY HAND:
3. Adjust the running count for the Ace side count (optional)
4. Estimate the size of the remaining deck
5. Calculate the true count
6. Divide the true count by 2 and add the result to the BSE
7. Multiply the result of No. 6 by your bankroll
8. Place your bet

Like any other repetitive task, step Nos. 3 through 8 can be done in a few seconds with practice. The same person who says he can't master counting can quickly determine tolerances off a blueprint. A person who says she couldn't guess the number of holes in a doughnut can estimate the grocery bill within two dollars by merely glancing at the full basket. With practice, anything is possible for anyone. And to start winning, all you need to do are step Nos. 1 and 8, omitting everything in between. Those can be added as you become a better player. Still, if you're having trouble with step No. 1, here's more help.

COUNTING AIDS

Even after going through the above steps to learn the running count, some of my students complain that they have trouble remembering the count from hand to hand. What's happening is that their short-term memory isn't being used properly or they are too easily distracted. For some it's a confidence problem. They want a crutch so that they don't have to depend purely on their own mental skill. Whatever your reason, there are a number of tricks for keeping the count with less mental effort.

One of the most ingenious of these is a little plastic wheel put out by a small company in Florida. The wheel is mounted in a little case much like an umpire's counter. There is an index mark that can be felt, and the numbers are embossed on the wheel in Braille. The number ascends the farther you go in either direction from the index mark. You can see what it is meant to do.

At the beginning of a deal, you center the index mark over a counting window. You then click the wheel forward or backward, depending upon whether you see low or high cards. When it is time to bet, you feel the number over the counting window and search for the location of the index mark to see if the number is plus or minus. This way you don't need to keep the actual number in your head; it is always "displayed" on the wheel.

My wheel worked perfectly in practice. After carrying it around for a few hours and playing with it while watching TV, the Braille numbers were easy to "read" with the thumb. The problem was that the wheel I had, clicked noticeably and had a squeak as I turned it. Also, my hand would have to be in my pocket or under the table constantly. This was obvious enough that I didn't want to try it in the casino. Also, with my first trip, I found that the running count could be kept easily without the wheel.

Other gimmicks for keeping the count all operate on this same principle—that is, you keep the count mechanically, then "read" the result at bet time. One of the best sources for these techniques comes from the book *21 Counting Methods to Beat 21* by Professor Koko Ita and published by the Gambler's Book Club. His methods can be used without drawing attention to yourself in the casino. Some of the best of these are:

CHIP COUNT

Most players are continually fooling with their chips, stacking and restacking them. If you do this seemingly carelessly and continuously (even between hands), you won't attract any undue attention. You might start with a single stack of ten chips, remove one with each ten you see, and add one with each small card you count. You could have two stacks, one for a plus count and one for a minus count, switching chips from stack to stack as the count changes. The approaches are endless, so figure out a method that works best for you.

The chip count is also an excellent way to keep the Ace side count. You might keep the running count in your head and use chips for the Ace. In a single-deck game, you can start out with a stack of four chips and remove one chip every time you see an Ace. When it comes time to make a bet, you can check the chips left in the stack and make the proper adjustment. This way you still need to remember only one number, yet you have increased the accuracy of your count.

POSITION COUNT

The plastic wheel described above is a good example of a position-count aid. Anytime you can have an object where there is an index position and you can determine how many positions you are ahead of or behind the index position, you can use this method. For example, you could have etch marks on the side of your lighter, the index mark "0" being deeper and in the center. With the count you would move up and down the lighter with your fingernail, going from notch to notch. You can use almost anything that has "positions"—the rivets on your mod blue jeans, a book of matches, placing your tongue behind a certain tooth, or moving your thumb back and forth along your fingers. Ita even suggests strapping a string of beads under your pants or dress just above the knee. The index bead is larger than the others. You merely move your finger left or right along the string and then count/feel the distance from the index bead. Once again, the list is limited only by your imagination.

CLOCK COUNT

We are all familiar with the position of the numbers on the face of a clock or watch. By positioning an item toward one of the twelve hours, you can track up to ±5 with a single item and ±11 with two. A chip can easily be used for this. Chips all have elaborate designs that clearly indicate what direction is up. A single chip can track up to ±5 by counting the straight-up twelve-o'clock position as "0." Rotating the chip to face one o'clock would represent +1; eleven o'clock would represent −1. Since +6 and −6 would be the same position, you could only go up to ±5 without confusion.

As you can see from the earlier table, two chips counting up to 11 each would give you capacity enough for nearly all the running-count situations you will encounter. One chip would be used for the negative numbers and one for the positive. Once again, the limit is ±11 because the twelfth position would correspond to zero and you wouldn't know which was correct.

The clock position can be used with any number of items common at the Blackjack table. You can read the placement of your cigarette in the ashtray, the position of your straw or stirrer in your glass or lying on the table, the direction your lighter points or where your finger is placed on a chip. In fact, any item that has a "top" can be used. The more common it is to the game and the more casual your handling of it is, the better off you will be.

Go ahead and use any of these tricks if they help you. Use them as long as you need them, but don't become dependent upon them. They are temporary crutches until you can count and remember unassisted. There is a tendency to stop trying to play without a counting aid. As long as you need aids for your initial count, you will have trouble moving on to better play. And better play means more winnings.

A WORD OF WARNING TO THE INEXPERIENCED

If you run to the nearest casino after reading this chapter without having also read Chapter Ten, then you run the risk of getting barred as one of a category of people the casinos fear most: card counters. It may seem ridiculous that a corporation with millions of dollars in cash and property assets should fear you, but such is the power of your current knowledge. Knowledge is power.

If you are asked to leave a casino, here is what you should do: LEAVE THE CASINO. Don't go with a guilty, "You got me!" attitude. Protest your innocence and ignorance but don't put up a fight. The hassle and legal problems you can cause for yourself aren't worth it. In most locations, there are many other casinos in which to play. It doesn't pay to play anywhere you're not wanted, rightfully or not. The casinos also realize that they sometimes bar noncounters accidentally and may drop the matter if given time to forget who you are.

As I instructed earlier, you should get all the details you can of the incident. Get the day, time, casino, table, dealer's name, and pit boss's name or description before you go. There have been lawsuits generated from being barred, and you may want the data later. For more information on the legal status of barring counters, see Chapter Twelve.

Isn't it amazing what a little knowledge will do to change your thinking? At the start of this book you were wondering how to keep from losing your shirt in the casino. Now you're worrying about how to keep from losing your privilege to play. Up to now, you only have half the picture. Chapter Eight will show you how to use your count information to vary the Basic Strategy to your advantage. With this step you will be a fully qualified counter.

EIGHT

Professional Casino Play: Hi-Opt I Play Strategy

Luck, that's when preparation and opportunity meet.

PIERRE TRUDEAU

It's truly amazing how quickly your ego can go from the heights of success to Death Valley. I was playing at a table once with a lovely older couple in their sixties who gave me one of the nicest compliments I have ever received at the tables. In watching them play I saw they used a fairly accurate Basic Strategy, which made the compliment mean even more.

My bet was twenty dollars for this hand and I drew 2,2 versus the dealer's 3 up card. Doubling was not allowed after splitting, so the Basic Strategy dictated that I hit the hand. As you will soon see, Basic Strategy can be improved upon. Since the count was +1, I followed the Hi-Opt I Play Strategy and split the hand for another twenty-dollar bet. As the turn of the cards would have it, I pulled a 10 on each 2 and was forced to stand. The couple groaned for me and resolved their hands.

I was groaning even more because not only had I doubled my money at risk, but also I had changed the count from an advantageous plus to a minus. To my great relief, the dealer proceeded to bust his hand. I nearly wrenched my arm trying to pat my back and thought to myself, "That was well played." The couple murmured approvingly. The man turned to me and said, "An expert couldn't have played it better."

I modestly thanked the man for his comment, but inside I responded as Lancelot had in the musical *Camelot, "C'est Moi!"* The man was absolutely right. An expert couldn't have played it better because an expert *had* played the hand. And that is what this book, and in particular, this chapter, is about: turning you into the same caliber of Blackjack expert.

Glowing from my small success and large ego stroke, I was now ripe for a quick trip to Death Valley. Later on in the same trip (but not that same session), I was playing at a one-deck table with one other man. He was a better player than the couple —he was following the accurate Basic Strategy perfectly. But he wasn't counting, since his bets didn't follow the condition of the deck.

He was watching me carefully because I seemed to make unusual plays and yet was doing all right. After I hit a hard 15 versus a dealer 10 up, the man became very concerned. He started making innocent comments on following hands I played: "Gee, that would be a good hand to double," or "Too bad you have to stand on a stiff like that."

I find it irritating when people tell me how to play my cards, so I told him quietly, "I appreciate the help you're trying to give me, but I prefer to play my cards on my own." That shut him up for a while, but then I stood on an 8,8 versus a dealer 10 instead of splitting the pair. This was too much for the man at the table and he started up his "helpful" commentary again. I believe everybody deserves one straightforward request before getting singed. It was now singe time.

I happened to glance at the dealer and saw that he was having great fun watching the two of us. Since there was no heat at the table, I didn't want to leave, but I wanted to be left alone. I turned to the player and told him, "Look, sport, as long as I'm betting my money, I intend to play the hands the way I see fit. I'll be more than happy to play my cards any way you see fit if you want to start betting for me. Do you understand?"

The man gave a start, then said, "So toss your money away like a jerk. I don't give a damn!" He quickly stood up and stomped off. I looked up at the dealer and saw him laughing at both of us. I told him, "Argh!" and put my bet out to continue what was once again a pleasant session.

So you can go from apparent expert to jerk in one trip with the Hi-Opt I system. Yet what has actually happened so far in this book is that you have gone *toward* the expert category instead of away from it. With the information in this chapter, you will be able to use the full application of the Hi-Opt I system. It is possible that your play can be so much more knowledgeable that your decisions will be totally beyond the understanding of any other player at the table.

HOW GOOD IS THE HI-OPT I SYSTEM?

I've been making a lot of promises so far that the Hi-Opt I system is the most simple powerful system available today. You saw a hint of this from Professor Griffin's figures in Chapter Seven. Although the Hi-Opt I system is not the very highest rated in either betting correlation or playing efficiency, it is near the top in both categories.

The definitive study of comparative systems performance was first published by Julian Braun in 1974 in his paper "The Development and Analysis of Winning Strategies for the Casino Game of Blackjack." The paper was updated in 1975, and material has been added since for inclusion in this book. In fact, most of the information in this next section has been graciously provided by Braun or paraphrased from his paper. Braun's and Griffin's independent studies both confirm the power of the Hi-Opt I system.

The performance figures in the above table come from Braun's general-purpose simulation computer program for evaluating *any* point-count system. The program produces a series of random "shuffles" that are repeatable, enabling different systems to be tested with the same "random" hands. The program allows Braun to specify the shuffle point, to vary the rules, to use up to four decks, and to have as many as four players against the dealer. The simulations in this table were for a single-deck game with a shuffle point at one-fourth deck remaining, Las Vegas Strip rules with no double after split, and head-on play versus the dealer. Head-on play was chosen to make the one-to-one systems comparisons more valid (extra players complicate the comparison).

To evaluate the effects of a wider betting range, a simple approach was used. The player bet either one unit or "n" units. On

COMPARATIVE SYSTEMS PERFORMANCE.

SYSTEM	LEVEL	NUMBER OF VALUES COUNTED	PLAYING EFFICIENCY	BETTING CORRELATION	PERCENT ADVANTAGE BETTING RANGES		
					FLAT	1 – 4	1 – 8
Hi-Opt I	1	5	.615 (.635)	.86 (.96)	.8%	2.1%	2.8%
Revere APC – 73	4	8	.657	.91	.8	2.1	2.8
Revere Pt. Ct.	2	8	.527*	.98	.6	2.1	2.8
Braun + –	1	7	.510*	.95	.7	2.0	2.8
Gordon	1	5	.574	.83	.7	2.0	2.7
Revere APC – 71	4	9	.523*	.995	.6	2.0	2.7
Revere Adv. + –	1	7	.592	.86	.5	1.6	2.2
Roberts 10 – Count	1	–	.621	.71	.5	1.5	2.1
Hi-Opt II	2	7	.671	.90	.9	2.3	3.1

PLAYING RULES: 1 deck
no double after split
Las Vegas Strip rules
Head-on play

NOTES: (1) Figures with * show systems including Ace in high/low count.
(2) Figures in ( ) show value with Ace side count.

the chart, "1–4" means "bet one unit most of the time and bet four units when the count is sufficiently favorable." In practice, a player's bets would increase gradually, but this is impractical to program and would create distortions in the comparisons. The actual head-on play yield should be slightly higher than these results show. The important point in this table is to see the *relative* power of the various systems. You will see *exactly* how the Hi-Opt I system performs shortly.

The systems included in this table were not chosen arbitrarily. First, they represent most of the commonly known and heavily marketed systems. Second, they represent the widest number of systems Braun has studied for any particular set of rules and number of decks. Many of these systems are quite expensive, yet are inferior in performance to the Hi-Opt I system.

Some of the results were disputed. When Braun's paper was first published, Revere claimed that his systems were not tested fairly. He thought his advanced point count would fare better with a larger percentage of bets made at the higher level (Braun had determined that about 20 per cent of the bets should be at the "n" level). In fact, the more often bets were made at the maximum, the worse the Revere Advanced Point Count performed.

For a time, there was a flurry of articles, letters to the editor, and correspondence about the low figures for Roberts' 10 count. Roberts had gotten the impression that Braun's simulation was for only ten thousand hands. In fact, every figure in the table is the result of a one-million starting-hand simulation. Owing to pair splitting, somewhat more than one million hands were actually played for each simulation run. Even so, one million hands is not enough to obtain an *exact* result. Using statistics, Braun calculated that *all* the simulation results were accurate within ±.3 per cent; with a 95 per cent confidence level they were accurate within ±.2 per cent for flat betting.

As you can see from the table, there is a very small difference among the systems' performances. Except for the Hi-Opt II, which is a more complicated second-level system designed for the very serious player, the Hi-Opt I has the highest performance of the group. The surprise when Braun's figures first came out was that the Hi-Opt I outperformed complicated fourth-level strategies like the Revere Advanced Point Counts. Despite the finer gradation in valuing cards, their performance did not show this extra counting effort to be an advantage.

If you combine the high relative performance of the Hi-Opt I system with the fact that it has the lowest level and fewest cards to count, you can see that you are holding the most powerful, simple, and usable system available.

HI-OPT I PLAYING PERFORMANCE

Game	Shuffle Point	Flat	Betting % 1–4	1–8
1 deck	.75	.8	2.1	2.8
4 decks	.80	−.2	.5	1.1
6 decks	.80	−.3	.4	1.0

Rules Options			
Surrender	.12	.25	n/a
Ace side count	n/a	.2	n/a
Double down after split	.05	.1	.2

RULES: Las Vegas Strip
Head-on play

This table shows how the Hi-Opt I system performs in a variety of playing situations. You can be certain from the previous table that it will be the highest performer (except for the Hi-Opt II) of any other system. Notice the dramatic effect of playing in a four-deck game. By increasing the betting range, you can overcome some of the disadvantage. Yet your expected yield is less than half that of a single-deck game even with a relatively aggressive one-to-eight betting range.

The effect of four decks is to reduce your advantageous situations. Braun found that the maximum would be correctly bet only about 12 per cent of the time in a four-deck game versus approximately 20 per cent with a single deck. This causes the greatly reduced yield.

The benefits (where available) of various rules options or playing changes are also shown in this table. Surrender offers you the greatest increase in yield; keeping an Ace side count runs close behind. Playing where doubling is allowed after the split offers a small gain, much as it does with Basic Strategy.

The survey results reported in the next table, while not as scientific as a one-million-hand simulation, offer a further indication of the benefits of the Hi-Opt I system. In 1976, the International Blackjack Club polled its members not only for their number of winning and of losing sessions, but also for the system they used and number of decks encountered in each playing session. The survey results provide an experimental indication of the better yield *in actual play* of the Hi-Opt I and of the reduction in advantage of multiple decks.

INTERNATIONAL BLACKJACK CLUB SURVEY
OF COUNTERS (1976).

HI–OPT PLAYERS

ONE DECK			TWO DECKS			FOUR DECKS		
WON	LOST	% WON	WON	LOST	% WON	WON	LOST	% WON
456	260	63.7	67	49	57.7	268	205	56.6

PLAYERS USING OTHER STRATEGIES

ONE DECK			TWO DECKS			FOUR DECKS		
WON	LOST	% WON	WON	LOST	% WON	WON	LOST	% WON
585	441	57.0	107	83	56.3	503	421	54.4

HI–OPT PLAYERS AND OTHER PLAYERS COMBINED

ONE DECK			TWO DECKS			FOUR DECKS		
WON	LOST	% WON	WON	LOST	% WON	WON	LOST	% WON
1,041	701	59.7	174	132	56.8	771	626	55.2

You might be wondering at this point why you should go to any trouble and devote any time to achieving a 1 to 3 per cent advantage. I've added several zeroes to the amount of my bankroll more than four times over with such an advantage, so don't ignore this tremendous edge. Some European Roulette wheels offer a little over 2.5 per cent house advantage, but are a solid casino moneymaker. Certain Craps bets yield about 1.4 per cent to the tune of thousands of dollars daily. Your Blackjack advantage can do the same for you. But for a moment, let's talk about the other side.

You might next be wondering how anyone can go broke in a casino when the casino advantage is so slight. It would appear when you start out with a hundred-dollar bankroll making five-dollar bets that it would take forever to go broke, since 2 per cent of your bankroll is only two dollars. The problem with this line of reasoning is that you are not calculating your expected losses correctly. A house edge under 5 per cent can quickly and easily strip you of your money.

Using the bankroll as the basis for counting how much you can expect to lose is a mistake. Your losses depend upon how much you are *betting*, not how much you have in your pocket. You may be betting much more than your entire bankroll each *hour* at the Blackjack tables. Here is how: Let's assume that the table is not full, so that the dealer can deal fifty to one hundred hands per hour. If you are betting $5.00 per hand, this is $250 to $500 in bets made per hour. If you are ranging your bets at all, your average bet can easily be $10 per hand. The total of all the money you're putting in the betting square can be as high as $1,000 per hour with this fairly modest betting scheme. In this situation, a 2 per cent disadvantage means an average loss of $20 per hour.

In any casino game, don't confuse your per cent disadvantage with how much of your bankroll you will part with. The reason your actual dollar losses are a much higher portion of your bankroll than the casino edge would indicate is that you usually bet your playing bankroll several times over at a single sitting. Your losses are gone forever, your winnings are bet again, so that the house odds can work on them a second time, a third time, and so on. Finally, when your bankroll gets small enough, the normal fluctuations of losses versus wins finally wipe you out. This is why the casinos can make your life so comfortable, even pay you to come, on such a "small" advantage.

Now you know why the casino is happy with a 1 to 3 per cent advantage, and ecstatic about 5 per cent. There's a ton of cash to be harvested with those numbers. Well, you're in the casino game now, too. With the information in this chapter and the previous one, you can achieve a 1 to 3 per cent advantage over the house. And with that, everything that was working for the casino except for stockholders and a bankroll of millions is now working for you. Your bankroll is being bet over and over. Only instead of it getting smaller and smaller, it is getting larger and larger.

I sometimes think about a classic old horror movie called *The Blob*. This little blob of outer-space goop lunched on humans, absorbing them by oozing over them, "eating" person by person. With each victim it got a little larger. It started out as a handful of gunk on some poor farmer's arm, but at the end it was wiping out whole movie theaters at a time. Not too fast on its goo, it moved slowly but surely. At the end, the authorities couldn't kill it or stop it; they finally froze it and sent the blob to the Antarctic for safekeeping.

I've always admired the blob. Nameless, faceless, without a history, it was a total enigma cutting a swath through humanity. What a rags-to-riches story! The blob's only mistake was in being too greedy for victims. It's the same with your Blackjack play. With your advantage, you can find victim after victim willing to ply you with drinks and entertainment so that you will win from them. At first, they will gladly help you add to your bankroll. The bigger your bankroll gets, the more you can bet. The more you bet, the faster your bankroll grows. But if you get too greedy, like the blob the authorities will put you too on ice.

How good is the Hi-Opt I system? For combining ease of play with an amazingly high performance, it's the best. For providing a significant enough advantage to make applying it in the casino worthwhile it is good enough for the casino operators to insist you not use it there any longer. Betting your bankroll over and over, it is all you need to turn your original stake into a blob.

YOUR EXACT ADVANTAGE WITH HI-OPT I

As you saw in the previous chapter, to bet using the Kelly Crite-rion you must know the exact advantage with each hand. Part of this is based upon the Basic Strategy Expectation that the particu-lar casino rules provided, and part is based upon the true count for betting. Now there is a third factor that will affect your advan-tage—varying from the Basic Strategy playing rules.

You actually have quite a bit of useful playing information as a result of keeping the true count for betting purposes. This count information can be used in determining how to play certain hands in which the Basic Strategy decision provides only a borderline advantage. Take for example the situation of holding a hard 12 versus a dealer 3. Basic Strategy says you should hit in this situa-tion. Yet you know that if there are an excess of 10s left in the deck, you have a higher chance of busting. But if there are few 10s remaining, then you have a better chance of improving your hand. Since you know the relative number of 10s to low cards from the Hi-Opt I count, you can use this information to deter-mine what is the best play. If the true count is plus (more 10s in the deck), you might break Basic Strategy and *stand*. If the true count is 0 or minus (more low cards), you might hit.

Another such situation is whether or not to double a hard 8 versus a dealer 6. Here the Basic Strategy indicates to hit and not double. But if the deck is rich in 10s, then the dealer has a higher chance of busting and you have a higher chance of hitting to hard 18. As you will see in the coming tables, you should double 8 versus a dealer 6 on a true count of +2 or higher.

Peter Griffin has calculated the gain for varying Basic Strategy rules depending upon the true count. The relationship between the true count and your gain is shown in the following chart. The more the true count varies from 0 (the assumption of Basic Strat-egy), the more it benefits you to modify your play.

Gain from using Hi-Opt I strategy as related to true count

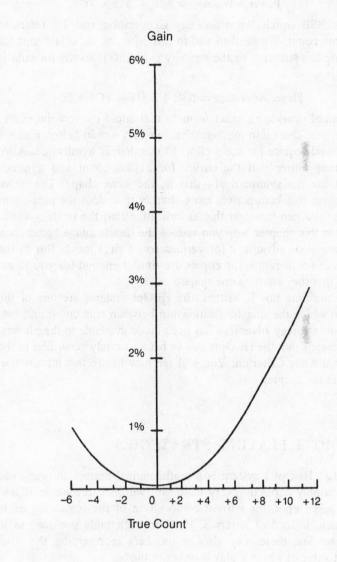

In Chapter Seven, the Hi-Opt I advantage was calculated by the formula:

$$\text{Player Advantage} = \text{BSE} + .515 \times \text{TC}$$

where BSE equals Basic Strategy Expectation and TC refers to the true count. We need to add to this equation an adjustment for varying the strategy, or the strategy gain (SG), so the formula is now:

$$\text{Player Advantage} = \text{BSE} + (.516 \times \text{TC}) + \text{SG}$$

I could provide an exact formula that could convert the curves in the gain chart into mathematics, but they would be too complicated and require far more effort to use than is worthwhile. Also, you may notice that the curves for a plus count and a minus count are not symmetrical—that is, the same shape. The curve for minus true counts rises more sharply than does the plus-count curve (you can interpret this as indicating that the strategy variations in this chapter help you reduce the disadvantage better than increase your advantage for various count situations). But in the ±6 true-count range, the curves are similar enough for you to assume that they are the same shape.

At the time this is written, the Hi-Opt systems are one of the few in which the specific relationship between true count and betting and strategy advantage has been made available to the players. This means that the Hi-Opts can be bet accurately according to the optimal Kelly Criterion. You will see how to use this information later in the chapter.

HI-OPT I PLAYING STRATEGIES

The full Hi-Opt I system is a mathematical marvel showing you how to play correctly every hand you will ever receive in Blackjack based upon the current composition of the remaining deck. As such, instead of letters S, H, D in each table position, as in Chapter Six, there may also be numbers representing the true-count value at which a play is or is not made.

HOW MUCH SHOULD YOU MEMORIZE?

If you are picturing each of the tables in Chapter Six with a number instead of a letter at every option and getting a little awed at this point, don't worry. The *full* Hi-Opt I system appears awesome at first, listing table values ranging from —19 to +26 in scores of positions. This can be too much for all but the most serious players with excellent memories.

The chance of having a true count at one of these extremes in actual play is so remote that it can be ignored. Table values at those levels are useful only to the academics and computer scientists who wish to study the game and its systems. The question you should have as a player is: "How many of the extremes can be ignored without greatly reducing the performance of the system?" To answer this, you need to know how frequently the hands that require a high index to be memorized occur.

For example, the table value for doubling 3,2 versus a dealer 3 up is +19. To determine whether or not that play is worth remembering, you need to know how likely it is that the count will reach +19 and how often you will be holding 3,2. Basic Strategy dictates that you hit this hand. The full Hi-Opt I strategy indicates that you double if the true count equals or exceeds +19. To calculate how often you will be in error by not knowing the proper table value and instead following Basic Strategy, you must combine the odds that the count will equal or exceed +19 when you are holding 3,2 vs. a dealer 3 up. You will receive a two-card hand of 3,2 vs. a dealer 3 up .07 per cent of the time and can expect the count to reach +19 an estimated .2 per cent of the time in a single-deck game with a shuffle point at one-fourth deck. This means you will misplay this hand with Basic Strategy about .00015 per cent of the time. Memorizing this play is a total waste of time.

This chapter presents the Hi-Opt I values between ±6 only. Limiting what you learn to ±6 is very advantageous because it offers a good trade-off between how much you have to memorize versus how great a coverage of possible situations you have. Using a ±6 range reduces the amount of table values to about a hundred, which is well within the reach of any motivated player who is willing to spend some time for memorizing. But the ±6 range also offers a surprisingly good coverage of the true counts you will see in actual play.

PER CENT OF TRUE COUNTS BETWEEN LIMITS FOR HI-OPT I (10,000 deals)

True Count Limits	1 Deck %	2 Decks %	4 Decks %	6 Decks %
At 0	17.9	11.7	22.5	29.0
Between ±1	40.0	41.5	55.7	61.2
Between ±2	57.4	59.6	72.2	77.4
Between ±3	69.3	70.8	84.1	86.6
Between ±4	76.6	79.6	91.6	91.5
Between ±5	82.2	85.7	95.6	95.2
Between ±6	87.2	89.6	97.3	97.5
Between ±7	90.3	93.3	98.1	98.4
Between ±8	92.6	95.2	98.7	99.2
Between ±9	94.7	96.6	99.3	99.6
Between ±10 or more	100.0	100.0	100.0	100.0

This table shows how widely the true count ranges for various deck levels. The figures were computed assuming head-on play with the shuffle point at one fourth of the cards remaining. At the four- and six-deck levels, you will have the perfect strategy memorized for over 97 per cent of the true counts that occur. At the one- and two-deck levels, your coverage drops under 90 per cent, but as you saw in the doubling example above, this doesn't always mean an incorrect play. In addition, many times the incorrect play offers only a slight reduction from the alternative. In the one-deck game with true counts outside ±6, you will often be making the correct play with Basic Strategy or will be making a play almost as good as the correct one.[1]

---

[1] As a side point, notice the figures in this table for a one-deck game versus those for a four-deck game. The count ranges outside the ± 5 range over

Still, there will be instances when you will not be making the correct play. The important question is: "How much does this affect my advantage?" Griffin recently completed a study especially for this book that establishes the results of memorizing a limited range of table values. His results were for a betting range of one to four in a single-deck game, so they could be compared to figures in the playing-performance table.

Hi-Opt I Count Range	*Player Gain %*
All values	2.1
± 6 only	1.9
± 3 only	1.7

This is a further indicator of the power of the Hi-Opt I strategy. Memorizing only the values between ±3 results in over 80 per cent of the player's optimum gain in a single-deck game. By limiting the table values to ±6, the performance of the system is over 90 per cent of the optimum. Many original Hi-Opt I users memorized only the values between ±3 and won several million dollars as a group. Their success is strong evidence for how powerful a seemingly small 1.7 per cent advantage can be.

For ease of memorization while still providing good true-count coverage and playing performance, the following charts show the values between ±6. The final benefit of the approach is accuracy. It's far more important always to play the strategy correctly in the ±6 true-count range than to make a few errors trying to play with the ±10-range strategy tables. Keeping the Hi-Opt I system manageable is the difference between having a perfect but unusable system and having an accurate *and* playable winning system.

---

13 per cent less often with four decks. As you observed in the previous figure, your strategy advantage is much larger when the count is highly positive or highly negative. You know from Chapter Seven that your betting advantage is better with the highly positive count. This is further indication of why going to four decks reduces the player's opportunities to win.

STANDING AND HITTING

The tables you are about to see are very similar to those in Chapter Six. Take a moment to go back to Chapter Six to familiarize yourself with the format. The plays are indicated by a matrix listing your hands on the left and the dealer's up card along the top. Once again you are to find the hand that you hold and move across the row until you are under the appropriate dealer-up card. The table will then indicate either a letter, as in the Basic Strategy, or a number. The letters indicate that a play should be made no matter what value the true count. The numbers are the Hi-Opt I playing-strategy index.

HI–OPT I STRATEGY: 4 Deck Hard Standing & Hitting.

YOU HOLD	DEALER UP CARD									
	2	3	4	5	6	7	8	9	10	A
18 or more	S	S	S	S	S	S	S	S	S	S
17	S	S	S	S	S	S	S	S	S	−6
16	S	S	S	S	S	H	6	4	0	H
15	−5	−6	S	S	S	H	H	6	3	H
14	−3	−4	−5	S	−6	H	H	H	H	H
13	−1	−2	−3	−4	−4	H	H	H	H	H
12	2	1	0	−1	−1	H	H	H	H	H

TO READ CHART: STAND if True Count ⩾ table number
HIT if True Count < table number

S = STAND   H = HIT

The strategy for hitting or standing with any hard hand over 11 is summarized in the above table. You are to *stand* in any situation when the true count IS GREATER THAN *OR EQUAL TO* (⩾) the table number. This is easy to evaluate with positive numbers. A +4 true count is obviously larger than a +2 table value. But what is the relationship between a −4 true count and a −2 table value?

If you dig back into your algebra, assuming it's still there to dig into, you might remember that numbers can be thought of as sitting on a line that looks like this:

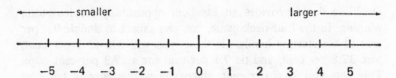

If you think of numbers and visualize this line, you will remember how to compare negative numbers. A —4 true count is *smaller than* a table value of —2. So if you held a hard 13 versus a dealer 3 and the true count was —4, you would HIT the hard 13. This makes sense considering deck composition, since your minus count tells you there is an excess of small cards, which can help you improve your hand.

HI—OPT I STRATEGY: 4 Deck Soft Standing & Hitting.

YOU HOLD	DEALER UP CARD									
	2	3	4	5	6	7	8	9	10	A
19 or more	S	S	S	S	S	S	S	S	S	S
18	S	S	S	S	S	S	S	H	H	1
17 or less	H	H	H	H	H	H	H	H	H	H

TO READ CHART: STAND if True Count ≥ table number
HIT if True Count < table number

S = STAND   H = HIT

This table gives the standing and hitting strategy for any soft hands containing Aces. There is only one playing variation from Basic Strategy, holding a soft 18 versus a dealer Ace. You would expect to hit normally, but the decision is a borderline one. If the true count is +1 or greater, then you are better off standing. You already know that the dealer doesn't have a 10 under the Ace up, or else you would have lost already. So you are keeping your soft 18 in the hope that the dealer will have to draw and bust a weak hand.

DOUBLING DOWN

Doubling down provides an excellent opportunity for long-term winning. In the four-deck game, you can expect to double 9.4 per cent of the starting hands. Of these, you will win 55.1 per cent, lose 37.8 per cent, and tie 7.1 per cent for a 17.3 per cent edge. This nets you 34.6 per cent, since you were wagering twice as much in doubling situations.

HI–OPT I STRATEGY: 4 Deck Hard Doubling.

YOU HOLD	DEALER UP CARD									
	2	3	4	5	6	7	8	9	10	A
11	D	D	D	D	D	D	−5	−4	−3	1
10	D	D	D	D	D	−6	−4	−1	5	4
9	1	0	−2	−4	−4	3	H	H	H	H
8	H	H	5	3	2	H	H	H	H	H
7 or less	H	H	H	H	H	H	H	H	H	H

TO READ CHART: DOUBLE if True Count ≥ strategy number
HIT if True Count < strategy number

H = HIT   D = DOUBLE

The hard-doubling strategy is shown above. A question that frequently comes up when examining this table is the rule for doubling 8 versus a dealer 5 up in a single-deck game. Some publications have listed this as a double-down play for Basic Strategy, usually with the qualifier, "except 6,2." This seems to contradict the above table. With your understanding of the Hi-Opt I count and strategy, you now know why this play is correct.

Basic Strategy assumes a continuing true count of 0. If you are holding 4,4 or 5,3 versus a dealer 6 up, then the Hi-Opt I count would be +3. But if you're 6,2, then the count is only +2, which is not enough to double, according to the table. Thus the exception is a refinement in playing strategy for use without counting. By understanding how the count affects playing decisions, the rule becomes obvious.

HI–OPT I STRATEGY: 4 Deck Soft Doubling.

YOU HOLD	DEALER UP CARD									
	2	3	4	5	6	7	8	9	10	A
A,9	S	S	6	5	5	S	S	S	S	S
A,8	6	4	3	1	1	S	S	S	S	S
A,7	1	−1	−5	D	D	S	S	H	H	*
A,6	1	−2	−5	D	D	H	H	H	H	H
A,5	H	3	−1	−5	D	H	H	H	H	H
A,4	H	5	−1	−4	D	H	H	H	H	H
A,3	H	5	1	−2	−4	H	H	H	H	H
A,2	H	6	2	−1	−2	H	H	H	H	H

TO READ CHART: DOUBLE if True Count ⩾ table number
*Follow 4 Deck Soft Standing Table

S = STAND   H = HIT   D = DOUBLE

The strategy for doubling soft two-card hands is shown in this table. You are never to double a soft hand against a dealer 7 or higher, just as in Basic Strategy. But there are a few surprises here that will bewilder the uninformed player. For example, it is to your advantage to double a soft 19 versus a dealer 5 or 6 if the deck is slightly positive (+1). You are taking advantage of the opportunity to draw a high card and let the dealer bust or draw to a low hand. Because you have doubled your wager, even though you may win a smaller percentage of hands with this play, you will win more because you are doubling the amount of money on your hand.

PAIR SPLITTING

The following table contains the four-deck pair-splitting rules assuming no double down is allowed after split. You will split 2.2 per cent of your starting hands. Pay particular attention to the rules for Aces and 8s. No longer do you always split these Now you may not split Aces with a count of −5 or below because there is too little likelihood of drawing a high card as the single card you will get on each Ace. While you are limited to a single weak hit, the dealer can go on to hit his hand repeatedly to a better total.

HI–OPT I STRATEGY: 4 Deck Pair Splitting

YOU HOLD	DEALER UP CARD									
	2	3	4	5	6	7	8	9	10	A
A,A	SP	SP	SP	SP	SP	SP	SP	SP	SP	−4
10,10	S	S	6	4	4	S	S	S	S	S
9,9	−1	−2	−3	−5	−3	6	SP	SP	S	6
8,8	SP	SP	SP	SP	SP	SP	SP	SP	5B*	SP
7,7	SP	SP	SP	SP	SP	SP	H	H	H	H
6,6	2	0	−1	−4	−5	H	H	H	H	H
5,5 4,4	see Hi–Opt I Strategy: 4 Deck Hard Doubling Table									
3,3	H	4	0	−2	SP	SP	H	H	H	H
2,2	6	1	−3	−6	SP	SP	H	H	H	H

TO READ CHART: SPLIT if True Count ⩾ table number
DO NOT SPLIT if True Count < table number

S = STAND　　　　H = HIT　　　　SP = SPLIT

*Split (8,8) vs. Dealer 10 if True Count ⩽ +5 (B = "below")

The 8s line contains a unique and special rule situation. Although all the tables up to this point are read as taking action if the true count is greater than or equal to the table index, the situation of 8,8 versus a dealer 10 is the opposite. In this case, you are to split 8,8 if the true count is LESS THAN or equal to the value. This is noted in the table by a capital "B," standing for "below." Again, let's examine what this means in terms of deck composition.

If the true count is +6 or higher, the table shows you should not want to split 8s versus a dealer 10. The reason is that the deck is *very* rich in 10s. You are likely to draw a 10 on one or both of your 8s, and the dealer is more likely to pull a 10 to match his first. You have taken a probable busting hand and turned it into two probable losing hands, since your 8s become

18s and the dealer's 10 becomes 20. So the "below" rule must be used in this case.

Also note that 4s and 5s should be played according to the hard-doubling table. In the four-deck game, these should not be split under any circumstances. This changes if doubling is allowed after a pair split. The new rules when this option is allowed are shown in the table below. To highlight the differences in that table relative to the table above, the changes are in italics. For example, there are no longer indices for splitting 2s or 3s versus a dealer 4 or 5. These should always be split if doubling is allowed, There are also rules for splitting 4s. Only 5,5 should be played according to the hard-doubling table.

HI-OPT STRATEGY: 4 Deck Pair Splitting
(when double down allowed after split)

YOU HOLD	DEALER UP CARD									
	2	3	4	5	6	7	8	9	10	A
A,A	SP	SP	SP	SP	SP	SP	SP	SP	SP	– 4
10,10	S	S	6	4	4	S	S	S	S	S
9,9	– 2	– 3	– 5	– 6	– 5	3	SP	SP	S	4
8,8	SP	SP	SP	SP	SP	SP	SP	SP	SP	SP
7,7	SP	SP	SP	SP	SP	SP	1	H	H	H
6,6	– 1	– 3	– 4	– 6	SP	H	H	H	H	H
5,5	see Hi-Opt I Strategy: 4 Deck Hard Doubling Table									
4,4	H	H	3	1	0	H	H	H	H	H
3,3	– 2	– 6	SP	SP	SP	SP	H	H	H	H
2,2	– 4	– 5	SP	SP	SP	SP	H	H	H	H

TO READ CHART: SPLIT if True Count ≥ table number
DO NOT SPLIT if True Count < table number

S = STAND   H = Hit   SP = SPLIT

When there is a question as to priorities—in other words, whether you split 4,4 or double it versus a dealer 5 when the count is +3—use the pair-splitting table first. A typical situation is whether to split or double 4,4 versus a dealer 5 with a true count of +3. The index for doubling is +3 and the index for splitting (where doubling is allowed after a split) is +1. In this case, you are to go ahead and split the 4s rather than double the hard 8.

SURRENDER

The true-count strategy for regular surrender is shown in the next table. Making the proper surrender plays can benefit the count player much more than the Basic Strategy player. As you saw in the effect-of-rules-variation table in Chapter Six, the Basic Strategy gain was only .06 per cent. In this chapter, the Hi-Opt I playing-performance table illustrates that the expected gain for the count player betting at various levels can be four times greater.

HI—OPT I STRATEGY: 4 Deck Surrender.

	DEALER UP CARD				
YOU HOLD	7	8	9	10	A
10,6	H	4	1	−2	0
9,7	H	4	1	−2	0
8,8	SP	SP	SP	1	SP
10,5	H	5	2	−1	1
9,6	H	6	2	0	2
8,7	H	6	2	1	2
10,4	H	H	6	3	5
9,5	H	H	6	3	6
8,6	H	H	5	3	5
7,7	SP	*	4	2	4
8,5	H	H	H	6	H
7,6	H	H	H	6	H

TO READ CHART:　SURRENDER if True Count ≥ table number
　　　　　　　　　　DO NOT SURRENDER if True Count < table number

H = HIT　　　SP = SPLIT

*See two previous tables.

In general, about two out of fifty-five hands should be surrendered. For these surrendered hands, Braun found that if they were played out, an average loss of 53.3 per cent would have occurred. Since you lose just 50 per cent of your bet with surrender, you are saving 3.3 per cent (53.3 — 50.0) with each surrendered hand. Now, ²⁄₅₅ of 3.3 per cent equals .12 per cent, which is the gain with a flat bet for the count player. This is how the flat-betting surrender gain was calculated for the playing-performance table. Braun also analyzed surrender gains for the one-to-four betting range as .25 per cent, but did not provide figures for the one-to-eight range.

The surrender table is read the same as the other tables with one exception: In considering whether or not to surrender 7,7 versus a dealer 8 up, you must refer back to the two previous tables; 7,7 is not to be surrendered in any game, and therefore you must determine the proper play from the appropriate pair-splitting tables.

Early Surrender

As you first saw in Chapter Six, correct early-surrender play can provide a significant gain for the Basic Strategy player. While proper Basic Strategy early surrender provides a gain of .62 per cent, no figures have been determined as of yet for the early-surrender count strategy shown in the table below. You can be certain that it *is at least as great as* the Basic Strategy gain, and in and by Braun's estimate, "a significant additional amount can be gained by the count player using appropriate indexes."

If you find the amount of numbers to be memorized in either early or regular surrender too numerous, you can simplify the tables with negligible loss in performance. For each hand value, estimate the index by choosing the largest algebraic number in the table. For example, you could surrender all hard 13s versus a dealer 10 on a true count of 4 or more (the largest of +3, +4, and +2). Remember the number line and that small negative numbers are greater in value than large negative numbers? If you wanted to pick the largest index for surrendering a hard 16 versus a dealer 10, you would choose −2 (the larger of −6 and −2).

There is one final consideration in using the surrender tables

HI–OPT I STRATEGY:
Modifications for Early Surrender.

YOU HOLD	DEALER UP CARD	
	10	A
(10,7)	5	always
(9,8)	–	always
(10,6) or (9,7)	–6	always
(8,8)	–2	always
Hard 15	–3	always
(10,4)	–1	always
(9,5)	0	always
(8,6)	–1	always
(7,7)	–2	always
(10,3)	3	always
(9,4)	4	always
(8,5) or (7,6)	2	always
Hard 12	–	always
(5,2)	–	always
(4,3)	–	always
Hard 6	–	–4
(A,5)	–	6
(3,2)	–	1
(2,2)	–	2

correctly. Students frequently look at the tables and then ask, "What takes precedence, pair splitting or surrender?" Unlike doubling, where pair splitting takes precedence, *surrender is always the highest-priority play*. You continue to play any hand *only* if the hand is *not* to be surrendered.

MODIFICATIONS FOR RULES VARIATIONS

An important consideration in using the Hi-Opt I system is its completeness in covering the wide range of Blackjack game conditions and rules variations. One of the more common of these in the Nevada game is when the dealer hits a soft 17. From the effects of rules variance in Chapter Six, you know that this option reduces your Basic Strategy expectation by .2 per cent because the dealer will improve his hand more often than not.

HI-OPT I STRATEGY: Modifications if Dealer Hits Soft 17

Option	Situation	New Strategy	
Hard standing	Hard 17 vs. Dealer A	−4	
	Hard 16 vs. Dealer A	3	
	Hard 15 vs. Dealer A	4	
	Hard 14 vs. Dealer 6	S	
	Hard 13 vs. Dealer 6	−5	
	Hard 12 vs. Dealer 6	−3	
Soft standing	Soft 18 vs. Dealer A	H	
Pair splitting	9,9 vs. Dealer 6	−4	(no double down after
	9,9 vs. Dealer A	5	split)
	9,9 vs. Dealer 6	−6	(double after split
	9,9 vs. Dealer A	3	allowed)

S = Stand   H = Hit

The rules in the above table modify the Hi-Opt I system strategy numbers for the dealer's hitting soft 17, as in downtown Las Vegas and in northern Nevada. If you examine the table, you will notice that you are more likely to stand on the stiff 12–16 hands listed than when the dealer stands on soft 17. On those hard or soft hands over 17, you are more likely to hit. You are also slightly more likely to split 9s versus a very good or a very bad dealer up card.

HI-OPT I STRATEGY: Modifications for One or
Two Decks

Option	Situation	New Strategy	
Hard standing	Hard 16 vs. Dealer 8	H	
	7,7 vs. Dealer 10	0	(single-deck game only)
	7,7 vs. Dealer 10	4	(two-deck game only)
Soft standing	Soft 18 vs. Dealer A	0	
Soft doubling	A,9 vs. Dealer 4	S	
	A,8 vs. Dealer 2	S	
	A,4 vs. Dealer 3	4	
	A,2 vs. Dealer 3	5	
Pair splitting	8,8 vs. Dealer 10	6B	(B = "below")
Surrender	10,6 vs. Dealer 8	5	
	9,7 vs. Dealer 8	5	
	8,8 vs. Dealer 10	2	
	10,5 vs. Dealer 8	6	
	8,7 vs. Dealer 8	H	
	8,7 vs. Dealer 9	3	
	8,7 vs. Dealer A	3	
	8,6 vs. Dealer A	6	
	7,7 vs. Dealer 10	−1	
	7,7 vs. Dealer A	3	
	8,5 vs. Dealer 10	6	
	7,6 vs. Dealer 10	6	
	7,6 vs. Dealer A	5	

S = Stand   H = Hit

The modifications for playing in a one- or a two-deck game are shown in this table (there are no modifications for a six-deck game). In general, you are to play more aggressively with the one- or two-deck rules. You are more likely to stand on certain numbers, more likely to double soft hands, and less likely to surrender certain hands.

ADVANCED BLACKJACK PLAYS

The strategies in this section detail advanced Blackjack plays for the serious player. Using the Hi-Opt I strategies already presented is enough for you to increase your win rate significantly. The following strategies should be learned and employed in the casino only after you are an accomplished player with as much as two or three years' experience as a winning counter.

STRATEGY-GAIN ADJUSTMENT

Rather than trying to evaluate another equation to calculate your exact advantage for Kelly Criterion betting you can use the curves shown previously in Chapter 6 to estimate the additional advantage you have from following the strategy tables in this chapter. For the ±6 true-count range, you can assume that the curves are basically the same. At the ±6 level, your gain is approximately 1 per cent. At a ±3 to ±4 count, your gain is only about .2 per cent, so the bulk of the advantage is in the three higher true-count points. Beyond ±6, the curves rise differently and dramatically. At a −11 true count, your gain from the Hi-Opt I *play* strategy only is about 5 per cent. With a +11 count, it is a still substantial 3 per cent.

One way to use the information in this curve if you want to be more accurate is to approximate your advantage mentally. As long as you are conservative, you won't be overbetting. Here are suggestions:

1. If the true count is in the ± 3 range (which will be a large portion of the time), ignore this adjustment.
2. If the count is between ±3 and ±6, give yourself .3 per cent per point (added onto .15 per cent for the ±3 range).

This sounds unwieldy, but in practice it becomes second nature very quickly. If you want an even rougher estimate, at ±4 your SG advantage is about .5 per cent; at ±6 it is about 1 per cent.

You can "fudge" or even ignore trying to estimate numbers in between.

If you were playing at Caesar's Palace casino in Las Vegas and were betting into a +4 true count, your advantage with the Hi-Opt I would be:

$$\text{Player advantage} = \text{BSE} + (.515 \times \text{true count}) + \text{SG}$$
$$= .17 + (.515 \times 4) + .50$$
$$= .17 + 2.06 + .5$$
$$= 2.73 \text{ per cent}$$

In practice, you would more likely round off the numbers and come up with:

$$\text{Player advantage} = .2 + (.5 \times 4) + .5$$
$$= 2.7 \text{ per cent}$$

At the MGM Grand in Las Vegas with a −6 true count, your advantage would be:

$$\text{Player advantage} = -.34 + (.515 \times -6) + 1.0$$
$$= -.34 - 3.09 + 1.0$$
$$= -2.43 \text{ per cent}$$

Rounding this off in play you would figure:

$$\text{Player advantage} = -.3 + (.5 \times 6) + 1.0$$
$$= -.3 - 3.0 + 1.0$$
$$= -2.3 \text{ per cent}$$

Rounding off the values to provide a quick and easy approximation is certainly accurate enough for use in the casino. When the count is plus, you only need to estimate the proper strategy-gain adjustment before placing your next bet. When the count is negative, you won't need to approximate anything because you will be betting table minimums.

ACE-SIDE-COUNT STRATEGY

The advantages of keeping an Ace side count for betting purposes was detailed in the previous chapter. In this chapter, we are concerned with the correct *playing* strategy, where the Ace behaves quite differently than for betting purposes.

Hard-doubling Factors

Knowing the proportion of Aces in the deck is particularly useful in determining whether or not to double down on a total of 10, 9, or 8 in close decisions. For example, if you are at the half-deck level and all four Aces are still in the deck, you have a surplus of two Aces. Accordingly, you have an extra true count of +4 (adding +1 for each Ace and applying the 2 multiplier for the half deck) for purposes of bet variation.

Since the Ace is very important as a potential card when doubling down on 10, you should give it an extra 50 per cent factor in this doubling-down situation. With two surplus Aces at the half-deck level, use an extra true count of +6 (150 per cent of +4) for determining if doubling down on 10 is merited.

The same type of Ace adjustment can be used to determine better whether or not to double down on a total of 9 or 8. Here you should use a 25 per cent factor for doubling on 9, and no factor for doubling on 8. So for all four Aces left at the half-deck level, we would have an extra true count of +5 (125 per cent of +4) holding a 9 and +4 when holding an 8.

Conversely, if there were *no* Aces left at the half-deck level, you should *subtract* 6, 5, or 4, respectively, from the true count to determine whether or not to double on a 10, 9, or 8 total. The factors applied to the Ace adjustment help you to play these hard-doubling hands more accurately.

Ace-multiparameter Tables

For the *highly skilled player* who wants every edge the Hi-Opt I can offer, the answer lies in the concept of multiparameter tables. Unlike the above approximation factors for a specific situation, the multiparameter tables indicate exactly how each 0-value card should modify the basic count. In this book, only tables for the Ace are included. Complete multiparameter tables are available from International Gaming.

In Chapter Seven, I told you that most Blackjack authorities felt that the Ace acts like a large card for betting and a small card for playing. The only fully accurate method of accounting for the effect of a shortage or excess of Aces is to specify an adjustment value for each player hand and dealer up card. These adjustments are presented in the following Ace multiparameter tables.

The values in the tables are the *adjustments* you should make in the *running count* whenever there is a DEFICIENCY of Aces —that is, when the deck has one *fewer* Ace than is normal you would add the appropriate table value to your *running count*. For example, you are playing the Hi-Opt I strategy and hold a 16 versus a dealer 10 up. One quarter of a single deck has been dealt out but two Aces came out in that quarter of the deck. Thus there is one less Ace than normal in the three-quarters deck remaining. The entry in the following table for a 16 versus 10 up is +1. So you would add 1 to whatever your running count is at that particular moment. When there is an *extra* Ace in the remaining deck, *subtract* each table value from your running count. In the above example, if three-quarters deck were remaining but NO Aces came out, you would *subtract* 1 from your running count when holding 16 versus a dealer 10 up. When there is TWICE the deficiency of Aces from normal, DOUBLE each table value before adding it to your running count, etc.

In general, positive values in the tables indicate that the Ace acts like a small card in that situation; negative values in the tables indicate that the Ace acts like a 10. For example, the Ace acts like a large card and is counted −1 in betting adjustments, but should be counted +1 when adjusting for the Ace in insurance decisions (because it is a non-10 and therefore a non-Blackjack card).

The Ace adjustments when holding hard totals of 10 to 17 are shown in the table below. Notice that when holding a 10, the Ace acts like a large card for playing purposes. In hand totals of 11 or more, the Ace has the effect of a small card (the table values are positive). And in a large portion of the hands, the effect is to stay neutral.

Soft-doubling Ace adjustments are listed in the table below.

HI–OPT I STRATEGY: Hard 10 to 17 Ace Adjustment.

	DEALER UP CARD									
YOU HOLD	2	3	4	5	6	7	8	9	10	A
17	0	1	1	1	1	3	5	3	2	0
16	1	0	0	1	1	2	1	1	1	0
15	0	0	0	0	1	1	0	0	0	0
14	0	0	0	0	1	1	0	0	0	0
13	0	0	0	0	1	1	0	0	0	0
12	0	0	0	0	1	1	0	0	0	0
11	1	1	1	1	1	1	1	2	1	1
10	−1	0	0	0	0	0	−1	0	−2	−1

Once again the values point out the dual nature of the Ace. For hands of A,7 or greater, the Ace affects your hand like a large card. This makes common sense, since any Ace improves the hand only slightly better than a 10. For lower-valued soft hands, the Ace is treated like a small card.

HI–OPT I STRATEGY: Soft Doubling Ace Adjustment.

	DEALER UP CARD					
YOU HOLD	2	3	4	5	6	7
A,9	−1	−1	−1	−1	0	−1
A,8	−1	−1	−1	0	0	0
A,7	−1	−1	0	0	0	−2
A,6	1	0	0	0	1	1
A,5	2	2	1	1	2	0
A,4	4	3	2	2	3	0
A,3	2	2	1	1	2	0
A,2	1	1	1	1	2	0

The multiparameter Ace information here is complete. No other Ace tables or values are needed. Also, every value in each table has been checked and double-checked for accuracy. Every value is correct according to computer calculations of Professor

Peter Griffin. I'm making such a point of this because many players find some of the table values difficult to accept.

There are similar multiparameter tables for each of the other four 0-value cards in the Hi-Opt I count (2,7,8, and 9), but they are not presented here. Although they are available from International Gaming, most players choose to keep separate track of the Aces only because of the large amount of effort required to keep track of *all* the zero-value cards. For the sophisticated player who can keep all of these additional counts and memorize the corresponding tables, the upper limit of Hi-Opt I accuracy is, again, a betting correlation of .98 and a playing efficiency of .891. This represents the upper bound of the ultimate capability of the Hi-Opt I system for an honest game of Blackjack from a single deck.

SURRENDER ADJUSTMENTS FOR DEALER 10 UP

The values in the previous tables for surrendering against a dealer 10 assume that the Aces remaining in the deck are at a normal number. If you are tracking the Aces, you can surrender with a lower count if the deck is Ace rich. If there are fewer Aces, you need a higher count to surrender. The information you need to know is how much lower or higher the count must be as a function of the Ace side count.

For the Hi-Opt I count, for each extra Ace remaining in the deck you should add .9 to the *running count*. If the Aces are below the normal level for that portion of the deck, you must subtract .9 from the running count. This adjustment is made for each Ace deficient.

Here's an example: Suppose two decks remain and there are exactly 10 Aces left. You hold 8,7 versus a dealer 10. The Hi-Opt I running count is +1. Your true count without adjustment is +½. So if you are not counting Aces, based on the entry in that previous table, you do not surrender.

If you are aware of the Ace side count, then you know that there are two more Aces than normal. Adding the .9 adjustment for each Ace, your new running count is +2.8 (+1 +2 × .9). The adjusted true count is 2.8/2 or 1.4. Since the surrender-table value for 8,7 versus a dealer 10 is +1, and your adjusted true

count is 1.4, you would make the better play of surrendering the
hand as a result of your Ace side count.

To be honest, the additional gain in such borderline situations
is very small. Failure to surrender in the indicated example costs
you very little. But when the number of Aces remaining deviates
from the normal amount by a comparatively large number, then
the Ace-adjustment calculation may become much more important
in achieving the optimum choice of strategy. In any case, you
should be fully aware of all of the intricacies of side counts
whether or not you are likely to apply them in the casino.

HOW TO LEARN THE HI-OPT I STRATEGY

If you have read this chapter straight through, then it would not
be unusual if you are glassy-eyed at the tables, strategies, variations, modifications, and side counts possible. Remember, you
can win money with Basic Strategy and the Hi-Opt I count, so
don't be in a hurry to master everything in this chapter at once.
Be patient, be thorough—take as long as a year or more to learn
all the chart values and procedures. You will still be winning in
the interim, if at a reduced rate.

You can approach learning the Hi-Opt I strategy according to a
time-management principle that I call "eating the elephant." If
one of those crazy TV game shows trundled up Elsie the elephant
and offered you a hundred thousand dollars if your family of four
could consume her in a year of dining, you would probably laugh
at the offer and take a different door. Yet if you gave it some
thought, you might be able to do it. Oh it might take a year of elephant steak, rack of elephant, elephant stew, roast elephant,
BBQ elephant, elephant kabob, elephant sandwiches, elephant
omelettes, etc. But you could do it.

This is the way to tackle any big job that looks overwhelming.
If you break up the work into smaller, more readily achievable
tasks, then you can see your progress from day to day, and you
get a feeling of accomplishment as you increase your knowledge.
More important in Blackjack, your play gradually becomes better

and better. But before you begin to carve up your personal pachyderm, you can make sure you have the smallest elephant to start with.

WHICH STRATEGY TO LEARN FIRST

When there are so many different strategies, each with modifications to the Hi-Opt I tables, you must carefully choose what you wish to memorize first. In most cases, what you memorize first will be remembered best throughout your playing days. In the chapter on Basic Strategy, I presented the four-deck system as the basis, and then listed modifications to the four-deck system for one, two, or six decks. This organization is used here for the same reasons. Four-deck games are the most common throughout the world. And four-deck strategy is more conservative if you suspect the honesty of the game. In Chapter Six I even suggested that you might want to use *only* the four-deck Basic Strategy, no matter how many decks were in play, so that you wouldn't confuse the various modifications. I promised that the penalty for using a different strategy was negligible.

PENALTY FOR USING STRATEGY DESIGNED FOR DIFFERENT NUMBER OF DECKS

1-deck Game	Shuffle Point	Flat %	Betting 1–4 %	1–8 %
Braun + − 1 Deck	.75	.7	2.0	2.8
Braun + − 4 Deck	.75	.6	2.0	2.7
4-deck Game				
Braun + − 4 Deck	.80	−.2	.5	1.1
Braun + − 1 Deck	.80	−.3	.5	1.0

RULES: Las Vegas Strip
         Head-on play

My advice is the same for playing the Hi-Opt I strategy. And I can prove that the penalty is indeed negligible. Braun wondered what the penalty is for using a strategy designed for a different number of decks. The table above shows the results of his one-million-hand simulations using the Braun + — count and strategy tables. The penalty is only .1 per cent when flat-betting or with widely ranging bets. If you are betting one to four units (which is more common than the other two extremes), then there is *no difference* in advantage.

Although the Braun + — count is a slightly different count than that for the Hi-Opt I, Braun has written that the slight penalty is consistent between systems. You will suffer little or no loss in performance by using one strategy for all the games. And that one system should be the four-deck strategy. Because of the increased difficulty of the tables, it is even more important than before not to become confused. By memorizing the four-deck strategy only, you will be greatly reducing and simplifying what you must know in the casino. You can learn the other modifications when you are completely comfortable with the four-deck strategy and want to be exact in your play.

HOW TO LEARN THE STRATEGY TABLES

Go back to review the Basic Strategy frequency-of-use table in Chapter Six. If you wish to rank the various tables by their frequency of use for two-card hands, the list is:

Hard-standing hitting	53.1%
Hard doubling	19.3
Soft standing and hitting	14.5
Pair splitting	13.1
Soft doubling	3.7
Surrender	3.6 (10.4 early surrender)

This closely matches a list that would result from ranking the plays according to Basic Strategy advantage. Although no statistics other than those given in this chapter exist for the various Hi-Opt I strategy tables, it is safe to assume that the relative advantages are similar to Basic Strategy ranking. If you intend to keep playing while you are learning the strategy tables, I suggest you learn the four-deck hard-doubling table directly after the standing-and-hitting table, and the four-deck pair-splitting table directly before the soft-doubling table. Then, depending upon where you intend to play and the rules in force there (check the Las Vegas rules table), you can memorize the next four tables, and if you want to be exact, the table for modifications for one or two decks. The Ace multiparameter tables should be learned last if at all.

The best way to learn any individual table is to memorize the small values first and then use them in casino play. Start with the hard standing and hitting table and learn only the values between and including ±2. This is a good point to get some playing time in because it gives you the opportunity to count, calculate the true count, and then play the correct strategy while you have only about eight table values from that table to remember. If you are comfortable with the table, you might learn all twenty-two numbers from it and then play.

When you have memorized all the table values in the ±2 range, then go back to learn the additional numbers in the ±4 range, then ±6. Again, this may take many months, but you are in no hurry. Of what importance are a few months when you are mastering a lifetime money-making skill? And as Griffin's study showed, you are gaining the bulk of the Hi-Opt I strategy's gain by the ±3 range numbers anyway. You will have a powerful winning system even before you complete your memorization work.

You have seen how to reduce the number of values you ultimately must learn, and can break these up into achievable segments so they can be learned gradually. So much for the *what* and *when* of learning the tables; now you can consider the *how*. The best and most productive use of your time is to study a little bit each day for a long period of time. Here is the approach I used. As a memory expert, I can attest that this method will result in the most accurate memorization for the least amount of your time invested. *Calendar* time may be quite long, but the total demand on your time is slight.

I first took the Hi-Opt I strategy in this book (in the full ±6 range) and studied the indices for several hours one afternoon. I wanted to have an intuitive *understanding* of what the indices meant. I wanted to feel at the gut level that the numbers made sense. For example, the line for hard 13 in the hard-standing-and-hitting table made sense to me. I was to stand at lower and lower counts—that is, more frequently—as the dealer's card got worse. (Remember the corresponding table in Chapter Six?) Even though I didn't *know* the numbers, I felt *comfortable* with them.

I next wrote up three-by-five index cards with one line of strategy on each. At the top of each card I wrote the play option and my hand. Across the card were the dealer's possible up cards, with the Hi-Opt I strategy numbers for that hand underneath. For the portion of tables I wanted to memorize, this amounted to thirty-eight cards. I decided to devote one day to each card. Each morning I set a card out to be carried with me that day. I glanced at it while shaving, I carried it with me in the car, and I looked at it at stoplights. I sat it up on my desk at the office and glanced at it throughout the day. On the way home I did the same thing.

What I was doing was taking advantage of the mind's ability to remember without having to try. I wanted that card to be remembered the same way we remember an incessant TV commercial. We don't *try* to retain it; the message just gets imbedded through endless repetition. This is the easiest, surest, most painless way to remember anything. I looked at that card over two hundred times on its day, more if I wasn't busy.

The second day, I reviewed the previous day's card in the morning and right before I went to bed in the evening. Again, I looked at it. I did not try to memorize it. As the days progressed, the review became longer because I was reviewing *all* the cards I had already spent a day with. At the end of the thirty-eight days, I had looked at each card several hundred times and reviewed each one anywhere from twice to seventy-six times. And I had never spent more than ten minutes a day reviewing the cards. The rest of the time was taken from the wasted minutes every day is filled with.

Review as often as you can. Carry the cards with you. If you are caught with a few minutes of waiting, or stuck in a freeway parking lot, pull out your three-by-five cards and review the strategy. Repeat! Up to now you have not yet tried to remember anything! But believe it or not, your work is well over half done. You have shoved the Hi-Opt I into your brain in much the way that "Sesame Street" shoves knowledge into the brains of unsuspecting kiddies.

Now it's time for the memory work. How long this takes

depends upon your innate memory ability and how well you've trained it. For most players, their memory is totally untrained so their genes are the telling factor. The easiest way to handle this raw memory work is endless detailed repetition. The most painless way to accomplish this is the quiz-card approach; this is used for memorization of multiplication tables.

For the full ±6 range with every option, you will need between two hundred and three hundred cards. Start out with the tables on hard standing and hitting through pair splitting in the ±2 range. This will mean having only thirty-six cards. On the front of the card put your hand and the dealer up card. On the back of the card write the correct play and the index number. For example, the front of one card would have:

Hard   16
Dealer 10 up

The back of the card would have:

Stand if true count $\geqq 0$

Go through your "flash cards" as often as you can until you know the answer correctly every time without having to think. As with memorization of multiplication tables, you want your memory to be instantaneous so you will be fast enough for casino play. When you know the ±2 range, add the cards for the ±4 range, etc. When you have the full ±6 range for these tables, learn the modifications that will help you in specific casinos where you intend to play.

No matter what your profession—housewife (it is a profession, don't let anybody kid you), factory worker, assembly-line member, auto mechanic, or office worker—this learning approach will work for you. There is always some location you look at frequently, be it a tool box or kitchen counter top. There are always a few moments on even the most busy assembly line to glance at your card. And there are always a few minutes in the morning and at night on the most hectic days for a brief card review. Using the Hi-Opt I playing strategy in these particular tables is easily within the capabilities of *any* motivated individual. It is about as difficult as learning to type sixty words per minute or memorizing the multiplication tables. It requires *much less* information to be remembered than is needed for most professions. Like amateur sports, Blackjack requires time and practice. But unlike a sport, Blackjack pays off in negotiable currency rather than plastic statues.

Once you have learned the Hi-Opt I strategy in the above manner, you will have it forever. If you haven't played for a while, you will only need to use your summary cards or flash cards to brush up and review before your next trip. With the knowledge that your memory work brings, you will have a lifetime skill that can never be taken away. By mastering the main strategies in this chapter, you will become a full practicing member of a profession the casinos label with dismay and fear: a COUNTER.

NINE

Blackjack Outside the Casino

At the card game, one of the boys looked across the table and said, "Now Reuben, play the cards fair. I know what I dealt you."

LYNDON B. JOHNSON

If you think gambling in a casino can be a tricky business, then you have a real shock coming. The situation is worse outside the casino. It's not unusual for a group of professional gamblers from Las Vegas to set up a special game for the sole purpose of stripping some rich mark of all his money, and they do it quickly, quietly, and smoothly. They politely split the take and head for the next sucker. The mark never has a chance because he is playing against *every* other player in the game.

The amount of play in private games is staggering if you consider it nationwide. Some of the Blackjack played outside the casino is for fun and some is for keeps. Much of it is honest but a significant portion is totally dishonest. What this chapter will do is teach you everything there is to know about the game outside the recognized casinos. Not only will you find the strategies for two variations of the home game, you will also learn about illegal underground games and about fund-raising club games.

You will even learn about one of the greatest Blackjack hustlers of all time: Lawrence Revere.

"PRIVATE" BLACKJACK

I got my first opportunity to play in an underground game as the result of a college class I was teaching in my hometown which I'll call University City. The class was the result of an interview about my harness-racing career that had been printed in a local paper. The article identified me as a winning bettor and horse owner who had consistently won over the years. The paper was even so kind as to print a rough picture of me showing my unshaven face and disheveled looks.

The next day my university was flooded with calls asking about "the professor who gambles." They literally begged me to offer a "how to win" course for gamblers. I designed a course on gaming and offered it through the adult-education evening program. The first class had fifteen students in it and covered racing and other forms of gambling. For the Blackjack portion, I was using Thorp's *Beat the Dealer* as the text.

Near the end of the class, we took a field trip to one of the local tracks to apply our knowledge and to bet according to my horse system. We were quite a sight at the track, a large group trooping to and from the windows, all betting different amounts on the same horse. The class won $928 that night, which earned us another newspaper article about "the class that learns how to win money." As a result, my second class had over ninety students in it, all eager to achieve the same success. This second class won at the track, too, as have all my classes since, because we really do our homework on the racing program.

It was in that second class that I met Joe. Joe was a lawyer and was very wealthy from real-estate and business holdings. He regularly went to Las Vegas and also frequented a number of the underground games in University City. Through Joe I met Peter, another wealthy player. Peter had made his money through a chain of reducing salons. Both of them had big money and liked to bet it whenever possible.

The private games were run just like in an organized casino except that instead of a "house," there was a sponsor. The sponsors were from varied backgrounds: a bookie, a businessman, a stock-market speculator, and several organized-crime figures. Each sponsor had "his" night of the week, so none of the games conflicted. When I started, it was possible to play six out of seven nights. The games floated from location to location, with word getting out the day before as to where the next game would be.

The game offered very favorable conditions at that time. The dealers dealt nearly to the end of a single deck. Typical Las

Vegas rules allowed doubling on any two cards and resplitting pairs. Table limits at that time were normally five dollars to two hundred dollars. In some of the bigger games, minimums were as high as twenty dollars. I saw tens of thousands of dollars change hands night after night.

The private games had another interesting feature: They were usually located in a plush suite of hotel rooms. The first game I went to I kept seeing players get up and leave the room for about twenty minutes. They would come back with silly grins on their faces and resume playing. As soon as one came back, another would wordlessly get up and leave. There seemed to be no pattern that I could discern to these comings and goings. But they never stopped.

Finally, I couldn't stand the suspense any longer so I asked Joe what was going on. He laughed and told me that every game had a free prostitute service as part of the "complimentaries." I made some sort of remark about, "Only twenty minutes?" and Joe laughed again. One of the prostitutes had told him that most of the men went for oral sex so that they could get back to the game faster. I was impressed. What better measure of a serious player is there?

At those first few visits to private games, I had a bankroll of only two hundred dollars, so I wasn't allowed to sit in. Instead, I stood behind Joe and watched the game. When the deck was significantly plus, I would give Joe some money to bet for me. After I had built up my bankroll to a thousand dollars in several weeks, I was allowed to sit and play. When Joe and Peter saw how regularly I was winning, they took me to one side and asked what I knew that they didn't.

I explained to them generally what you have just finished reading. The private games were ridiculously easy to win in because there were no countermeasures against winning players. The games were totally honest. In fact, I once caught a dealer named Frankie picking up the cards in a high–low stack. I stopped the game and complained about it. When the sponsor came over Frankie explained that an old-time Las Vegas dealer had told her it was the best way to pick up the cards, so that's why she did it that way. She didn't even know she was cheating. The sponsor did, though, and he told her to stop!

Joe, Peter, and I decided to play as a team in the coming months. I was the team leader and acted as the official counter. They followed my betting patterns closely, but on a much larger scale. On a high plus, Peter would bet fourteen hundred dollars (two hundred dollars maximum on seven hands). Before we teamed up, I had won about fifty thousand dollars over a five-month period. During that time, Peter had won about two hundred thousand dollars with a betting-variation count only (he was also lucky). Unfortunately, when we teamed up, Joe and Peter got greedy. The games began to get scared of us because we were winning so heavily. The sponsors started watching us closely and figured out that Joe and Peter were following my betting lead. In about three weeks, I was effectively barred from all the games. They didn't kick me out, I was just never told where any of the games were going to be held. When Peter and Joe kept winning, although at a reduced rate, they soon received the same treatment.

During those five months, I had some interesting experiences. Once I was eating in a restaurant with a gambler we called "The Druggist." He had made about three million dollars in the late fifties betting on Thoroughbreds. He now owned a very famous restaurant in University City. If you can picture Humpty Dumpty with a Santa Claus face, then you know what The Druggist looks like.

As we were having dinner at his restaurant, I noticed two men in suits eating quietly over in the corner. At the end of their meal, they got up and walked over purposefully. As they approached, The Druggist said to me, "Listen to this." The Druggist plucked the check out of one of the men's hand and said, "What can I do for you, Detective, other than buy you a meal?"

The two diners were local policemen from the missing-person's bureau. The detective pulled out a photograph and asked us, "Do either of you know this man?" I recognized the picture as one of the regular Blackjack players whom we called "The Ox." Both of us blankly shook our heads "No" and I asked noncommittally, "Why are you looking for him?"

The detective told us, "His wife has reported him missing and wants us to track him down." The Druggist and I expressed our regret at not being able to help and watched the two march off. I turned to The Druggist and asked him what was going on.

"He's not missing," The Druggist chuckled. "His wife doesn't know where he is and wants to find out if he's with his old mistress or if he has gotten a new one. So she sent the cops out after him." The Druggist was right. The Ox later told me he was with his new "girlfriend." And people wonder why the police get frustrated.

Once I was in a game that was busted. Barry, a new guy in the private-casino business, tried to start up a game on Monday night. Monday was open, and this was before the advent of "Monday Night Football," so there was no conflict with any other established competition. Barry offered a first-class game. The players were treated to free wine and steak dinners as well as to other social-sexual amenities. That first week, Barry netted about two thousand dollars from the game, so he decided to have another game the following Monday.

I was there again. At about 12:30 A.M. eight plainclothes police officers crashed through the double doors of the suite. They grabbed all the chips and money, and collared Barry and one of the dealers. The police asked all the players for their identification, wrote it down, and let us go uncharged. Since many of the players carried false IDs (I don't), they were totally out of danger at that point. The police were only interested in the sponsors, fortunately, so nothing further came of the incident. Barry managed to get off, but one of the dealers had a criminal record and was jailed briefly. Barry, true to the unwritten code of sponsors, reimbursed the players for all their money that was confiscated by the police. We later found out that his problem was that he didn't pay off the right people in the Police Department. All the other games had someone high up who would tip off a coming police raid in time to clear the hotel.

Another night's sponsor was named "Mr. C." Mr. C. met with a similar bit of misfortune because he couldn't control his gambling losses. Mr. C.'s main business had been running junkets to a major Las Vegas casino. He was finally fired for gambling all the profits away at the Craps table (the casino didn't want the host to be so uncontrolled). On one of his last trips, the police put a bug in Mr. C.'s car when it was parked at the University City airport.

When he returned, they heard him discuss his bookmaking operation and promptly arrested him. They found a safety-deposit key on him and went and opened the box. Inside the police found ninety thousand dollars in cash. At this point, Mr. C. didn't want to take the fall alone, so he implicated three senior police officials who had been tipping him off about the raids. The end result was that Mr. C.'s next eighteen months were all planned for him. The three police officials were forced to resign.

So Joe, Peter, and I all ended our private-game play barred, but big winners. Joe is still a successful lawyer and gambler. Peter sold his reducing-salon chain and quickly went to Costa Rica because he "forgot" to pay the Canadian IRS the capital-gains tax. Recognizing a worthwhile scam when he saw one, Peter started a beauty wrinkle-remover franchise scheme and once again skipped to Costa Rica when the U.S. IRS got peeved over a similar oversight. The last I heard Peter settled out of court with the U.S. IRS with Joe's help. But Peter is still wanted in Canada. So much for the company you keep in private Blackjack games.

PRIVATE BLACKJACK AND LAWRENCE REVERE

I first learned of the late Lawrence Revere when a student brought in a copy of his book *Playing Blackjack as a Business* to one of my classes. We were all impressed with the book and its beautiful colored strategy charts. As a teacher, I was particularly interested in Revere's statement in the back of the book that said that he welcomed all people who are interested in Blackjack to come to visit him at his home in Las Vegas, where he gave private lessons. I wrote to him immediately and told him when I was coming. He replied on the back of a three-by-five inch index card, as was his custom. Little did I know that I was going to meet one of the truly original characters still around in gambling. Damon Runyon is probably turning over in his grave at having missed this live one. Unfortunately, I didn't know what a costly lesson I was about to learn from the late Mr. Revere.

When my plane touched down in Las Vegas several weeks later, I took the junket bus to the Sahara, my hotel. I checked my bags, then immediately took a taxi to Revere's house. You can imagine my excitement as I stood at his door about to meet this famous author and gambling expert. When the door opened to my knock, I was momentarily left speechless. I had pictured this man as looking something like Tyrone Power in the movie *The Mississippi Gambler*. Instead, I found a diminutive, pale, freckled-faced little man dressed in a faded blue shirt and wrinkled trousers.

He immediately led me to his Blackjack table, gave me some chips, and asked me to start playing. He was dealing from a single deck. After watching me for several minutes, he began pointing out mistakes that he felt I was making. A master intimidator, he was trying to make me feel very anxious and he was succeeding. He said that I had a lot to learn and that I shouldn't gamble in the casino until I learned how to count properly, learned the Basic Strategy, and learned how to handle myself at a Blackjack table.

I didn't care for what I heard. I had been to Las Vegas several times and had won every time using the information in Thorp's book. I had been playing regularly with even greater success in the private games in University City. I went home after this first meeting a winner again.

Once I got home and recuperated from my junket, I began to think about what Revere had said. I decided that I could still improve my game, and that he did offer valuable knowledge. I would just ignore the useless sales pressure and keep the nuggets. On subsequent trips to Las Vegas, I made it a point to stop by and see him for further "lessons," as he called our conversations. As a Blackjack analyst, I also systematically purchased and evaluated each of his systems. In fact, before Braun's work, I managed to learn the complicated Revere Advance Point Count but found that I was making too many errors with it under casino conditions for it to be of any value to me.

Revere then advised that I learn his new Advanced Plus-minus strategy. I purchased it with the intent of using it, but then I already had a strategy I felt was better, the Hi-Opt I. Later studies proved me correct. I decided to learn the Hi-Opt I since it was as powerful as the new Revere count and much simpler to use.

What kind of man was Lawrence Revere? Most either loved him or hated him. To many casinos, he was barred as a "4." (Casinos rate players on a 1-to-4 scale: 1 = good, 2 = acceptable, 3 = undesirables such as counters, and 4 = cheaters.) Revere used to be a dealer and knew lots of casino people. He was very good at being able to make deals to cheat casinos. On the other hand, he would sometimes work with casinos in identifying which players were counters. I believe the best way to view Revere is as a true original.

Revere was ruthless in a physically harmless sort of way. He would never hurt you physically. All he wanted was *all of* your money. He once told me, "It doesn't matter who wins or loses, only who ends up with the money." The concept of cheating didn't apply to a man like Revere, because the game he was playing had no rules. Author Robert Ringer defines three types of people: the "honest" person—out to get all your chips and says so; the "dishonest" person—out to get all your chips but says he's on your side; and the "incompetent" person—he is really on your side but ends up with all your chips anyway. Revere alternated between the first two but never was the incompetent.

Having little formal education, Revere made the most of his abilities by being ingenious and resourceful. Through students who came for lessons, he would find out about private Blackjack games in all parts of the country. When I first met him, he asked me if there were any games in University City. I told him that there was at least one game nearly every night of the week in some hotel there. He persuaded me to invite him up and take him to these games. Not understanding the capabilities and motivations of a man like Revere at this time, I innocently invited him up for a visit.

The first time up he suggested that my friend Joe and I each give him a thousand dollars and he would play for us. The agreement was that we would split the profits at the end of the evening. We were eager to take him up on this offer. Who wouldn't want this world-famous expert playing for us? The conditions were also good. It was a two-deck game and the number of players varied from two to six at the table.

As the evening progressed, Revere's bankroll was going up and down. About two hours into the game, he motioned me into the bathroom. He told me that he needed more money because he was losing. I was reluctant to give him any more after the initial thousand. Suddenly he pulled the 5 of Hearts and the 5 of Clubs out of his pocket and threw them from the window to the street below. He said that he took the 5s out of the deck and that we were going to have a great advantage now. I watched the two 5s floating down and agreed that it was a beautiful sight. With the larcenous heart of the typical sucker, I gave him another five hundred dollars. He then went over and talked to Joe and suggested that Joe now sit in the game, since a number of the other players had left. He would signal Joe with his knee when Joe was to vary from the Basic Strategy.

The two of them played for three more hours and then quit. We all went downstairs, got into Joe's Cadillac, and headed for Revere's motel. On the way, Revere asked Joe to stop outside a store so he could get some cigarettes. Revere was gone quite a long time. He finally returned and we arrived at his motel minutes later. He started to empty out his pockets to divide the loot and suggested Joe do the same. Joe pulled out $625; he had won $125. Revere pulled out $400 and some odd dollars in crumpled bills. It appeared he lost over $2,000.

I say "appeared" because I was shocked. I was very surprised that Revere didn't have more money because I had been watching the game from behind him for the whole evening and it didn't appear that he lost at all. I had figured he broke even. We later found out that he *didn't* lose that much. The people dealing the game told us Revere lost about $250. We suspect that Revere hid the extra money somewhere on his person when he went in to buy cigarettes.

I decided to be very careful and not let Revere handle any more of my money in the future. I also told all my friends to whom I had previously recommended Revere to not let him handle their money either. One of these friends, a millionaire from Arizona, called me later and told me how upset Revere got when they were both in Panama. Revere suggested the same kind of partnership and my friend refused. This was evidently a standard scam Revere used.

Joe was not as suspicious of Revere as I was and continued to invite him to University City to play in other games. In fact, Joe set up a game in which he was the dealer and invited other wealthy regular players to the game in one of the city's fanciest hotels on one Wednesday evening. Joe told me that Revere was bringing a friend of his, "Bill," from Los Angeles to help him with the game. The whole thing sounded like a setup to me so I told Joe to leave me out. Although Bill was ostensibly present to deal, he would be playing in the game first. I told Joe that if he wanted to borrow some money from me to increase his bankroll as a dealer I would be glad to lend him a few thousand. But I didn't want to learn the same lesson twice. I wanted to stick to only the advantage my skill gave me. I was and will always be a player.

Joe went on with the game just the same. There were six to eight players at the game throughout most of the evening, including Bill and Revere. Joe was dealing the game and Bill would constantly ask to shuffle the cards even though he was a player. Bill, it turned out, was a "mechanic" brought in especially by Revere. Since it was all prearranged for Bill to manipulate the deck, Joe innocently let him shuffle. In their ignorance, none of the players even thought to question the practice. To shorten a sad story, the players lost all of their money to Joe.

When Joe got tired of dealing, Revere quickly offered to deal. Like a fool, Joe sat down and started to play. Some fresh players came in and Bill still continued to shuffle as before. I don't know exactly what happened next. Joe told me later that he lost about fifteen thousand dollars to Revere that evening. The other players lost about twenty thousand dollars combined. Revere and Bill split the thirty-five thousand dollars and Joe was left with some very hostile former friends and business associates.

Joe was a naïve glutton for punishment. He continued to invite Revere to University City. The final game to which Joe invited Revere had fantastic rules. You could double any number of cards at any time, five cards under 21 beat a Blackjack, you could split any number of times and resplit. You could resplit Aces and draw any number of cards to Aces and so on. There was only one hitch: Blackjack was paid off at even money instead of three to two. When Revere found out about this rule he was furious. He said it was impossible to win with this and tore into

Joe for not telling him about the rule before Revere came up. Revere even went so far as to demand that Joe pay Revere's air fare—Revere had no shortage of gall. Joe suggested what Revere could do with his request for air fare, and that was the last time Joe invited Revere to University City.

As a result of our dealings with each other, Revere wrote a number of myths that require a bit of clarification. First, no one has ever accepted my fifty-thousand-dollar challenge, including Revere or his friends. Although he had never approached me about it, Revere claimed that he did accept my challenge and I refused to carry it through. Incidentally, if he had taken up my challenge and took the role of the dealer, I would have asked that the deck be laid flat on the table and that one card be dealt at a time very slowly and from the top. I would demand this because Revere showed Joe and me that he could deal seconds during one of his lessons.

Second, Revere has claimed that I am not a winning player. He is only partly correct here. I was a winning player until I got to know him. After we met, I noticed that I began losing against the same dealers I had consistently won against before. Later on I found that he in fact worked for some of the casinos and fingered people that were threats to the casinos. Revere later admitted to me that he sometimes worked teaching dealers how to spot counters. The contradiction of his association with casino management and personnel and his being a Blackjack teacher was understandable since he was a former dealer and pit boss with many industry contacts.

Third, the statements Revere made about the power of the Hi-Opt I in his advertisements are simply not true. Revere could not comprehend how a simple system like the Hi-Opt I could be so much more powerful than some of his complex systems. The power of Hi-Opt I has been proven by independent experts such as Julian Braun and Professor Peter Griffin and verified by Professor Walter Schneider to be *at least as* powerful as any other two-hundred-dollar system in existence. Ken Uston's teams have also shown the power of the Hi-Opt I by winning over one million dollars with it in casinos throughout the world. I don't feel too badly about Revere's criticisms of me, since he devoted a whole chapter of his book to a venomous attack slamming nearly every system or authority who has contributed to the Blackjack scene in recent years except himself. (Stanley Roberts has even won a libel suit over Revere's remarks.)

Nonetheless, I have to admit somewhat ruefully that knowing Revere was worthwhile. Revere was truly a professional gambler —he let nothing stand in his way of getting money. From Revere I learned that professional gambling could be a ruthless, no-holds-barred profession, and I had the dubious privilege of seeing an expert practice his craft. This kind of gambling is not for me.

FINDING PRIVATE GAMES

If you are interested in playing in private games and live in a big city, nose around for a game. In most places, the illegal casinos are alive and well. In New York, for example, an International Blackjack Club member sent me a flier, excerpts of which state:

> CARD PARTY every Saturday, Sunday, Monday, Tuesday, and Thursday evenings at 7:30 P.M. Park your car free at the Midwood Parking Lot at Coney Island Avenue. One of *our* cars will be waiting to drive you from and to your car. . . . Four decks out of a shoe, real casino chips, splits, double downs, played on professional tables and cushioned stools for your comfort. Dealt by a trained young man or woman in uniform. By far the best game in town.

If you are not enthused with the idea of becoming a participant in a "victimless crime," you might want to take advantage of other private games that let you play legally. These usually take the form of "Las Vegas nights" and are organized to help some socially acceptable group raise money. The only problem is that you won't be playing with real money. You buy play money, often ten thousand dollars for five dollars in actual currency, and play a typical casino game.

Play goes on for several hours, with the Blackjack table minimums gradually raised to five thousand dollars then to ten thousand dollars toward the end of the night. The games are stopped about midnight and the real payoff begins. The normal procedure is to auction off a large number of donated or purchased gifts to the assembled players. With winnings in hand, you bid your funny money on whatever item you want in competition with other winners.

This is a terrific gimmick for the sponsoring organization. The items are usually donated or bought at a discount, the "casino" keeps the typical portion of the players' money, and then the big winners dutifully drive up the price of the best goods through an auction. Since many of the items have a minimum bid (if the organization is smart), the sponsors not only make money on the entrance fee and on player losses at the tables, but also they don't have to "sell" all the items if the players' winnings aren't sufficient.

I play in Las Vegas nights for relaxation and for practice. The playing session is too short to guarantee my being able to win enough to buy a big prize. The tables are normally very crowded (often going more than the casino maximum of seven to a table), and the dealing very slow because of the inexperience of the volunteers. Nonetheless, it is an excellent place to practice any of the playing strategies in this book under conditions similar to those in a real casino. And if you are a winning player, you are likely to be able to buy at least a small prize.

Since most of my friends know of my Blackjack work, I normally let them combine my winnings with theirs so that they can bid on a bigger gift. I can just see the headline in the sponsor's bulletin if I didn't contribute to the cause. "Charity's fund-raising event raided by professional Blackjack player!" Fortunately, you have no such problem and can use the information in this book to bid on and cart home anything your winnings will buy.

"NO HOUSE" BLACKJACK

There is another form of Blackjack outside the casino that I have dubbed "no house" Blackjack. This is the typical game played at home where there is no casino or house to be the dealer and benefit from the advantage of holding the deal full time. My first exposure to the home game was at a neighborhood barbeque. As the sun went down and the children were being sent home to bed our host suggested we sit down for a friendly game of Blackjack. My next-door neighbor gave me a quick grin because he was the only one who knew I was a professional player. I got him to one side and asked that he keep quiet about it and just let me play without suspicion. I promised him I would split any of my winnings evenly with the table at the end of the game. He laughed and pointed out that if I lost he might also save me the embarrassment if he was feeling generous.

I made an excuse about not having any money with me and headed back to my house. What I really wanted to do was take a few moments to look at some material I had recently received from Julian Braun. Braun had sent me the only known version of the correct Basic Strategy for the home game of Blackjack. I was eager to try it in play but not eager enough to win at the expense of the people I live near—thus the reason for passing the winnings back if the strategy was as powerful as I thought. I spent a few minutes reviewing the summary charts for standing, doubling, and splitting, and then went back to my neighbor's house.

The rules in the game we were playing were very typical of most home games. One deck is used and the dealer wins ties. Blackjack pays off two to one but no insurance is offered. Splitting pairs and doubling down are allowed, with one card only on split Aces. Any five-card hand was an automatic winner. We arbitrarily set the table limits as one dollar to twenty-five dollars, which made for an interesting game when you were the dealer facing the possibility of six or seven twenty-five-dollar bets per hand. This group was fairly conservative.

THE HOME DEALER

As you saw in an earlier table, the player losing ties gives the dealer an extra 9 per cent advantage over the Basic Strategy player. Most players understand this and realize the value of being the dealer. If you are playing with a group that doesn't, you can volunteer for the "bothersome" duty. In most cases the beginning deal is decided randomly by cutting for high or low card. Thereafter, the deal shifts on some regular fashion every certain number of hands or at every Blackjack.

The last method is the most common. A typical rule is that whoever gets a Blackjack becomes the dealer. If the dealer Blackjacks, he keeps the deal. If a player is dealt a Blackjack, then that player deals next. If both player and dealer Blackjack, then the dealer keeps the deal. If two players get Blackjack, then the player nearer to the left of the dealer gets the deal.

We cut the cards and I turned over a Queen. No one else cut over an 8 so I began to deal. Another rule we agreed upon was that any dealer errors meant that the dealer had to pay the board. In big games in Europe, I have seen where a player will pay a professional dealer to handle the cards while the player handled only the money because this penalty is so severe. Even in our little neighborhood game, I could tell some of the players were relieved that I would have to handle the cards until everyone got into the rhythm of the game. I was careful not to show my familiarity dealing Blackjack or my delight at being able to deal immediately.

OPTIMUM DEALER STRATEGY against good players is to STAND ON ALL 17s. When the dealer is allowed flexibility, Braun found that the dealer's edge can be increased slightly by HITTING SOFT 17 WITH AN ACE UP and STANDING ON SOFT 17 WITH A 2 THROUGH 6 UP. I suggested to the other players that the dealer hit his hand as he saw fit and they agreed.

The game can be dealt in any manner the players see fit—all down, all up, or a mixture. When the dealer can hit or stand at his own discretion, it is to the players' advantage to have an all-down game and to the dealer's to have the game up. The players must bust first and as dealer you can see the exact hands you have to beat in an up game. In a down game, you have no idea of the player hands and should hit or stand according to the rules above. A common variation is one card down and the following cards up, which can also give you a good indicator of the player hands when it comes your turn to hit or stand. Our game was to be all down so I decided to follow the Braun's dealer strategy for hard and for soft 17.

I started this game with one of the hottest streaks I have ever had as a home-game dealer. In all, you can expect a Blackjack to occur once every twenty-one hands or so. We had five players at the table so the deal should have changed every four or five rounds on the average. I kept the deal through eleven Blackjacks! In eight of these, I dealt a Blackjack to myself; the other three I had a Blackjack when another player had one, and so I kept the deal. My neighbor was looking at me quizzically and began watching my hands closely. When I caught his eye I shrugged in answer to his silent question and only later managed to convince him that I wasn't a card mechanic.

During this hot streak, all the players were moaning and groaning except the man to my right. I won very little throughout this stretch because everyone decided I was hot and was betting minimums except this man. He was betting five dollars and twenty-five dollars randomly and winning almost all of the twenty-five-dollar bets and losing most of the five-dollar ones. I was breaking everyone else and making this guy rich. In their misery, the rest of the players didn't notice this guy taking me to the cleaners.

Selling the Deal

On my eleventh Blackjack, I decided that the situation had gotten sticky enough. I had managed to keep very little of what I had won and had made everyone but the guy next to me mad. He was busy throwing chips in his pocket. So I decided to utilize another option of the home game, selling the deal. Like any other financial decision, if you think you can get a player to pay you more than you think something is worth, then you sell it. After my hot run of dealing, I was hoping one of the players would be willing to lay out too much money for the privilege of dealing.

The value of holding the deal depends upon factors such as number of players, size of bets, and overall skill of the players. Against average-to-good players you can estimate your advantage as about 10 per cent. If on the average you will be dealing 21 hands until the next Blackjack and let's assume the average table bet is $10, then you can expect to win 10 per cent of the total $210 bet (21 hands times $10 per hand) or $21. Therefore you might be willing to sell the deal for any bid over $21.

But if there are four other players, one out of five times you can expect to deal yourself a Blackjack and not have to give up the deal. You have a chance of winning $21 all over again. If you are playing with only one player, then double your win estimate because of this factor. If the table is full, you should only increase your win estimate by about 10 to 20 per cent. With five players at the table, and a $5.00 average bet between them, I figured the deal was worth about $13 (.10 dealer win rate times 21 hands times $5.00 per hand bet average times 1.25 dealer Blackjack factor estimate). I didn't go through all these detailed mental gymnastics as I played; I merely want to show you where the figures come from. In the game, I decided to accept any bid over $15. Because of my hot streak, the deal looked better than it actually was and I sold it for $30 after two players bid the price up.

In general, any time you want to sell the deal, just estimate the total amount of bets the players are likely to make in the next 21 *hands* (not rounds!) and divide by 10. If someone beats that figure, then you are statistically better off to sell the deal.

After I sold my deal, the Blackjacks began coming up in a more random fashion so that everyone had a chance to act as the house. In one instance, I managed to buy the deal very cheaply because the player didn't have enough bankroll to cover the bets on the table. In fact only two of us—me and the man on my right—were in any financial shape to act as the dealer. The man didn't want to deal unless forced to and always sold the deal. The rest were down after my long win streak.

"NO HOUSE" BASIC STRATEGY

When I was not dealing I tried to follow the old poker maxim of minimizing my losses and maximizing my gains by playing Braun's "no house" Basic Strategy. To my knowledge, Braun's is the first complete and correct Basic Strategy for the game. With it, I knew I had a 7 per cent disadvantage with respect to the dealer. This is an impossible game to beat without being able to deal after getting a Blackjack.

The following Basic Strategy charts are in the format used throughout the book. Player hands are shown on the left, and the dealer's possible up cards are listed across the top. The following table shows the hard-standing and -hitting rules for the no-house game.

"NO HOUSE" BASIC STRATEGY: 1 Deck Hard Standing & Hitting.

YOU HOLD	DEALER UP CARD									
	2	3	4	5	6	7	8	9	10	A
18 or more	S	S	S	S	S	S	S	S	S	S
17	S	S	S	S	S	S	S	S	S	H
16	S	S	S	S	S	H	H	S	S	H
15	S	S	S	S	S	H	H	H	S	H
14	S	S	S	S	S	H	H	H	H*	H
13	S	S	S	S	S	H	H	H	H	H
12	S**	S	S	S	S	H	H	H	H	H

Exceptions: *STAND on (7,7) vs. Dealer **10**
HIT (10,2) vs. Dealer **2

S = STAND   H = HIT

You can see that this table and the corresponding one in Chapter Six are very similar. If you have already memorized the Basic Strategy for the casino game, then this section should be very simple to learn by concentrating only on the differences. In the home game you must stand on hard 12 versus a dealer 2 or 3 (with one exception) and also stand on lower values versus a dealer 9 or 10. You must stand as low as 15 or 16 against a dealer 10 or 9, respectively, because the home game places more importance on the dealer busting. Merely tying the dealer is a loss. Since you are unlikely to beat the dealer's 10 up hand with a 15 or 16, you are better off standing and hoping for a bust.

"NO HOUSE" BASIC STRATEGY: 1 Deck Soft Standing & Hitting

YOU HOLD	DEALER UP CARD									
	2	3	4	5	6	7	8	9	10	A
19 or more	S	S	S	S	S	S	S	S	S	S
18	S	S	S	S	S	S	H	H	H	H
17 or less	H	H	H	H	H	H	H	H	H	H

S = STAND   H = HIT

There is only one change in soft standing and hitting at home. Comparing the above table to the one on page 173 shows that in the no-house game you must hit a soft 18 against a dealer 8 up. In the casino game you would stand on this combination.

Hard doubling rules for the no-house game are also similar to casino rules. The two main differences between the following table and its companion casino table are that you do not double a hard 9 versus a dealer 3 up and do not double a hard 10 against a dealer 9 up. It makes sense that your doubling should be more conservative, since the dealer wins ties and you are more likely to lose your doubled bet.

"NO HOUSE" BASIC STRATEGY: 1 Deck Hard Doubling.

YOU HOLD	DEALER UP CARD									
	2	3	4	5	6	7	8	9	10	A
11	D	D	D	D	D	D	D	D	D	H*
10	D	D	D	D	D	D	D	H**	H	H
9	H	H	D	D	D	H	H	H	H	H
8 or less	H	H	H	H	H	H	H	H	H	H

Exceptions: *DOUBLE (6,5) vs. Dealer A
**DOUBLE (8,2) vs. Dealer 9

H = HIT   D = DOUBLE

The two exceptions in this table are easily understood if you know the Hi-Opt I count. It is to your advantage to double a hard 11 versus a dealer 10 only if your hard 11 is made up of 6,5. These are both low cards, which give you a plus-count situation. With these cards in your hand, you are more likely to draw a high-value card such as a 10, resulting in an unbeatable total. You know the dealer doesn't have Blackjack, since the hand is being continued after the peek. In doubling 8,2 versus a dealer 9 up, you have a similar situation. No 10-value cards are showing. Even though you don't have a plus-count situation, you are in a better position with a 10 total than the dealer with a 9 up. So you are betting more in an advantageous situation.

"NO HOUSE" BASIC STRATEGY: 1 Deck Pair Splitting.

YOU HOLD	DEALER UP CARD									
	2	3	4	5	6	7	8	9	10	A
A,A	SP	SP	SP	SP	SP	SP	SP	SP	SP	SP
10,10	S	S	S	S	S	S	S	S	S	S
9,9	SP	SP	SP	SP	SP	S	SP	S	S	S
8,8	SP	SP	SP	SP	SP	SP	SP	S	S	H
7,7	S	SP	SP	SP	SP	SP	H	H	S	H
6,6	S	SP	SP	SP	SP	H	H	H	H	H
5,5	D	D	D	D	D	D	D	H	H	H
4,4	H	H	H	SP	H	H	H	H	H	H
3,3	H	SP	SP	SP	SP	H	H	H	H	H
2,2	H	H	SP	SP	SP	H	H	H	H	H

S = STAND   H = HIT   D = DOUBLE   SP = SPLIT

This table shows the proper pair-splitting strategy in the no-house game. In general, you will split pairs, particularly higher-value pairs, slightly *less* frequently than in the casino. Although you still always split Aces, you don't always split 8s. This puts most casino players in shock. You also don't split 9s against a dealer 9 or split 2s, 3s, and 7s against certain dealer low cards, as you do in the casino. All this is because of the dealer winning ties.

You are also more conservative in doubling soft hands. The following table shows that you double only against the worst dealer up cards, 4, 5, or 6. The rules for soft doubling against a dealer 5 or 6 are the same as in the table in Chapter Six, but the only additional doubling you are allowed in the no-house game is holding a soft 17 or 18 versus a dealer 4 up. You must be much more careful about getting additional money on the table in the no-house game.

A special rule that is common in the home game and rare in the casino is the "N-card Automatic Win" rule. "N" is usually five to seven cards, a number chosen and agreed upon at the start of the game. Anything less than five happens too frequently to be fair and anything more than seven happens too rarely to be in-

"NO HOUSE" BASIC STRATEGY: 1 Deck Soft Doubling.

YOU HOLD	DEALER UP CARD									
	2	3	4	5	6	7	8	9	10	A
A,8 or more	S	S	S	S	S	S	S	S	S	S
A,7	S	S	D	D	D	S	H	H	H	H
A,6	H	H	D	D	D	H	H	H	H	H
A,5	H	H	H	D	D	H	H	H	H	H
A,4	H	H	H	D	D	H	H	H	H	H
A,3	H	H	H	D	D	H	H	H	H	H
A,2	H	H	H	D	D	H	H	H	H	H

S = STAND   H = HIT   D = DOUBLE

teresting. The rule allows for an automatic player win if he or she draws a hand containing a specified number of cards without busting. In the five-card version, you may wish to vary Basic Strategy and hit a four-card stiff on the chance of winning automatically.

"NO HOUSE" BASIC STRATEGY: One-deck, Five-card Automatic-win Rule Modifications

HIT four-card hard 16 or 17 vs. dealer 7 or higher
ALWAYS HIT four-card hard 15 or lower
HIT three-card hard 12 vs. dealer 2, 3, and 7 or higher
NEVER SPLIT 2, 2

The Basic Strategy for a five-card automatic-win rule is listed in the table above. Once again, the computer-generated rules make good card sense. It's to your advantage to hit a four-card hard 16 or 17 versus a dealer 7 or higher and all four-card hard stiffs since these hands are very likely to be beaten. Your best hope lies in drawing a small card and collecting a sure win. You want to hit a three-card hard 12 against certain dealer up cards for much the same reason. Finally, never split 2,2. This is nearly your best pair on the way to a five-card hand without busting.

Aces are even better if you want to get a five-card nonbusting hand, but they yield more for you if you split them and get more money on the table.

"NO HOUSE" BASIC STRATEGY: 1 Deck Summary
(No 5—card Rule).

YOU SHOW	DEALER UP CARD									
	2	3	4	5	6	7	8	9	10	A
min hard std #'s	12[1]	12	12	12	12	17	17	16	15[2]	18
min soft std #'s	18	18	18	18	18	18	19	19	19	19
min hard dbl #'s	10	10	9	9	9	10	10	11[3]	11	—[4]
pair splitting										
9,9	SP	SP	SP	SP	SP	S	SP	S	S	S
8,8	SP	SP	SP	SP	SP	SP	SP	S	S	S
7,7	S	SP	SP	SP	SP	SP	H	H	S[2]	H
6,6	S	SP	SP	SP	SP	H	H	H	H	H
4,4	H	H	H	SP	H	H	H	H	H	H
3,3	H	SP	SP	SP	SP	H	H	H	H	H
2,2	H	H	SP	SP	SP	H	H	H	H	H
max soft dbl #'s	—	—	18	18	18					
min soft dbl #'s	—	—	17	13	13					

NOTES: ALWAYS Split (A,A)
NEVER Split (5,5) or (10,10)

Exceptions: [1] HIT (10,2) vs. Dealer 2
[2] STAND on (7,7) vs. Dealer 10
[3] DOUBLE (8,2) vs. Dealer 9
[4] DOUBLE (6,5) vs. Dealer A

S = STAND   H = HIT   SP = SPLIT

The table above shows a summary of all the no-house Basic Strategy charts in a format similar to the one in Chapter Six. It is probably easiest for you to learn the charts in this format as you did in Chapter Six. Once again, you can get the most benefit from your study time if you learn the plays from the top of the chart down. And you will get most of the Basic Strategy benefit by memorizing the first three lines. Pair splitting and soft doubling can be learned only if you play enough at home to warrant the extra study effort. Using the casino pair-splitting strategies will cause only a minor reduction in accuracy of play.

Here's what using the proper no-house Basic Strategy will do for you. If you are playing with knowledgeable gamblers who know the casino Basic Strategy, then you will have at least a 9 per cent advantage over them when you are *dealing*. Since it is extremely unlikely that the players in a home game will be this skilled (look at the level of play in a casino), your advantage will probably be even higher. When you are *playing*, Braun's no-house Basic Strategy puts you at a 7 per cent disadvantage at the most. If the dealer varies from the optimal dealer strategy, your disadvantage is smaller.

So with the information in this section, you will be dealing with at least a 9 per cent advantage and playing with at most a 7 per cent disadvantage for a tidy 2 per cent numerical edge over the other players IF THEY ARE GOOD ENOUGH TO KNOW CHAPTER SIX. What is more likely is that they will be the same caliber of players (or worse) who support the casinos and that your advantage will be many times greater.

In my neighborhood game, the players were all very poor with little knowledge of Blackjack. I might as well have brought a gun to the game and gotten the fleecing over with in sixty seconds. Instead it took four hours to kill the game because everyone was betting so conservatively after my hot opening dealing streak. Although the bets rarely went above five dollars per hand, I was up over two hundred dollars when we broke up. The gentleman to my right was back down to about fifty dollars ahead, and everyone else was down. As we got up to leave I stopped everyone and explained that the game hadn't been fair because I had some information that wasn't available to the other players. I pocketed my original stake and suggested my neighbors split the winnings I had gotten "unfairly." To no surprise, not one player gave me an "Aw, shucks. You won it fair and square." They gave me the fish eye, grabbed their share, and took off counting their fingers and toes.

I normally feel that if you put your money on the table then you take your chances. But in this case, and with these people, I felt I needed to keep peace in the valley. What the session did do was convince me that the no-house game Basic Strategy is a powerful winning tool in any amateur game. I've since been able to bring winnings home regularly as an occasional player on the "Let's try something other than poker tonight" circuit.

"NO HOUSE" BLACKJACK AND THE HI-OPT I

If you are like most players, you were thinking about the pattern of Chapters Six, Seven, and Eight, and racing ahead to the topic of this section. Yes, the Hi-Opt I can be applied to the no-house game to your advantage, but not as much as you might think. In the no-house game, there are three applications of the Hi-Opt I instead of two. In addition to betting and playing strategy, the Hi-Opt I can help in better playing your dealer hands when you are allowed to hit or stand at your discretion.

First consider using the Hi-Opt I count for betting variation as a player. Recall that the player advantage for betting purposes at any point in time for the casino game can be expressed by Griffin's equation:

Player Advantage = Basic Strategy Expectation + (.515 × true count)

Although Professor Griffin has not computed the exact true count factor for the home game, we can use the casino factor to estimate betting levels. In the no-house game, this equation reduces to:

Player Advantage = −7.0 per cent + (.515 × true count)

This means that the player may have an advantage over the dealer only when the true count is +14 or greater. The deck reaches a +14-or-more level so infrequently that in theory you should rarely (if ever) bet more than the game minimum. The only reason for raising your betting level occasionally is to seem like "one of the boys" or to keep the game loose and the bets flowing. Ideally, you want to make small bets without drawing attention to yourself.

The second potential application for the Hi-Opt I system is in varying your playing strategy from the no-house Basic Strategy. Because of the dealer winning ties, this no-house strategy will be different from the Hi-Opt I casino strategy you learned in Chapter Eight. Unfortunately, the demand for special no-house strategy tables based upon the Hi-Opt I count has not been sufficient to justify the effort and expense of determining the proper Hi-Opt I strategy modifications.

What you can do is use the casino Hi-Opt I strategy as an approximation for the no-house game. As you saw with the Basic Strategy, the no-house rules are very similar to the casino rules. You are not likely to have the exact correct play in all situations, but you will gain at least a portion of the benefit by varying from the Basic Strategy decisions that are the same for both types of games.

Finally, you can take the Hi-Opt I true count into consideration when you are dealing and have the option of hitting or standing on any hand. When the true count is 0 or negative, you can follow the optimal dealer rule of standing on 17 or greater. If the count is plus, you may wish to stand on a stiff and hope to tie or beat the players without risking a bust. The higher the true count, the lower a value you may stand on. This is another area where the exact mathematical analysis has not been completed.

I normally pay close attention to the playing habits of the people in the game. If there are a number of "no bust" players and the count is plus, I will not risk a hit on stiffs of 15 or 16. If the players are good, then I will stick closely to optimal play unless the true count varies outside the ±5 range. In dealing no-house games I feel that this has helped me more than hurt me, but I have no idea what exact benefit in percentage I gain.

By using the correct no-house Basic Strategy in this chapter and at least considering the Hi-Opt I count information, you will be a tough customer to beat in the home Blackjack game. Casino experience has shown that the *take* (that is, per cent of money bet kept by the casino) averages about 17 per cent. When you are dealing, you can reasonably expect this level of winnings or more. If you play according to this chapter, you will suffer a take of at most only 7 per cent, giving you a realistic 10 per cent gain in home-game betting against casino-quality players. Although the total amount of money in the home game is far less than in the casino, the greatly increased win percentage and the absence of "countermeasures" make the game worthwhile. Being dealt down to the last card and using multiple hands with "end play" are just two of the favorable possibilities for the counter. So don't ignore the substantial winnings you can accumulate in no-house games.

The no-house game is becoming more and more popular. One recent development was reported to me by an International Blackjack Club member in Ottawa, Canada. A recent Canadian court ruling has made it possible for anyone to open up a legal Blackjack game in Canada provided the shoe is passed around from player to player in some manner so that there is no fixed house. As a result the club member has started up a legal casino that is open several times a week and bars no one. I expect that there will be a lot of these legal Blackjack games in all the major cities in Canada in the near future.

A similar type of home game is also legal in Oregon at this time. At the option of local city and county government, social gambling can be made lawful as long as the house percentage goes to the dealer and all players have the opportunity to deal. Rules vary, but generally are restrictive with doubling on 10 or 11 only. Some special options such as three 7s or 6,7,8 of the same suit payed off double, but the dealer still retains a healthy edge by winning pushes. So far these games are for small stakes— maximum bets are generally in the five dollar to ten dollar range. Nonetheless, the popularity of home Blackjack seems to be increasing so that the strategies in this chapter will be of more and more importance.

BENEFITING FROM THE INEXPERIENCED DEALER

I remember sitting in a downtown Las Vegas casino one evening with a young man dealing. It was near the end of the shift right before the final dealer session. The dealer was very quick and had been giving us a fair and entertaining game so far. On one hand he had a 5 card up and casually peeked underneath it to see if he had a 10. Several of the other players started with surprise and I said, "What's going on?"

The dealer was very embarrassed by his mistake. He kept apologizing and explained that he was on cold medicine (pronounced "code bedicid" in his condition) and was tired and groggy at the end of his shift. This type of error is forgivable because it was perfectly innocent and didn't hurt the players.

I saw another incident that was much more serious. At the dealer change we were given a nice young woman dealer who obviously hadn't been working too long. What happened was that after only about five minutes at the table she had "busted" on a five-card hand of 21 and paid the table. Not all the players noticed it, but I did. I was eager to see what was going to result, since a pit boss hadn't seen the error.

About three hands later there was a phone call at the pit-boss station. The boss listened for a short time and got a disgusted look on his face and hung up. He stomped over to an idle dealer and had him follow to our table. When the pit boss arrived, he got our dealer's attention and with a wave of his thumb, said, "Get outta here." The poor dealer blanched and left immediately. Evidently the eye in the sky had seen the mistake and notified the pit boss.

There's one thing common about harmful mistakes in Blackjack. If you make a mistake, the dealer will often quietly take your money. If he makes a mistake, he will quietly take your money. Now, I don't know what your philosophy of gambling is, but I'll tell you mine. If I am giving away my bankroll through making mistakes, then that is my problem and no one else's. Conversely, I've got enough work trying to increase my bankroll without worrying about yours too. Mistakes are things we both pay for, a system that Nature has been successfully using for millions of years. Although dealer errors will happen in a casino (particularly on some of the islands), they are much more likely to occur in the sponsored games or in private home games where the dealers are untrained. This is why this section is included in a chapter on Blackjack outside the casino.

EXPOSED HOLE CARD

One of the most advantageous errors for the player is when the dealer inadvertently exposes the hole card. Braun calculated that the player's advantage in a one-deck casino game with typical rules is 9.9 per cent, and in the no-house game is 2.1 per cent. No matter what game you are playing, use the extra information to its fullest. If the dealer shows you a standing hand (17 or better), hit yours until you tie his or bust. If the dealer shows a stiff, double nearly every possible hand and split all but 4s and 5s. You can approximate the proper exposed-hole-card strategy for dealer two-card 11 or under by considering that total as the dealer's up number and playing accordingly.

Braun calculated the first exposed-hole-card Basic Strategy for the casino game and gave it to Thorp for inclusion in *Beat the Dealer*. The table below shows a simplified version of that strategy for playing dealer hands. The pair-splitting rules and soft-doubling strategies were omitted here in order to make the memorization effort reasonable for the gain. Also, certain rules were simplified where there are multiple strategies for a particular dealer hand value.

Thorp mentioned in *Beat the Dealer* that Braun had also calculated the correct exposed-hole-card strategy for the "no house" game. For some reason, Thorp chose not to include that in his book. I called Braun to inquire about the strategy, and Julian told me that he had also given it to Epstein for inclusion in *The Theory of Gambling and Statistical Logic*. The following table details this home-game Basic Strategy for an exposed hole card.

If you closely examine this and the previous table, you will see that the strategies make good Blackjack sense. For hard- or soft-standing hands, you must hit until you tie in the casino game and hit until you win in the home game. For stiff dealer hands you must depend upon the dealer to bust by not chancing a bust yourself. And on certain dealer stiffs you can double all the way down to a two-card 5.

You might also notice that you stand more readily in the home game when the dealer has a two-card total of 11 or under. For example, you stand on a hard 13 versus a dealer 11 in the casino game, but stand on a 12 in the same situation in a home game. This is because you have little chance of beating a home dealer 11 with a stiff and must hope for a dealer bust. So in this case it is better for you to take a smaller chance of busting yourself.

These two tables should be fairly easy to learn because of the

"EXPOSED HOLE CARD" BASIC STRATEGY:
1 Deck Casino Game.

DEALER CARDS	PLAYER STRATEGY		
HARD HANDS	MINIMUM HARD STANDING NUMBERS	MINIMUM SOFT STANDING NUMBERS	MINIMUM HARD DOUBLING NUMBERS
20	20	20	–
19	19	19	–
18	18	19	–
17	17	18	–
16	12	18	5
15	12	18	5
14	12	18	5
13	12	18	7
12	12	18	8
11	14*	18*	–
10	16*	19	11
9	17*	19	10
8	17	18	10
7	17	18	10*
6	12	18	9*
5	13	18	10
4	14	18	10
SOFT HANDS			
A,9	20	20	–
A,8	19	19	–
A,7	18	19	–
A,6	17	18	–
A,5	13	18	9
A,4	13	18	10
A,3	14	18	10
A,2	15	18	10
A,A	16	18	11

*Simplification

"EXPOSED HOLE CARD" BASIC STRATEGY:
1 Deck "No House" Game.

DEALER CARDS	PLAYER STRATEGY		
HARD HANDS	MINIMUM HARD STANDING NUMBERS	MINIMUM SOFT STANDING NUMBERS	MINIMUM HARD DOUBLING NUMBERS
20	21	21	–
19	20	20	–
18	19	19	–
17	18	18	–
16	12	19*	5
15	12	19*	5
14	12	18*	5
13	12	18*	7*
12	12	18*	8
11	13*	18*	–
10	14*	19	–
9	15*	19	10
8	15*	19	10
7	14*	18	10
6	12	18*	10*
5	12	18	10
4	13	18	10
SOFT HANDS			
A,9	21	21	–
A,8	20	20	–
A,7	19	19	–
A,6	18	18	–
A,5	12	19	10
A,4	12	18	10
A,3	13	18	10
A,2	14	18	11
A,A	15	18	11

*Simplification

regular pattern to the numbers. If you wish, you can skip memorizing the rules for soft dealer hands, since these make up only
about 10 per cent of all dealer hands. Whatever you choose to
learn, you will know how to play any hands correctly where the
dealer has an exposed hole card no matter what type of game you
are in.

EXPOSED NEXT CARD

Another common error with dealers is to expose the next card accidentally. This can happen when the dealer is trying to keep the
game moving and triggers a new card out when the player signaled a stand, or when the dealer accidentally grabs two cards
from a new deck. In the home game, the last card is often optional,
so you can accept it or take your chances on the next card.

In any case, you have the opportunity to play the next card
with perfect knowledge. If the standard procedure isn't to burn
any exposed cards, then you can stand or draw with complete
safety. If the card helps you make a hand with a high total versus
the dealer up card, then you might consider doubling. For example, if you were holding a 13 and the exposed card was a 7, you
shouldn't hit, you should double to a sure 20 (if doubling is allowed on any two cards).

PAYOFF ERRORS

Studies of retail-store cashiers have shown that a money error is
most often made to the benefit of the customer. In other words,
you will be given too much change more frequently than you will
be shortchanged. It's much the same with the dealer in Blackjack.
A majority of the money errors are made in favor of the player.
When you are playing against an inexperienced or tired dealer,
you should be alert for payoff errors.

One of the most common mistakes is incorrectly paying off a
natural. Most people aren't too comfortable with ratios (3 to 2),
with percentages (150 per cent), or with fractions (1½). For example, quickly now, what is the correct payoff for a natural when
the player bet $25? $130? $175? They are $37.50, $195, and
$262.50, respectively. Even if the chips are sized against the

stacks properly, making a payoff of $262.50 requires real skill to be done quickly, skill that new dealers may not have.

Whenever and wherever you are playing Blackjack, always count your payoffs carefully before handling your money. Once you have touched the chips, any errors you claim will be suspect as sleight-of-hand cheating tricks. All you will have done is call attention to yourself. If you visually check the payoff and then call any errors to the dealer's attention, there will be no doubt as to your honesty.

New dealers have a hard enough time handling the cards properly and counting the hand values. If you find a dealer having difficulty handling money, some professional gamblers suggest you sit down and start betting weird amounts and hope for a natural. If you mix your chips in the stack, putting the more expensive ones on top, they feel the dealer may pay off with an equal-size stack of the higher-valued chip.

MISCOUNTING HANDS

Dealers seem to make the most errors in counting five-card hands. The dealer doesn't count two- or three-card hands—from experience and repetition he knows the value of these hands just by looking at the cards. Four-card hands are nearly the same. Six-card hands are rare enough and complex enough that most dealers will spread the cards and carefully count the hand. But the five-card hand is right in between what the dealer can count easily and what must be counted carefully. If you find a dealer counting five-card hands at a glance, then you have an error waiting to happen.

Some players even try to increase dealer errors by standing on five-card 22s with a satisfied remark like, "That's just what I needed" when the fifth, busting card comes. If the dealer is in a hurry he or she may assume you had a 21 and pay you off accordingly. The same type of trick can be used with five-card 20s or 16s to make the dealer think you have a better hand than you actually do. I don't mind taking advantage of incompetence, but forcing dealer errors isn't my style of play. Still, some players delight in being the quick-change artists of the casino.

I have one final bit of advice about playing against an inexperienced dealer. Try to avoid sitting at a table with a bunch of novices. Playing with unskilled Blackjack players can be a very trying experience. I've seen beginners do incredible things like standing on 11 or less and trying to split a two-card "pair" made up of A,8, etc. In such a game, the dealers get almost paranoid about the rotten players and start plowing through the game counting and double-checking everything. With a crazy player at your table, the dealer errors are less likely to help you.

Unfortunately, the new dealers at casinos are most often assigned to the lower-limit tables, and the better dealers to the higher-limit games. Novice players stick to the small-limit tables, so the normal playing habits are working against you in the casino getting good table partners against a poor dealer. In a privately sponsored game, or in a home game, this is not such a problem, because the dealer is much less skilled than in a casino. So be alert as to the profit potential of errors in any game you play.

I enjoy Blackjack outside the casino immensely. If I had to rank the ease of winning money playing Blackjack my list would be:

1. No-house home game
2. Privately sponsored house game
5. Casino game

You might notice that there is no 3 and no 4 on my list. This is to emphasize that the first two games are incredibly easy to win in compared to the third. The home game is a much better opportunity than poker because there are many excellent poker players but few knowledgeable Blackjack players. Although the privately sponsored games know they can be beaten, they aren't used to seeing the professional-level Blackjack player and don't use countermeasures to such a degree as the casino.

Blackjack is the fastest-growing casino game in the world for one reason: It gives the player the most action for his or her money. This popularity is contributing to the interest in playing Blackjack outside the casino in house and no-house forms. To the player using the information in this chapter, Blackjack outside the casino can be your very own personal cash machine for as long and as often as you want to play.

TEN

Tips for Hi-Opt I Players

He who holds the least to fortune is in the strongest position.

MACHIAVELLI

I never cease to be amazed at the places and situations in which I find good game conditions. On one disastrous trip, I found them right under the nose of a pit boss! I was making a quick stop in Las Vegas for about six hours on my way out to Los Angeles for a speech. It was only about a half hour before I had to leave for the airport and I was way down. I had lost three playing-session bankrolls in separate sittings and I had to leave soon.

I decided to try one more shot at a nearby casino since the casino I was in was packed to the maximum. There was hardly a seat free. As is often the case, the casino next door was nearly empty. I sat down at an empty table and began to play. The dealer was bored stiff, and silently began to deal after curtly handling all of my "get friendly" questions. It was a one-deck game; the dealer was extremely fast and wasn't too careful about how far he dealt into the deck. I began winning immediately.

Nervously glancing at my watch, I only hoped I had enough time to get even before I had to leave. To my dismay, though, the pit boss came over and started talking to the dealer. The last thing I wanted was a pit boss hampering my play. At least the conversation was very interesting. They talked about the NCAA basketball championships that were going on at the time, about good Italian restaurants, about people they knew. I was hearing lots of juicy gossip. But better yet, I was playing even more aggressively without any problem.

The reason my play went unnoticed was that the pit boss talking to the dealer was leaning with his back up against the table

The dealer was turned toward the pit boss and watching for my signals out of the corner of his eye. He played the cards almost absent-mindedly and made the proper payoffs. His real attention was on the conversation. I was happy for the cloak of invisibility and distraction because the dealer was dealing near the end of the deck and no one was monitoring my bets. In the short period before I had to leave, I made up all my losses and gained about half a session's bankroll. I had perfect game conditions with a pit boss standing at my table!

The difference between just playing with the Hi-Opt I system and playing profitably with the Hi-Opt I system is often very fine. The tips in this chapter can help you achieve the best possible results in casino play. Following the organization in Chapter Five, "How to Play Smart (Without a System)," you will learn how to manage yourself, stay ahead of the dealer, and keep clear of the casino bosses.

MANAGING YOURSELF

No matter how powerful the system, be it the Hi-Opt I or any other, it pales in significance next to our ego. The most difficult aspect of systems play in the casino is that it is almost impossible not to begin using our own "hunches" and ignore the system. The way to conquer this urge is to handle the judgment playing decisions according to a predetermined plan. How many hands to play, how much to bet, and money-management techniques should all be decided before sitting down. You can even plan when to go to the bathroom!

GOING TO THE BATHROOM

When your body hears the call of the bathroom, don't just arbitrarily leave. If you are in the middle of a long shoe game, wait until the count is negative before going. Why leave when you have a favorable positive count?

I make it a practice to visit the washroom often when I play in a shoe game. As soon as the true count reaches —5, I leave and

stay in the washroom as long as I think it will take until the
dealer reaches the end of the shoe. I time my return so that I
come back when he is shuffling the cards. This way, I gain an
extra advantage by playing fewer hands in negative situations
without attracting undue attention to myself by withholding bets.
The player who drinks can be expected to go to the bathroom.
The player who jumps in and out of a game while watching all
the cards will quickly be shuffled up on every time he sits down
with a large bet.

This happened to me and a friend in Atlantic City. The twenty-
five-dollar-minimum table where we sat was full. I was ranging
my bets from twenty-five dollars to four hundred dollars (one to
sixteen) while seated next to third base (my favorite position); my
friend, Mike, was playing on my right. The count quickly went to
—4, so I bet the twenty-five-dollar minimum. Mike said, "Deal
me out" to the dealer. She hesitated, looked him in the eyes, then
went by him.

About six hands later, the count reached +4. Mike shoved out
sixteen green chips (four hundred dollars). Since I had won a
two-hundred-dollar bet on the previous hand, I let four hundred
dollars ride. Unfortunately, the pit boss was watching Mike. The
boss came up in back of the dealer and whispered loudly, "Cut
the deck in half." She did this after immediately shuffling. I drew
back the four hundred dollars and played one twenty-five-dollar
chip off the top of the fresh shoe, won, and quit, pulling Mike
away from the table. I told him at the bar that he had spoiled a
good situation for us by jumping in and out of the game. He
agreed. As a result of his bet, though, we could no longer play
against that dealer and pit boss.

PICKING THE RIGHT GAME CONDITIONS

A question that often comes up from my students is, "What is
more important: playing strategy or playing conditions? Is it better to play accurately or to play in a more advantageous game?"
The answer is that it is MUCH more important to play in the
right type of game than it is to play whatever strategy you are
using, Basic Strategy or Hi-Opt I, perfectly. As long as you have
the right type of game and can range your bets, you will win at a

very quick rate no matter which system you use. Even if you are playing the Basic Strategy with occasional errors, you *will win money* with bet variations.

Of course, the more powerful your playing strategy and the more accurately you apply it, the better. Though you can double your advantage with a powerful strategy such as the Hi-Opt II (see Chapter Twelve), *in theory,* inaccuracies or lack of power in the playing strategy can be mostly compensated for by increasing the range of your bets. This is convenient, since it is much easier to bet than it is to learn how to play accurately.

Your Bet Range

In the fifties and early sixties, knowledgeable players took hundreds of thousands of dollars from unwitting casinos. These experts would range their bets from the dollar minimums to the fifty-dollar table limit, playing one to seven hands at a time depending upon the end-play conditions. The disadvantage of a large bet range now is in being cheated, shuffled up on, or barred as a counter. Because of their desire to win large amounts of money without consistently being barred, all professionals use a smaller bet range than one to fifty, along with a very powerful strategy like the Hi-Opt I or II.

Recent research has clarified the exact relationship between betting range and winnings. In one of the outstanding papers presented at the Fourth Conference on Gambling at Reno, Nevada, in December 1978, Joel H. Friedman of the Operations Research Department at Stanford University identified some of the considerations in his paper "Choosing a Blackjack Game." Friedman graciously did some further work on his charts for this book, and it is these charts that follow.

All of Friedman's charts were determined from one-hundred-thousand-deck simulations of games using the Hi-Opt II system with an Ace side count (this explains why some of the curves are so high in comparison to the figures you have seen for the Hi-Opt I). The study assumed typical Las Vegas Strip rules and that the player could see every other player hand for counting purposes. The betting scheme allowed the player to range his bets from 1 unit to "N" units when the deck was favorable. "N" was allowed to take on varied values as the favorability of the deck changed.

This is a much more accurate betting scheme than either the 1 or "N" approach used by Braun or the 0 or 1 approach used by Gwynn and Seri.

Player gain as shuffle point and bet range vary.

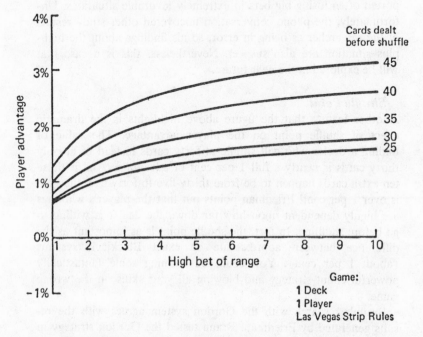

The figure above shows the results for a one-deck game played head-on with the dealer. There are a number of important features to be observed here. The first is that the performance curves begin to level off. The difference between a betting range of one to five and that of one to ten is only a few tenths of 1 per cent. The major benefit comes from raising your bets to the one-to-four range. Since high betting variation brings casino countermeasures, Friedman concludes that you should avoid betting ratios over five to one.

At the time this is being written, there is new research going on concerning what happens when the count is extremely positive. Although Friedman's charts suggest that performance rises asymptotically to some ultimate number, there is some evidence that this may not be the case. I recently received a phone call from a researcher who had simulated high plus situations and measured the results. His findings were that the player is actually at a *disadvantage* when the count is a *very* high plus. This agrees with the feelings of myself and many other players who have reported often losing big bets in extremely favorable situations. Unfortunately, the phone conversation uncovered other study results of the researcher as being in error, so his findings about the high-plus situation are also suspect. Nevertheless, this is a case that will be explored in the near future.

Shuffle Point

Another feature that the figure above highlights is the dramatic effect of shuffle point on the player advantage. The value of finding a dealer who will shuffle at forty cards instead of at only thirty cards is nearly a full 1 per cent of advantage. And if those ten extra cards happen to be from thirty-five to forty-five, the gain is over 1 per cent! Friedman points out that the player's winnings are highly dependent upon how far down the dealer is willing to go before shuffling. In fact, the shuffle point is as important as the difference between approximate or exact Blackjack systems (about 1 per cent). You could be learning some fantastically powerful count strategy and blowing all your skills on the wrong game.

Braun's research with the Gordon system agrees with the results generated by Friedman. Braun tested the Gordon strategy in a one-deck game with a shuffle point of .8 instead of the .75 reported in the comparative-systems-performance table in Chapter Seven and used a true count of +2 to increase the bet. This reduced the per cent of hands at the high bet from 20 to 17 per cent, but nevertheless increased the player's gain from 2.0 to 2.2 per cent for a one-to-four range, and from 2.7 to 3.0 per cent at a one-to-eight range. He also tried the Gordon strategy in a four-deck game dealt to the 90 per cent level with 13.5 per cent of the hands at the high bet. This resulted in a .4 per cent gain for both the one-to-four and one-to-eight ranges.

Number of Decks

Throughout the book you have seen statistics showing the penalties for playing in multiple-deck games. The figure below illustrates this effect once again. The shuffle points for one deck or for two decks are equivalent in percentage terms, but vastly different in performance. The loss from playing in a two-deck game instead of a one-deck game is severe. The difference between playing in a two-deck game with a shuffle point at eighty cards or in a one-deck game with a shuffle point at forty cards (equivalent levels) is over 1.2 per cent at the one-to-five bet range. This is further reason always to play in a game with the fewest decks possible.

Player gains for 1 and 2 decks as shuffle point and bet range vary.

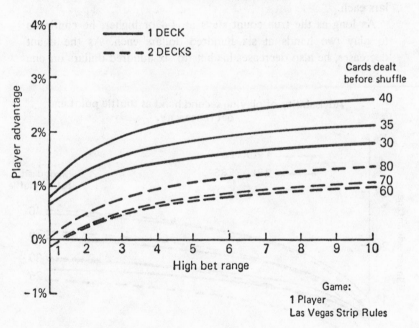

PLAYING MULTIPLE HANDS

Sometimes you will see a player betting two or more hands. Many students have asked me if this can help the systems player, guessing that multiple hands offer a protection against losing because one hand will cancel out the other. Professor Epstein has estimated that this is true only 25 per cent of the time. He showed that if you are going to lose a single hand, you will probably lose both hands 75 per cent of the time, and if you are going to win a single hand, you will probably win both 75 per cent of the time.

The most successful professional Blackjack player I know plays the four-deck game this way: At the start of a fresh deal, he plays two hands at twenty-five dollars each. If the count is slightly positive (+1), he changes to playing only one hand at fifty dollars. As the count increases, he increases the size of his wager, playing a single hand until the true count reaches +4. Then, if he won his last hand (which by this time is usually three hundred dollars), he lets the six hundred dollars ride. Should he win the next hands, he now will move to playing two hands at six hundred dollars each.

As long as the true count stays at +4 or higher, he continues to play two hands at six hundred dollars each. As the count decreases, he also decreases his bets to six hundred dollars on one

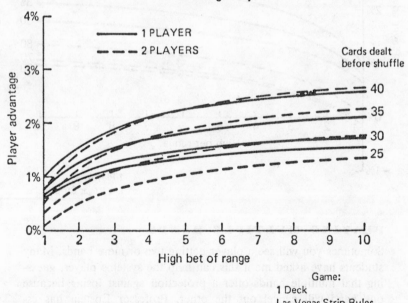

Advisability of playing second hand as shuffle point and bet range vary.

hand only, then down to three hundred dollars, down to one hundred dollars, then fifty dollars, and finally twenty-five dollars. The betting is always done gradually up or down to avoid attracting attention. He never plays more than two hands.

The advantage in playing multiple hands in a four-deck game is that it helps camouflage your betting range in a positive deck. Instead of ranging a single-deck hand from one to ten, you can range two hands from one to five or higher and attract less attention while getting more money out on the table. I used to recommend not playing two hands in single-deck games, but Friedman's studies have caused me to change that advice.

This figure shows the results for one player and for two players superimposed. There are several features of this figure to notice. First, the performance range for two players is wider than for one player. At twenty-five cards the two player total is lower, and at forty cards it is higher. Friedman concludes that the two-player game is more sensitive to shuffle point than head-on play is. Therefore you should avoid the high-cutoff dealer all the more when you are not playing head-on.

The surprising feature of the figure above is that the performance curves cross for shuffle points of thirty, thirty-five, and forty cards. Although Friedman informed me that exact crossover points were difficult to determine and not very important since the curves crossed so gradually, the differences in the one-to-four range and in the five-to-ten range are readily apparent. This leads to three conclusions:

1. If you are forced into using a low bet range because of casino pressure, play one hand head-on.
2. If you can bet a wide range without the casino getting worried, play two hands.
3. If you are not able to play head-on, you MUST bet a wider range to take full advantage of your system.

METHODS OF BETTING

Even with a smaller bet range, you must vary your bets carefully to avoid attracting attention, particularly if you are winning consistently. I have had dealers shuffle up on me in downtown Las

Vegas during the day when I would range my bets from one dollar to four dollars. The wagering methods in this section are also meant to protect you from the wild fluctuations that so often occur in Blackjack. By following these methods, you have little risk of being ruined (losing your entire bankroll) in an honest game.

There are five basic methods presented here. You can choose whichever one best suits your personal style, bankroll, and the type of game you intend to play in. As you become more comfortable in managing your bets with control, you may wish to experiment with modifications to the methods. The variations are almost infinite.

The important point is this: *The player who adopts the wagering advice and methods given here not only will keep his or her starting bankroll, but also will start winning money and continue to win as long as he or she continues playing.* As long as you are not cheated, you can never ultimately lose; you will only win because you have the long-term advantage previously owned only by the casino. You should appreciate what a monumental achievement it is never to stand a chance of long-term losing at a gambling game against an honest house. If you don't believe you are a winner with my methods, start playing in an honest game at home with your friends and prove it to yourself.

Method 1

Wager the same amount with every hand. This is known as FLAT betting, the most conservative method of betting possible. Your bet never changes, regardless of the count. Using Basic Strategy, flat betting is only a break-even proposition in most single-deck games and a slight loser in multiple-deck games (unless the casino has the "surrender" option). If you wish to win consistently, this method can be used only with a powerful playing strategy such as the Hi-Opt I or Hi-Opt II. Either of these strategies will produce close to a 1 per cent gain on flat bets in a single-deck game.

The advantage of flat betting is that you become completely ignored as a systems player (unless you are betting table maximums). The casinos have only barred one player who flat-bet.

But he made half a million dollars *before* he decided to flat-bet in order to prolong his playing career. Flat betting did allow him to play one more year. Method 1 is suggested for players betting twenty-five-dollar-or-larger chips.

Method 2

Method 2 is for single-deck play only. Start with either one- or two-unit bets, then follow the diagram below (our thanks to Dr. Koko Ita for the idea of the diagrams). This is another conservative method for players betting twenty-dollar units or greater amounts. It is extremely unlikely that you would ever get barred using this method because of its low-profile nature and limited gain. In order for this method to yield a worthwhile hourly profit, it too should be used with one of the Hi-Opt strategies.

Method 2. For single deck play.

Your first bet is one or two units:

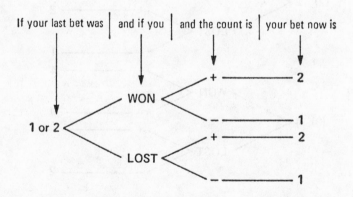

Method 2 is recommended for 20 or more dollar unit chip bettors.

Method 3

This betting method can be used in single- or double-deck play. Using it, five-dollar and twenty-five-dollar-unit-chip bettors can range their wagers from one to four units.

Method 3. For single or double deck play.

Your first bet is one unit:

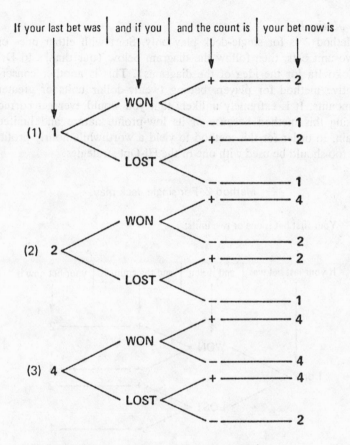

| If your last bet was | and if you | and the count is | your bet now is |

Method 3 is recommended for 5 and 25 dollar unit chip bettors.

Method 4

This method is suitable for play with any number of decks. It is a more aggressive betting approach, ranging from two to eight units (which looks like one to four to the casino, since the casino doesn't know what your unit is). Method 4 is recommended for

two-dollar and five-dollar-unit-chip bettors. The only exception to
the chart is when using Method 4 against four or more decks. In
this instance, your first bet should be two units, not four.

Method 4. For single, double or multiple deck play.

Your first bet is 4 units. Follow steps (1) and (2) of method 3 unless:

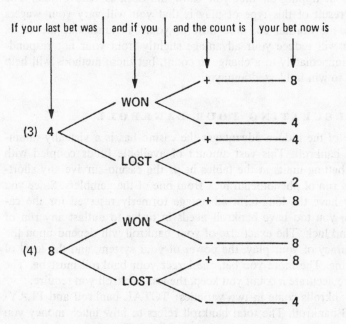

If your last bet was | and if you | and the count is | your bet now is

(3) 4 — WON — + ———— 8
          — ———— 4
        LOST — + ———— 4
          — ———— 2

(4) 8 — WON — + ———— 8
          — ———— 8
        LOST — + ———— 8
          — ———— 4

Method 4 is recommended for 5 dollar unit chip bettors and for 2 dollar unit
chip bettors. When using Method 4 against 4 or more decks your first bet
should be 2 (not 4) units.

Method 5

Method 5 is a slight modification to Method 4 for four- or six-
deck play only. Your first bet is always two units. The only
difference is that when you win an eight-unit bet, place the eight
units you have just won on a second hand if the count is plus.
You may want to play two hands in a multiple-deck game when
you have an advantage. Playing two hands gives that 25 per cent

advantage in balancing wild fluctuations against losing all sixteen units in one hand.

As you can see from the charts, the key is to let your winnings ride up into larger bets when the deck is advantageous. Letting winnings ride is a normal bet for any gambler, and doesn't attract the attention of a suspicious pit boss the way a sudden increase does. The charts also show you how to reduce your bets gradually without tipping off that you know the deck is unfavorable. The net result of this type of play is that you will vary your wagers with the normal ebb and flow of your "fortunes" at the table. This will reduce your advantage slightly from your not responding immediately to a change in count, but these methods will help you to win in blessed anonymity.

CALCULATING YOUR BANKROLL

One of the hidden advantages the casino has is a virtually unlimited bankroll. This vast amount of available funds coupled with the betting limits at the tables helps the casino survive any short-term run of phenomenal luck from one of the gamblers. Since you now have the long-term advantage formerly reserved for the casino, you too have bankroll needs in order to outlast any run of casino luck. The exact size of your bankroll will depend upon the accuracy of your play, the power of your system, and the level of betting. The more you bet, the larger your bankroll must be. The more accurate a count you keep, the less bankroll you require.

Bankrolls come in two varieties: TOTAL bankroll and PLAY⤸ ING bankroll. The total bankroll refers to how much money you should accumulate to use in gambling. The size of your total bankroll depends upon the size of your bet and the type of point count used. The following table shows the multipliers required for each type of count used.

Effect of Count Method on Total Bankroll

Betting-count Method	Bankroll (in units)
True count	50 × largest bet
Running count	100 × largest bet
Plus count	200 × largest bet

Keeping an accurate running count cuts the required size of your bankroll in half. Performing the division to keep the exact true count again halves the bankroll requirements. Starting with an adequate bankroll will nearly eliminate your being wiped out by a bad streak of luck.

The playing bankroll is the amount of money you need for *one playing session*. You aren't expected to carry around your total bankroll (that could be dangerous). You only need several small playing bankrolls for each day. The size of the playing bankroll depends upon the method of betting you use. Although the values in the table below are recommended, there are no hard-and-fast rules here. If you don't like the methods recommended, make up a playing bankroll that is comfortable for you.

Playing-bankroll Requirements

Betting Method	Bet Range	Playing Bankroll
1	Flat	8
2	1–2	10
3	1–4	16
4	2–8	32
5	2–16	64

The playing bankrolls are in terms of units. Do not lose more than one playing bankroll in any one session. If you suspect the dealer is cheating, quit *before* losing your entire playing bankroll to him.

Help control your losses with this little trick. When sitting down at the table, buy as few chips as possible. Buy only half or one quarter of the number of units needed for your playing bankroll. For example, if you are using Method 5, buy only sixteen units worth of chips instead of the sixty-four required. You can buy more later should you need to, which helps maintain the impression you are a loser. The more times you have to buy chips, the bigger a loser you seem, even if you are pocketing winnings under the table and asking for more change. I like to pocket part of my winnings at the end of a dealer shift. This gives me the opportunity to ask for more change during the next session without the dealer realizing I have been winning. The other reason to cash only a portion of your chips is so you never show the casino how much money you have. The less you show, the smaller a threat you seem to them. This is how they see you.

The next table shows a summary of the features of the five betting methods. The total bankrolls were calculated by multiplying the proper factor from the Betting Method 2 table by the top of the bet range. For example, the running-count bankroll for Method 3 was: $4 \times 100 = 400$ units. Although the Hi-Opt I is rated as "necessary" for only two of the methods, it is highly recommended in all cases.

BETTING-METHODS SUMMARY

	1	2	3	4	5
Decks	1	1	1,2	1,2,4	4,6
Units bets	$25+	$20+	$5,25	$2,5	$2,5
Range	flat	1–2	1–4	2–8	2–16
Playing bankroll (units)	8	10	16	32	64
True-count total bankroll (units)	200	100	200	400	800
Running-count total bankroll (units)	200	200	400	800	1,600
Plus-count total bankroll (units)	200	400	800	1,600	3,200
Hi-Opt strategy necessary?	yes	yes	no	no	no

STAYING AHEAD OF THE DEALER

Once you are fully in control of yourself, you can focus on controlling the dealer. Many players who come to me for lessons complain that most dealers work so fast that the players can't concentrate and lose track of the cards. There is no excuse for this because it is very easy to slow down the dealer.

SLOWING DOWN THE DEALER

A lot of players are intimidated by the dealer. The majority of dealers intimidate these players on purpose. Here is how they do it. If you happen to sit down alone at a table and begin to play, you'll notice that the dealer will start dealing quite slowly. Then, very, very gradually, he (or she) will pick up the pace of the deal. From hand to hand, shuffle to shuffle, his speed will increase. He's getting you into his rhythm of play. This is so gradual that most players are unaware of the change.

What they do become aware of is a feeling of being rushed. Since few players are willing to admit they can't play as fast as the dealer, they begin to play an inferior brand of Blackjack. They stand more often, split pairs less often, and don't get as many big bets out as frequently as they otherwise would. Don't let this happen to you.

It is very easy to slow the dealer down for your play, since the dealer cannot pass you up until you have given your stand signal. So from the beginning, play at your pace and ignore the dealer's rhythm. Be very methodical and clear in your hand signals. Look at your cards carefully before giving your signal. After a short time, this careful mode of play will become your natural rhythm, one that the dealer will adjust to.

He won't adjust to it willingly unless you tip him. One dealer at the twenty-five-dollar tables on the Strip tried the speed-up routine early one morning head to head. As his pace increased, I continued my methodical play, thinking each play through. At first he looked disgusted, as if I were a novice with more money than brains. Then he got bored, looking off into the casino between cards and watching for my signal out of the corner of his eye. He sighed like the best soap-opera Romeo, as if my method of play were driving him into a stupor. Despite his attitude, I continued because the cards were running well. And after a few tips and several hundred dollars in profit for me, he realized I was there to stay. He finally brightened up and we had a decent conversation as I played.

There is just one warning to slowing the dealer down: Don't overdo it. If you irritate the dealer or other players at the table, you are only hurting your chances of winning. You needn't disrupt the flow of the game to give yourself time. Often a delay of a second or two is enough to gather your thoughts and choose the correct play. This will never bother anybody at the table.

PLAYING THE DEALER HEAD-ON

The best time to play is when the tables are not crowded. The *ideal* situation is to play alone at a table, as I was doing above at the Flamingo. There are many advantages to head-on play:

1. More hands per hour. When you sit alone, you get to play more hands per hour. The more hands you play, the more money you will turn over per hour. Naturally, the more money you turn over, the more you will win.

2. You see all the cards. You often miss seeing all of the cards when you play with others in a down game. If people at your

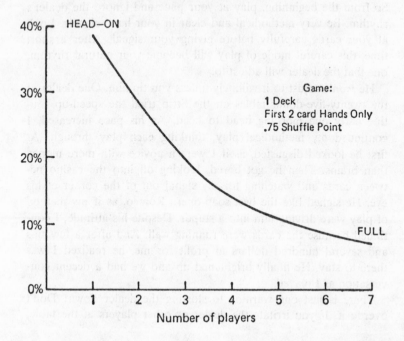

Percent of time observed true count equals actual true count as number of players varies.

Game:
1 Deck
First 2 card Hands Only
.75 Shuffle Point

HEAD–ON

FULL

Number of players

table are hiding their hands, your count will be inaccurate. With an inaccurate count, you may be playing and betting inaccurately. This takes away from your optimum advantage.

As this is written, I am just beginning computer studies on the effects of not seeing the other players' cards. At this point, all I have available are frequencies for various situations. More valuable would be the effect on the player gain from not seeing all the cards, much as Friedman did for evaluating the effects of shuffle point and bet range. What is available at this time, though, shows that the error in not seeing all the cards is greater than most players imagined.

The figure above shows the results of a simple simulation covering the first two card hands dealt each round for ten thousand deals. The simulation recorded the number of hands the player's true count (seeing his two cards and the dealer's up card only) equaled the actual true count (assuming full knowledge of all the cards including the dealer's hole card). The per cent of time the player knew the correct true count after every player had the first two cards is shown by the curve.

When I saw how infrequently the player knew the actual true count, I modified the simulation program to evaluate what the average error was as the number of players increased. The relationship between number of players and average amount of error turned out to be roughly linear. Although no figures for the amount of gain lost by not playing head-on are currently available, the average error is striking. With a full table, the preliminary simulations suggest that your true count for playing the hand is normally wrong by an average of three points. This can't help but result in playing-strategy errors.

3. You conserve mental energy. The more players at your table, the more mental effort is required to watch and count all the cards. With a full table of seven players, it takes seven times the energy per (your) hand to keep track of cards than with only you at the table. What is also unfortunate is that this additional mental energy is required to play fewer hands per hour. So it takes more effort to win less money.

4. More hands are dealt between shuffles. Shuffling is a waste of your playing time. While rest time is valuable, you can't win

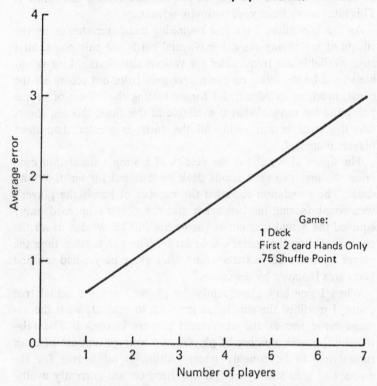

Weighted average of error between observed and actual
true count as number of players varies.

Game:
1 Deck
First 2 card Hands Only
.75 Shuffle Point

while the cards are being shuffled. More importantly, with fewer
shuffles, higher count values often result.

5. *Less bother from other players.* Other players can bother
you in many different ways. They can distract you innocently by
asking if the seat next to you is empty, or by trying to start up a
conversation. They can alienate the dealer by not tipping when
they win or by complaining when they lose. If the dealer decides
to take out his anger on another player, the whole table suffers
because it is easier for him to deal himself winners than to deal
losers to a particular player.

If you are a nonsmoker, a smoker joining your table can quickly
kill your concentration. Unfortunately, most Blackjack players

smoke due to the tension created by the game and the availability of free cigarettes (as a nonsmoker, I would have killed several cigar smokers and gone for a defense of justifiable homicide if I could have been certain of getting a nonsmoking judge).

If the other players at your table are bad, it can be taxing on your self-control. When I first started to play winning Blackjack, I sat in constant amazement at the way people gave their money away in ignorance. Although you should know (as a professional) that the play of someone else at the table has no effect on your hand in the long run, it can be quite upsetting when someone takes the card you needed against the odds. I was at the Riviera once and had four hundred dollars on the table after doubling down with two hundred dollars. A poor player on my right took a 10 I needed for my 11 double-down hand by drawing to his 14 against a dealer 6! I lost the four hundred dollars. No matter how tough a player you are, it is difficult to maintain your composure in such situations. It is better to avoid them from the beginning.

A crowded table also draws more attention from the pit boss, especially if you are the biggest bettor there. This is not good for your playing longevity. Not only will he be able to watch your betting, but he may even ask you your name and where you are from. A crowded table also reduces your control over the game. You cannot speed up or slow down anything more than your decision if there are others at your table. You won't get to cut the deck as often, which is a missed opportunity, as you will see.

The only disadvantage of head-on play has nothing to do with the dealer. The problem is that the pit boss or other observer can watch you more easily, since you are the only one at the table.

Finding Head-on Play

With all these advantages in head-on play, the challenge is to find an empty table. Empty tables in crowded casinos are little help. Most people seem to have an aversion to sitting at an empty table, while you prefer one. But once you sit down, the table isn't empty anymore, and others will join you in short order.

The best time to find a dealer alone is on the graveyard shift from midnight to eight o'clock in the morning. On weekdays, the tables are very quiet between 3:00 A.M. and 10:00 A.M. On weekends, you have to wait until after 4:00 A.M. to play this shift. It is getting more difficult to find good conditions on this shift because the casinos like to close down tables after the midnight-show crowd leaves. This way they force the players to pack together at the few tables that remain open.

A potential problem on the graveyard shift is that the casinos are alert to finding counters playing at this time. But if you play after 5:00 A.M., the dealers are more tired. They have already worked five hours and are looking forward to going home. They are physically weaker and mentally more lazy, dealing slower and not taking the extra effort to cheat you at this time.

Other favorable times to play are during show times, when most people are watching the high-priced entertainment. This is usually from about 8:00 P.M. to 9:30 P.M. and from midnight to 1:30 P.M. The new shift at noon is also a good time because many casinos open most of their tables at noon. You can usually play for up to two hours thereafter before the tables become crowded.

In general, it is best to avoid playing on weekends. Las Vegas, Reno, and Lake Tahoe are all overcrowded then. The only places you can find ideal conditions during weekends are on the outskirts of town.

In terms of seasons of the year, the winter months are much better than the summer months. Tourists pack the casinos during the summer, then return home once the vacation season is over. The deadest time of the year is the first three weeks in December. The playing conditions during this short period are absolutely perfect.

Although there are no other specific times at which playing conditions are best, there is one tip in locating good conditions. I have found that some casinos are uncrowded at exactly the same time as other casinos are jammed. When the MGM Grand or the Dunes is crowded, the Flamingo is often dead. When the Riviera and the Circus Circus are jumping, the Stardust or the Frontier may be quiet. When the Sahara is full, the Hilton or the Landmark can be good places for a head-on game. As soon as the casino becomes crowded, try the place next door.

THE "BURN CARD" AND THE BOTTOM CARD

There are other tricks to staying ahead of the dealer. You gain an extra advantage if you can get a glimpse of the burn card and/or the bottom card in a hand dealt game (single- or double-deck). After the deck has been shuffled by the dealer and cut by one of the players, the dealer takes the top card (burn card) and places it underneath the last card in the deck (bottom card). Depending upon where you are sitting, you can often get a glimpse of one of these cards. The best seats for this are the ones at about a forty-five-degree angle from the dealer, the second seat or the second-to-last seat. Which card you might see depends upon the seat you are sitting in and whether the dealer is left- or right-handed. I prefer to sit in the second-to-last seat next to third base. This position allows me more time to think about my plays while still affording a good view of the deck.

The advantage of seeing either of the two cards comes from your being able to count this extra card before the first card is dealt. Should one of these two cards turn out to be a plus card, then you know that you automatically have the advantage at the start. You might place a larger wager in the beginning of a one-deck game. Should your glimpse show you a negative card, you can place your minimum bet before the deal begins or quit.

Even dealers with sloppy burn motions can be clever about timing the move. At its worst, it is still a quick move. And your distractions are multiplied during the break for shuffles, as players change tables, waitresses stop for drink orders, and conversations begin. One young woman dealer I played against was not very dextrous with the cards. Her burn motion practically let me count the spots on the card. What she would do, though, is make her burn move suddenly and randomly. After her shuffle and cut, she would pick up the deck and converse while squaring the sides. She would then burn the card within the next few seconds, sometimes immediately, sometimes after a slight delay. Naturally, you look at someone as they speak. At first I missed about half of her burns as I was lulled and distracted into seeing only the closing part of her motion, when it was too late. I finally started concentrating on her hands the minute she picked up the deck and then saw the burn card consistently.

Don't worry about seeing the burn card in a shoe game. Here the dealer simply takes the top card and places it in the discard rack. It is almost impossible to get a glimpse of the burn card in a shoe game because the dealer slides it over the top of the table. The face of the card never leaves the felt. Sometimes, however, the plastic discard tray will give you a reflection of the burn card as it is placed in the tray. Continue to be alert.

CUTTING THE DECK PROPERLY

There are certain ways to cut the deck that can add to your advantage, particularly when you are playing head-on with the dealer. In head-on play, the dealer will often face you so that he won't have to deal sideways. If you are sitting to one side trying to see the burn or bottom cards, your viewing angle is destroyed. You can get the dealer to twist his body around to a more favorable angle with the cut.

Instead of placing the half you pick up right beside the remaining half, put it about a foot away. This forces the dealer to twist slightly to pick up your half of the deck. If you make this a quick, careless motion, plopping the deck down with style, the dealer is not likely to get irritated. The advantage to you is that the dealer is frequently not in the same position as he was originally. With your cut you have made him shift the angle at which he is holding the deck in relation to your line of sight. You have to experiment on exactly which side to place your half of the deck after you have cut it with different dealers in order to get them to move around.

Another important move is to cut the deck where it resists cutting. In most decks, there are certain places where it is easy to cut the deck. There, one of the cards is bent, creating a larger-than-normal space between it and the next card. We know that these cards are normally a 10 or an Ace. Why? Because, as you read in Chapter Five, these are the cards that are bent when they are the dealer's "up" card. To review, whenever an Ace or a 10 is "up" for the dealer, he must have a look at his "down" card to see if he has a Blackjack. The gaps from bent cards can be quite prominent if the deck has been in play for several hours.

If you are not aware of this condition, you will most likely cut the deck where it breaks the easiest and put one of the bent cards out of play on the bottom of the deck. Conversely, if you cut the deck where it resists cutting, you will be more likely to cut a small card to the bottom of the deck, where it is safely out of play. This is much to your advantage.

There are also some gains from proper cutting in a shoe game. If you are keeping a running point count from the start of a shoe until the dealer hits the plastic cut card, you should wind up with a plus count about half of the time (if you don't, find another table). This means that the cards left in the shoe (usually about one deck) are advantageous to you. *Keep your eyes on these remaining undealt cards.* Follow that clump of cards through the dealer's entire shuffle. You will soon notice that your clump of cards will be shuffled into only *half* of the remaining cards because the dealers usually do not shuffle as thoroughly as they should. The positive count you identified stays in one half of the shoe.

When the dealer slides the cards to you for cutting, what you want to do is cut the positive half of the deck into the front of the shoe. To do this, place the red card directly in front of the positive clump. When the dealer shifts the cards from behind the cutting card to the front, you will have a positive deck from the beginning. Since your original positive deck has been shuffled into another, unknown deck, *divide the ending count by 2* and begin your betting accordingly. After several hands have been played, you can then adjust your count back to normal, since the 10s-rich part of the deck has been passed. Although it sounds complicated, with practice you will make this advanced Blackjack play with ease (this play can't be applied in Atlantic City, because the dealers shuffle the shoe end more thoroughly than in Nevada).

CHOOSING A SHOE GAME

Lots of players think that a shoe insures them of not being cheated. As you read in the discussion about illegal shoes, this is not always the case. But there are other ways to cheat with a shoe. One friend of mine reported having a very unsuccessful playing session in Panama. He was suspicious for reasons we will soon see, so when the time for a shoe change of cards came, he asked the pit boss for the used cards as souvenirs. The pit boss didn't want to give him the cards, but my friend kept pestering him. Since he was a high roller and getting insistent, the pit boss finally gave in and handed him the four decks. When my friend got back to his room, he started sorting through the cards and arranging them on the bed. He found that four 10s and two Aces had been removed! It was suddenly obvious why he had been losing.

The first thing to do is use the Hi-Opt I count to find out whether all the cards are in the shoe. Without being obvious, stand back from the table at the start of a fresh shoe and count until the red cut card is hit. Make a mental note of the count you are left with. Repeat the operation several times, continuing your count at the start of each shoe. Your final net figure should be close to 0. If your net is a +4 or more, then you can be suspicious that some of the 10s are missing from the shoe. Don't play at that table. Go to another table and repeat the procedure. Better still, go to another casino. If you are satisfied that all the 10s are in the deck, then count the Aces. There should be four Aces for every deck dealt out.

I was playing at one Strip casino with little success. I became suspicious when the count seemed always to be positive at the reshuffle. In the interests of science and my curiosity, I quit playing (also to save my bankroll) and started watching the game closely. The count was plus nearly 70 per cent of the time at the shuffle point. The pit boss suddenly came over with new cards for the table. It might have been a coincidence, but I think I was watching the cards too intently and alerted the pit boss that I was suspicious. I stayed ten minutes or so after the new cards went into play to feign innocence and left a slightly poorer player for the experience.

If you are satisfied after watching the cards and the dealer for anything suspicious, you are almost ready to sit down. Wait until the dealer starts a fresh shoe, get the count, and don't sit down until the count is plus. Then bet your maximum bet. This is a neat maneuver, but don't expect to get away with it more than once in any casino on any one day. If the dealer doesn't shuffle up on your bet, you are likely to have the pit boss or dealer closely watch your play. It is simply not worth the risk of getting barred by engaging in this practice too often in the same casino.

ELIMINATING A NEGATIVE SHOE

If you experience a negative count near the beginning of the shoe, you can get rid of it faster by playing the absolute table minimum bet on two or more hands. This gets a lot of cards out of the shoe quickly but not at a minimum cost. You are best off playing only one hand at a time during a negative count. What you want is to use the most number of cards per bet when the house has an advantage. Arbitrarily assuming an average of three cards per hand (whether dealer or player), you use up six cards per bet playing head on. Nine cards are used if you play two hands, only four and one half cards per bet. Therefore, the only time you might want to play more than one hand is when you are facing positive counts.

KEEPING CLEAR OF THE CASINO

When I first learned to play winning Blackjack, I was very much afraid of getting detected as a winning player and being barred. I began to feel anxious every time I sat down at the table. Many other players have admitted to me that they feel the same way. *Do not be afraid of getting barred.* They will only bar you if they cannot cheat you. If you have been losing lately, you have no risk whatsoever. Out of the millions of gamblers who have played Blackjack in the past fifteen years, only several hundred are barred. If you are a good enough player to avoid being cheated and win openly and consistently, then you might begin to worry about it. If you don't win *openly,* your chances of getting barred are practically 0.

Do what many players do: Adopt a spy mentality. Spies are unobtrusive. They don't bother anybody. They are quiet and polite. They look like the natives, dress like the natives, and talk like the natives. They never stand out. They pretend to have the same values as the natives. The men like money and women. They follow at least one sport and are up on politics. The women are giggly and nervous, raving about the shows.

Spies are well trained for their job. They are so well trained, the training never shows. They look casual, but the brain is functioning at a very rapid rate. They are aware of everything around them at all times. They use their training, experience, and determination to get the job done. The job is to win money in a casino steadily and smoothly for a long time.

There are many techniques you can use to camouflage your play so as not to get barred. The major ways the casino identifies systems "spies" is usually from the way they appear, the way they bet, or because they tip off that they are counting. All of the suggestions listed in this section are designed to make you seem like just another gambler, happily giving your money to the casino.

THE INVISIBLE PROFESSIONAL

As you play winning Blackjack, you want to be like the "little man upon the stair" from the childhood poem:

> I saw a man upon the stair,
> The little man that wasn't there.
> He wasn't there again today,
> Oh how I wish he'd go away!

By following these rules, the casino will feel the same way about you.

1. Don't attract attention in any way. A number of careless Blackjack players attract attention by the way they handle their cards. Since there are constantly players who try to cheat at Blackjack, the dealers are instructed to watch any unusual moves on the part of the players. Some cheaters mark cards with special paint that they get from underneath their fingernails. Others bend cards, crimp them, or mark them by cutting them with their fingernails. Players have even been caught trying to switch decks and bring new cards (Aces, for example) into the game. Therefore, think about how you hold your cards. Don't make any unnecessary or suspicious moves. Hold your cards still and in plain view of the dealer and keep your fingernails clean and well trimmed.

You should also avoid any other unusual behavior in the casino. One young man attracted enormous pit-boss attention at a Sahara table where I played by furtively using a small reference card as a guide. There were two others in the casino playing the same way, and they would have conferences in the middle of the floor, playing openly as a team. The pit bosses clustered around any table where one of them sat, nearly breaking their necks to see what was on one of the cards. Although the team was up several thousands of dollars, the casino bosses let them play on once they found out that the "system" was based on ESP. Seeing this, the bosses knew the short-term run of luck would not last forever and the house percentage would win out in the end.

The reason I played under all this attention was that I was totally ignored with all the concern over the team player at my table. I was ranging my bets much wider than if I were playing alone or at a regular table. In a similar situation, one professional talked about making a large win when playing with Sammy Davis, Jr. Davis came up to his table and began betting five hundred dollars on several hands at once. This drew a tremendous crowd, which Davis regaled with funny stories, impressions, and quips. In the meantime, the professional won about two thousand dollars ranging his bets aggressively, safely in the shadow of the great entertainer.

2. Dress like a tourist. It is important not to stand out in any way in terms of dress. For example, in Las Vegas the weather is extremely hot for most of the year. Most men wear short-sleeved shirts, and women wear light blouses. But the type of clothes differs from the Strip to downtown. Although all the tourists wear casual clothes, the Strip crowd dresses better than the downtown crowd. You would fit in well downtown if you wore a short-sleeved checkered cowboy shirt with Levi's or plain, dull slacks. Expensive jewelry is definitely out, as is a sports jacket. Strip tourists wear more expensive and brighter casual clothes, and showgoers can get away with a sports jacket. I like to be comfortable when I play, so I normally stick to muted sports clothes on the Strip, and jeans and a shirt downtown.

3. Hide your pen and pad. Whenever I play downtown I wear

a Timex watch, and take the Cross pen out of my shirt and hide it
in my pants pocket, where it won't be seen (see "The Keeping of
Records" in Chapter One). Dealers and pit bosses are very alert
when it comes to players' apparel and jewelry, including pens.
Regular gamblers don't carry pens—they never need one. If you
carry a pen, the dealer can quickly infer that you are some kind
of systems player recording details of your sessions. Casinos don't
like people who keep track of their wins and losses. They like
people who happily gamble without being aware of how much
they are losing.

4. *Smile.* If you are supposed to be losing happily, smile! If
you look serious or glum while playing, you may alert the house.
I'm not the smiling type when I gamble. I actually had to practice
in front of a mirror in order to learn how to smile while concentrating on the cards. Try to be happy at the table. If you must
talk, don't complain. Dealers are sick of hearing complaining
players, the curse of every shift. Speak up if the dealer has made
a mistake, but don't gripe or complain unnecessarily. Exercise
control always.

5. *Drink while you play.* If you can hold your liquor, drink
while you play. Casinos love drunks, so they provide you with all
the free drinks you want. In fact, they make them stronger than
the drinks served at the bar to nongamblers. If you can drink
well, then you will draw suspicion away from yourself. Some
players have mastered the Hi-Opt I so well that they get drunk on
purpose when they play. They become winning drunks!

Unfortunately, I do not drink. At first I would order either a
Diet Pepsi or an Orange Julius, which always got a big laugh out
of the dealers and pit bosses. If you are a nondrinker, the Orange
Julius is a completely nonalcoholic drink, something like a milk-
shake. In addition to the unwanted attention from the casino, or-
dering this drink often created conversation for me at the table,
as other players would like the looks of the drink and talk to me
about it.

Now I use several techniques to look like I'm drinking. At the
start of a session, I may order an orange juice or soda and carry
it to the table with me. I can nurse this for quite a while, taking
small sips as I play. If I have to order a nonalcoholic drink at the

table, I try to do it right before the dealer change when the pit boss is elsewhere. Then the new dealer has no idea what I have in the glass, only that I have one. As I move from table to table, I sometimes water the drink down in a short stop in the washroom. This way I can keep from attracting attention by reordering less often. My philosophy is that I can dull my brain with funny substances at home if I want to, but I'm at the casino to win money gambling.

6. *Minimize talk at the table.* Talking can not only disturb your concentration in keeping track of the cards, it also can shorten your playing days. You don't want to give your identity away to the dealer or the pit boss, who often can tell where you are from just by your accent. I have often had my hometown identified in my trips to Las Vegas. Also, the more you talk, the more it encourages others at your table to talk.

What is worse, though, is that the pit boss will often come up to a table and ask your name and where you're from. Pit bosses are instructed to get this information from any players who are betting large amounts of money. Once they get it, they can phone Central Credit Agency to check you out. It has information such as whether you've ever been on a junket, how much money you lost, how you paid, whether by check or by cash, where you played, and so on. Therefore, if you want to protect your anonymity and prolong your playing life, don't talk at the table. If you must, be brief and polite.

7. *Have an alias.* If you have a persistent pit boss who wants your personal information, use an alias. Most big bettors I know use different names when they are gambling. A number of them even have several passports. There is a saying in the casinos that nobody gives his right name in Las Vegas.

You can even establish credit under a different name. My banker is particularly understanding as I have several business and personal accounts with him under both my real name and my gambling pseudonyms. As long as he knows what name I will be using, he can verify my credit line when the casino calls up for credit approval. I have not yet had to use falsified identification, but many of the big bettors have several sets with them at all times in case the casino cage requires it.

342 THE WORLD'S GREATEST

DISGUISING YOUR BETS

If you follow the above suggestions, it will be extremely difficult for the casino to identify you as a winning player from your appearance and the way you conduct yourself. You still may give yourself away by the way you bet.

The following is an internal memo from a major East Coast casino that was first reprinted in a recent issue of the *Rouge et Noir News:*

SUBJECT: Definition and Descriptions Identifying Professional Card Counters and Exclusion of Professional Card Counters

A. There are various methods in recognizing professional card counters. The following three are the most obvious to casino managements:

1. The identification of a professional card counter can be accomplished by personal publications by the individual, information transmitted by sources in the industry, and self-acclamation.

2. The observation of any persons playing in concert with other persons as a team.

3. A player who systematically will accelerate his betting with recognized counting methods.

B. After the on-duty shift boss or casino manager has identified a patron playing at our Blackjack tables as a professional card counter, the following procedures will be observed when requesting said patron to refrain from playing Blackjack:

1. On-duty compliance officer will be notified of the presence of an identified professional card counter.

2. Upon notification, the compliance officer or casino shift boss will contact the TV surveillance room and request surveillance of the patron and table game in question.

3. The compliance officer will notify a representative of the Division of Gaming Enforcement and an inspector of the Gaming Commission of the proposed exclusion of the patron.

4. The patron will be read the exclusion notification applicable to the exclusion of professional card counters, and the compliance officer will further inform the individual that the exclusion only refers to the Blackjack tables. A log will be maintained by the Security Department of all actions taken pursuant to these instructions.

(Signed)

Rouge et Noir went on to observe:

> . . . The key move to identify card counters is a sudden large increase in bet size followed by a reduction to previous betting levels. Card counters would be well advised to mask bet-size increases with particular attention to the reduction phase as well.
>
> . . . The win rate is penalized somewhat by the masking procedure but the probability of being barred should decrease enough to make the more conservative approach more profitable.

The five betting methods discussed earlier in this chapter will help lessen your risk, but may not eliminate it if you are winning. The following tips will make your betting patterns more difficult to discover:

1. Don't always open a new deal with the minimum bet. This is most applicable to multiple-deck games, where the casinos know they have built-in advantage at the start of a new deal. If you raise your bets only toward the end of the deal, you will be tipping yourself off as a counter. My advice is to bet two units sometimes instead of the minimum one unit or to play two hands with a minimum on each at the beginning of multiple-deck games in order to throw the house off.

2. Quit at the end of a shoe if your last bet was large. If your last bet in the old shoe was large and your first bet in the new shoe is small, it will be quite obvious to the dealer and the pit boss that you are keeping track of the cards. I recommend two other options at this point. First, you can follow the advice above and leave your bet alone. True, you will be giving up a small advantage in the long run by beginning the play with a large wager against the shoe. However, you will be able to continue playing in that particular casino. The second option is to leave the table after a big bet at the end of a shoe. This might be a good time for a washroom break or to move on. With either option, you avoid changing your bet at the shuffle.

3. Don't be the biggest bettor at your table. Pit bosses are instructed to watch the biggest bettor at any table. As the example with Sammy Davis, Jr., showed, having a larger bettor present is a good screen for your actions. Don't be the only one at a downtown casino betting five dollars at the one-dollar tables, or twenty-five-dollar chips at the five-dollar tables. You will be the center of everyone's attention, much to your detriment.

4. Don't jump your bet. The dealers and pit bosses have learned to watch erratic betting more than any other feature of Blackjack play. Jumping your bet is a sudden increase from a steady bet of one unit to a bet of three or more units as the deck becomes positive. The betting methods earlier were designed to let you "parlay" your winnings into an increased bet. This is simply to let the winnings ride on the next hand when you have an advantage. The only exception to this that the casino people will tolerate is a jump from one to two units, because it is so small. Otherwise, use one of the betting methods or parlay your winnings.

5. Don't vary your bet with a pit boss watching. A few serious players I know resort to flat betting when the pit boss is watching. Whatever level of bet they had continues on each hand until the boss leaves. In some cases, if they are using one of the advanced strategies, such as the Hi-Opt I or Hi-Opt II, they even change to the Basic Strategy temporarily while being watched. As a reminder, although there is nothing you can do about it, don't think that you are not being observed just because the pit boss walks away. Every major casino uses an eye in the sky.

HIDING YOUR COUNTING EFFORT

Your final concern in playing and winning in secrecy is hiding your counting effort. The casinos realize that you must keep track of the cards to win consistently, so they are alert for any signs that a player is counting the cards. These final tips will conceal your actions from the casino personnel.

1. Don't move your lips. This seems ridiculously obvious. Nevertheless, have you ever watched yourself in the mirror playing Blackjack? I've seen myself. It's amazing how serious you can appear when playing. Your lips will often unconsciously move unless you have practiced and trained yourself to keep your lips motionless as you count. If you keep your lips closed, your tongue will sometimes move, but this is undetectable by the casino observer. If you can't stop your lips, you can chew on gum, a toothpick, or a cigarette to hide lip movement.

2. Don't move your head. Many counters give themselves away by moving their head while they follow the cards being dealt

around the table. This is also something common to many amateur Blackjack players. Again, practice in front of a mirror, or
ask a friend in the casino to watch your head to see if it moves as
you are following the cards.

This is another reason why one of the two seats near each end
is preferred. You can watch the entire table from this perspective
without having to move your head. Since you have the total scene
in view, don't count the cards as they are coming out of the
dealer's hand and falling on the table. Wait until all of the
players' hands are dealt and then count *all* the cards as you see
them. Most players prefer this method because it is easier to keep
an accurate count and you don't have to move your head back
and forth.

3. Don't hold up the game. Some new systems players unwittingly hold up the game as they try to find the count and determine the best play. As they struggle with their decision, you can
almost see the gears turning. You must learn how to play
smoothly—a skill that will come with practice. Slowing down the
dealer is vastly different from slowing down the game for the entire table. If you are playing against a fast dealer and cannot keep
the count, you might want to find another dealer. If you sit near
third base, you may not need to slow down the dealer or move
because you will have much more time to think as the other
players complete their hands.

4. Avoid leaving the betting spot empty. Another tipoff to the
casino that you are counting is always waiting until the dealer's
hand has been played and bets paid before placing your next bet.
The novice counter waits so that he or she will have the exact
count for betting purposes. You should consider occasionally keeping the spot in front of you full when playing with others at your
table. When some of them have to play after your hand has
busted, you should not always wait to see the results of their
hands before placing your next bet on the spot.

It's true that you may not have an accurate value of the count
for betting purposes. But you can estimate the probable value of
the count. Even though this does take away slightly from your
advantage when your estimate of the count turns out to be incorrect, it is better to have something on the spot than to be on it
yourself.

There are two final pieces of advice that apply to all winning

Blackjack players. Use the feelings of the casino personnel toward women to your advantage. Most of the casino personnel feel that women are good for one thing, like the Italian executive who said, "The only way a woman will ever get into this executive suite is on the couch." If you are a woman player and can play up the "dumb broad" aspect, you have a winning advantage no man can hope to match. It will take much longer for the casino to suspect a giggly, "confused" woman of being a systems player. Let them go ahead and pay for their chauvinistic ideas.

A good way for a man to draw attention away from himself as a winning player is to play with a woman companion. The pit bosses love couples. They usually assume that the man can't play well, that he's not serious about winning money because he's got his wife or girlfriend with him. If your companion knows at least the Basic Strategy, her beneficial presence will be very inexpensive.

I know one professional player who not only taught his female traveling companion the Basic Strategy, but also worked out a series of hand signals for her to raise the size of her bets. One of his clever maneuvers is to have her betting two hundred dollars when the count is a high plus while he is betting only fifty dollars. During a high positive count, it's easy for the dealer to realize that most of the 10s are still in the deck. When he sees the man betting small and the woman betting big, he really becomes confused and assumes the man doesn't know what he is doing. After all, "Why would a man trust a dumb broad with all that money? He must be dumb or weak to be dominated by the woman."

My last piece of advice for the winning player is: *Don't play for more than thirty minutes in any one casino.* The dealer and the pit boss are constantly on the lookout for winning players. Obvious winners are either shuffled up on, cheated, or barred. The less time you spend winning in one casino, the longer your playing life will be. I know some players who will play through one shoe in a multiple-deck game and then leave the casino, win or lose. Others playing in single- or double-deck games will leave as soon as they have won several large wagers.

Some players quit after playing only five minutes in a casino. These players may come in, watch a game in progress, wait until the count is positive, then place a large wager. They keep on playing while the count is positive, then leave when the dealer shuffles up or the count turns negative. The bet can't be too large, though, or the dealer will immediately shuffle up.

If you are not worried about getting barred, there is a different method you can use. It's my current style of play, since I am easily recognized in most casinos in Las Vegas. Whenever I am allowed to play in a casino like any regular player, without countermeasures, I will stay and keep playing until I start to lose some larger wagers. Sometimes I've played for as long as two hours because I kept winning. I stay, gradually increasing the size of my bets and trying to win as much money as possible at one sitting. If you are not concerned with getting barred, I recommend you try playing the same way.

So now you have the tips that can extend your winning Blackjack career indefinitely. By controlling yourself, staying ahead of the dealer, and keeping clear of the suspicious casino, your systems play will continue undetected. But you don't have to take my word for it. The casinos will prove every point for me if you only give them the chance. I hope you don't!

ELEVEN

Playing Courtesy of the Casino

By the way, how about a player's trying to win based on astrology, the occult, soothsayers, or parapsychology rather than mathematics?

Well, which does the casino use—astrology, the occult, soothsayers, parapsychology, or mathematics?

R. T. BARNHART

Here I go again! I am about to take off on another junket to Las Vegas. This is nothing new; I've done it thirty-three times before. I made a phone call two weeks ago and I'm on. All I have to do now is show up at the airport on Wednesday at 10:00 A.M. Absolutely everything has been arranged for me. My free plane ticket is waiting at the airport. A seat has been especially reserved for me on the charter, and my bags will be automatically tagged and taken care of by Max the junket runner. A room has been assigned to me in the resort in Las Vegas.

I will get a VIP personal credit card on arrival compliments of the casino. This card will allow me to see every show in the hotel, and will permit me to eat in any cafe and restaurant on the premises as a preferred guest. It will cover any companion I may wish to entertain, male or female. I can also order anything I may want sent to my room—breakfasts, liquor, complete gourmet dinners, etc.

Most importantly, the card will allow me simply to sign for five thousand dollars' worth of casino chips to gamble with. That one thin, little plastic card will get me everything I mentioned for

FREE. All I have to do is sign, and, of course, obtain the card in the first place. Maybe you're thinking, "If he can get one, maybe I can, too." So you want to know how I rate such a card? It's ridiculously easy.

Years ago, when I first started teaching my class on gambling, I taught the students the theory of Craps and Blackjack. In the middle of one of my lectures, a very strange thing happened. One of the students interrupted and told me I didn't know what I was talking about. I was stunned and I felt my face go red. No daytime student has ever challenged my teaching. But this was a nighttime class of adults. He jeered, "I bet you've never even been to a casino." I had to agree.

At this point another student, Terry, came to my rescue. He said he would take me on a junket to Las Vegas with him so that I could test Thorp's theories of Blackjack (since we were using Thorp's book). I agreed to go, but as a full junket member—as a player—not as a guest. Here is where the story of a junket really begins.

GETTING STARTED ON JUNKETS

The rule is that you must first be recommended by a player who is already an established junket gambler. Terry was such a person and provided me with the necessary recommendation. Terry is a salesman who goes on junkets two or three times a year. His credit is good. This means that on the occasions when he has lost money his check was always honored. Terry recommended me to Max, who is a travel agent specializing in junkets.

I got Max's phone number from Terry, called Max, and told him I wanted to go on the next trip. He suggested I talk to my bank manager and get him to send a letter stating that I had credit for three thousand dollars (the sum is five thousand dollars now due to inflation and other things, like greed on the part of the casinos). Credit for three thousand dollars meant that should I lose that much, the bank would guarantee payment. Luckily, I had an understanding bank manager, and the credit was easily arranged. Some bank managers are less co-operative. They actually want you to take out a loan for the amount of credit you need guaranteed for the junket!

The arranging of credit is the most critical part of becoming a regular on the junket lists. Once you have established credit in one casino (through your travel agent), then you can establish similar credit in almost any other casino in Las Vegas, or the world. The new casino will check your credit with your old casino or with the Central Credit Agency in Las Vegas. When the new casino gets the information it wants, simply that every check you ever wrote for a casino was good and did not bounce, you are automatically granted credit for the same amount as your original sum.

A credit application card may be easily obtained at the cashier's cage of any casino or from a travel agent who runs junkets. In fact, you will probably be getting such applications in the mail right after you get back from the first junket. News travels fast among junket agents. They all want a piece of you so badly that they will often fight over players.

In return for your casino privileges, there are certain requirements. Currently you are required to make twenty-five-dollar minimum wagers at Blackjack. (In 1970, the minimum was only five dollars.) Second, you are expected to gamble at least several hours each day. Third, the casino prefers you to use all of your credit—that is, they want you to bet all your money, five hundred dollars, or a thousand dollars, at each gambling session and to keep on drawing such amounts until you have drawn out your whole credit line. Don't misunderstand, they don't expect you to lose your entire five thousand dollars. All they want is for you to gamble with it an appreciable length of time. They know that you are sure to lose a large chunk of it if you are like the average junketeer. According to their experience with house percentages, they know you will probably lose at least 20 per cent of the "drop."

So this is what is expected of you. What if you lose your first five hundred dollars, get scared, and refuse to lose any more? If you stop gambling, what will they do to you? Most of the time they will do absolutely nothing to you on that trip. The casino will simply put your name down very low on their VIP list so that the next time you call asking to go on a junket the agent will say that he has no room. If you believe him and decide to wait until the next trip he will tell you the same thing again.

If you persist in trying to get back on a junket and tell the agent that you really want to go again, he may be kind enough to tell you that the casino felt that you "didn't use your credit enough" on the last trip. If you give him your word to use it all on the next trip, he will telephone the casino (long distance, yet!) and inform them of this. "They may give you another chance," he says. It's supposedly out of his hands. "It's up to them," he continues. He'll try to convince them that you are a "good" player. He is on your side, etc.

The likely outcome of this exchange is that nine out of ten times you will get back on the junket. What he was using on you is known as the "negative sell"—making it seem hard for you to get what you really want, even though he is in a desperately competitive situation for high rollers. The real truth is that neither the casino nor the agent want to lose your business. After all, on this trip you may get drunk and lose your entire five thousand dollars. This will more than make up for your first trip's light play.

The casinos make it easy for you to lose very *much* very *comfortably*. The atmosphere is purposely designed to draw your chips from you. The cocktail waitresses, courteous dealers, dim, hypnotizing lighting, easy-come, easy-go attitude about the chips, twenty-four-hour gambling, and the glamor attached to being a VIP, a big shot who gets everything for free, are all a part of their big plan to get your money.

Many Blackjack players will not go on a junket because they feel too much pressure to play. They don't want to gamble three thousand or five thousand dollars' worth of chips even if they can afford to. If you can't stand the pressure of junket gambling, I recommend that you pay your own way and play where you like. I personally do not like to go to certain casinos because of their attitude. Foreign casinos are the worst for pressure because they make you cash in your chips (if you have any left) *after each playing session*. This way they know exactly how much you have won or lost. Should you wind up a winner by the end of the trip they will make a note of this and try to prevent you from repeating it on the next visit.

Please don't let this scare you, because I'm not putting junkets down. After all, I'm about to go on another one. Some people have learned how to survive and profit on a junket; others get buried every time they go. These latter souls are most often Craps players. Over a four- or five-day period of shooting Craps, it is simply impossible to come out a winner. The house percentages in Craps will not permit it. There are rare exceptions—about as rare as surviving a twenty-story fall. There is only one way to survive and prosper on a junket, and that is to learn how to play Blackjack. You don't need to learn how to play professionally. All you need to learn is enough to get the percentages on your side, as shown in Chapter Seven. Way back in 1970 I learned how to win well enough to come out ahead the first five times I went on junkets. The roof fell in on the next trip.

On the sixth trip they found out I was a *counter*. From that time on I never played there again. I was using a simple point count then with Basic Strategy and betting in direct proportion to the running count. After winning on the first three trips, I began to bet more boldly. By the sixth trip I was ranging my bets between the $5 minimum and a $150 maximum bet, betting two hands at $75 per hand. At the time, I knew only a few of the tips in Chapter Ten, and did not realize that the pit bosses don't like players to range their bets that widely. In my innocence, I didn't think they would object so strenuously to my winning on a junket. I thought all they wanted was action, and I gave them plenty of action! I played at least ten hours each day and I loved it all because I would win almost every day.

I did not believe that there was cheating in Las Vegas, only that I seemed to win more often against certain dealers. Even though I had read about cheating in Thorp's book, I thought that they only cheated people who bet a lot of money or who were big threats to them. I never thought I fit those categories, nor had I seen any suspicious play, so why should I have suspected cheating? After identifying the tough dealers, I played only against the easier ones. Looking back on it, this is probably why I was so successful in winning. There were two dealers that were exceptionally good to play against, Ron and Mike. Ron still deals there today. Mike is now a pit boss at a rival casino.

I was playing against Mike and betting my $5.00 to $150. One of the pit bosses rushed over and told Mike to shuffle up when I had two $75 bets out. Mike shuffled up so I removed my bets and started with $5.00 again. I kept on playing and eventually had $150 out once more. By this time, the pit boss had walked over to the head pit boss, who was standing by the desk in the center of the Blackjack pit. I knew they were talking about me because they were both looking at me and one of them got red in the face and started to shake. I didn't pay too much attention to it, I just kept on playing and winning.

The next thing I saw was the head pit boss coming over to my table with the manager of the casino. I knew him because he had made several show reservations for me in other casinos on previous trips. As he came over I said, "Hi, how are you?"

He said, "Hello." That's all. He was very pleasant, just stayed for a minute and walked away with the head pit boss. I thought nothing of it at the time. Since I had won enough that day and was tired, I then quit.

The next morning was my final session before the junket charter left. I make it a rule not to play on the final morning because I am usually very tired from four days of play. However, I wanted to win enough to buy a new radio for my car, so I took out $200 and decided to play until I was $125 up. Since neither Mike nor Ron started work until noon, I had to play against the other dealers.

I tried three different dealers and couldn't win against any of them. I lost almost my entire $200. The last dealer I played against was one of the tougher dealers. As he began to take my money, he told me to take it easy, that I had won enough on this trip. I didn't realize how good his advice was, that he was actually trying to help me. You see, I was now a marked man. I had been pointed out to him and the other dealers as a counter, and the dealers were instructed not to let me win. I have never won in this casino since then and rarely play there anymore. I go in about once a year just to see what I can do. I am usually recognized within about five minutes and then I am shuffled up on after each hand until I leave.

These countermeasures were not unique to this one casino. One of my other junket trips was to a casino that had only four-deck games. After the first two days I was ahead about $300, betting $5.00 to $25. On the third day I got an extremely high positive count during an early-evening session and won $1,600 in about fifteen minutes. I was betting $100 chips during the high count. At the end of the run, I took a twenty-minute break for a cold drink at the bar.

When I returned, I noticed the dealer stopping the game and shuffling after only about ten minutes. He had dealt out only two decks. I asked, "Hey, what are you doing that for?" He didn't answer so I looked at his name tag and said, "Mickey, what's happening?"

"Just following orders from the boss," he answered.

Can you imagine this casino's attitude toward my winning? This was my first time in the casino and I had a lucky run. They did not know me as a winning player, yet they cut off half the shoe. These people weren't sportsmen, they were cowards with no class. When a casino backed by millions of dollars is afraid of a single gambler they have not seen before, they are running scared.

The moral of my early playing days is not to give yourself away as a winning player. I quickly learned to disguise myself to the casino using the procedures in the previous chapter. Junkets are no problem once you know how to handle yourself. The information in the rest of this book teaches you how to gamble successfully on a junket and get all of your expenses paid for while walking away with the casino's money.

There are other pitfalls to gambling on a junket. One of the worst I have ever been on was to the Flamingo and had nothing to do with my advantage at the tables. I had gotten a nice room on the ground floor at the Flamingo, but it was not single occupancy. I shared the room with a cricket in the air-conditioning vent. He kept me up the first night with his incessant chirping. I banged on the grate and ceiling and did everything I could to get him out but with no success.

I called room service and asked them to remove the cricket. I didn't want to change rooms because I was still new to junket travel and I didn't want to attract attention or seem ungrateful. I figured room service could take care of it for me.

That afternoon, after a morning of play fogged with fatigue, I returned to my room for a nap. To my great relief, there was no cricket. That night was another matter. He managed to get in the shag rug and continue his noisy way. I must have beaten every square inch of that carpet looking for that damn cricket but I never got him. The end result is that the cricket was with me the

whole trip. It was just one of those things. In retrospect, I should
have moved. The hotel people kept telling me they got it but I
kept finding it again at night.

That is one trip I don't remember very well because I was in a
daze the whole time. I lost twenty-seven hundred dollars in four
days, all over a lousy cricket. For all I know, he's still there helping the casino. I'll never be that shy about asking for a new room
again to get away from any bothersome distraction.

A junket I remember only too well is my recent one to Haiti. I
should have known it would be a different sort of trip from the
way it started. The couple my wife and I were traveling with
didn't bring their passports because the agent said they didn't
need one. Without a passport, they were refused entry. The Haitian authorities were going to ship our friends to Puerto Rico on
the next flight. They were finally allowed to enter Haiti after
about an hour and a half of haggling between the hotel representative and the government personnel at the airport. Evidently,
the governmental climate is still not too good there.

Our trip into Port-au-Prince was a real eye-opener. The first
thing that hits you is the great poverty. Everything is black or
gray, like an A-bomb hit it. The cars and buildings are old and
decrepit. With a per-capita income of about two hundred dollars
per year, the streets swarm with beggars and peddlers trying to
sell you stuff. Most of it appears hand-made but it is junk mass-
produced in factories.

There are two major hotels where we were. One is in the city
and caters to locals, and the other, the Royal Haitian Hotel, is on
the outskirts of the city and caters to tourists. The hotel is very
old but "renovated." The accommodations were far from first-
class, much less Holiday Inn class. The air conditioner was so
noisy that we couldn't run it at night or it would keep us awake.
The water dripped in the bathrooms. The beds were old, small
single beds with bad mattresses and springs. The food in the hotel
tasted OK, and only three of the four of us got diarrhea.

The poverty there is deplorable. We were warned not to give
the beggars anything or we would be swamped by hordes of them.
A taxi driver, upon learning we were there to gamble, told us that
the casino in Haiti is run by the Mafia. I asked him what Mafia it
was, the Jewish, Italian, or Irish Mafia. At this he suddenly became cautious and said, "Me no can tell. These are little stories

that we do not tell to strangers." He went on to explain that there are two religions in Haiti, Catholic and voodoo. He was beginning to make me wish I had brought some long pins and a doll of the agent with me.

The junket had sounded good when we first ran across it. Each couple had to put up one thousand dollars in front money with the chance of getting some of it back depending upon the action we gave the casino. The agent promised that if the men gambled three hours per night with a bet range between twenty-five and five hundred dollars and averaging fifty dollars per bet the casino would cover air fare, accommodations, and food. We were to pay for any bottled wine, liquor, gratuities, and the 10 per cent government tax on the total bill.

The Blackjack rules are very unfavorable. They deal four decks out of a shoe with the dealer putting one quarter of the deck out of play *before* dealing. There is no soft doubling, no resplitting of pairs, no double after pair splitting, and hard doubling restricted to 9, 10, and 11. Insurance is allowed for up to half your bet and you can surrender against any up card other than an Ace. With these rules, we were facing a Basic Strategy Expectation of nearly a full 1 per cent *against* us. The game was going to be very tough to beat.

The casino personnel were a real mixture. The manager was an Italian, the pit bosses British, and the dealers were all locals. The dealers were very cold, never smiling. The pit bosses were fairly friendly and a delight to listen to with their British accents. It got to be a joke with our little group. Whenever we wondered what to do next someone would mimic the pit bosses and say, "Why doeunt we shoofle oop?"

At least the game was honest. The only questionable tactic I saw was that one dealer would occasionally shuffle only half the deck and leave the other half undisturbed. This was infrequent enough that it could be ignored. Who needs to take chances cheating with the rules they had going for them? And as you will see, they reduced any other risk by the countermeasures they used.

The first night my friend Norm and I were just another pair of players to the casino. We had already decided never to come back to Haiti, so we figured to win as much as we could during the trip and not worry about being barred. It was one of those nights that happen every so often. I won $6,770 in four hours varying my bets from $25 to $500 (one to twenty). Norm was down at first, so I told him to put his knee close to mine and I would signal when to deviate from Basic Strategy. He then won $1,400 with a smaller range of $25 to $200. The dealers had been cutting off one-half deck from the top and dealing down to one-half deck before shuffling. As our winnings mounted, they began to cut more off the top. When they were finally cutting a full deck off the top, Norm and I quit for the evening.

The second night I knew they were going to get tougher with us. From that night on we almost continually had a pit boss at our table full time. Every time the count was plus, the boss would have the dealer shuffle up. Once the count was an incredible +31. I had $500 out and pulled a Blackjack. The player on my right, an older man from Wisconsin, congratulated me for the play. I was feeling good about it too when I heard the boss order the dealer to shuffle even though there were more than two decks remaining.

I was sick that this incredible situation was lost. The count had gotten so high so fast, yet it was all history now. After that last Blackjack win, the dealers started to burn a full deck off the top and shuffle up at one deck remaining as a matter of course. With these conditions I lost about $450 that evening, which was all right because I was thinking about that $1,000 I wanted back. As long as I could keep my losses from here on out under my deposit, then I would be ahead by continuing to play.

The third night was disastrous for us. As fortunate a run as we had the first night, we had a nearly equally bad night this evening. I kept getting bad hands while the dealer made his. He was drawing to 20 or 21 consistently or not busting. To show you the typical turn of events at the table, another junket member was playing (none too accurately) at third base and won $11,000 over the same period I lost $1,000. The cards were just falling right for him.

The only bright spot of the evening came when I suddenly got a strong marijuana smell. I needed comedy relief at this point so I said loudly to no one in general, "OK, who's smoking grass in here?" A little old lady next to me started laughing and told me they were herbal cigarettes her doctor had put her on after forty years of smoking Pall Malls. She had to get them at the health store. She went on to say that she was always getting in trouble because of them and had even been arrested once. When she was there, the casino always smelled like pot. I didn't mind; she was fun to be with and played intelligently. She told me she won about $200 each night because she wasn't greedy and quit as soon as she had her nightly quota.

During this third night of play, not only did the dealer cut off a full deck at the front and back of the shoe, but also he shuffled up *any time* I put a large bet out. So once when the count got negative, I asked the pit boss, "Hey, how about a shuffle?" He said, "OK," so the dealer shuffled away a —17 count for me. A little later, I was making a small comeback and won a $200 double down early in the deal. When the dealer started to shuffle up automatically after my win, I asked, "How about dealing one or two more hands?"

The boss replied, "We will keep shuffling when we think it's appropriate. You may request a shuffle any time you wish." I thought for a moment and decided that was as fair as it was going to get. At the end of our play that night, the casino returned $800 of our deposit and kept $200.

The fourth night I planned to request shuffles whenever the count was fairly negative. If they were going to take away the positive situations, I could do the same with the negatives. Early in the evening it was crowded so we could sit down at a $25-minimum table with a young dealer named Fritz and without the usual pit boss. Fritz evidently hadn't been told about us because we got a good game. I was up several hundred when they noticed me and took Fritz off duty and gave us one of the toughies. At least he was alternating with two younger guys who were fairly easy to deal with. I would have won more but the bosses kept the tables crowded by closing down half-full ones.

Norm and I stayed fairly even for the whole night, so we kept playing. We finally closed the casino down about 3:30 A.M. It was really funny; over fifteen of the casino personnel were there watching us, even the strolling guitar player. They were like a group of vultures watching a life-and-death conflict take place. I thought at the time that we needed a director and a camera because it would have made a good movie scene.

The fifth night we got a much better game for some unknown reason. They shuffled up only two or three times and often let the game go to one-half deck at the end. We got to talking with one of the pit bosses and found that he was from my home country, their "token," as he called it. When even *he* ordered a shuffle after I had won $200 on a hand, I asked him, "How can you do that to a friend, a fellow countryman?"

He grinned and told me, "Just following orders from the boss. We'll deal you all the cards you want but you can only range your bets from one to five."

I told him, "No one can beat this game under these conditions."

"We're not sure, so I'm just following orders," he explained. We got to talking to him and he continued, "I beat this game when I play." We told him the rules are better in Las Vegas, but he felt he could make more money as a pit boss in Haiti than as a player in Las Vegas. For the local economy, he's probably very well paid.

Later that evening I found myself in the buffet dinner line with two of the other pit bosses. To my surprise, they apologized for having to be so tough on me. "We figure you are better than average so we can't give you a good game," one told me. I argued that I was a big shooter. I liked to gamble; just look at the $1,000 loss I took. I suggested that they would lose a lot of high rollers with their tough game. But they told me that the casino was getting all the action it could handle as it was. The sad part is that it looks as though they are right.

The final night of play I managed to break even and was grateful to be able to leave with as much winnings as I still had. Overall, we were treated very politely as tourists but very rudely as players. With all the excessive shuffle-ups that accompanied us whenever we sat down, it surprised me that there were no complaints. The other players took whatever type of lousy game was offered like sheep being led to the slaughter. The only way such a casino will mend its ways is if informed players take their business elsewhere for a more even game. Fortunately, you have everything you need to be informed about at your fingertips.

If I had to rate other casinos in the area to Haiti, I would say that the Bahamas are approximately a hundred times nicer and that Aruba is two hundred times nicer than Haiti. I hope you have gotten the picture on Haiti. I don't plan on going back even though it was a winning trip.

GETTING YOUR SHARE OF CASINO COMPLIMENTARIES

Casinos are no different than other businesses. They want to increase their revenue while reducing their expenses. But they also realize that they have to spend promotional money. Giveaway programs are popular with any business if they work properly. Like the dime store's "one-cent sale" or a "two-for-one bonanza" at the supermarket, the business hopes that the promotion will cause the customer to shop and spend additional money there.

The way it works in casinos is with complimentaries ("comps") and air-fare refunds. Casinos compete aggressively with each other for the business of high rollers who consistently lose thousands of dollars in their favorite casinos. As on a junket, they are willing to let the player enjoy the hotel services free just for the shot at his gambling losses. Players who qualify for this free hospitality don't have to depend upon a junket operator; they are welcome any time they want to come.

COMPS AS A PER CENT OF TOTAL DEPARTMENTAL REVENUES

	Room	Food	Beverage
Las Vegas Strip Casinos			
Gross revenues: $1,000 to $10,000	6.0	19.4	61.3
$10,000 to $20,000	4.4	9.9	45.3
$20,000 and over	26.2	22.9	31.1
Downtown Las Vegas Casinos			
Gross revenues: $1,000 to $10,000	10.6	49.1	80.8
$10,000 and over	10.9	17.6	63.8
Reno/Sparks Casinos			
Gross revenues: $1,000 to $10,000	3.6	10.4	61.0
$10,000 and over	6.7	12.3	56.9
South Lake Tahoe Casinos			
Gross revenues: $1,000 and over	10.3	9.2	43.4

Lest you think that the freebies given out by the casino are too small or infrequent for you to try for, look at the above table. The information is taken from the *Nevada Gaming Abstract,* published yearly by the Nevada State Gaming Control Board (these reports are available at no charge and contain a wealth of statistical data on Nevada casino gaming). Most of the information in this section was taken from *Rouge et Noir News'* analysis of last year's *Abstract* and published comments about proper comp procedures. Its summary of the *Abstract* provides an insight into the importance casinos place on comps and how much they spend providing them to favored players.

Casinos spend much more money on comps than on junkets. The next table shows the comparison of comps versus junkets for various Nevada areas and different-size casinos. Veteran casino gamers have found that comp conditions vary not only from area to area but also from casino to casino within any one area. And comp practices in individual hotels change with management shuffles and profit-improvement drives. So you have to shop around on an individual basis.

COMPS VERSUS JUNKETS AS A PER CENT OF HOTEL/CASINO GROSS REVENUES

	Comps	*Junkets*
Las Vegas Strip Casinos		
Gross revenues: $1,000 to $10,000	4.6	0.5
$10,000 to $20,000	3.2	2.6
$20,000 and over	9.8	4.1
Downtown Las Vegas Casinos		
Gross revenues: $1,000 to $10,000	5.8	—
$10,000 and over	5.3	—
Reno/Sparks Casinos		
Gross revenues: $1,000 to $10,000	8.6	—
$10,000 and over	7.0	—
South Lake Tahoe Casinos		
Gross revenues: $1,000 and over	7.0	0.8

If you have been gambling in Nevada for some time or are new to casino gaming, an important question is: "How can you get the comps and air-fare refunds you are entitled to?" Using comps, you can greatly increase your gambling bankroll right at the start by not having to pay your own expenses. The average player spends about $150 a day staying in a Strip hotel that could be better spent at the tables playing Blackjack.

If you don't want to take the junket route, the best approach to getting the most comp for your gaming dollar is to bring your stake with you in cash. If the amount is substantial (at least several thousand dollars), you should deposit the funds in the casino cage. This has several advantages. First, it is safer! Probably the most serious lapse in security for most players is to keep a large amount of cash or chips in their room overnight. Hotel rooms are not secure enough to prevent theft. You should deposit the bulk of your cash in the cage (or safety deposit box) before going to bed. The money can easily be retrieved at your convenience.

The second advantage of using cash at the cage is the casino attitude. A cash player who deposits and uses five thousand dollars in the cage in most casinos will get as much in comps as a credit player with a ten-thousand-dollar credit line. Upon depositing your stake, you should ask to be introduced to the casino credit host. The recommended procedure is to tell that host that you like the resort and would like to bring your business there if things work out well.

The casino host will be glad to hear this, but will make no commitment until he or she sees your action. By depositing your funds at the cage, you can draw against the funds at the tables. The standard procedure is to ask for chips in five-hundred-dollar or one-thousand-dollar increments. You're not going to get a high customer rating unless you play with green (twenty-five-dollar) chips as a minimum. Don't ask for anything in the way of comps the first day of play, but charge your food expenses to your room in the hope that the casino will pick up the bill before you leave.

Once you have demonstrated your "action" at the tables over several playing sessions, you can approach the host about a comp in the gourmet restaurant or in the showroom. While many casinos will comp out-of-hotel shows for their best customers, these are the hardest comps to get. The easiest comp is for a hotel show at which no food is served. The proper etiquette is for you to ask whether the host can take care of you at a particular show. Hosts have a problem justifying to their management a comp for more than a party of two, so don't ask to bring along your children unless you're really a high roller.

If the host co-operates, you will be told to use the "invited guest" entrance, letting you skip the long waiting line of those with regular reservations. Unless the host has said that he'll comp the show, you won't know whether the casino is picking up the tab until you check in with the maître d'. When he checks the reservations, you'll notice that some of the names are printed in red (or some other different color)—these are the comped reservations. If you're concerned whether or not the show is comped, just ask the maître d' and he'll be glad to tell you.

If after a number of playing sessions you still don't know what comps your table action merits, you should ask the credit host. If the hotel standards are higher than your action merits, you should shop around to see if you can get a better deal. If you don't qualify for high-roller treatment ordinarily, you can still get special treatment at times. The easiest thing is to get a line pass for the showroom to avoid waiting in line. Just ask the pit boss where you're playing for one. In resorts that do not have line passes, the supervisor will tell you that he'll walk you in when you're ready to go. A good time to ask for a show or gourmet-restaurant reservation from a credit host or pit boss is when you're on a plus count streak and your bet levels are higher than normal. Even a five-dollar-chip player can be making large bets at a "hot" table.

One thing to remember with comps: Don't abuse the privilege. Casinos are particularly sensitive about room-service charges and extra guests in the showroom or restaurant. Although the resorts want their guests to enjoy themselves, they resent even high rollers who use comp privileges to host big parties or stock their private wine cellar at home.

If you're a substantial credit customer and the resort doesn't comp your hotel bill, you might try a trick other gamblers have found successful. Deduct the hotel bill from the amount due the casino and pay the balance promptly. When you try this make sure that you enclose a note stating that the hotel apparently made a mistake in not comping the bill and you're adjusting for the error. Your only risk is that if you are unreasonable the casino may cancel your credit.

Another question that comes up is whether or not to tip the credit host. Hosts cannot accept cash, but they are human and do appreciate being remembered. Very few players go to the trouble of writing a letter of thanks to a generous casino host or a note of commendation to his boss. Small gifts may also get surprising results. A gift of something that is connected with your business or geographical area and that isn't ostentatious can help enhance this valuable relationship.

The important thing to remember is that even when a host wants to go out of his way to be extremely generous, he needs your help. Comps have to be justified to the casino, so you can get the best results by making your largest bets when a marker is issued. In many casinos, the player's action is noted on the marker, so it is your betting immediately after the marker is issued that is most likely to be recorded.

In choosing which comps you want, consider the host. Out-of-hotel comps are the hardest for the host to justify. The host must cash in on friendships in other resorts for difficult comps, done for only the most favored customers. Instead, arrange your schedule to use the local gourmet restaurants. But even if popular out-of-hotel show comps are impossible to get, you can still get reservations to those out-of-hotel "full" shows.

Sometimes all it takes is a little persistence. I had attended a conference at a resort in Reno. Since I had deposited five thousand dollars in cash at the cage and used much of it, I was hoping to get full RFB (room, food, and beverage) and air-fare refund. I ran into a problem the second-to-last day before I was to leave. One of the managers there was a former pit boss who knew me as a counter from my early junket days in Las Vegas. He saw me and immediately had the dealers shuffling up whenever I played. Since then, I had been careful to play only when he was off duty.

When I went to ask about being comped and refunded, I was told by a secretary that the manager was not there. She looked at their records and told me I was not rated for comps. She glanced

over the floor and suddenly said, "Oh there he is." It turned out
he was the man who knew me. When she offered to bring him
over, I thanked her, left my name, suggested I could see him
later, and quickly took off.

I knew what my mistake was. I had been taking markers as
recommended, but I had been buying them back with my winnings. When the casino rated me, it looked as if I had not played
enough with my stake. And with the credit manager being an old
opponent I knew I had little chance of being comped if he had
anything to say about it. Fortunately, he didn't know me by
name.

After scouting the manager's office the next day right before I
was to leave for the airport, I decided to give it one more try. I
saw he was once again out on the floor so I went up to his secretary and asked again, keeping my back to the gaming tables. She
picked up the phone and punched several numbers. Out of the
corner of my eye I saw the phone on the floor ring and watched
the manager pick it up. He glanced over to where I stood as they
talked, so I turned away completely, praying he wasn't the
friendly type and wouldn't come over. After a few seconds, I
heard the secretary say, "OK," and hang up.

The end result was that I got my air fare of $470 refunded and
escaped undetected. I happily paid my hotel bill and left before
the manager realized what happened. In general, the casino wants
your business. If the credit host thinks you are a serious player
and intend to come back, he might make a marginal decision in
your favor in the hopes that you will return for another chance at
losing your stake. It never hurts to ask!

There is one final point to remember: The casino owners make
money only if they comp or allow junkets for losers. If you are
suspected of being a counter, you run the risk of having to pick
up the full tab for your trip. The best approach is to be certain
what the rules are before you go. If being comped depends upon
the "action" you provide, then you shouldn't be billed as long as
you were playing enough at the right levels. But if there are no
clear agreements and if the casino personnel just don't like the
skill they see you playing with, *you* will pay for your trip and
never be invited back.

COMPS PRACTICES IN LAS VEGAS

Rouge et Noir News continually monitors gaming conditions at the world's casinos. Several years ago, *Rouge et Noir* conducted a survey of casino comp practices. Although the information in this section is likely to be out of date before you read it, the practices reported here should give you an idea of what you can expect in trying to play for free. Here are the preliminary results of the *Rouge et Noir* survey:

Aladdin: The hosts at the Aladdin have been generous in the past, but because of the legal problems mentioned earlier in the book the operation has been taken away from the owners by the state and put in the hands of a state-appointed manager. The profits still accrue to the current owners, and the casino manager is under pressure to keep profits at precrisis levels. Should a choice have to be made, long-term customer relations from liberal comps could be sacrificed for short-term profits from smaller expenses. In any case, the resort will be sold soon, so any effort you make to build a good relationship will go down the drain when the resort changes hands. Since the new management is likely to have been installed by the time you read this, the Aladdin could be one of your shopping stops.

Caesar's Palace: Caesar's is expanding its casino-promotion program with new offices scheduled to open in various parts of the country. At this time, Caesar's is looking for high rollers with a ten-thousand-dollar credit-line minimum, but they are willing to offer quite a bit in return. You might call Caesar's Palace directly for the name and telephone number of the casino-promotion office serving your area.

Castaways: This is not one of the Strip's top resorts, but many gamers don't spend that much time in their rooms anyway. If this is your case, then the other hotel features are not of prime importance. Such gamers can work out a comp-and-air-fare-reimbursement package directly with the general manager. You should ask him what he can offer you for your typical playing stake and table habits. Ask him specially if he will approve comps should you get lucky and win.

Desert Inn: This Summa property hopes to capture a good part of the highest of the high rollers visiting Las Vegas. The Desert Inn has attracted some of the elite gamblers, but the economies of the small operation requires the casino to dip down into the ten thousand dollars and even lower credit lines, with cash players of five thousand dollars getting VIP treatment. The Desert Inn is a top facility and one you might consider if you're in the high-roller category.

Dunes: As this is written, the Dunes is coming out from under an airlines strike that halted all of its junket trips. As a result, the casino win is falling behind last year's figures. As a general rule, anytime there is an airline strike of one of the carriers that fly to Las Vegas or handle charters for junkets, you can wheel and deal exceptional comp-and-air-fare refunds from the player-starved resort. Even during normal times, the Dunes is one of the more generous dispensers of comps and of air-fare reimbursement. However, the Blackjack conditions are tough in the Dunes.

Flamingo: As a part of the Hilton operation, the Flamingo has operated as a "grind joint," with the high rollers being serviced by the Las Vegas Hilton. But the Flamingo is growing in size and stature, so this is one you can try if you can't get what you want from one of the independents.

Frontier: This hotel has had an aggressive junket program and relatively generous comp practices. Recently, though, a drive to improve "bottom line" performance has forced the casino to cut back on comps. As with most management practices, this can change for the better or worse at a moment's notice. The Frontier casino has always been a tough casino for counters to win in.

Las Vegas Hilton: With its loyal established clientele, the Hilton has abandoned the regular junket approach in favor of individual travel arrangements. The VIP treatment at the Hilton for most hopefuls comes only after the casino has had a good chance to evaluate your play.

MGM Grand: The giant hotel/casinos invariably get tied up in a ridiculous amount of paperwork. As a result of the extra work, such resorts like to take a good look at a customer before the gamer qualifies for comps. The way to short-circuit the paperwork here is to join the VIP list via the casino's junket program. If you know someone who is already one of the MGM's junket guests, a recommendation will help get you on a flight. Even without a recommendation you can approach the junket rep, but you should first make certain the rep knows that you are willing to be charged if the casino doesn't agree that you qualify as a player. I have always been treated with courtesy and respect at the MGM and have never lost there.

Marina: Rouge et Noir's information on the Marina is incomplete at this time. Numerous junket agents have filed with the state and been approved as representatives of the Marina, but reports on the junkets are not available. In general, the Marina should have lower junket and comp standards than the top Strip resorts, but that hasn't been verified. The only problem is that International Blackjack Club surveys consistently report the Marina as next to impossible to win in.

Sands: As the most successful Summa operation in Las Vegas, the Sands can afford to be selective. As in the MGM Grand case, the junket route is your best bet to secure VIP treatment. Once you qualify as a well-rated junket guest, you are in a good position to switch to individual travel.

Tropicana: At this time, the Tropicana has just completed its new tower. In general with any hotel, the best time to approach a resort is right after a room expansion has been completed. They are eager to have additional gamers fill the extra rooms and tend to relax their comp and junket standards until the new facility regularly meets their occupancy rates. Playing conditions here have been changing faster than a newborn's diapers.

Other Gaming Areas: Comps, junkets, and individual travel arrangements are sales tools expected to generate additional profits greater than the expenses. In Atlantic City, for example, player demand exceeded supply to such an extent that Resorts International has not had to spend much for promotion. In the first seven months of its Atlantic City operation, Resorts refunded a total of $162 to one player for travel expenses. The Resorts casino win in the area of $150 million would have necessitated $6 million of junket expenses on the Las Vegas Strip. While the Atlantic City casinos will have to increase their promotional activity, this won't become a major factor until many more casinos open up. Las

Vegas conditions won't prevail in Atlantic City until late 1981 at the earliest, if ever.

Summer and fall are the off-seasons in the Caribbean. Most casino junket programs include wives free or at a nominal charge at these times of year. Some casinos also lower their junket playing requirements for the nonpeak period, as illustrated by the Caribbean minijunket program described below:

	Regular	*Minijunket*
Period	Monday to Thursday	Monday to Thursday
	Thursday to Monday	Thursday to Monday
Front money	$5,000 to casino	$3,000 to casino
	$600 to agent; $500	$600 to agent; $500
	returned at casino in	returned at casino in
	nonnegotiable chips	nonnegotiable chips
Minimum		
wagers	$50 minimum	$20 minimum
Wives	Air fare only	$150 total charge

So if you think you are paying money you should be playing with, then get to work. Contact your favorite casino directly, ask your gaming acquaintances, or watch the sports pages of your newspaper, where junket ads often appear, for information. With the proper use of junkets, comps, and refunds, you can let the casinos be your benefactors at the tables *and* at the hotel.

TWELVE

Staying Ahead of the Game

To be great, you must stand on the shoulders of giants.

SIR ISAAC NEWTON

I hate to hear someone tell me how naïve, ignorant, dull, slow, unskilled, etc., they are. I often end up losing money to such a person. As any good hustler knows, the less your opponent thinks of you, the better. The problem with the information you have learned in the past eleven chapters is that you have become one hell of a knowledgeable Blackjack player. And that isn't always easy to hide, even if you follow every tip in Chapter Ten.

DEVELOPING YOUR "ACT"

It's also not easy to let someone think you are ignorant. One of the thrills of being a good Blackjack player is knowing what is going on at the table and getting some respect from the dealers, who usually know quality when they see it. Still, you're better off letting everyone think you are a well-heeled dolt. Whatever you want the casino people to think, you must appear to be something other than a winning Blackjack player if you want to keep on making money at the tables. The Blackjack pros call this false image your "act."

I recently returned from a trip to Nassau, where I stayed at the Ambassador Beach hotel which houses the Playboy casino. (As a side note, I don't recommend staying there. The hotel is government-owned and its policy of automatically billing a 15 per cent tip robs the employees there of any incentive to provide good service. In the off season, service was poor. I can only imagine what it must be like during the peak period.) Since I was new to the Playboy, I decided to try out a new act on them. In it I was to be the typical poor player who regularly visited Las Vegas and thought he knew what was going on but really didn't.

What made the plan more interesting was that my wife had recently learned the Basic Strategy and had not yet applied it in the casino. This would be her first chance to play "under fire" at the five-dollar tables. During one session as we played side by side, I would explain to her how this game was different than what I was used to in Las Vegas and appeared to be "showing her the ropes." In reality, I was keeping up this patter while counting and betting. She would follow my betting lead to a lesser degree so that our play appeared unrelated.

After a few minutes, I decided it was time for several mistakes. Having some one-dollar chips from our Blackjacks, I put six chips in the betting square. The dealer glanced at the stack and neutrally said, "Sir, you must bet in even multiples of five dollars. You have six dollars on the table." I acted embarrassed and quickly removed a chip. Later on I tried to double on a soft 18, which was not allowed. I told my wife that it was done that way in Vegas as the pit boss looked on. All I wanted was to seem like a sloppy player with his wife.

Later on we were playing against a delightful Bunny dealer named Naomi. She warmed up when my wife played, and Naomi began talking to us good-naturedly. At one point, my wife drew a 4,4 against Naomi's 6 up in the four-deck game. Since doubling down was allowed after splitting, I suggested to my wife that she split her 4s. She did and Naomi said, "Don't listen to him."

"What do you mean?" I said. "Splitting 4s is OK if you can double down afterward." I caught myself giving too much away and bit my tongue.

Naomi countered, "No, it isn't. I dealt in Britain, where it's not allowed to split 4s. And they do things there to help the player." She turned to my wife and repeated with a conspiratorial stage whisper, "Don't listen to him. He doesn't know what he's talking about." The woman pit boss watching this just smiled while we all laughed. My wife won one hand and lost one hand so no one could make any points there.

Later on at a different table with a different pit boss, I decided it was time to make a few more errors. Once again I shoved out six one-dollar chips to see what would happen. I was going to tip the dealer and wanted to find out how he would handle this. This dealer was much different than the first with whom I tried this. He let the bet stand, and when I lost he collected the whole six dollars without a word. This pit boss behind him walked up and said loud enough for my wife to hear, "That guy didn't really put six chips out there, did he?" The dealer nodded yes, and they both laughed at me right in front of my face. What the dealer didn't realize was that he had just dealt himself out of any tips for a measly one dollar that went to the house.

From that point on, I could vary my bets at will without the slightest heat from anyone. For an entire week, I had nearly perfect playing conditions unmarred by paranoid pit bosses. Later on in the week I was particularly curious and wanted really to push them with an error and see what happened. So during a shuffle, which occurred even in the middle of a hand, I absent-mindedly swapped out my five-dollar chip and replaced it with five one-dollar chips. The dealer nearly jumped out of his skin. I once again apologized and explained that I wasn't used to having the deal stopped during a hand. I told them the Las Vegas casinos I went to finished the hand after the cut card was encountered.

All in all, I had a terrific time with this "act," except that my ego took a beating. I could see that in a way, I was reinforcing the egos of the Playboy casino personnel because of my apparent stupidity. Any time casino personnel are prepared to laugh at their customers while they are sitting there, the casino has to be fairly arrogant. And I don't worry about any casino people who read this book picking me out because there are plenty of genuinely rotten players making the same kind of mistakes plus those I detailed in Chapter Two. Picking out one phony idiot is a hopeless task.

Who knows what I'll be next time? I've been a scruffy tourist, conservative businessman, gambling addict on an emotional binge, pleasant junketeer just looking for a little action. You name it. The closer you are to some common cliché like the drunk or penny-ante housewife player, the easier it will be to go undetected. If you can't think of an act, look around the casino. You will see a cross section of people unmatched in any other

business. Somewhere out there is a personality for you to put on
and hide who you are and what you know. Once you find an act
to mask the serious business of your counting, you will be home
free.

KEEPING UP WITH THE GAME

Gambling is one of the fastest-changing industries in all the
world. With gambling at the bare beginnings of a phenomenal
boom, trying to keep up with the latest events can be a full-time
job. If you want to maintain your edge as a winning Blackjack
player you will need to stay abreast of important developments as
they occur. Whether you approach Blackjack as a diversion, a
hobby, or a business, the sources in this section can keep you on
the winning track.

IMPORTANT NAMES IN BLACKJACK RESEARCH

I've mentioned a number of people throughout the book, people
who have all contributed to creating the strategies you have seen
and to evaluating their power fairly. As a student of Blackjack,
you can be certain that any time you see these names quoted as a
source you are getting valuable and accurate information:

Julian H. Braun

An employee of IBM Corporation, Braun is commonly recognized as the world's greatest authority on computer-devised
Blackjack strategies. His work *The Development and Analysis of
Winning Strategies for the Casino Game of Blackjack* is a recognized classic. Most modern systems of value are based upon
Braun's computer-programming work. His programs are responsible for the correct Basic Strategy and Count Strategy in books
such as Thorp's *Beat the Dealer,* Revere's *Playing Blackjack as a
Business,* Epstein's *The Theory of Gambling and Statistical
Logic,* and Humble's *Blackjack Gold* and *Blackjack SuperGold*
books. Braun's programs are also responsible for the Basic Strategy given in this book and for the powerful Hi-Opt I and Hi-Opt
II strategies.

Braun has been a frequent contributor to various gambling periodicals but has become more interested in other fields such as the commodity markets. He has provided analyses for new options such as the early-surrender rule in Atlantic City and is one of the most respected sources of Blackjack systems ratings. His most recent publication is the book, *How to Play Winning Blackjack*.

Joel H. Friedman

Joel Friedman is a newcomer to the group of respected Blackjack analysts. Currently a graduate student in operations research at Stanford University, Friedman first came to prominence with his paper "Choosing a Blackjack Game," presented at the Fourth Conference on Gambling (more on the conferences later). The paper showed Friedman's grasp of the practical problems of the player by posing and answering several important and original questions. He was also very gracious in providing additional material in adapting his graphs for inclusion in Chapter Ten of this book.

When I quizzed Joel on his future plans, he told me that his study of Blackjack is continuing, but explained that the current work must be kept confidential at this stage. Whatever he is completing, it is likely to be of immediate assistance to the player.

Peter A. Griffin

Peter Griffin bills himself as a professor of mathematics and gambler in residence at his university. As well respected as Braun when it comes to rating Blackjack systems, Griffin pioneered the statistical approach of evaluation as opposed to the simulation approach used by Braun. Griffin's paper "Use of Bivariate Normal Approximations to Evaluate Single-parameter Card-counting Systems in Blackjack" was first presented to the Third Conference on Gambling. In it, Griffin introduced the concepts of "playing efficiency" and "betting correlation" in comparing systems.

An avid student of the game, Griffin is also the source of the multiparameter-tables concept, and has computed complete multiparameter strategies for both the Hi-Opt I and Hi-Opt II. His work analyzing the power of the Hi-Opt I with reduced count ranges is the first of its kind ever to be done for any system. He has also recently written an excellent book, *The Theory of Blackjack,* published by the Gamblers Book Club.

Edward O. Thorp

Edward Thorp was one of a handful of scientists studying the game of Blackjack in the early sixties. The work by Baldwin, Cantey, Maisel, and McDermott in using calculators to compute the proper Basic Strategy had been analyzed further by people like Richard Epstein and Allan Wilson. But Thorp had the insight also to question what the strategy should be as the composition of the deck changed. The results of this research were first presented to the public in the classic best seller (and still selling) *Beat the Dealer.*

These days, Thorp is not as active as he once was in Blackjack, but still authors articles on such subjects as Backgammon, Roulette, and the stock market.

Allan N. Wilson

Allan Wilson was another one of the scientists to be interested by the Baldwin group's work. In the late 1950s, Wilson began to write his own analysis program to determine the Basic Strategy and accurate expectation with the simulation approach and was the first to come up with the nearly correct Basic Strategy Expectation value of 0.0 per cent. The first edition of his book *The Casino Gambler's Guide* was published one year before the second edition of *Beat the Dealer.* In correspondence with me, Wilson justifiably calls his book one of the half-dozen outstanding books of all time on casino-gambling odds. In fact, many of the book's features have not been duplicated in numerous later volumes that have appeared. Several of the gambling "truths" that appear throughout this book are the result of Wilson's initial analyses and application of statistical principles to Blackjack.

You can't go wrong if you depend upon information generated by any of the Blackjack experts mentioned above. There are many other competent and respected names in the field of Blackjack research and analysis who aren't listed. Their omission in no way is meant as a judgment or ranking. The experts listed were either important in the development or rating of the Hi-Opt systems or provided significant data on winning Blackjack.

IMPORTANT ORGANIZATIONS COVERING BLACKJACK

I'm always surprised how little regular players know about the various organizations that supply gambling information. Even the vacation player can benefit from using some of the following sources. The regular player should seriously consider each of these organizations to see how their products might be of assistance to his or her game.

Gamblers Book Club

The Gamblers Book Club (630 South Eleventh Street, Las Vegas, NV 89101; 1-800-634-6243) is not a club, but a store founded and operated for many years by two very warm and conscientious people, John and Edna Luckman. John has been a dealer and pit boss, and he is noted for publishing rare gaming books. He has been involved in gaming for many, many years. After leaving the casino, John started the bookstore as a means of making gaming information easily available to all who seek it. His philosophy was that every system should cost only a few dollars and proved it with his low-priced *Facts of . . .* series of booklets. John is also a collector of old books on gaming, and his store is your best source for finding any new, old, or out-of-print books or periodicals on gaming. The marketing director of the GBC is Howard Schwartz. Howard is frequently quoted in news articles and is one of the most knowledgeable individuals on current events and publications in gaming.

The GBC published over ninety titles itself and has nearly every other gaming book that has ever been written. It can supply literally hundreds of titles under fifteen classifications: poker, casino, sports, racing, card games, backgammon, probabilities, history, biography, sociology, psychology, novels, slots, magic, and if that didn't cover everything, miscellaneous. In all there are over a thousand new book titles. The GBC can also supply back issues or out-of-print items such as the only three issues of the magazine *Gamblers World* or reprints such as Houdini's *Right Way to Do Wrong*. There are over two thousand used titles in addition to a complete collection of periodicals, newsletters, and papers.

The GBC also published two periodicals, *Systems & Methods* and *Casino & Sports*. The first was dedicated to pari-mutuel gaming and the second to casino and sports book wagering. While these are no longer published, back issues are available on a limited basis and are worth the investment for a serious gamer.

In late 1984 the GBC sold the publication rights for its own books to Casino Press in New York. Casino Press has come out with a catalogue of GBC publications and as of yet has not published any of its own editions of GBC titles.

The GBC is still the world's largest bookstore of gaming publications. Approximately 15 percent of its business comes from local visitors, and the rest from mail order. There are over fifty thousand people on the worldwide mailing list, and about fifteen thousand individuals placed orders last year. If the GBC doesn't have a publication, it probably doesn't exist. The extensive GBC catalogue covers every imaginable facet of gaming and makes for interesting reading. Write for catalogue information, call the 800 number, or visit the store when you are in town.

Lance Humble's International Gaming, Inc.

International Gaming, Inc. (P.O. Box 73, Thornhill, Ont. L3T 3N1, Canada) is the organization established by Lance Humble to disseminate important information concerning the world of gaming. It offers a wide range of both systems and information to the general public.

International Blackjack Club (IBC) The IBC is dedicated to better Blackjack by providing a communications medium for players from around the world. The IBC newsletter contains information on playing conditions in specific casinos, players' experiences, news of casino openings and junkets, book and systems reviews, and general information, plus answers to questions on gaming. A new feature of the newsletter is the "Winning Edge" column, containing winning tips in Blackjack and other games such as Poker, Gin, horse racing, and sports wagering. The newsletter is a consumer's guide to systems and casinos. If you want to see what the IBC newsletter looks like before subscribing, write IGI and it will send you information on obtaining a sample copy.

Hi-Opt I and II. For the very serious player wishing to have the complete table values for the Hi-Opt I system (and thus gain the final .2 per cent in performance), IGI still sells the Hi-Opt I for seventy-five dollars. Purchasers of the Hi-Opt I system also receive the current issue of the IBC newsletter and a complimentary copy of the complete Hi-Opt I multiparameter tables.

For the player wishing the highest practicable gain over the casino, IGI also sells the complete Hi-Opt II strategy. The power of the Hi-Opt II was shown in the table in Chapter Eight. Recent studies by Edward Thorp, Peter Griffin, and Julian Braun have shown that it was *not possible* for the computers to construct a more powerful strategy than the Hi-Opt II that was at the same time practical for casino play. Thus the Hi-Opt II will ALWAYS remain the *most powerful, practicable Blackjack strategy ever devised.* The complete Hi-Opt II costs two hundred dollars.

Although the Hi-Opt II is more powerful than the Hi-Opt I, it contains fewer tables—only six. The tables are composite in that they apply to all games—single-, double-, four-, five-, six-, or eight-deck games. There are only slight modifications for one- or two-deck games. The "price" for the extra is that the Hi-Opt II is slightly more complex. It is a second-level system counting three more cards than the Hi-Opt I. The Hi-Opt II strategy is the preferred system among professional Blackjack players today.

With the purchase of a Hi-Opt II system come the Hi-Opt II multiparameter tables and one-year membership in the International Blackjack Club. Also included are direct consultation privileges with Dr. Humble. All Hi-Opt II purchasers receive Dr. Humble's unlisted telephone number.

Multiparameter tables. For owners of this book, or for previous purchasers of the Hi-Opt I or II systems, the full multiparameter tables are available separately.

Pari-mutuel betting information. International Gaming is also actively analyzing gaming systems other than those for Blackjack. The following products or services are also available from IGI:

1. A point method for profit taking at the harness races (free research report)

2. *Harness-racing Gold* (systems book)
3. Advanced point method for harness-racing prediction (system)
4. Power approaches to thoroughbreds (winning angles)

CCA Enterprises

CCA Enterprises (P.O. Box 1205, Ballwin, MO 63022) is the organization established by Carl Cooper to provide personnel training to a wide range of public, private, and educational organizations. The firm specializes in personal-productivity topics such as memory development, interpersonal communications, creativity, and time management. The learning techniques for Blackjack taught in this book are an outgrowth of a memory course CCA Enterprises developed for a governmental agency. CCA's gaming activities include:

Basic Blackjack seminar. Several gaming organizations have chosen to establish full-time gambling schools in many of the large cities. These often close soon after the initial group of serious gamers who can afford the high tuition costs have passed through the course. CCA Enterprises, in conjunction with International Gaming, has developed a reasonably priced one-day seminar that teaches the fundamentals of casino play, Basic Strategy, and the Hi-Opt I count. The one-day seminar provides the start to becoming a winning player. Further information on seminar content and scheduled dates and cities can be obtained from CCA Enterprises.

"The World's Greatest Blackjack Reference Wheel." Many students of the Blackjack seminar have asked for an easy-to-use reference for the Basic Strategy and Hi-Opt I playing strategy. CCA Enterprises also markets a handy reference "wheel" providing this information. The player merely lines up a rotating card under the proper player hand and reads the correct strategy through a viewing window. One side of the card shows the Basic Strategy, the other shows the Hi-Opt I index number.

The card is an excellent learning tool for mastering and reviewing the correct Blackjack strategies but would not be appropriate for casino play because of its size and the obvious nature of its use. CCA Enterprises can provide a more detailed description and current price information.

"The World's Greatest Blackjack Program." Home computers first made an appearance in 1977, and are rapidly gaining use in the development and teaching of proper strategies for Blackjack and other forms of gaming. "The World's Greatest Blackjack Program" was designed by CCA Enterprises and programmed by home computer expert Warren Irwin.

WGBJP provides for every rule variation including the home game. It teaches Basic Strategy, the Hi-Opt I count and strategy, and has additional programs for developing visual and card-counting skills. It also plays a real-life game with up to four players using actual card images and sound effects. The program is available through most home computer retailers.

RGE Publishing

One of the most refreshing personalities in blackjack is Arnold Snyder of RGE Publishing (#1067, 2000 Center Street, Berkeley, CA 94704). Snyder, founder of the "first church of blackjack," writes with puckish humor on all facets of the game. He is noted for attending gaming symposiums disguised in full beard and bowler to thwart casino observers. If there isn't a current controversy or fight among experts, Snyder will invent one. If no one is criticizing Snyder enough, he will write his own. The serious side of Snyder is also quickly evident. For example, Snyder was the first to isolate the mathematically most important factors in determining favorable playing conditions.

RGE's main publication is *Blackjack Forum,* a fifty-page (with small type) magazine filled with irreverent satire, articles, correspondence, and timely reviews. Each issue is crammed with information invaluable to winning blackjack. Regular correspondents update the current gaming situation at all popular North American locales. There are "how to" articles such as reading the dealer. Results of mathematical studies are also included where appropriate.

Other regular features of *Blackjack Forum* help even casual players. These include "The Las Vegas Advisor" section, which is filled with tips on casino promotions like low-cost meals and free offers. The "Best Bets" and "Burn Joints" features detail current playing conditions at favorable and difficult-to-beat casinos. If you are interested in other publications, the "Digest" section provides an overview of the contents of every other major blackjack publication. Finally, there is an entertaining and informative "Letters to the Editor" section, and a "Counters Classified" section for those wanting to meet other counters. All in all, if there is only one publication to which you plan to subscribe, this should be it.

RGE publications also include books such as *The Blackjack Formula, Reading the Dealer,* and the highly rated *Blackbelt in Blackjack.* RGE too stocks other important blackjack materials such as video programs, meeting notes, and back issues to other selected publications. Arnold Snyder is one of the most knowledgeable and interesting experts currently writing about blackjack. Write RGE for further information.

Rouge et Noir News

It's hard to say enough about this publication. Published by Walter Tyminski, *Rouge et Noir News* (P.O. Box 6, Glen Head, NY 11545) is a complete newsletter of the world of casino gambling. The monthly copies provide truly first-class investigative reporting on casino operations, ownership, finances, legal positions, irregularities, and political involvement. Tyminski has sources where the subjects of his articles didn't know they had places. The *News* also provides objective reviews of casino books and systems, and contains a Las Vegas casino show guide. I think you can understand the worth of the *News* based upon the number of times you have seen me quote from it in this book.

Rouge et Noir also publishes or sells a number of other books and one other magazine, *Resort Management Report.* The report is written for professionals in the gambling resort industry, investors, the financial community, and the media. The report provides in-depth reporting and analysis on management, financial, legal, and governmental-control aspects of casino gaming. Information about any of the Rouge et Noir products can be obtained by writing Walter Tyminski.

SRS Enterprises, Inc.

SRS Enterprises (1018 N. Cole Ave., Hollywood, CA 90038)
publishes *Gambling Times* magazine, possibly the best gambling
magazine ever offered. *Gambling Times* contains authoritative
articles, fiction, humor, and news written by some of the best
gambling writers in the world. Not limited to casino gaming, the
Times has articles on all aspects of gambling worldwide.

If I had any criticism of the content, it would only be that
sometimes articles describe systems for games that absolutely cannot be beaten with systems such as Craps or Roulette. But even
then, the *Times* makes no promises beyond their "Systems Shop."
The *"Gambling Times* Systems Shop" buying service contains
only systems that have the *Times'* seal of approval. I'm proud to
say that both the Hi-Opt I and II have earned *GT*'s seal.

Subscription information for *Gambling Times* can be obtained
by writing SRS Enterprises at the above address.

If you subscribed to all of the periodicals described above, you
would be one tough gambler to deal with. What I suggest you do
is take the time to write the organizations for the material that
sounds interesting and then determine the proper level of information you need to play on an informed basis. The only mistake
you can make is to decide that you don't need *anything* and pass
up all of them. What you will be missing is very likely to hurt you
somewhere along the line.

GAMBLING EVENTS

There are several Blackjack events you should be aware of. One
is a conference where gaming professionals meet to exchange
ideas, and the other is the result of a stunning promotional idea
for the casino. Let's start first with the casino event because once
again the player is encouraged to make a poor financial decision.

Tournament Blackjack

The American public is generally aware of the famous annual
"World Championship of Poker" event because of the regular
newspaper and TV coverage it has received each year. An organization named World Championship of Blackjack, Inc., came up
with the idea of running a similar contest for Blackjack players,
and interested the Sahara management in offering the tourney.

The first WCB was run at the Las Vegas Sahara in December of 1978 and was a total success, drawing over 1,400 entries.

The rules are enticing for a player hoping to win the tournament. The game is single-deck dealt face up to a full table. Betting limits are $5.00 to $500. Playing rules are typical Las Vegas Strip, with resplitting allowed. To insure no advantage in seating position, a rotating marker is used to determine the betting and dealing order. The player directly in front of the marker begins the betting, and the other players bet in turn.

In the first round, players are divided into table groups of seven for a two-hour playing session. Each participant is required to buy in at each round with $500. The player with the highest winnings at each table at the end of the round proceeds to the next round. Remaining players can keep any winnings (or suffer any losses). Since Blackjack authors or teachers are barred from entry, amateur players have a fair chance of moving up. The total announced prize package of the first tourney was $125,000, so the championship seemed like a great opportunity for the average player.

If you ignore the fun factor or snob appeal of being able to tell your friends you were a contestant and work strictly on logic, the tourney is a bad bet. The entry fee is $250 ($225 is submitted early) per participant. With exactly 1,408 entries in December 1978, this meant the tourney grossed between $317,000 and $352,000 in entry fees. With an announced prize package of $125,000, this is a tidy initial profit of over $200,000. The difference comes out of the contestants' pockets. The player could expect to win only $89 ($125,000 divided by 1,408 players) for his or her $225 or $250 entry fee.

The Sahara might counter with the fact that there were numerous other tournament expenses. Although this is true, the casino was actually doing itself a big favor. December is the slowest time of year in Nevada, so the Sahara was filling rooms that would have stood empty. The food and beverage services of the resort made more money than would have been otherwise possible. The Sahara might also counter that it could expect to lose at the tournament Blackjack tables because of skilled players and perfect conditions. This is true. In fact, they did lose a little. But the Sahara management later said that they made up the difference through increased action at the other games as a result of the championship crowd. Finally, the promotional benefit of the national TV coverage by NBC was worth many thousands of dollars in advertising.

The December 1978 event was so successful that WCB, Inc., and the Sahara announced an even bigger event for July 1979. Called "The $125,000 Sahara Summer Blackjack Classic," tournaments were to be run simultaneously at the Sahara resorts in Las Vegas, Reno, and Lake Tahoe, with the championship round taking place in Las Vegas. WCB officials tallied about 1,900 entries for this second event. If you do the division for average winnings per participant, the total was down to $66 per person for the same $250 entry fee.

If you are a serious bettor only interested in the expected return on your gaming dollar, I suggest you skip this type of event. The payout is worse than that of the most greedy slot machines, and the tournament format puts too much weight on luck. A two-hour round is hardly long enough for the difference in skill among players to be determined. The winners of the first three tournaments (held up to the time this was written) characterized themselves as "not an experienced player," "never really studied the game," and "I never read a book on Blackjack and I'm not a card counter." What happens is that a player who is "hot" will win the round and move on. Also, as a systems player you risk being identified as a winner. Do you think the Sahara will welcome you back into their casino and let you play unhindered once you have established yourself as a winning counter? I wouldn't want anyone to jeopardize hard-earned skills for a one-in-two-thousand shot at big money.

Nonetheless, if you want to involve yourself in one of the most carefully conceived and slickly promoted gambling events in history, then World Championship Blackjack (WCB) may be for you. The very fact that anyone can win has given the WCB tourneys a tremendous growth in popularity. While the December 1978 Championship had 1,400 entries, the 1979 Championship had 2,500 at three Nevada locations, and projections for later years was for 5,000 eager entrants. Trying to cash in on a good promotion, the WCB people eventually expanded to three tournaments per year in March, May, and September. The plan was to expand to monthly tournaments.

It didn't take long for the casino industry to realize that tournament blackjack had caught the public's attention. Always looking for ways to increase casino traffic, and realizing that Atlantic City was siphoning off many serious players, several other casinos announced tournaments. There was then a court fight over whether WCB owned all rights to the tournament concept, which was lost by WCB.

Soon there were numerous blackjack tournaments with a dizzying array of options and promotions. There were cash and merchandise prizes, early-bird drawings, second-chance tournaments for first-round losers, and mixed doubles tournaments. Prize money was still linked to attendance, though, and did not provide a good expected-winnings bet.

It was inevitable that the heavy competition among the casinos for the tournament players nearly killed the concept. The choice of tournaments was nearly overwhelming for the average gamer. The current situation is that there are all types of tournaments available. For example, in 1986 Four Queens, Marina, and the Sands had all sponsored tournaments. Also, Royal and Lady Luck casinos held weekly minitournaments requiring only a small buy-in.

For a minitournament, the buy-in is currently $25. First prize varies from $750 to $1,200 for a preliminary-round win, and up to $5,000 for a final-round win. Some casinos adjust these amounts if they do not have a full complement of entrants, others award standard amounts regardless of the number of players. Typically, the house returns in prize money only 75 to 80 percent of the total entry fees. So the "house edge" for a filled tournament, or a tournament where prize money is adjusted for the number of entrants is quite steep. Conceivably, a minitournament offering prizes could *lose* money on a slow night with few entries. You might wish to find out the number of entrants before you sign up for this style of tournament—some nights may pay better than others.

In the larger tournaments, particularly those with champions from different sites competing equally in the finals, you might want to choose your entry location carefully. You will likely get a better playing schedule at Reno or Lake Tahoe preliminaries. And there are usually three times as many entrants at Las Vegas editions. There is much less competition at the other sites, yet qualifiers have an equal chance with Las Vegas champions.

A final twist to the tournament scene is the "match play" format. Here you compete with another individual and not a whole table of opponents. This reduces the luck factor and provides a better test of skill. Any of these formats provide a poor bet but can result in exciting entertainment. Try a minitournament the next time you have an opportunity and see what you think.

Conference on Gambling

Every two years there is a national conference of gambling. The third conference was held at Caesar's Palace in 1976, and the fourth was held at the MGM Reno in 1978. The conference was usually scheduled in December, to take advantage of the slow season at the resorts. The fifth was held in Lake Tahoe in October 1981. I highly recommend this conference to anyone interested in Blackjack and other games.

In previous conferences, papers were presented (and distributed free to the audience) by experts such as Braun, Griffin, Heath, Schneider, and Thorp. There were papers on poker, football, baseball, the psychology of gambling, horse racing, cheating, etc. Several of the papers usually describe winning systems or evaluate systems for the reader.

The conference is open to the public. The public is also invited to submit papers for presentation. This conference is not a bunch of academics blowing dust off reams of computer printouts and high-level math. The papers are generally of high value to players at all levels. In addition, the conference gives the perfect opportunity to meet and trade notes with some of the world's greatest gaming experts. The personal contacts I've made at the conferences have been extremely valuable.

For information on the gambling conferences, you can write: Dr. Bill Eadington, Department of Economics, University of Nevada at Reno, Reno, NV 89057. If you are interested in copies of papers from previous conferences you can contact Dr. Eadington or check with Walter Tyminski at Rouge et Noir. All the papers that were presented at the First Conference on Gambling have been published in book form by Charles C Thomas, Publisher. The book is titled *Gambling and Society*. A beautiful hardcover volume embossed in gold, it is a true collector's item.

THE CURRENT STATUS OF GAMBLING

In the United States, the demand for gambling has never been greater, and analysts peg gaming as one of the big growth industries in the next ten years. If the results of the New Jersey casino openings are any indications, the demand is not even close to being met. At this point, here are the number of states involved in various forms of gambling:

Bingo	39
Horse racing	31
Lotteries	15
Dog racing	13
Numbers	8
Card rooms	7
Jai alai	5
Sports books	3
Off-track betting	2
Casinos	2

So far, fifteen states have expressed interest in or are considering legalized casino gambling. They are: California, Connecticut, Delaware, Florida, Hawaii, Illinois, Louisiana, Maine, Maryland, Massachusetts, Michigan, New York, Pennsylvania, Rhode Island, and Washington. Formal proposals for various forms of legalized gambling, including casino-style, are proceeding through official channels in New York, Florida, Louisiana, Pennsylvania (Pocono Mountains sector only), Massachusetts (local-option legislation), and California (various initiative petitions).

While everyone is looking at the benefits of increased employment, raised property values, higher tax bases, and state cuts of the casinos' profits, the New Jersey experiment has shown that there are also some problems. In a June 10, 1979, article, *Parade* magazine reported:

> Street crime is up 25 per cent and offenses like murder, assault, and armed robbery are increasing. Organized crime—which formerly shunned the town because there were no pickings—is making a determined effort to infiltrate vending-machine, liquor, real-estate and other auxiliary businesses that surround gaming, say state officials.

Despite any potential problems, governments worldwide are eager to cash in on the so far insatible demand for gambling opportunities. Following is a summary of the gambling situation worldwide from an article entitled "The Gambling Explosion" courtesy of John Luckman at the Gamblers Book Club:

CANADA

In Ontario last year, a couple received a five-hundred-thousand-dollar lottery prize with a ticket purchased via a credit card. That's not so much: Lotto Canada offers twelve first prizes of one million dollars each (ten dollars per ticket). Horse-racing wagering totals more than one billion dollars a year (not counting illegal bets placed through the neighborhood book). Bingo, football, hockey, and baseball games are also popular. Federal and provincial governments share in the profits. A Canadian official said, "We sell dreams and expectations."

For the casino gambler, there are the games at the Calgary Stampede and the Edmonton Exhibition in addition to "no house" games in the western provinces. I feel that year-round casino gambling isn't far off.

MEXICO

It's regarded as better than even money that casino-style gaming will come to Mexico within three years. Miguel Aleman, Mexico's No. 1 political figure other than President Lopez Portillo, told tourist officials in Mexico City that gambling is a certainty for Mexico. The biggest lure is the estimated quarter-billion-dollar annual tax revenues gaming would produce. Mexico City? Not a chance, said Aleman. Acapulco is where it'll happen.

SOUTH AMERICA

There's a state-run lottery in almost every South American country; most have casinos or horse racing, or both. The Boy Scouts participate by singing out the results as numbered balls emerge from the drum at the Loteria Nacional in Buenos Aires. Telephone employees share in under-table payoffs during busy Argentina weekends as business gets so heavy that extra lines are needed to the bookies' offices (householders complain that their telephones go dead on Saturday morning, then "mysteriously" come back into service Sunday night). Brazilians bet approximately 1.6 million cruzeiros every day on an illegal numbers game, *jogo do bicho,* featuring animal pictures instead of numbers so the illiterate can participate. Put it this way: You can get some action on some kind of game almost anywhere in South America.

THE NETHERLANDS

Two casinos operate here (at Zandvoort and Valkenburg), Dutchmen only recently having discovered gambling as a source of governmental revenue. The national lottery is the biggest game of chance, with lotto, soccer pools, and horse racing also on the menu. Total amount wagered annually: three hundred million dollars. The government keeps all net profits.

SWITZERLAND

It's difficult to go broke here as Swiss law forbids wagers exceeding two dollars. Lotteries, soccer, and a handful of privately owned casinos are in vogue at present. Average per-capita annual wagering: twenty dollars.

BELGIUM

A highly placed government official says privately, "Gambling is the only industry in Belgium that functions well." Horse racing, both domestic and foreign, is popular. Also a national lottery, trapshooting and archery contests (!), and eight casinos. Cock fighting, a crime, is popular in the small Liège region villages. Bird singing attracts substantial wagering; the birds (roosters or male canaries) are placed in cages covered with black cloth; fans bet on which birds crows or sings longest when the cloths are whipped away (eight million bet annually on this sport). Belgium's known betting total: five hundred million Belgian francs a year.

WEST GERMANY

A third of all West Germans (approximately twenty million) play the national lottery each Saturday night; there's a six-hundred-thousand-dollar first prize, and winning numbers are flashed on TV screens. Germans also go for the slots, casinos (twenty-one at the moment), and horse racing. The national lottery is up 22 per cent over earlier figures.

GREAT BRITAIN

Britains bet $5.5 billion a year on soccer, horses, dog races, bingo, and other games of chance. The weekly soccer pools attract 15 million bettors (average bet: $.40) who gamble $450

million annually. Winnings are not tax-free; the government gets
its cut right off the top by sucking up 40 per cent of all moneys
wagered. Bingo is a blast, with 18,000 clubs operating. The lottery mania hasn't won the fancy of the English. Privately run casinos have a modest membership total of about 300,000. The
government doesn't see betting as harmful. There are few reports
of organized-crime involvement. Average annual per-capita betting in Britain: $125. The reduced-fare jet-travel boom is causing
British gaming authorities to advocate more liberal playing rules
to attract the international gaming set.

FRANCE

The most popular sport is horse racing: 2.6 billion francs is
wagered annually, of which all but a pittance is bet through cafes,
licensed to make book. Biggest turf event: the Tierce, where bettors try to pick win, place, and show horses (Saturdays and Sun-
days only). Seven million people bet this offering weekly. There
is also the weekly national lottery, loto (a numbers game), and
(for the upper crust) casinos that also feature theaters, cabarets,
and fashionable restaurants. France has 147 casinos. Your winnings aren't taxed.

MONACO

Fabled Casino de Monte Carlo gaming is for tourists only (the
first tourists were the Russian aristocracy, escaping the Commu-
nist Revolution in 1917). The Loew's hotel chain (United States)
participates fifty-fifty with the government in a new casino that
opened in mid-1975. Publicity through the generations has helped
perpetuate this Mediterranean principality as a mecca for gamblers
everywhere. Arabs are heavy gamblers here.

ITALY

Gambling is up about 20 per cent, with Italians betting about
$600 million a year on lotteries, soccer pools, and the horses. All
gaming is operated by the federal government except the casinos,
which are run by the very greedy cities. These are real money-
makers, but the feds won't let local politicos open any more casinos. (The most recent one was started back in 1951!) Italy,
hard hit by depression and governmental instability, is betting

more during the hard times as people seek a windfall. That's what the government believes, anyway.

MIDEAST

The Koran, the Islamic holy book, strictly forbids gambling, so in the Mideast it's a potpourri of wealth, stealth, and travel. Casino play is for tourists *only*. Wealthy oilmen from Saudi Arabia, Kuwait, and the Persian Gulf do their gaming at Cairo, Beirut, and Damascus. (Socialist Syria operates a casino near the Damascus airport, to avoid missing any prospective wagers, from which the state profits handsomely. The fabled Casino du Liban is again open in once-beautiful Beirut, now a civil-war rubbish pile—the action isn't what it once was.) The Lebanese can play if they can prove they make more than seven thousand dollars a year—these fortunates enjoy European soccer, pools, poker (newly popular), and, biggest of them all, the Syrian national lottery. Some Mideast governments totally ignore the Koran and operate lotteries for the unwashed man on the street. All these have lotteries, highly visible or low-key: Egypt, Jordan, Lebanon, and Syria.

JAPAN

The Japanese rank near the top of world gambling fans: $14 billion wagered each year, with horse racing getting the most action ($5.7 billion). Boat racing attracts a surprising $4.1 billion, and the $.33 lottery gets a lot of action, offering a top payoff of $33,333. Gambling is growing so fast in Japan that it's impossible to keep tabs on it: Government-run lotteries showed a 47 per cent increase in 1978 alone. The government builds schools and highways with its gambling revenues.

SINGAPORE

The Chinese, traditional gambling enthusiasts, find many ways to beat the antigaming law on this island nation. They get their bets down in coffee houses and on the streets. Mah-jongg, Chinese chess, and board games are popular. Children risk real currency on spider fights. Police look the other way when people gather over their gaming boards. There are no reliable estimates as to Singapore's total betting "handle."

U . S . S . R .

Gambling for money is strictly against Soviet law, so the government itself hustles lottery tickets in banks and parks, at newsstands and on the subway, as a means of "dampening inflation" and soaking up the public's extra cash. The Soviet national lottery is called "Money and Goods," with everything from automobiles to guitars as noncapitalistic prizes. In six Soviet cities, there's horse-race betting only on race days (twice weekly). At Moscow's Hippodrome track, six to eight bookmakers flourish without police opposition. There are reports of card sharks plying their trade in the Black Sea resort vacation sector.

Racing through the alphabet, here are some other countries or areas in which gaming flourishes: Antigua, Argentina, Aruba, Australia, Austria, Bahamas, Belgium, Bonaire, Bulgaria, Chile, Colombia, Curaçao, Dominican Republic, Ecuador, Egypt, Ghana, Greece, Haiti, Korea, Lebanon, Macao, Malaysia, Morocco, Panama, Philippines, Portugal, Puerto Rico, Saint Maarten, Spain, Surinam, Turkey, Uruguay, and Yugoslavia.

THE FUTURE OF BLACKJACK

I recently had an interesting conversation with a man called "Babe." We were sitting in the usual din at a large Italian wedding talking about gambling in general and Las Vegas in particular. He suddenly leaned back and told me:

> The only way to say it is that Las Vegas is going downhill. When the gangsters controlled the place it was much better. They knew how to run a scam. A good thief never takes everything; he always leaves the sucker with a little so he'll be back. I remember talking to a farmer during World War II who had been under both German and Russian occupation. He told me the Germans came around every week with a list and took just enough so that they could come back and fill the same list the next week. The Russians, on the other hand, swept in and took everything so there was no more for anybody. Well, the Las Vegas casinos are the Russians of gambling.
>
> The trouble is the place is run by accountants with one hand on their computer and the other in the till. All they care about is the bottom line and the hell with the patron. So the players are going elsewhere. Food is expensive, shows are outrageous, and the free entertainment in the lounges has been cut back because it's too costly. Even slots are going up in price. Now they're losing the little

old lady who faithfully drops two hundred dollars a trip several times a year. The bettors aren't as stupid as the casinos might think.

I had to laugh at Babe wishing the crooks were back in control, but I agreed that casino gambling has changed drastically. As long as the supply falls short of the demand, the casinos are going to be in the driver's seat. But there are signs that this is about to change. In the East, the huge success of the Atlantic City casinos has brought real worry into the executive suites in Nevada. The gasoline shortage of 1979 (and who knows how much longer) has restricted the flow of gamers from the West Coast, leaving Las Vegas stranded. If this continues, at some point greed will become tempered by reality. Only by making the game more attractive can the nation's casinos maintain their growth and profitability in the next five to ten years.

On the other side, what can you expect in the way of future Blackjack systems? If you are thinking of trying to use the current level of miniature computer technology, it's already been done. Using five small computers specially built into pairs of shoes, inventor Keith Taft and team organizer Ken Uston masterminded a win of $130,000 in a short period in 1977. When one of their two-person teams was discovered in Harvey's Club in May 1977, the team stopped operating with the computer.

The computer was confiscated and sent to the FBI in Washington. Five months later, the FBI determined that the computer was not a cheating device and made use of the normal information any player had. Charges were dropped after this pronouncement. In an article following these events, I wrote in the IBC newsletter:

Epstein estimates in the 1977 edition of his book *The Theory of Gambling and Statistical Logic* that if the Blackjack game were played perfectly with every card being kept track of according to its exact denomination, a player would have a flat bet advantage of 5 per cent in a single-deck game. I doubt whether this instrument presently in use yields this high an advantage. I estimate that the advantage is probably closer to 3 per cent on a flat-bet basis [I later found out that the advantage was 2.5 per cent]. Against multiple decks the advantage would be approximately twice that of the Hi-Opt II with the same bet ranges.

I am against this kind of instrument for playing Blackjack for the simple reason that it will ruin the game for all of us. I agree with

Walter Tyminski of *Rouge et Noir News* that such devices should be outlawed in casinos.

After my comments appeared, I received a long letter from Ken Uston, a portion of which is included below:

> Since we've always been able to beat the game utilizing ethical, legal methods, I decided to leave the Blackjack computer business shortly thereafter [are arrest]—even though it had not been established that the use of computers is illegal. Similarly, my teams have *never* resorted to "playing with help," marking cards, utilizing "cold decks," or using any of the myriad ways of cheating the house.

I was able to witness a demonstration of an electronic computer device being used to play Blackjack recently. Generally, I was not impressed. Portable computers have been in use both in the casinos and outside of casinos and laboratories to my knowledge since 1966. As a trial for this version, I began dealing a game and played the Hi-Opt II system while the computer made its plays. After going through several single decks, I discovered that every decision made by the computer matched the dictates of the Hi-Opt II. In other words, I could see no advantage in using this computer for improving the accuracy of my play. In any case, I estimate that there are about a dozen of these devices still bouncing around the casinos of the world and more likely to follow as technology continues to improve. I can only hope that these people ultimately make the same decision as Ken Uston, or the casinos will change the game enough to ruin it for all of us.

Along these lines, in 1986 the Nevada judicial system has decided the issue of on-body computers. In the years since the first edition of this book, several versions of computers were used in casinos, some individuals were caught, and their equipment was confiscated by the house. The courts initially ruled that such computers were "cheating devices" and that their use in the casino was cause for arrest. At this time anyone using such a device is gambling with far more than a bankroll.

There is no doubt that the game of Blackjack has been more difficult to win at than in Thorp's days, or even in the early seventies. Yet more and more tables are available every year, making the competition for players keener and keener. From a systems standpoint, "necessity is the mother of invention." At this very moment more powerful approaches to Blackjack are being investigated in computer centers in several North American universities.

THE FUTURE OF GAMBLING

Gambling is a painless form of taxation; therefore it will always have a future. No one has ever been voted out of office for taxing a casino. I foresee a time not too far in the future when anyone will be able to view live and bet on any sporting event in the United States, and on most major events in the world. The technology is almost here with Radio Shack reportedly bringing out a roof antenna for about $400. Rooftop receivers are allowing casinos to get satellite signals of hundreds of TV stations simultaneously. If you wish to bet on a televised horse race in Kentucky, you might be able to see how you did as it is run. A little farther in the future, you will be able to view and bet in the privacy of your home through a combination TV computer terminal. Everyone who wants one will have a gaming account that is automatically credited or debited as necessary. In its search for new sources of income, the government will want to make it as easy as possible for you to wager. As for growth, financial analysts suggest that the gambling industry is now at the stage fast foods were twenty years ago.

It's important to realize that there will always be hope for gamblers. They may have to change names. They may have to learn more about probability theory. They may have to devote additional hours to learning a more powerful strategy. They may want to get together with other players to form a team. They may have to invest more money in devices or information to make them better gamers. Nevertheless, as long as the following saying holds, there will always be a way to make money through gambling. You've just finished the most powerful book ever written on the game of Blackjack. Now how much money are you going to let it win for you?

Everyone wants to learn how to improve themselves—
as long as they really don't have to do it.

ANONYMOUS

SELECTED
BIBLIOGRAPHY

ANDERSEN, IAN. *Turning the Tables on Las Vegas.* New York: Vanguard, 1976.

ANDERSON, EDDIE. *Las Vegas 1978.* Las Vegas: Oracle, 1977.

ARCHER, JOHN. *The Archer Method of Winning at 21.* Hollywood: Wishire, 1978.

BRAUN, JULIAN H. "The Development and Analysis of Winning Strategies for the Casino Game of Blackpack." Chicago, 1975.

————. *How to Play Winning Blackjack.* Chicago: Data House Publishing, 1980.

COLLVER, DONALD I. *Scientific Blackjack.* New York: Arco, 1977.

COOPER, KEN. *Nonverbal Communication for Business Success.* New York: AMACOM, 1979.

EINSTEIN, CHARLES. *How to Win at Blackjack.* Las Vegas: Gamblers Book Club, 1976.

EPSTEIN, RICHARD A. *The Theory of Gambling and Statistical Logic.* New York: Academic Press, 1977.

FORTE, STEVE. *Reading the Dealer.* Berkeley, Calif.: RGE, 1986.

FRIEDMAN, JOEL H. "Choosing a Blackjack Game," report to the Fourth Conference on Gambling, Reno, 1978.

GOODMAN, MIKE. *How to Win.* New York: Holloway, 1971.

GRIFFIN, PETER A. "The Use of Bivariate Normal Approximations to Evaluate Single-parameter Card-counting Systems," report to the Third Conference on Gambling, Las Vegas, 1976.

————. *The Theory of Blackjack.* Las Vegas: Gamblers Book Club, 1979.

HUMBLE, LANCE. *Blackjack SuperGold.* Toronto: International Gaming, 1979.

ITA, KOKO. *21 Counting Methods to Beat 21.* Las Vegas: Gamblers Book Club, 1976.

MOODY, ROBERT. *Las Vegas Sensibly.* San Diego: Harmand, 1975.

NOLAN, WALTER I. *Facts of Blackjack.* Las Vegas: Gamblers Book Club, 1976.

PATTERSON, JERRY L. *Blackjack: A Winner's Handbook.* Vorhees, N.J.: Echelon, 1977.

REVERE, LAWRENCE. *Playing Blackjack as a Business*. Secaucus, N.J.: Lyle Stewart, 1977.

Rouge et Noir News, staff. *Winning at Casino Gaming*. Glen Head, N.Y.: Rouge et Noir, 1975.

SNYDER, ARNOLD. *The Blackjack Formula*. Berkeley, Calif.: RGE, 1981.

SNYDER, ARNOLD. *Blackbelt in Blackjack*. Berkeley, Calif.: RGE, 1983.

THORP, EDWARD O. *Beat the Dealer*. New York: Vintage, 1966.

USTON, KEN. *One-third of a Shoe and How You Can Win at Blackjack in Atlantic City and Nevada*. Wheaton, N.J.: Uston Institute of Blackjack, 1979.

USTON, KEN, AND RAPOPORT, ROGER. *The Big Player*. New York: Holt, Rinehart & Winston, 1977.

WILSON, ALLAN N. *The Casino Gambler's Guide*. New York: Harper & Row, 1970.

APPENDIX A

Glossary of Blackjack Jargon

While all of the terms used in this book are explained in the text, you may be reading or reviewing certain passages and find a word that is not self-explanatory or that seems to have a Blackjack meaning different from normal English usage. Following is a list of these terms and their definitions for your reference:

ACT the personality a winning Blackjack player assumes in order to disguise the fact that he is a counter.

ACTION the total amount of money bet—for example, one hundred bets of five dollars each is five hundred dollars in action.

BASIC STRATEGY the computer-devised playing rules for a player who is not tracking cards. Also called the zero-sum strategy.

BLACKJACK a two-card hand of Ace and 10-value card that is normally paid off as a premium bet. This is an automatic casino winner if untied by another Blackjack.

BURN CARD usually a single card from the top that is removed from play before the dealer begins dealing after a shuffle.

BUST draw enough cards so that the total exceeds the maximum of 21.

COUNTER a player who keeps track of the cards played through counting the number of cards by categories and playing accordingly.

FIRST BASE the seat farthest to the right of the player (and at the left of the dealer), which is dealt to first and must play first.

FLAT BET betting the same amount from hand to hand regardless of the play of the cards.

HARD TOTAL   a hand value in which no Ace is counted as an 11.

HEAD-ON   playing alone against the dealer.

HIT   asking for another card from the dealer.

HOLE CARD   the dealer card that remains face down (or undrawn) until all the player hands have been resolved.

MARKER   an IOU the player signs at the table in return for casino chips.

MECHANIC   a person who is adept at manipulating cards; normally a cheat.

NATURAL   another word for a Blackjack. A two-card hand of Ace and 10 that is paid at a premium.

PAT HAND   a hand value of 17 or greater.

PEEK   the process of looking at a card. Normally, the dealer is said to peek when looking for a possible natural with an Ace or 10 up card. A cheating dealer will try to peek to determine the value of the top card of the undealt deck.

POOR   the deck is said to be poor in certain values of cards if there is smaller-than-normal percentage of that card value present.

PUSH   a situation in which the player and dealer attain the same hand value. In the casino game it is a tie; in the no-house game the dealer wins the tie.

RICH   the deck is said to be rich in certain values of cards if there is a larger-than-normal percentage of cards present.

SHILL   a casino employee who plays in order to stimulate interest and betting in the game.

SOFT TOTAL   any hand value in which an Ace is counted as 11.

STAND   receive no more cards from the dealer.

STIFF   a nonpat hand that can be busted if hit. Hand values are 12 to 16.

THIRD BASE   the seat farthest to the left of the player (and at the right of the dealer), which is dealt to last and must play last.

TOKE   a tip given directly to or bet for the dealer.

APPENDIX B

Basic Strategy Summary Charts

BLACKJACK BASIC STRATEGY: 4+ Deck Summary
(double after split).

YOUR HAND:	DEALER SHOWS									
	2	3	4	5	6	7	8	9	10	A
min hard std #'s	13	13	12	12	12	17	17	17	17	17
min soft std #'s	18	18	18	18	18	18	18	19	19	19
min hard doubling	10	9	9	9	9	10	10	10	11	—
pair splitting										
9,9	SP	SP	SP	SP	SP	S	SP	SP	S	S
7,7	SP	SP	SP	SP	SP	SP	H	H	H	H
6,6	SP	SP	SP	SP	SP	H	H	H	H	H
4,4	H	H	H	SP	SP	H	H	H	H	H
3,3	SP	SP	SP	SP	SP	SP	H	H	H	H
2,2	SP	SP	SP	SP	SP	SP	H	H	H	
soft doubling										
max #'s	—	18	18	18	18					
min #'s	—	17	15	13	13					
surrender	(9,7), (10,6) vs. Dealer A, 10, 9									
	(9,6), (10,5) vs. Dealer 10									
	(8,7) vs. Dealer 10 in 6 deck game only									

NOTES: ALWAYS Split (A,A) and (8,8)
NEVER Split (10,10) and (5,5)

BLACKJACK BASIC STRATEGY: 1 Deck Summary
(no double after split).

YOUR HAND:	DEALER SHOWS									
	2	3	4	5	6	7	8	9	10	A
min hard std #'s	13	13	12	12	12	17	17	17	17*	17
min soft std #'s	18	18	18	18	18	18	18	19	19	18
min hard doubling	9	9	9	8	8	10	10	10	11	11
pair splitting										
9,9	SP	SP	SP	SP	SP	S	SP	SP	S	S
7,7	SP	SP	SP	SP	SP	SP	H	H	S*	H
6,6	SP	SP	SP	SP	SP	H	H	H	H	H
3,3	H	H	SP	SP	SP	SP	H	H	H	H
2,2	H	SP	SP	SP	SP	SP	H	H	H	H
soft doubling										
max #'s	17	18	18	18	19					
min #'s	17	17	13	13	13					
surrender	(10,6) vs. Dealer A, 10									
	(9,7), (9,6), (10,5) and (7,7) vs. Dealer 10									

NOTES: ALWAYS Split (A,A) and (8,8)
        NEVER Split (10,10), (5,5) and (4,4)

*STAND on (7,7) vs. Dealer 10

BLACKJACK BASIC STRATEGY: 1 Deck Summary
(double after split).

YOUR HAND:	2	3	4	5	6	7	8	9	10	A
	DEALER SHOWS									
min hard std #'s	13	13	12	12	12	17	17	17	17*	17
min soft std #'s	18	18	18	18	18	18	18	19	19	18
min hard doubling	9	9	9	8	8	10	10	10	11	11
pair splitting										
9,9	SP	SP	SP	SP	SP	S	SP	SP	S	S
7,7	SP	SP	SP	SP	SP	SP	SP	H	S*	H
6,6	SP	SP	SP	SP	SP	SP	H	H	H	H
4,4	H	H	SP	SP	SP	H	H	H	H	H
3,3	H	SP	SP	SP	SP	SP	H	H	H	H
2,2	SP	SP	SP	SP	SP	SP	H	H	H	H
soft doubling										
max #'s	17	18	18	18	19					
min #'s	17	17	13	13	13					
surrender	(10,6) vs. Dealer A, 10									
	(9,7), (9,6), (10,5) and (7,7) vs. Dealer 10									

NOTES: ALWAYS Split (A,A) and (8,8)
NEVER Split (10,10) and (5,5)

*STAND on (7,7) vs. Dealer 10

BLACKJACK BASIC STRATEGY: 2 Deck Summary
(no double after split).

YOUR HAND:	2	3	4	5	6	7	8	9	10	A
			DEALER	SHOWS						
min hard std #'s	13	13	12	12	12	17	17	17	17	17
min soft std #'s	18	18	18	18	18	18	18	19	19	19
min hard doubling	9	9	9	9	9	10	10	10	11	11*
pair splitting										
9,9	SP	SP	SP	SP	SP	S	SP	SP	S	S
7,7	SP	SP	SP	SP	SP	SP	H	H	H	H
6,6	H	SP	SP	SP	SP	H	H	H	H	H
3,3	H	H	SP	SP	SP	SP	H	H	H	H
2,2	H	H	SP	SP	SP	SP	H	H	H	H
soft doubling										
max #'s	—	18	18	18	18					
min #'s	—	17	15	13	13					
surrender	(9,7) and (10,6) vs. Dealer A, 10									
	(9,6) and (10,5) vs. Dealer 10									

NOTES: ALWAYS Split (A,A) and (8,8)
       NEVER Split (10,10), (5,5) and (4,4)

*DOUBLE only (6,5) and (7,4) vs. Dealer A.

BLACKJACK BASIC STRATEGY: 2 Deck Summary
(double after split).

YOUR HAND:	2	3	4	5	6	7	8	9	10	A
			DEALER SHOWS							
min hard std #'s	13	13	12	12	12	17	17	17	17	17
min soft std #'s	18	18	18	18	18	18	18	19	19	19
min hard doubling	9	9	9	9	9	10	10	10	11	11*
pair splitting										
9,9	SP	SP	SP	SP	SP	S	SP	SP	S	S
7,7	SP	SP	SP	SP	SP	SP	H	H	H	H
6,6	SP	SP	SP	SP	SP	H	H	H	H	H
4,4	H	H	H	SP	SP	H	H	H	H	H
3,3	SP	SP	SP	SP	SP	SP	H	H	H	H
2,2	SP	SP	SP	SP	SP	SP	H	H	H	H
soft doubling										
max #'s	—	18	18	18	18					
min #'s	—	17	15	13	13					
surrender	(9,7) and (10,6) vs. Dealer A, 10									
	(9,6) and (10,5) vs. Dealer 10									

NOTES: ALWAYS Split (A,A) and (8,8)
NEVER Split (10,10) and (5,5)

*DOUBLE only (6,5) and (7,4) vs. Dealer A

4 DECK BASIC STRATEGY FOR 21

DOUBLE DOWN		DLR UP	PAIR SPLITTING		STANDING ON	
Soft	Hard				Hard	Soft
	11	A	A			19
	11	10				
	11	9	9	8	17	
	11	8				
	10	7	7			
			3			
18 To 13	11	6	A			
		5	9		12	18
18 To 15	10	4	2	6	8	
18 To 17	9	3				
			7		13	
	11 10	2				

Surrender (9,7) & (10,6) to Dlr. 9, 10, A UP
(9,6) & (10,5) to Dlr. 10 UP

Format Courtesy Gamblers Book Club

4 DECK BASIC STRATEGY FOR 21

DOUBLE DOWN		DLR UP	PAIR SPLITTING		STANDING ON	
Soft	Hard				Hard	Soft
	11	A	A			19
	11	10				
	11	9	9	8	17	
	11	8				
	10	7	7			
			3			
18 To 13	11	6	A			
		5	9		12	18
18 To 15	10	4	2	6	8	
18 To 17	9	3				
			7		13	
	11 10	2				

Surrender (9,7) & (10,6) to Dlr. 9, 10, A UP
(9,6) & (10,5) to Dlr. 10 UP

Format Courtesy Gamblers Book Club

Cut out, place in wallet or behind the cellophane of a cigarette pack, etc.

Affix on watchband or inside match-book cover.